Frommer's®

Santa Fe, Taos & Albuquerque

Here's what the critics say about Frommer's:

"Amazingly easy to use. Very portable, very complete."
— *Booklist*

♦

"The only mainstream guide to list specific prices. The Walter Cronkite of guidebooks—with all that implies."
— *Travel & Leisure*

♦

"Complete, concise, and filled with useful information."
— *New York Daily News*

♦

"Hotel information is close to encyclopedic."
— *Des Moines Sunday Register*

Other Great Guides for Your Trip:

Frommer's New Mexico

Frommer's Irreverent Guide to Santa Fe

Frommer's USA

Frommer's®

7th Edition

Santa Fe, Taos & Albuquerque

by Lesley S. King

Macmillan • USA

ABOUT THE AUTHOR

Lesley S. King grew up on a ranch in Northern New Mexico, where she still returns on weekends to help work cattle. She's a freelance writer and photographer and a contributor to *New Mexico Magazine*—as well as an avid kayaker and skier. Formerly the managing editor for *The Santa Fean,* she has written about food and restaurants for the *New York Times,* the Anasazi culture for United Airline's *Hemispheres* magazine, ranches for *American Cowboy,* and birds for Audubon. She is also the author of Frommer's *New Mexico.*

MACMILLAN TRAVEL

A Simon & Schuster Macmillan Company
1633 Broadway
New York, NY 10019

Find us online at **www.frommers.com**

ISBN 0-02-862367-3
ISSN 0899-2789

Editor: Neil E. Schlecht
Production Editor: Donna Wright
Photo Editor: Richard Fox
Design by Michele Laseau
Digital Cartography by Raffaele DeGennaro and Gail Accardi
Page Creation by: Bob LaRoche, David Pruett, and Linda Quiqley

SPECIAL SALES

Bulk purchases (10+ copies) of Frommer's and selected Macmillan travel guides are available to corporations, organizations, mail-order catalogs, institutions, and charities at special discounts, and can be customized to suit individual needs. For more information write to Special Sales, Macmillan General Reference, 1633 Broadway, New York, NY 10019.

Manufactured in the United States of America

Contents

List of Maps

Acknowledgments

The author wishes to thank her assistant, Julia Ward, who helped greatly with fact checking and bringing new ideas to the project.

An Invitation to the Reader

In researching this book, we discovered many wonderful places—hotels, restaurants, shops, and more. We're sure you'll find others. Please tell us about them, so we can share the information with your fellow travelers in upcoming editions. If you were disappointed with a recommendation, we'd love to know that, too. Please write to:

Frommer's Santa Fe, Taos & Albuquerque, 7th Edition
Macmillan Travel
1633 Broadway
New York, NY 10019

An Additional Note

Please be advised that travel information is subject to change at any time—and this is especially true of prices. We therefore suggest that you write or call ahead for confirmation when making your travel plans. The authors, editors, and publisher cannot be held responsible for the experiences of readers while traveling. Your safety is important to us, however, so we encourage you to stay alert and be aware of your surroundings. Keep a close eye on cameras, purses, and wallets, all favorite targets of thieves and pickpockets.

What the Symbols Mean

✪ Frommer's Favorites

Our favorite places and experiences—outstanding for quality, value, or both.

The following abbreviations are used for credit cards:

AE	American Express	EURO	Eurocard
CB	Carte Blanche	JCB	Japan Credit Bank
DC	Diners Club	MC	MasterCard
DISC	Discover	V	Visa
ER	enRoute		

Find Frommer's Online

Arthur Frommer's Outspoken Encyclopedia of Travel (www.frommers.com) offers more than 6,000 pages of up-to-the-minute travel information—including the latest bargains and candid, personal articles updated daily by Arthur Frommer himself. No other Web site offers such comprehensive and timely coverage of the world of travel.

Introducing Northern New Mexico

This land, once the site of live volcanoes and cataclysmic ground shifts, has a tumultuous character that not only marked the past but continues to inform the present. Northern New Mexico witnessed the epic clash of Spanish, Native American, and Anglo cultures; today, disparate but overlapping identities continue to negotiate for space. But, just as geological mutations gave rise to a desert and mountain landscape that is by turns austere and lushly beautiful, cultural conflicts have produced immeasurable richness and hard scars. Today, it is a land of immense cultural diversity, creativity, appreciation for the outdoors, and a place where people very much pursue their own paths.

The center of the region is Santa Fe, a hip, artsy city that wears its 400-year-old mores on its sleeve. Nestled on the side of the **Sangre de Cristo Mountains,** it's an adobe showcase of centuries-old buildings that hug the earth. Many of these are artist studios and galleries set on narrow streets, ideal for desultory browsing. And then there's upstart Taos, the little arts town and ski center of just 5,000 people that lies wedged between the 13,000-foot Sangre de Cristo Mountains and the 700-foot-deep **Rio Grande Gorge.** Taos is a place of extreme temperatures and temperaments. Winter snows here bring light powder, excellent for skiing; spring's warmth fattens the rivers with runoff, allowing for terrific rafting and kayaking; and summer and fall are full of sun, great for a variety of outdoor activities. *Taoseños,* the locals, eschew regular work schedules—some businesses even shut down on good ski days. Albuquerque is the big city, New Mexico style, where people from all over the state come to trade. You'll see cowboys and Native Americans with pickups loaded with everything from saddles to swing sets to solar windmills, heading in all directions.

Not far from these three cities are the 19 settlements and numerous ruins of the Native American Pueblo culture, an incredible testament to the resilience of a proud people. And through it all weave the **Manzano, Sandia, Sangre de Cristo,** and **Jemez mountains,** multimillion-year-old reminders of man's recent arrival to this vast and unique landscape.

Northern New Mexico

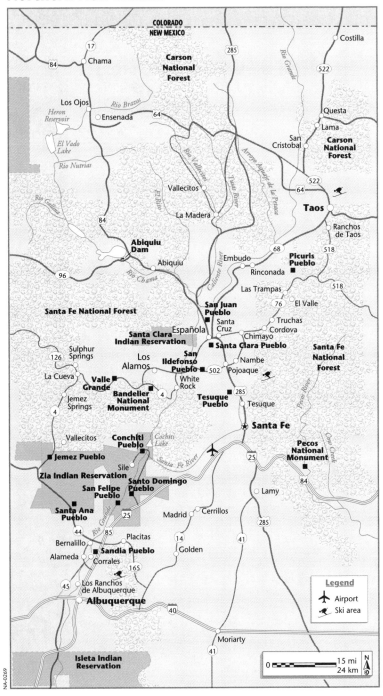

1 Frommer's Favorite Northern New Mexico Experiences

- **High Road to Taos.** This spectacular 80-mile route into the mountains between Santa Fe and Taos takes you through red painted desert, villages bordered by apple and peach orchards, and the foothills of 13,000-foot peaks. You can stop in Cordova, known for its wood-carvers, or Chimayo, known for its weavers. At the fabled Santuario de Chimayo, you can rub healing dust between your fingers. You'll also pass through Truchas, a village stronghold on a mountain mesa 1½ miles above sea level.

- **Pueblo Dances.** These native dances, related to the changing cycles of the earth, offer a unique chance to see how an indigenous culture worships and rejoices. The winter dances (around Christmastime) focus mainly on animals such as the deer and turtle. Taos is noted for the deer dance, during which men wearing antlers and hides come down from the hills at dawn. The Matachine dances, which depict the Spanish conquest of the Indians, are performed by both Hispanic and Pueblo communities and are also a worthwhile experience. San Juan Pueblo usually does this dance on Christmas morning. In late August or early September, San Ildefonso Pueblo performs the corn dance. Throughout the year other pueblos celebrate the feast days of their particular saints, so you're likely to catch a dance at any time of year—all in the mystical light of the Northern New Mexico sun.

- **Santa Fe Opera.** One of the finest opera companies in the United States—thought by some to rival New York City's Metropolitan—has called Santa Fe home for 41 years. Performances are held during the summer months in a hilltop, open-air amphitheater. In 1999, you can see such classics as *Carmen* by Bizet and *Idomeneo* by Mozart. Usually there is a Strauss opera; in 1999 it will be *Ariadne Auf Naxos*. And for the less traditional-minded, there's *Countess Maritza* by Kalman and *Dialogues of the Carmelites* by Poulenc. If you're lucky, you may see lightening bolts strike in the distance during the performance.

- **Taos Ski Valley.** World renowned for its difficult runs (such as Al's) and the ridge where skiers hike for up to 2 hours to ski fresh powder, Taos has long been a pilgrimage site for extreme skiers. Today, this Southwestern play spot with a Bavarian accent is no longer a well-guarded secret. Over the years, the ski area has opened up new bowls to accommodate intermediate and beginners too (though many beginners I've spoken to seem daunted by the mountain's verticality).

- **Museum of International Folk Art.** Santa Fe's perpetually expanding collection of folk art is the largest in the world; it contains 130,000 objects from more than 100 countries. You'll find an amazing array of imaginative works, ranging from Hispanic folk art *santos* (carved saints) to Indonesian textiles and African sculptures.

- **Chaco Canyon.** Though it's a long drive west of Santa Fe, it's worth a visit to these spectacular ancient ruins set in a beautiful canyon—a site believed to be the center of Anasazi culture. An ancient people best known for pottery making, the Anasazi lived in the area from around A.D. 850 to around 1200. Remains of 800 rooms exist here, many built on top of each other in structures that once towered four and five stories high. Most spectacular is Pueblo Bonito, with its giant kivas (underground chambers used by the men especially for ceremonies or councils); the structure was once a religious gathering place for Indians all over the area.

- **Sandia Peak Tramway.** The world's longest tramway ferries passengers 2.7 miles, from Albuquerque's city limits to the summit of the 10,378-foot Sandia Peak. On the way, you'll likely see rare Rocky Mountain bighorn sheep and birds of prey. In the summer, you may see hang gliders taking off from the giant precipice to soar in the drafts that sweep up the mountain. Go in the evening to watch the sun burn its way out of the western sky, then enjoy the glimmering city lights on your way down.
- **Kodak Albuquerque International Balloon Festival.** The world's largest balloon rally assembles more than 850 colorful balloons and includes races and contests. Highlights are the mass ascension at sunrise and the special shapes rodeo, in which balloons in all sorts of whimsical forms, from liquor bottles to milk cows, rise into the sky. As befits the sponsor, the festival is a photographer's delight. During the "balloon glow," hundreds of balloons take flight after dark.
- **Bandelier National Monument.** Along with Puye Cliff Dwellings, these ruins provide a spectacular peek into the lives of the Anasazi Pueblo culture, which flourished in this area between A.D. 1100 and 1550—considerably later than the apex of Chaco Canyon. (Recent findings suggest that some Chaco residents ended up at Bandelier.) Less than 15 miles south of Los Alamos, the ruins spread across a peaceful canyon. You'll probably see deer and rabbits as you make your way through the canyon to the most dramatic site, a kiva and dwelling in a cave 140 feet above the canyon floor—reached by a climb up long pueblo-style ladders.
- **Northern New Mexican Enchilada.** The food here is unique, reflecting the rich cultural heritage of the region. And few things are more New Mexican than the enchilada. You can order red or green chile, or "Christmas"—half and half. Sauces are rich, seasoned with *ajo* (garlic) and oregano. Unlike Mexican food in other locales, New Mexican cuisine isn't smothered in cheese and sour cream, so the flavors of the chiles, corn, and meats can really be savored. Enchiladas are often served with *frijoles* (beans), firmer than the refried bean paste you might be used to getting in Tex-Mex restaurants. They're also served with *posole* (hominy) and *sopaipillas* (fried bread), both culinary elements derived from local native cultures.
- **The Galleries Along Canyon Road.** Originally a Pueblo Indian route over the mountains and later an artists' community, Santa Fe's Canyon Road is now gallery central—the arts capital of the Southwest. The narrow one-way street is lined with more than 100 galleries, in addition to restaurants and private residences. You can visit the elaborate gardens of El Zaguán, where native plants mingle with roses and irises, or the quaint shops of Gypsy Alley, where buildings date back to 1753. Artwork on display (and for sale) ranges from the beautiful to bizarre. You can step into artists' simple studio-galleries as well as refined galleries showing world-renowned artists' works, such as paintings by Georgia O'Keeffe and sculpture by Frederic Remington. Be sure to stop for lunch at one of the streetside cafes.
- **Pecos National Historical Park.** It's hard to rank New Mexico's many ruins, but this one, sprawled on a plain about 25 miles east of Santa Fe, is one of the most impressive, resonating with the history of the Pueblo Revolt of 1680, the only successful revolt of indigenous people in the New World. You'll see evidence of where the Pecos people burned the mission church before joining in the attack on Santa Fe. You'll also see where the Spanish conquistadors later compromised, allowing sacred kivas to be built next to the reconstructed mission.

- **Rio Grande Gorge.** A hike into this dramatic gorge is unforgettable. You'll first see it as you come over a rise heading toward Taos, a colossal slice in the earth formed during the late Cretaceous period 130 million years ago and the early Tertiary period, about 70 million years ago. Drive about 35 miles north of Taos, near the village of Cerro, to the Rio Grande Wild River Area. From the lip of the canyon, you descend through millions of years of geologic history on land inhabited by Indians since 16,000 B.C. You're liable to encounter raccoons and other wildlife, and once you reach the river you'll see fishermen, rafters, and kayakers. There you can dip your toes in the fabled *Rio*. If you're visiting during spring and early summer, and like an adrenaline rush, be sure to hook up with a professional guide and raft the Taos Box, a 17-mile stretch of class IV white water.
- **María Benitez Teatro Flamenco.** Flamenco dancing originated in Spain, strongly influenced by the Moors; it is a cultural expression held sacred by Spanish Gypsies. The passionate dance is characterized by intricate toe and heel clicking, sinuous arm and hand gestures, *cante hondo* or "deep song," and expressive guitar solos. A native New Mexican, María Benitez was trained in Spain, where she returns each year to find dancers and prepare her show. Through her fluid movement and aggressive solos, she brings a contemporary voice to this ancient art. This world-class dancer and her troupe perform at the Radisson Hotel in Santa Fe from July through early September.
- **Old Town.** Albuquerque's commercial center until about 1880, Old Town still gives a remarkable sense of what life was once like in a Southwestern village. You can meander down crooked streets and narrow alleys and rest in the cottonwood-shaded Plaza. Though many of the shops are now very touristy, you can still happen upon some interesting shopping and dining finds here. Native Americans sell jewelry, pottery, and weavings under a portal on the plaza.

2 Northern New Mexico Today

On rock faces throughout northern New Mexico, you'll find circular symbols carved in sandstone, the wavy mark of Avanu the river serpent, or the ubiquitous Kokopelli playing his magic flute. These petroglyphs are constant reminders of the enigmatic history of the Anasazi, the Indians that inhabited this area from A.D. 1100 until as late as 1550. Part of my fascination with this land is the mysterious presence of these ancient people even today. Excavations continue in the area; the other day, right on a highway shoulder between Santa Fe and Española, I saw archaeologists excavating two sites, brushing away dirt to expose kivas and ancient walls.

The Spanish conquistadors, in their inimitable fashion, imposed a new, foreign order upon the resident Native Americans and their land. They brought with them a rich culture bolstered by a fervent belief in spreading Catholicism. As an inevitable component of conquest, they changed most Native American names— today, you'll find a number of Native Americans with Hispanic names—and renamed the villages "pueblos." The Spaniards' most far-reaching legacy, however, was the forceful conversion of Indian populations to Catholicism, a religion that many Indians still practice today. In each of the pueblos you'll see a large, often beautiful Catholic church, usually made with sculpted adobe. The churches, set against the ancient adobe dwellings, are symbolic of the melding of two cultures. During the holiday seasons here you'll see Pueblo people perform ritual dances outside their local Catholic church.

The mix of cultures is today very much apparent in Northern New Mexican cuisine. When the Spaniards came to the New World, they brought cows and sheep. They quickly learned to appreciate the indigenous foods here, most notably corn, beans, squash, and chiles. Look also for such Pueblo dishes as the thin-layered blue piki bread, or *chauquehue,* a thick corn pudding similar to polenta.

GROWING PAINS   Northern New Mexico is experiencing a reconquest of sorts, as the Anglo population soars, and outside money and values again make their way in. The process continues to transform New Mexico's three distinct cultures and their unique ways of life, albeit in a less violent manner than during the Spanish conquest.

Certainly, the Anglos—many of them from large cities—add a cosmopolitan flavor to life here. The variety of restaurants has greatly improved, as have entertainment options. For their small size, towns such as Taos and Santa Fe offer a broad variety of restaurants and cultural events. Santa Fe has developed a strong dance and drama scene, with treats such as flamenco and opera that you'd expect to find in New York or Los Angeles. And Albuquerque has an exciting nightlife scene downtown; you can walk from club to club and hear a wealth of jazz, rock, country, and alternative music.

Yet many newcomers, attracted by the adobe houses and exotic feel of the place, often bring only a loose appreciation for the area. Some tend to romanticize the lifestyle of the other cultures and trivialize their beliefs. Native American symbology, for example, is employed in ever-popular Southwestern decorative motifs; New Age groups appropriate valued rituals, such as sweats (in which believers sit encamped in a very hot, enclosed space to cleanse their spirits). The effects of cultural and economic change are even apparent throughout the countryside, where land is being developed at an alarming rate, often as lots for new million-dollar homes.

Transformation of the local way of life and landscape is also apparent in the stores continually springing up in the area. For some of us, these are a welcome relief from Western clothing stores and provincial dress shops. The down side is that city plazas, which once contained pharmacies and grocery stores frequented by residents, are now crowded with T-shirt shops and galleries appealing to tourists. Many locals in these cities now rarely visit their plazas except during special events such as fiestas.

Environmental threats are another regional reality. Nuclear waste issues form part of an ongoing conflict affecting the entire Southwest, and a section of southern New Mexico has been designated a nuclear waste site. Much of the waste would pass through Santa Fe; the problem necessitated construction of a bypass that will, when completed, direct a great deal of transit traffic around the west side of the city.

Still, new ways of thinking have also brought positive changes to the life here, and many locals have directly benefitted from New Mexico's expansion, influx of wealthy newcomers, and popularity as a tourist destination. Businesses and industries, large and small, have come to the area. In Albuquerque, the Intel Corporation now employs over 5,000 workers, and *Outside* magazine recently relocated from Chicago to Santa Fe. Local artists and artisans also benefit from growth. Many craftspeople—furniture makers, tin workers, and weavers—have expanded their businesses. The influx of people has broadened the sensibility of a fairly provincial state. The area has become a refuge for many gays and lesbians, as well as for political exiles, such as Tibetans. With them has developed a level of creativity and tolerance you would generally find in very large cities but not in smaller communities such as these.

CULTURAL QUESTIONS   Faced with new challenges to their ways of life, both Native Americans and Hispanics are marshaling forces to protect their cultural identities. A prime concern is language. Through the years, many Pueblo people have begun to speak more and more English, with their children getting little exposure to their native tongue. In a number of the pueblos, elders are working with school children in language classes. Some of the pueblos, such as Santa Clara, have even developed written dictionaries, the first time their languages have been presented in this form.

Many pueblos have introduced programs to conserve the environment, preserve ancient seed strains, and protect religious rites. Since their religion is tied closely to nature, a loss of their natural resources would threaten the entire culture. Certain rituals have been closed off to outsiders, the most notable being the Shalako at Zuni, a popular and elaborate series of year-end ceremonies.

Hispanics, through art and observance of cultural traditions, are also embracing their roots. In Northern New Mexico you'll see, adorning many walls, murals that depict important historical events, such as the Treaty of Guadalupe Hidalgo of 1848. The **Spanish Market** in Santa Fe has expanded into a grand celebration of traditional arts—from tin working to santo carving. Public schools in the area have bilingual education programs in place, allowing young people to embrace their Spanish-speaking roots.

Hispanics are also making their voices heard, insisting on more conscientious development of their neighborhoods and rising to positions of power in government. When she was in office, former Santa Fe mayor Debbie Jaramillo made national news as an advocate of the Hispanic people, and Congressman Bill Richardson, Hispanic despite his Anglo surname, was appointed U.S. ambassador to the United Nations.

GAMBLING WINS & LOSSES   Gambling, a fact of life and source of much-needed revenues for Native American populations across the country, has been a center of controversy for a number of years. In 1994, Governor Gary Johnson signed a compact with tribes in New Mexico, ratified by the U.S. Department of the Interior, to allow full-scale gambling. Tesuque Pueblo was one of the first to begin a massive expansion, and many other pueblos followed suit.

In early 1996, however, the State Supreme Court ruled that without legislative action on the matter, the casinos were operating illegally. Native Americans remained resolute in their determination to forge ahead with the casinos. Demonstrations of community strength, by the Pojoaque Pueblo and others, ultimately made an impact on legislators. In 1997, lawmakers agreed to allow gaming by Indian as well as fraternal and veteran organizations.

Many New Mexicans are concerned about the tone gambling sets in the state. The casinos are for the most part large and unsightly, neon-bedecked buildings that stand out sorely on some of New Mexico's most picturesque land. Though most residents appreciate the boost that gambling can ultimately bring to the Native American economies, many critics wonder where gambling profits actually go—and if the casinos can possibly be a good thing for the pueblos and tribes. Some detractors suspect that profits go directly into the pockets of outside backers.

A number of pueblos and tribes, however, are showing signs of prosperity, and they are using newfound revenues to buy firefighting and medical equipment and to invest in local schools. According to the Indian Gaming Association, casinos directly employ over 4,000 workers and pump over $260 million in revenues into the state's economy. Isleta Pueblo has built a $3.6-million youth center, money which their lieutenant governor says came from gambling revenues. Sandia Pueblo has built a $2-million medical and dental clinic and expanded its police department. Their Governor, Alex Lujan, calls these projects "totally funded by gaming revenues."

SANTA FE   This is where the splendor of diverse cultures really shines, and it does so in a setting that's unsurpassed. There's a magic in Santa Fe that's difficult to explain, but you'll sense it when you glimpse an old adobe building set against blue mountains and giant billowing thunderheads or when you hear a ranchero song come from a low-rider's radio and you smell chicken and chile grilling at a roadside vending booth. Although it's quickening, the pace of life here is still a few steps slower than the rest of the country. We use the word *mañana* to describe the pace—which doesn't mean "tomorrow" exactly, it just means "not today." There's also a level of creativity here that you'll find in few other places in the world. Artists who have fled big-city jobs are here to follow their passions, as are locals who grew up making crafts and continue to do so. Conversations often center around how to structure one's day so as to take advantage of the incredible outdoors while still making enough money to survive.

Meanwhile, Santa Fe's precipitous growth and enduring popularity with tourists have been the source of conflict and squabbling. Outsiders have bought up land in the hills around the city, building housing developments and sprawling single-family homes. The hills that local populations claimed for centuries as their own are being overrun, while property taxes for all skyrocket. On the positive side, however, local outcry has prompted the city to implement zoning restrictions on where and how development can proceed. Some of the restrictions include banning building on ridgetops and on steep slopes and limiting the size of homes built.

Santa Fe's last mayor, Debbie Jaramillo, was one of the first local politicians to take a strong stand against growth. A fiery native of Santa Fe, she came into office as a representative of *la gente* (the people), and set about discouraging tourism and rapid development. She took a lot of heat for her positions, which to some seemed xenophobic and antibusiness. The mayor initially failed to offer tax breaks or incentive money to some businesses interested in settling in the area, but by the time she left office had softened her position on development. The newly elected mayor, Larry Delgado, has taken a middle-of-the-road approach to the issue; Santa Feans are waiting to see how this affects the local economy and the future of the city's development.

TAOS   A funky town in the middle of a beautiful, sage-covered valley, Taos is full of narrow streets dotted with galleries and artisan shops. You might find an artist's studio tucked into a century-old church or a small furniture maker working at the back of his own shop.

More than any other major Northern New Mexico community, Taos has successfully opposed much of the heavy development slated for the area. In 1987, locals vociferously protested plans to expand the airport so that commercial airlines could fly in; plans have been stalled indefinitely pending environmental impact statements. In 1991, a $40 million golf course and housing development slated for the area was met with such community dissent that its developers eventually desisted. It's hard to say where Taos gets its rebellious strength; the roots may lie in the hippie community that settled here in the '60s, or possibly the Pueblo community around which the city formed. After all, Taos Pueblo was at the center of the 17th-century Pueblo Revolt.

Still, changes are upon Taoseños. The blinking light that for years residents used as a reference point has given way to a real traffic light. You'll also see the main route through town becoming more and more like Cerrillos Road in Santa Fe, as fast-food restaurants and service businesses set up shop. Though the town is working to streamline alternate routes to channel through-traffic around downtown, there's no feasible way of widening the main drag because the street—which started out as a wagon trail—is bordered closely by historic buildings.

ALBUQUERQUE   The largest city in New Mexico, Albuquerque has born the brunt of the state's most massive growth. Currently, the city sprawls over 16 miles, from the lava-crested mesas on the west side of the Rio Grande to the steep alluvial slopes of the Sandia Mountains on the east, and north and south through the Rio Grande Valley. New subdivisions sprout up constantly.

Despite the growth, this town is most prized by New Mexicans for its genuineness. You'll find none of the self-conscious artsy atmosphere of Santa Fe here. Instead, there's a traditional New Mexico feel that's evident when you spend some time in the heart of the city. It centers around downtown, a place of shiny skyscrapers built around the original Route 66, which still maintains some of its 1950s charm.

The most emblematic growth problem concerns the **Petroglyph National Monument** on the west side. The area is characterized by five extinct volcanoes. Adjacent lava flows became a hunting and gathering place for prehistoric Native Americans who left a chronicle of their beliefs etched in the dark basalt boulders. Some 15,000 petroglyphs have been found in this archaeological preserve. Now, there's a push to carve out a highway corridor right through the center of the monument. Opponents have fought the extension for nearly a decade. Some Native American groups, likening the highway to building a road through a church, oppose the extension on grounds that the petroglyphs are sacred to their culture. U.S. Interior Secretary Bruce Babbitt has refused to give permission for the road to go through. Senator Pete Domenici, however, has introduced a bill into the Senate that would allow the road to be built. The bill must be approved by Congress before construction can begin.

Northern New Mexico's extreme popularity as a tourist destination—it was the "in" place to be through much of the '80s—has dropped off. Though many artists and other businesspeople lament the loss of the crowds, most people are glad that the wave has subsided. It's good news for travelers too, who no longer have to compete so heavily for restaurant seats or space when hiking through ruins. Though parts of Northern New Mexico have lost some of the unique charm that attracted so many to the area, the overall feeling is still one of mystery and a cultural depth unmatched in the world. People here recognize the need to preserve the land and what New Mexicans have traditionally valued as integral to their unique lifestyle.

3 History 101

The Pueblo tribes of the upper Rio Grande Valley are believed to be descendants of the Anasazi, who from the mid-9th to the 13th centuries lived in the Four Corners Region—where the states of New Mexico, Arizona, Colorado, and Utah now meet. The Anasazi built spectacular structures; you get an idea of their scale and intricacy at the ruins at **Chaco Canyon** and **Mesa Verde.** It isn't known exactly why the Anasazi abandoned their homes (some archaeologists suggest it was due to drought; others claim social unrest), but most theories suggest that they moved from these sites to areas like Frijoles Canyon (**Bandelier National Monument**) and **Puye,** where they built villages resembling the ones they had left. Then several hundred years later, for reasons not yet understood, they moved down from the canyons

Regional Historical Interest

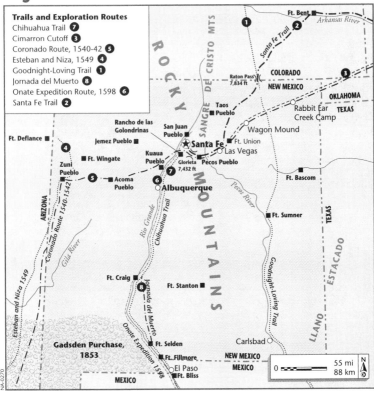

Trails and Exploration Routes

Chihuahua Trail ❼
Cimarron Cutoff ❸
Coronado Route, 1540-42 ❺
Esteban and Niza, 1549 ❹
Goodnight-Loving Trail ❶
Jornada del Muerto ❽
Onate Expedition Route, 1598 ❻
Santa Fe Trail ❷

onto the high, flat plain next to the Rio Grande. By the time the Spaniards arrived in the 1500s, the Pueblo culture was well established throughout what would become Northern and Western New Mexico.

Architectural style was a unifying mark of the otherwise diverse Anasazi and Pueblo cultures. Both built condominium-style communities of stone and mud adobe bricks, three and four stories high. Grouped around central plazas, the villages they constructed incorporated circular spiritual chambers called kivas. As farmers, the Anasazi and Pueblo peoples used the waters of the Rio Grande and its tributaries to irrigate fields of corn, beans, and squash. They were also the creators of elaborate works of pottery.

THE SPANISH OCCUPATION   The Spanish ventured into the upper Rio Grande after conquering Mexico's Aztecs in 1519–21. In 1540 Francisco Vásquez de Coronado led an expedition in search of the fabled Seven Cities of Cíbola, coincidentally introducing horses and sheep to the region. Neither Coronado nor a succession of fortune-seeking conquistadors could locate the legendary cities of gold, so the Spanish concentrated their efforts on exploiting the Native Americans.

Franciscan priests attempted to turn the Pueblo people into model peasants. Their churches became the focal points of every pueblo, with Catholic schools an essential adjunct. By 1625 there were approximately 50 churches in the Rio Grande Valley. (Two of the Pueblo missions, at Isleta and Acoma, are still in use today.) The Pueblo, however, weren't enthused about doing "God's work" for the Spanish— building new adobe missions, tilling fields, and weaving garments for export to

Mexico—so soldiers came north to back the padres in extracting labor. In effect, the Pueblo people were forced into slavery.

Santa Fe was founded in 1610 as the seat of Spanish government in the upper Rio Grande. Governor Don Pedro de Peralta named the settlement La Villa Real de la Santa Fe de San Francisco de Asis (The Royal City of the Holy Faith of St. Francis of Assisi). The **Palace of Governors** has been used continuously as a public building ever since—by the Spanish, Mexicans, Americans, Confederate troops (briefly), and Pueblos (1680–92). Today it stands as the flagship of the state museum system.

Decades of resentment against the Spanish colonials culminated in the Pueblo occupation. Uprisings in the 1630s at Taos and Jemez left village priests dead and triggered savage repression. In 1680, a unified Pueblo rebellion, orchestrated from Taos, succeeded in driving the Spaniards from the upper Rio Grande. The leaders of the revolt defiled or destroyed the churches, just as the Spanish had destroyed their religious symbols. They took the Palace of the Governors, where they burned archives and prayer books, and converted the chapel into a kiva. They also burned much of the property in Santa Fe that had been built by the Europeans and laid siege to Spanish settlements up and down the Rio Grande Valley. Forced to retreat to Mexico, the colonists were not able to retake Santa Fe until 12 years later. Bloody battles raged for the next several years, but by the beginning of the 18th century Nuevo Mexico was firmly in Spanish hands.

It remained so until Mexico gained its independence from Spain in 1821. The most notable event in the intervening years was the mid-1700s departure of the Franciscans, exasperated by their failure to wipe out all vestiges of traditional Pueblo religion. Throughout the Spanish occupation, eight generations of Pueblos had clung tenaciously to their way of life. However, by the 1750s the number of Pueblo villages had shrunk by half.

ARRIVAL OF THE ANGLOS   The first Anglos to spend time in the upper Rio Grande Valley were mountain men: itinerant hunters, trappers, and traders. Trailblazers of the U.S. westward expansion, they began settling in New Mexico in the first decade of the 19th century. Many married into Pueblo or Hispanic families. Perhaps the best known was Kit Carson, a sometime federal agent, sometime scout, whose legend is inextricably interwoven with that of early Taos. Though he seldom stayed in one place for long, he considered the Taos area his home. He married Josepha Jaramillo, the daughter of a leading Taos citizen. Later, while based in Taos, he became a prime force in the final subjugation of the Plains Indians. The Taos home where he lived off and on for 40 years, until his death in 1868, is now a museum.

Wagon trains and eastern merchants followed Carson and the other early settlers. Santa Fe, Taos, and Albuquerque, already major trading and commercial centers at the end of the Chihuahua Trail (the Camino Real from Veracruz, Mexico, 1,000 miles south), became the western termini of the new **Santa Fe Trail** (from Independence, Missouri, 800 miles east).

Even though independent Mexico granted the Pueblo people full citizenship and abandoned restrictive trade laws instituted by their former Spanish rulers, the subsequent 25 years of direct rule from Mexico City were not peaceful in the upper Rio Grande. Instead, they were marked by ongoing rebellion against severe taxation, especially in Taos. Neither did things quiet down when the United States assumed control of the territory during the Mexican War. Shortly after General Stephen Kearney occupied Santa Fe (in a bloodless takeover) on orders of President James Polk in 1846, a revolt in Taos in 1847 led to the slaying of the new governor of New Mexico, Charles Bent. In 1848, the Treaty of Guadalupe Hidalgo officially transferred title to New Mexico, along with Texas, Arizona, and California, to the United States.

Aside from Kit Carson, perhaps the two most notable personalities of 19th-century New Mexico were priests. Father José Martinez (1793–1867) was one of the first native-born priests to serve his people. Ordained in Durango, Mexico, he jolted the Catholic church after assuming control of the Taos parish: Martinez abolished the obligatory church tithe because it was a hardship on poor parishioners, published the first newspaper in the territory (in 1835), and fought large land acquisitions by Anglos after the United States annexed the territory.

On all these issues Martinez was at loggerheads with Bishop Jean-Baptiste Lamy (1814–88), a Frenchman appointed in 1851 to supervise the affairs of the first independent New Mexican diocese. Lamy, on whose life Willa Cather based her novel *Death Comes for the Archbishop,* served the diocese for 37 years. Lamy didn't take kindly to Martinez's independent streak and, after repeated conflicts, excommunicated the maverick priest in 1857. But Martinez was steadfast in his preaching. He established an independent church and continued as Northern New Mexico's spiritual leader until his death.

Nevertheless, Lamy made many positive contributions to New Mexico, especially in the fields of education and architecture. Santa Fe's Romanesque **Cathedral of St. Francis** and the nearby Gothic-style **Loretto Chapel,** for instance, were constructed under his aegis. But he was adamant about adhering to strict Catholic religious tenets. Martinez, on the other hand, embraced the folk tradition, including the craft of *santero* (religious icon) carving and a tolerance of the Penitentes, a flagellant sect that flourished after the departure of the Franciscans in the mid–18th century.

With the advent of the **Atchison, Topeka & Santa Fe Railway** in 1879, New Mexico began to boom. Albuquerque in particular blossomed in the wake of a series of major gold strikes in the Madrid Valley, close to ancient Native American turquoise mines. By the time the gold lodes began to shrink in the 1890s, cattle and sheep ranching had become well entrenched. The territory's growth culminated in statehood in 1912.

Territorial governor Lew Wallace, who served from 1878 to 1881, was instrumental in promoting interest in the arts, which today flourish in Northern New Mexico. While occupying the Palace of the Governors, Wallace penned the great biblical novel *Ben Hur.* In the 1890s, Ernest Blumenschein, Bert Phillips, and Joseph Sharp launched the Taos art colony; it boomed in the decade following World War I when Mabel Dodge Luhan, D. H. Lawrence, Georgia O'Keeffe, Willa Cather, and many others visited or established residence in the area.

During World War II, the federal government purchased an isolated boys' camp west of Santa Fe and turned it into the **Los Alamos National Laboratory,** where the Manhattan Project and other top-secret atomic experiments were developed and perfected. The science and military legacy continues today; Albuquerque is among the nation's leaders in attracting defense contracts and high technology.

4 Land of Art

It's all in the light—or at least that's what many artists claim drew them to Northern New Mexico. In truth, the light is only part of the attraction: Nature in this part of the country, with its awe-inspiring thunderheads, endless expanse of blue skies, and rugged desert, is itself a canvas. To record the wonders of earth and sky, the early natives of the area, the Anasazi, imprinted images (in the form of petroglyphs and pictographs) on the sides of caves and on stones, as well as on the sides of pots they shaped from clay dug in the hills.

Today's Native American tribes carry on that legacy, as do the other cultures that have settled here. Life in Northern New Mexico is shaped by the arts. Everywhere you turn you'll see pottery, paintings, jewelry, and weavings. You're liable to meet an artist whether you're having coffee in a Taos cafe or walking along Canyon Road in Santa Fe.

The area is full of little villages that maintain their own artistic specialties. Each Indian pueblo has a trademark design, such as **Santa Clara's** and **San Ildefonso's** black pottery and **Zuni's** needlepoint silverwork. Bear in mind that the images used often have deep symbolic meaning. When purchasing art or an artifact, you may want to talk to its maker about what the symbols mean.

Hispanic villages are also distinguished by their artistic identities. **Chimayo** has become a center for Hispanic weaving, while the village of **Cordova** is known for its *santo* (icon) carving. Santos, *retablos* (paintings), and *bultos* (sculptures), as well as works in tin, are traditional devotional arts tied to the Roman Catholic faith. Often, these works are sold out of artists' homes in these villages, allowing you to glimpse the lives of the artists and the surroundings that inspire them.

Hispanic and Native American villagers take their goods to the cities, where for centuries people have bought and traded. Under the portals along the plazas of Santa Fe, Taos, and Albuquerque, you'll find a variety of works in silver, stone, and pottery for sale. In the cities, you'll find streets lined with galleries, some very slick, some more modest. At major markets, such as the **Spanish Market** and **Indian Market** in Santa Fe, some of the top artists from the area sell their works. Smaller shows at the pueblos also attract artists and artisans. The **Northern Pueblo Artists and Craftsman show** at Santa Clara Pueblo in July continues to grow each year.

Drawn by the beauty of the local landscape and respect for indigenous art, artists from all over have flocked here, particularly during the 20th century. And they have established locally important art societies; one of the most notable is the **Taos Society of Artists.** An oft-repeated tale explains the roots of this society. The artists Bert Phillips and Ernest L. Blumenschein were traveling through the area from Colorado on a mission to sketch the Southwest when their wagon broke down north of Taos. The scenery so overwhelmed them that they abandoned their journey and stayed. Joseph Sharp joined them, and still later came Oscar Berninghaus, Walter Ufner, Herbert Dunton, and others. You can see a brilliant collection of some of their romantically lit portraits and landscapes at the Van Vechten Lineberry Museum in Taos. The 100th anniversary marking the artists' broken wheel was celebrated in 1998.

A major player in the development of Taos as an artists' community was the arts patron Mabel Dodge Luhan. A writer who financed the work of many an artist, in the 1920s Luhan held court for many notables, including Georgia O'Keeffe, Willa Cather, and D. H. Lawrence. This illustrious history goes a long way to explaining how it is that Taos—a town of less than 5,000—has more than 90 arts-and-crafts galleries and more than 100 resident painters.

Santa Fe has its own art society, begun in the 1920s by a nucleus of five painters—who became known as **Los Cinco Pintores.** Jozef Bakos, Fremont Ellis, Walter Mruk, Willard Nash, and Will Shuster lived in the area of dusty Canyon Road (now the arts center of Santa Fe, with more than 1,000 artists, countless galleries, and many museums). Despite its small size, Santa Fe is, remarkably, considered the third largest art market in the United States.

Perhaps the most celebrated artist associated with Northern New Mexico was **Georgia O'Keeffe** (1887–1986), a painter who worked and lived most of her later years in the region. O'Keeffe's first sojourn to New Mexico in 1929 inspired her sensuous paintings of the area's desert landscape and bleached animal skulls. The house where she lived in Abiquiu (42 miles northwest of Santa Fe on US 84) is now open for limited public tours (see chapter 10 for details). The **Georgia O'Keeffe Museum** in Santa Fe, the only museum in the United States entirely dedicated to a woman artist, opened in Santa Fe in 1997.

Santa Fe is also home to the **Institute of American Indian Arts** and the **School of Indian Art,** where many of today's leading Native American artists have studied, including the Apache sculptor Allan Houser (whose works you can see near the State Capitol building and in other public areas in Santa Fe). The best-known Native American painter is R. C. Gorman, an Arizona Navajo who has made his home in Taos for more than 2 decades. Now in his late 50s, Gorman is internationally acclaimed for his bright, somewhat surrealistic depictions of Navajo women. A relative newcomer to national fame is Dan Namingha, a Hopi artist who weaves native symbology into contemporary concerns.

If you look closely, you'll find notable works from a number of local artists. There's Tammy Garcia, a young Taos potter who year after year continues to sweep the awards at Indian Market with her intricately shaped and carved pots. Cippy Crazyhorse, a Cochiti, has acquired a steady following of patrons for his silver jewelry. All around the area you'll see the frescoes of Frederico Vigil, a noted muralist and Santa Fe native. From the village of Santa Cruz comes a new rising star named Andres Martinez, noted for his Picasso-esque portraits of Hispanic village life.

For the visitor interested in art, however, some caution should be exercised; there's a lot of schlock out there targeting the tourist trade. Yet if you persist, you're likely to find much inspiring work as well. The museums and many of the galleries are excellent repositories of local art. Their offerings range from small-town folk art to works by major artists who show internationally.

5 Architecture: A Rich Melting Pot

Northern New Mexico's distinctive architecture reflects the diversity of cultures that have left their imprint on the region. The first people in the area were the Anasazi, who built stone and mud homes at the bottom of canyons and inside caves (which look rather like condominiums to the modern urban eye). **Pueblo-style adobe architecture** evolved and became the basis for traditional New Mexican homes: sun-dried clay bricks mixed with grass for strength, mud-mortared, and covered with additional protective layers of mud. Roofs are supported by a network of *vigas*—long beams whose ends protrude through the outer facades—and *latillas,* smaller stripped branches layered between the *vigas*. Other adapted Pueblo architectural elements include plastered adobe-brick kiva fireplaces, *bancos* (adobe benches that protrude from walls), and *nichos* (small indentations within a wall in which religious icons are placed). These adobe homes are characterized by flat roofs and soft, rounded contours.

Spaniards wedded many elements to Pueblo style, such as portals (porches held up with posts, often running the length of a home) and enclosed patios, as well as the simple, dramatic sculptural shapes of Spanish mission arches and bell towers. They also brought elements from the Moorish architecture found in southern Spain: heavy wooden doors and elaborate corbels—carved wooden supports for the vertical posts.

With the opening of the Santa Fe Trail in 1821 and later the 1860s gold boom, both of which brought more Anglo settlers, came the next wave of building. New arrivals contributed architectural elements such as neo-Grecian and Victorian influences popular in the middle part of the United States at the time. Distinguishing features of what came to be known as **Territorial-style** architecture can be seen today; they include brick facades and cornices as well as porches, often placed on the second story. You'll also note millwork on doors and wood trim around windows and doorways, double-hung windows, as well as Victorian bric-a-brac.

Santa Fe Plaza is an excellent example of the convergence of these early architectural styles. On the west side is a Territorial-style balcony, while the Palace of Governors is marked by Pueblo-style vigas and oversized Spanish/Moorish doors.

Nowhere else in the United States are you likely to see such extremes of architectural style as in Northern New Mexico. In Santa Fe, you'll see the Romanesque architecture of the **St. Francis Cathedral** and **Loretto chapel,** brought by Archbishop Lamy from France, as well as the railroad station built in the **Spanish Mission style**—popular in the early part of this century.

Since 1957, strict state building codes have required that all new structures within the circumference of the Paseo de Peralta conform to one of two revival styles: Pueblo or Territorial. The regulation also limits the height of the buildings and restricts the types of signs permitted. It also requires buildings to be topped by flat roofs. In 1988, additional citywide standards were established in an effort to impose some degree of architectural taste on new developments.

Albuquerque also has a broad array of styles, most evident in a visit to Old Town. There, you'll find the large Italianate brick house known as the **Herman Blueher home** built in 1898; throughout Old Town you'll find little placitas, homes, and haciendas built around a courtyard, a strategy developed not only for defense purposes but also as a way to accommodate several generations of the same family in different wings of a single dwelling. **The Church of San Felipe de Neri** at the center of Old Town is centered between two folk Gothic towers. This building was begun in a cruciform plan in 1793; subsequent architectural changes resulted in an interesting mixture of styles.

Most notable architecturally in Taos is the **Taos Pueblo,** the site of two structures emulated in homes and business buildings throughout the Southwest. Built to resemble Taos Mountain, which stands behind it, the two structures are pyramidal in form, with the different levels reached by ladders. Also quite prevalent is architecture echoing colonial hacienda style. What's nice about Taos is that you can see historic homes inside and out. You can wander through **Kit Carson's old home;** built in 1825, it's an excellent example of a hacienda and is filled with a fine collection of 19th-century Western Americana. Taos Society artist **Ernest Blumenschein's home** is also a museum. Built in 1797 and restored by Blumenschein in 1919, it represents another New Mexico architectural phenomenon: homes that were added onto year after year. Doorways are typically low, and floors rise and fall at the whim of the earth beneath them. The **Martinez Hacienda** is an example of a hacienda stronghold. Built without windows facing outward, it originally had 20 small rooms, many with doors opening out to the courtyard. One of the few refurbished examples of colonial New Mexico architecture and life, the hacienda is on the National Historic Registry.

As you head into villages in the north, you'll see steep pitched roofs on most homes. This is because the common flat-roof style doesn't shed snow; the water builds up and causes roof problems. In just about any town in Northern New Mexico, you may detect the strong smell of tar, a sure sign that another resident is laying out thousands to fix his enchanting but frustratingly flat roof.

Today, very few new homes are built of adobe. Instead, most are constructed with wood frames and plasterboard, and then stuccoed over. Several local architects are currently employing innovative architecture to create a Pueblo-style feel. They incorporate straw bails, pumice-crete, rammed earth, old tires, even aluminum cans in the construction of homes. Most of these elements are used in the same way bricks are used, stacked and layered, then covered over with plaster and made to look like adobe. Often it's difficult to distinguish homes built with these materials from those built with wood-frame construction. West of Taos a number of "earth-ships" have been built. Many of these homes are constructed with alternative materials, some bermed into the sides of hills, utilizing the earth as insulation and the sun as an energy source.

A visitor could spend an entire trip to New Mexico focusing on the architecture. As well as relishing the wealth of architectural styles, you'll find more subtle elements everywhere. You may encounter an oxblood floor, for example. An old Spanish tradition, oxblood is spread in layers and left to dry, hardening into a glossy finish that's known to last centuries. You're also likely to see coyote fences—narrow cedar posts lined up side by side—a system early settlers devised to ensure safety of their animals. Winding around homes and buildings you'll see *acequias,* ancient irrigation canals still maintained by locals for watering crops and trees. Throughout the area you'll notice that old walls are whimsically bowed and windows and floors are often crooked, constant reminders of the effects time has had upon even these stalwart structures.

6 Anthropology 101: Beliefs & Rituals

Religion has always been a central, defining element in the life of the Pueblo people. Within the cosmos, which they view as a single whole, all living creatures are mutually dependent. Thus, every relationship a human being may have, whether with a person, animal, or even plant, has spiritual significance. A hunter prays before killing a deer, asking the creature to sacrifice itself to the tribe. A slain deer is treated as a guest of honor, and the hunter performs a ritual in which he sends the animal's soul back to its community, so that it may be reborn. Even the harvesting of plants requires prayer, thanks, and ritual.

The Pueblo people believe that their ancestors originally lived under the ground, which, as the place from which plants spring, is the source of all life. According to their beliefs, the original Pueblos, encouraged by burrowing animals, entered the world of humans—the so-called "fifth" world—through a hole, a sipapu. The ways in which this came about and the deities that the Pueblo people revere vary from tribe to tribe. Most, however, believe this world is bounded by four sacred mountains, where four sacred colors—coral, black, turquoise, and yellow or white—predominate.

There is no single great spirit ruling over this world; instead, it is watched over by a number of spiritual elements. Most common are Mother Earth and Father Sun. In this desert land, the sun is an element of both life and death. The tribes watch the skies closely, tracking solstices and planetary movements, to determine the optimal time for crop planting.

Ritualistic dances are occasions of great symbolic importance. Usually held in conjunction with the feast days of Catholic saints (including Christmas Eve), Pueblo ceremonies demonstrate the parallel absorption of Christian elements without the surrendering of traditional beliefs. To this day communities enact medicine dances, fertility rites, and prayers for rain and for good harvests. The spring

Danse Macabre

The Dance of the Matachines, a ritualistic dance performed at Northern New Mexico pueblos and in many Hispanic communities, can be seen as a metaphor for the tribulations and richness of this land. It reveals the cultural miscegenation, identities, and conflicts that characterize Northern New Mexico. It's a dark and vivid ritual in which a little girl, Malinche, is wedded to the church. The dance, depicting the taming of the native spirit, is difficult even for historians to decipher.

Brought to the New World by the Spaniards, the dance has its roots in the painful period during which the Moors were driven out of Spain. However, some symbols seem obvious: At one point, men bearing whips tame "El Toro," a small boy dressed as a bull who has been charging about rebelliously. The whip-men symbolically castrate him and then stroll through the crowd pretending to display the dismembered body parts, as if to warn villagers of the consequences of disobedience. At another point, a hunched woman-figure births a small troll-like doll, perhaps representative of the union between Indian and Hispanic cultures.

The Dance of the Matachines ends when two *abuelo* (grandparent) figures dance across the dirt holding up the just-born baby, while the Matachines, adorned with bishoplike headdresses, follow them away in a recessional march. The Matachines' dance, often performed in the early mornings, is so dark and mystical that every time I see it my passion for this area deepens. The image of that baby always stays with me, and in a way represents New Mexico itself: A place born of disparate beliefs that have melded with the sand, sage, and sun and produced incredible richness.

and summer corn, or tablita, dances are among the most impressive. Ceremonies begin with an early-morning mass and procession to the Plaza; the image of the saint is honored at the forefront. The rest of the day is devoted to song, dance, and feasting, with performers masked and clad as deer, buffalo, eagles, or other creatures.

Visitors are usually welcome to attend Pueblo dances, but they should respect the tribe's requests not to be photographed or recorded. It was exactly this lack of respect that led the Zunis to ban outsiders from attending many of their famous Shalako ceremonies.

Catholicism, imposed by the Spaniards, has infused Northern New Mexico with an elaborate set of beliefs. This is a Catholicism heavy with iconography, expressed in carved santos (statues) and beautiful retablos (paintings) that adorn the altars of many cathedrals. Catholic churches are the focal point of most Northern New Mexico villages. When you take the high road to Taos, be sure to note the church in **Las Trampas,** as well as the one in **Ranchos de Taos;** both have 3- to 4-foot-thick walls sculpted from adobe and inside have an old-world charm, with beautiful retablos decorating the walls and vigas (roof beams) holding up the roofs.

Hispanics in Northern New Mexico, in particular, maintain strong family and Catholic ties, and they continue to honor traditions associated with both. Communities plan elaborate celebrations such as the *quinciniera* for young girls reaching womanhood, and weddings with big feasts and dances in which well-wishers pin money to the bride's elaborately laced gown.

If you happen to be in the area during a holiday, you may even get to see a religious procession or pilgrimage. Most notable is the **pilgrimage to the Santuario de Chimayo,** an hour's drive north of the state capital. Constructed in 1816, the sanctuary has long been a pilgrimage site for Catholics who attribute miraculous healing powers to the earth found in the chapel's anteroom. Several days before Easter, fervent believers begin walking the highway headed north or south to Chimayo, some carrying large crosses, others carrying nothing but a small bottle of water, most praying for a miracle.

In recent years, New Mexico has become known (and in some circles, ridiculed) for **New Age pilgrims and celebrations.** The roots of the local movement are hard to trace. It may have something to do with Northern New Mexico's centuries-old reputation as a place where rebel thinkers come to enjoy the freedom to believe what they want. Pueblo spirituality and deeply felt connection to the land are also factors that have drawn New Agers. At any rate, the liberated atmosphere here has given rise to a thriving New Age network, one that now includes alternative churches, healing centers, and healing schools. You'll find all sorts of alternative medicine and fringe practices here, from aromatherapy to rolfing—a form of massage that realigns the muscles and bones in the body—and chelation therapy, in which an IV drips ethylene diamine tetra-acetic acid into your blood to remove heavy metals. If those sound too invasive, you can always try psychic surgery.

New Age practices and beliefs have given rise to a great deal of local humor targeting their supposed pyschobabble. One pointed joke asks: "How many 12-steppers does it take to change a lightbulb?" Answer: "None. They just form a support group and learn to live in the dark." For many, however, there's much good to be found in the movement. The Dalai Lama visited Santa Fe because the city is seen as a healing center and has become a refuge for Tibetans. Notable speakers such as Ram Das and John Bradshaw also frequently talk in the area. Many practitioners find the alternatives—healing resources and spiritual paths—they are looking for in the receptive Northern New Mexico desert and mountains.

7 Chiles, Sopaipillas & Other New Mexican Specialties

Northern New Mexicans are serious about eating, and the area's cuisine reflects the amalgam of cultural influences found here. Locals have given their unique blend of Hispanic and Pueblo recipes a rather prosaic, but direct, label: "Northern New Mexico Cuisine."

Food here isn't the same as Mexican cuisine or even those American variations of Tex-Mex and Cal-Mex. New Mexican cooking is a product of Southwestern history: Native Americans taught the Spanish conquerors about corn—how to roast it and how to make corn pudding, stewed corn, cornbread, cornmeal, and posole (hominy)—and they also taught the Spanish how to use chile peppers, a crop indigenous to the New World, having been first harvested in the Andean highlands as early as 4000 B.C. The Spaniards brought the practice of eating beef to the area.

Waves of newcomers have introduced other elements to the food here. From Mexico came the interest in seafood. You'll find fish tacos on many menus as well as shrimp enchiladas and ceviche. New Southwestern cuisine combines elements from various parts of Mexico, such as sauces from the Yucatán Peninsula, and fried bananas served with bean dishes, typical of Costa Rica and other Central American locales. You'll also find Asian elements mixed in, such as pot stickers in a tortilla soup.

You Say Chili, We Say Chile

You'll never see "chili" on a menu in New Mexico. New Mexicans are adamant that *chile,* the Spanish spelling of the word, is the only way to spell it—no matter what your dictionary might say.

I'm inclined to think chile with an "e" is listed as a secondary spelling only as a courtesy to New Mexicans. We have such a personal attachment to this small agricultural gem that in 1983 we directed our senior U.S. senator, Pete Domenici, to enter New Mexico's official position on the spelling of chile into the *Congressional Record.* That's taking your *chiles* seriously.

Chiles are grown throughout the state, in a perfect climate for cultivating and drying the small but powerful red and green New Mexican varieties. But it is the town of Hatch, New Mexico, that bills itself as the "Chile Capital of the World." Regardless of where you travel in the state, chiles appear on the menu. Virtually anything you order in a restaurant is topped with a chile sauce. If you're not accustomed to spicy foods, certain varieties of red or green chiles will make your eyes water, your sinuses drain, and your palate feel as if it's on fire—all after just one forkful. *Warning:* No amount of water or beer will alleviate the sting. (Drink milk. A sopaipilla drizzled with honey is also helpful.)

But don't let these words of caution scare you away from genuine New Mexico chiles. The pleasure of eating them far outweighs the pain. Start slow, with salsas and chile sauces first, perhaps rellenos (stuffed peppers) next, followed by rajas (roasted peeled chiles cut into strips). Before long, you'll be buying chile ristras (chiles strung on rope) and hanging them up for decoration. Perhaps you'll be so smitten that you'll purchase bags of chile powder or a chile plant to take home. If you happen to be in New Mexico in the fall, you'll find fresh roasted green chile sold. In the parking lots of most grocery stores and at some roadside stands, you'll smell the scent of roasting chile and see large metal baskets full of peppers rotating over flames. If you have a means of freezing the chile before transporting it home, you can sample the delicacy throughout the year. This will certainly make you an expert on the difference between chile and chili.

The basic ingredients of Northern New Mexico cooking are three indispensable, locally grown vegetables: **chile, beans,** and **corn.** Of these, perhaps the most crucial is the chile, whether brilliant red or green and with various levels of spicy bite. Green chile is hotter if the seeds are left in; red chile is green chile at its ripest stage. Chile forms the base for the red and green sauces that top most Northern New Mexico dishes such as enchiladas and burritos. One is not necessarily hotter than the other; spiciness depends on where and during what kind of season (dry or wet) the chiles were grown. You'll also find salsas, generally made with jalapeños, tomatoes, onions, and garlic, used for chip dipping and as a spice on tacos.

Beans—spotted or painted pinto beans with a nutty taste—are simmered with garlic, onion, cumin, and red chile powder and served as a side dish. When mashed and refried in oil, they become *frijoles refritos.* **Corn** supplies the vital dough for tortillas called *masa.* New Mexican corn comes in six colors, of which yellow, white, and blue are the most common.

Even if you are familiar with Mexican cooking, the dishes you know and love are likely to be prepared differently here. The following is a rundown of some regional dishes, a number of which are not widely known outside the Southwest:

biscochito   A cookie made with anise.

carne adovada   Tender pork marinated in red chile sauce, herbs, and spices, and then baked.

chile relleños   Peppers stuffed with cheese, deep-fried, then covered with green chile sauce.

chorizo burrito (also called a "breakfast burrito")   Mexican sausage, scrambled eggs, potatoes, and scallions wrapped in a flour tortilla with red or green chile sauce and melted Jack cheese.

empañada   A fried pie with nuts and currants.

enchiladas   Tortillas filled with peppers or other foods.

fajitas   Strips of beef or chicken sautéed with onions, green peppers, and other vegetables and served on a sizzling platter.

green chile stew   Locally grown chiles cooked in a stew with chunks of meat, beans, and potatoes.

huevos rancheros   Fried eggs on corn tortillas, topped with cheese and red or green chile, served with pinto beans.

pan dulce   A Native American sweetbread.

posole   A corn soup or stew (called hominy in other parts of the South), sometimes prepared with pork and chile.

sopaipillas   A lightly fried puff pastry served with honey as a dessert or stuffed with meat and vegetables as a main dish. Sopaipillas with honey have a cooling effect on your palate after you've eaten a spicy dish.

tacos   Served either in soft tortillas or crispy shells.

tamales   Made from cornmeal mush, wrapped in husks and steamed.

vegetables and nuts   Despite the prosaic name, unusual local ingredients, such as piñon nuts, jicama, and prickly pear cactus, will often be a part of your meals.

8 Recommended Books

Many well-known writers have made their home in Northern New Mexico in the 20th century. In the 1920s, the most celebrated were **D. H. Lawrence** and **Willa Cather,** both short-term Taos residents. Lawrence, the romantic and controversial English novelist, spent time here between 1922 and 1925; he reflected on his sojourn in *Mornings in Mexico* and *Etruscan Places.* Lawrence's Taos period is described in *Lorenzo in Taos,* which his patron, Mabel Dodge Luhan, wrote. Cather, a Pulitzer-prize winner famous for her depictions of the pioneer spirit, penned *Death Comes for the Archbishop.* This fictionalized account of the 19th-century Santa Fe bishop, Jean-Baptiste Lamy, grew out of her stay in the region.

Many contemporary authors also live in and write about New Mexico. John Nichols, of Taos, whose *Milagro Beanfield War* was made into a Robert Redford movie in 1987, writes insightfully about the problems of poor Hispanic farming communities. Albuquerque's Tony Hillerman has for 2 decades weaved mysteries around Navajo tribal police in books such as *Listening Woman* and *A Thief of Time.* The Hispanic novelist Rudolfo Anaya's *Bless Me, Ultima* and Pueblo writer Leslie Marmon Silko's *Ceremony* capture the lifestyles of their respective peoples. Of the desert environment and politics, no one wrote better than the late Edward Abbey; his *Fire on the Mountain,* set in New Mexico, was one of his most powerful works.

OTHER SUGGESTED READING   Excellent works about Native Americans of New Mexico include *The Pueblo Indians of North America* (Holt, Rinehart &

Winston, 1970) by Edward P. Dozier and *Living the Sky: The Cosmos of the American Indian* (University of Oklahoma Press, 1987) by Ray A. Williamson. Also look for *American Indian Literature 1979–1994* (Ballantine, 1996), an anthology edited by Paula Gunn Allen.

For general histories of the state, try Myra Ellen Jenkins and Albert H. Schroeder's *A Brief History of New Mexico* (University of New Mexico Press, 1974) and Marc Simmons's *New Mexico: An Interpretive History* (University of New Mexico Press, 1988). In addition, Claire Morrill's *A Taos Mosaic: Portrait of a New Mexico Village* (University of New Mexico Press, 1973) does an excellent job of portraying the history of that small New Mexican town. I have also enjoyed Tony Hillerman's (ed.) *The Spell of New Mexico* (University of New Mexico Press, 1976) and John Nichols and William Davis's *If Mountains Die: A New Mexico Memoir* (Alfred A. Knopf, 1979). *Talking Ground* (University of New Mexico Press, 1996), by Santa Fe author Douglas Preston, tells of a contemporary horseback trip through Navajoland exploring the native mythology. One of my favorite texts is *Enchantment and Exploitation* (University of New Mexico Press, 1985) by William deBuys. A new, very extensive book that attempts to capture the multiplicity of the region is *Legends of the American Southwest* (Alfred A. Knopf, 1997) by Alex Shoumatoff.

THE ARTS   *Enduring Visions: 1,000 Years of Southwestern Indian Art,* by the Aspen Center for the Visual Arts (Publishing Center for Cultural Resources, 1969), and Roland F. Dickey's *New Mexico Village Arts* (University of New Mexico Press, 1990) are both excellent resources for those interested in Indian art. If you become intrigued with Spanish art during your visit to New Mexico, you'll find E. Boyd's *Popular Arts of Spanish New Mexico* (Museum of New Mexico Press, 1974) to be quite informative.

2

Planning a Trip to Santa Fe, Taos & Albuquerque

As with any trip, a little preparation is essential before you start. This chapter will provide you with a variety of planning tools, including information on when to go and how to get there.

1 Visitor Information

Numerous agencies can assist you with planning your trip. The Tourism and Travel Division of the **New Mexico Department of Tourism** is located in Room 751, 491 Old Santa Fe Trail, Santa Fe, NM 87503 (☎ 800/545-2040). Santa Fe, Taos, and Albuquerque each has its own information service for visitors (see the "Orientation" sections in chapters 4, 11, and 15, respectively).

Information about Northern New Mexico is also available on the Internet. For general New Mexico information, try **www.swcp. com/nm/.** A new and valuable resource for information on outdoor recreation is the **Public Lands Information Center,** located on the south side of town at 1474 Rodeo Rd., Santa Fe, NM 87505 (☎ 505/438-7542). Under one roof, adventurers can find out what's available on lands administered by the National Forest Service, Bureau of Land Management, Fish and Wildlife Service, National Park Service, Bureau of Reclamation, Army Corps of Engineers, NM Department of Game and Fish (which sells hunting and fishing licenses), and NM State Parks Division. The Information Center collaborates with the NM Department of Tourism. Its main Web site address is **www.publiclandsinfo.org,** but it has links to 261 separate sites, which can be found by looking up either a particular activity or agency.

For Internet addresses of individual cities' visitor centers, see chapters 4, 11, and 15.

2 When to Go

THE CLIMATE Forget any preconceptions you may have about the New Mexico "desert." The high desert climate of this part of the world is generally dry but not always warm. Santa Fe and Taos, at 7,000 feet above sea level, have midsummer highs in the 80s and lows in the 50s. Spring and fall highs run in the 60s, with lows in the 30s. Typical midwinter daytime temperatures are in the low 40s, and overnight lows are in the teens. Temperatures in Albuquerque, at 5,300 feet, often run about 10°F warmer.

The average annual precipitation ranges from 8 inches at Albuquerque to 12 inches at Taos and 14 at Santa Fe, most of it coming in July and August as afternoon thunderstorms. Snowfall is common from November through March and sometimes as late as May, though the snow seldom lasts long. Santa Fe averages 32 inches total annual snowfall. At the high-mountain ski resorts, as much as 300 inches (25 feet) of snow may fall in a season—and stay.

Average Temperatures (°F) and Annual Rainfall (inches)

	Jan High–Low	Apr High–Low	July High–Low	Oct High–Low	Rainfall (inches)
Albuquerque	46–28	69–42	91–66	71–45	8.9
Santa Fe	42–18	62–33	85–56	65–38	14.0
Taos	40–10	64–29	87–50	67–32	12.1

NORTHERN NEW MEXICO CALENDAR OF EVENTS

January

- **New Year's Day.** Transfer of canes to new officials and various dances at most pueblos. Turtle Dance at Taos Pueblo (no photography allowed). January 1. Call ☎ **800/793-4955** for more information.
- **Winter Wine Festival.** A variety of wine offerings and food tastings prepared by local chefs take place mid-January in the Taos Ski Valley. Call ☎ **505/776-2291** for details.

February

- **Candelaria Day Celebration, Picuris Pueblo.** Traditional dances. February 2. Call ☎ **505/587-2519** for more information.
- ✪ **Winter Fiesta.** Santa Fe's annual retreat from the midwinter doldrums appeals to skiers and nonskiers alike. Highlights include the Great Santa Fe Chile Cookoff; ski races, both serious and frivolous; snow-sculpture contests; snow-shoe races; and hot-air balloon rides.

  The festival takes place at the Santa Fe Ski Area the first weekend in February. Most events are free. Call ☎ **800/777-2489** or 505/984-6760 for information.
- **Mt. Taylor Winter Quadrathlon.** Hundreds of athletes come from all over the West to bicycle, run, cross-country ski and snowshoe up and down this mountain. Mid-February. For information call ☎ **800/748-2142.**
- **Just Desserts Eat and Ski.** Cross-country skiers skate from point to point on the Enchanted Forest course near Red River tasting decadent desserts supplied by area restaurants. Late February. Call ☎ **505/754-2366.**

March

- **Fiery Food Show.** This annual trade show, which takes place in Albuquerque in early March, features chiles and an array of products that can be made from them. Call ☎ **505/298-3835** for details.
- **Rio Grande Arts and Crafts Festival.** A juried show featuring 200 artists and craftspeople from around the country takes place at the State Fairgrounds in Albuquerque during the second week of March. Call ☎ **505/292-7457** for more information.

April

- **Easter Weekend Celebration,** Nambe, San Juan, and San Ildefonso Pueblos. Celebrations include masses, parades, Corn Dances, and other dances, such as the Bow and Arrow Dance at Nambe. Call ☎ **800/793-4955** for information.

- **Easter Sunday Celebration,** Indian Pueblo Cultural Center, Albuquerque. Traditional dances are performed by Native Americans. Call ☎ **505/843-7270.**
- **American Indian Week,** Indian Pueblo Cultural Center, Albuquerque. A celebration of Native American traditions and culture. Begins late in the second week of April. Call ☎ **505/843-7270.**
- **Gathering of Nations Powwow,** University Arena, Albuquerque. Dance competitions, arts-and-crafts exhibitions, and Miss Indian World contest. Mid- to late April. Call ☎ **505/836-2810.**

✪ **Taos Talking Picture Festival.** Filmmakers and film enthusiasts gather to view a variety of films, from serious documentaries to lighthearted comedies. You'll see locally made films as well as those involving Hollywood big-hitters. Each year 5 acres of land is given as a prize to encourage filmmakers to take a fresh approach to storytelling. In 1998, the festival's Land Grant Award went to Native American filmmaker Chris Eyre. His film *Smoke Signals,* shown opening night, is the first Native-written and -directed film to be introduced into national distribution. The festival's 1998 Cineaste Award went to Latino filmmaker Moctesuma Esparza, whose work includes *Selena, The Disappearance of Garcia Lorca*, and *The Milagro Beanfield War.*

Events are held in mid-April at venues located throughout Taos and Taos County. Contact the Taos Talking Picture Festival, (7217 NDCBU) 1337 Gusdorf, Suite F, Taos, NM 87571. (☎ **505/751-0637;** Fax 505/751-7385. www.taosnet.com/ttpix/. E-mail: ttpix@taosnet.com).

May

✪ **Taos Spring Arts Festival.** Contemporary visual, performing, and literary arts are highlighted during 2 weeks of gallery openings, studio tours, performances by visiting theatrical and dance troupes, live musical events, traditional ethnic entertainment, a film festival, literary readings, and more.

The festival is during the first 2 weeks in May at venues throughout Taos and Taos County. Tickets are available from many galleries and from the Taos County Chamber of Commerce, P.O. Drawer I, Taos, NM 87571 (☎ **800/732-TAOS** or 505/758-3873).

- **¡Magnifico! Albuquerque Festival of the Arts.** This celebration features various visual and performing-arts events held throughout the year. In mid-May the performing arts are honored in several locations. For a schedule of all events, call ☎ **800/733-9918** or 505/842-9918, ext. 3353.

June

- **Rodeo de Taos,** County Fairgrounds, Taos. Fourth weekend in June. A fun event featuring local and regional participants. Call the Taos County Chamber of Commerce for more information (☎**800/732-TAOS** or 505/758-3873).

✪ **New Mexico Arts and Crafts Fair.** This is the second-largest event of its type in the United States. More than 200 New Mexico artisans exhibit and sell their crafts, and there is nonstop entertainment for the whole family. Hispanic arts and crafts are also on display.

The fair is held at the State Fairgrounds in Albuquerque the last weekend in June (on Friday and Saturday from 10am to 10pm and on Sunday from 10am to 6pm). Admission cost varies. For information, call ☎ **505/884-9043.**

- **Taos Poetry Circus.** Poetry readings, lectures, seminars, and several poetry bouts highlight this spirited event the second week in June. It culminates in the "World Championship Poetry Bout." For information call ☎ **505-758-1800.**

- **Prestigious Few Car Club Car Show.** See amazing low-riders of all types in Española, the "low-rider capital of the world." Call ☎ **505/753-9926** or 505/988-2233 for information.

July

- **Fourth of July celebrations** (including fireworks displays) are held all over New Mexico. Call the chambers of commerce in specific towns and cities for information.
- **Picuris Arts and Crafts Fair,** Picuris Pueblo. Traditional dances and other events. Proceeds go to the restoration of the San Lorenzo Mission. The first weekend in July. Call ☎ **505/587-2519** for details.
- **Santa Fe Wine Festival at Rancho de las Golondrinas.** This event in early July boasts live entertainment and wine tastings presided over by hosts dressed in period clothing. Call ☎ **505/892-4178.**
- **Rodeo de Santa Fe.** This 4-day event features a Western parade, rodeo dance, and four rodeo performances. It attracts hundreds of cowboys and cowgirls from all over the Southwest who compete for a sizable purse in such events as brahma bull and bronco riding, calf roping, steer wrestling, barrel racing, trick riding, clown and animal acts, and a local version of bullfighting in which neither the bull nor the matador is hurt.

    The rodeo grounds are at 2801 Rodeo Rd., off Cerrillos Road, 5½ miles south of the Plaza. The rodeo goes from the first weekend following the Fourth of July (starting at 7:30pm Wednesday through Saturday; also at 2pm on Saturday). For tickets and information, call ☎ **505/471-4300.**
- **Taos Pueblo Powwow.** Intertribal competition in traditional and contemporary dances. The second weekend in July. Call ☎ **505/758-9593** for more information.
- **Eight Northern Pueblos Artist and Craftsman Show.** More than 600 Native American artists exhibit their work at one of the eight northern pueblos. Traditional dances and food booths. The third weekend in July. Call ☎ **505/852-4265** for location and exact dates.

✪ **Fiestas de Santiago y Santa Ana.** The celebration begins with a Friday night mass at Our Lady of Guadalupe Church, where the fiesta queen is crowned. During the weekend there are candlelight processions, special masses, music, dancing, parades, crafts and food booths, and Corn Dances at Taos Pueblo (no photography allowed).

    Taos Plaza hosts events on the third weekend in July. Most events are free. For information, contact the Taos Fiesta Council, P.O. Box 3300, Taos, NM 87571 (☎ **800/732-8267**).

✪ **The Spanish Markets.** More than 300 Hispanic artists from New Mexico and southern Colorado exhibit and sell their work in this lively community event. Artists are featured in special demonstrations, while an entertaining mix of traditional Hispanic music, dance, foods, and pageantry creates the ambience of a village celebration. Artwork for sale includes *santos* (painted and carved saints), textiles, tin work, furniture, straw appliqué, and metalwork.

    The markets are found at Santa Fe Plaza in Santa Fe the last full weekend in July. For information, contact the Spanish Colonial Arts Society, P.O. Box 1611, Santa Fe, NM 87504 (☎ **505/983-4038**).

August

✪ **The Indian Market.** This is the largest all–Native American market in the country. About 800 artisans display their baskets and blankets, jewelry, pottery, wood carvings, rugs, sand paintings, and sculptures at rows of booths. Sales are brisk. Costumed tribal dancing and crafts demonstrations are scheduled in the afternoon.

Visit the Indian Market at Santa Fe Plaza, surrounding streets, and De Vargas Mall during the third weekend in August. The market is free but hotels are booked months in advance. For information, contact the Southwestern Association on Indian Affairs, P.O. Box 1964, Santa Fe, NM 87501 (☎ **505/983-5220**).

- **Music from Angel Fire,** Angel Fire. World-class musicians perform classical and chamber music. Last week in August to first week in September. Call ☎ **505/377-3233** for information and schedules.

September

- **Gourmet Jubilee,** Angel Fire. Farmer's market highlighting New Mexico–made products as well as wines. Cooking classes and dinners are available. Early September. Call ☎ **800/446-8117** for information.
- **New Mexico Wine Festival at Bernalillo,** near Albuquerque. New Mexico wines are showcased at this annual event. Wine tastings, art show, and live entertainment. Labor Day weekend. For schedule of events, call ☎ **505/892-4178.**
- **Velarde Apple Festival.** Apple growers sell their bounty in this village on the way to Taos. You'll find cider, apple sauce, and other tasty treats, as well as ristras and elaborate dry chile, gourd, and flower arrangements. Call ☎ **505/852-2310.**
- ✪ **La Fiesta de Santa Fe.** An exuberant combination of spirit, history, and general merrymaking, La Fiesta is the oldest community celebration in the United States. The first fiesta was celebrated in 1712, 20 years after the peaceful resettlement of New Mexico by Spanish conquistadors in 1692. La Conquistadora, a carved Madonna credited with the victory, is the focus of the celebration, which includes masses, a parade for children and their pets, a historical/hysterical parade, mariachi concerts, dances, food, and arts, as well as local entertainment on the Plaza. Zozobra, "Old Man Gloom," a 40-foot-tall effigy of wood, canvas, and paper, is burned at dusk on Friday to revitalize the community.

  The Fiesta is on the first Friday after Labor Day. For information, contact the Santa Fe Fiesta Council, P.O. Box 4516, Santa Fe, NM 87502-4516 (☎ **505/988-7575**).
- ✪ **New Mexico State Fair and Rodeo.** One of America's top-10 state fairs, it features parimutuel horse racing, a nationally acclaimed rodeo, entertainment by top country artists, Native American and Spanish villages, the requisite midway livestock shows, and arts and crafts.

  The Fair and Rodeo, which lasts 17 days starting in early September, are held at the State Fairgrounds in Albuquerque. Advance tickets can be ordered by calling ☎ **505/265-1791** for information.
- **Enchanted Circle Century Bike Tour.** Five hundred cyclists usually turn out to ride 100 miles of scenic mountain roads. All levels of riders are welcome, though not everyone completes this test of endurance. The weekend following Labor Day weekend. Call ☎ **505/754-2366.**
- **¡Magnifico! Albuquerque Festival of the Arts.** Art of Albuquerque, a juried show, is held at the Albuquerque Museum in mid-September. For details, call ☎ **800/733-9918** or 505/842-9918, ext. 3353.
- ✪ **Taos Fall Arts Festival.** Highlights include arts-and-crafts exhibitions and competitions, studio tours, gallery openings, lectures, films, concerts, dances, and

stage plays. Simultaneous events include the Old Taos Trade Fair, the Wool Festival, and San Geronimo Day at Taos Pueblo.

The festival is held throughout Taos and Taos County from mid-September (or the third weekend) through the first week in October. Events, schedules, and tickets (where required) can be obtained from the Taos County Chamber of Commerce, P.O. Drawer I, Taos, NM 87571 (☎ **800/732-8267**).

✪ **Old Taos Trade Fair,** Martinez Hacienda, Lower Ranchitos Road, Taos. This 2-day affair reenacts Spanish colonial life of the mid-1820s and features Hispanic and Native American music, weaving and crafts demonstrations, traditional foods, dancing, and visits by mountain men. The last full weekend in September. Call ☎ **505/758-0505.**

✪ **San Geronimo Vespers Sundown Dance and Trade Fair,** Taos Pueblo. A mass and procession; traditional Corn, Buffalo, and Comanche Dances; an arts-and-crafts fair; foot races; and pole climbs by clowns. The last weekend in September. Call ☎ **505/758-1028** for details.

October

✪ **Kodak Albuquerque International Balloon Fiesta.** The world's largest balloon rally brings together more than 800 colorful balloons and includes races and contests. There is a mass ascension at sunrise. Various special events are staged all week.

Balloons lift off at Balloon Fiesta Park (at I-25 and Alameda NE) on Albuquerque's northern city limits during the second week in October. For information call ☎ **800/733-9918.**

✪ **Taos Mountain Balloon Rally and Taste of Taos.** The Albuquerque fiesta's "little brother" offers mass dawn ascensions, tethered balloon rides for the public, and a Saturday parade of balloon baskets (in pickup trucks) from Kit Carson Park around the Plaza. Taste of Taos includes food and product fairs, chile cookoffs, and the creation of the world's biggest burrito. The last full weekend in October. Call ☎ **800/732-8267** for more information.

• **El Rito Artists Studio Tour.** Wander around this Northern New Mexico artist's colony about 30 minutes from Española and find some excellent arts-and-crafts buys. Early October. Call ☎ **505/581-4430.**

November

• **Dixon Art Studio Tour.** Northern New Mexico's most notable village studio tour takes place in early November. Walk the main street that winds through hills planted with fruit trees, and wander into artists' homes and studios. Some excellent arts-and-crafts finds. Call ☎ **505/579-4651.**

✪ **Weems Artfest,** State Fairgrounds, Albuquerque. Approximately 260 artisans, who work in mixed media, come from throughout the world to attend this fair. It's one of the top-100 arts-and-crafts fairs in the country. A 3-day weekend in mid-November. For details, call ☎ **505/293-6133.**

✪ **Festival of the Cranes.** People come from all over the world to attend this bird-watching event just an hour south of Albuquerque at Bosque del Apache National Wildlife Refuge, near Socorro. Call ☎ **505/835-0424.**

December

• **¡Magnifico! Albuquerque Festival of the Arts.** In mid-December, two holiday concerts are given in the historic San Felipe de Neri Church in Old Town. For a schedule, call ☎ **800/733-9918** or 505/842-9918, ext. 3353.

• **Christmas in Madrid Open House.** Even if you never get out of your car, it's worth going to see the spectacular lights display this village creates. You'll also find strolling carolers, entertainment, and, believe it or not, Santa Claus. Various days during December. Call ☎ **505/471-1054.**

✪ **Yuletide in Taos.** This pre-Christmas event, throughout Taos, emphasizes New Mexican traditions, cultures, and arts, with carols, festive classical music, Hispanic and Native American songs and dances, historic walking tours, art exhibitions, dance performances, candlelight dinners, and more.

Yuletide is throughout December. Events are staged by the Taos County Chamber of Commerce, P.O. Drawer I, Taos, NM 87571 (☎ **800/732-TAOS**).

✪ **Canyon Road Farolito Walk,** Santa Fe. Locals and visitors bundle up and stroll Canyon Road, where streets and rooftops are lined with *farolitos* (candle lamps). Musicians play and carolers sing around *luminarias* (little fires) and sip cider. Christmas Eve. Call ☎ **505/983-7317** for information.

• **Torchlight Procession,** Taos Ski Valley. Bold skiers snake down Al's Run in the dark while carrying golden fire. December 31. Call ☎ **505/776-2291** for information.

• **Winter Spanish Market,** Sweeney Convention Center, Santa Fe. See the Spanish Markets in July (above) for more information. The first full weekend in December. Call ☎ **505/983-4038.**

3 Health & Insurance

HEALTH One thing that sets New Mexico apart from most other states is its elevation. Santa Fe and Taos are about 7,000 feet above sea level; Albuquerque is more than 5,000 feet above sea level. The reduced oxygen and humidity can precipitate some unique problems, not the least of which is acute mountain sickness. In its early stages you might experience headaches, shortness of breath, loss of appetite and/or nausea, tingling in the fingers or toes, lethargy, and insomnia. It can usually be treated by taking aspirin as well as getting plenty of rest, avoiding large meals, and drinking lots of nonalcoholic fluids (especially water). If it persists or worsens, you must return to a lower altitude. Other dangers of higher elevations include sunburn and hypothermia, and these should be taken seriously. To avoid dehydration, drink water as often as possible.

It is important to monitor your children's health while in New Mexico. They are just as susceptible to mountain sickness, hypothermia, sunburn, and dehydration as you are.

Other things to be wary of are *arroyos,* or creek beds where flash floods can occur without warning in the desert. If water is flowing across a road, *do not* try to drive through it, because chances are the water is deeper and is flowing faster than you think. Just wait it out. Arroyo floods don't last long.

Finally, if you're an outdoorsperson, be on the lookout for snakes—particularly rattlers. Avoid them. Don't even get close enough to take a picture (unless you have a very good zoom lens).

INSURANCE Before setting out on your trip, check your medical insurance policy to be sure it covers you away from home. If it doesn't, it's wise to purchase a relatively inexpensive traveler's policy, widely available at banks, travel agencies, and automobile clubs. In addition to covering medical assistance, including hospitalization and surgery, the policy should include the cost of an accident, death, or repatriation; loss or theft of baggage; the cost of trip cancellation; and guaranteed bail in the event of an arrest or other legal difficulties.

4 Tips for Travelers with Special Needs

FOR FAMILIES Children are often given discounts that adults, even seniors, would never dream of. For instance, many hotels allow children to stay free with their parents in the same room. The upper age limit may vary from 12 to 18.

Youngsters are almost always entitled to discounts on public transportation and admission to attractions. Though every entrance requirement is different, you'll often find that admission for kids 5 and under is free and for elementary-school-age children it's half price; older students (through college) may also be offered significant discounts.

FOR SENIORS Travelers over the age of 65—and in many cases 60, sometimes even 55—may qualify for discounts not available to the younger adult traveler. Some hotels offer rates 10% to 20% lower than the published rate; inquire at the time you make reservations. Many attractions give seniors discounts of up to half the regular adult admission price (most New Mexico ski areas offer free skiing for seniors in their 70s). Get in the habit of asking about discounts. Seniors who plan to visit national parks and monuments in New Mexico should consider getting a **Golden Age Passport,** which gives anyone over 62 lifetime access to any national park, monument, historic site, recreational area, or wildlife refuge that charges an entrance fee. Golden Age Passports can be obtained at any National Park Office in the country. There is a one-time $10 processing fee. In New Mexico, contact the **National Park Service Office of Communications** (☎ **505/988-6011**) for more information.

If you're retired and are not already a member of the **American Association of Retired Persons (AARP),** consider joining. The AARP card is valuable throughout North America in your search for travel bargains.

In addition, there are 30 active **Elderhostel** locations throughout the state. For information, call New Mexico Elderhostel at ☎ **505/473-6267.**

A note about health: Senior travelers are often more susceptible to changes in elevation and may experience heart or respiratory problems. Consult your physician before your trip.

FOR STUDENTS Always carry your student identification with you. Tourist attractions, transportation systems, and other services may offer discounts if you have appropriate proof of your student status. Don't be afraid to ask. A high school or college ID card or International Student Card will suffice.

Student-oriented activities abound on and around college campuses, especially at the University of New Mexico in Albuquerque. In Santa Fe, there are two small four-year colleges: the College of Santa Fe and the liberal arts school St. John's College.

FOR TRAVELERS WITH DISABILITIES Throughout the state of New Mexico measures have been taken to provide access for the disabled. Several bed-and-breakfast inns have made one or more of their rooms completely wheelchair accessible, and in Taos there is a completely wheelchair-accessible trail in the state park. If you call the **Developmental Disabilities Planning Council** (☎ **800/552-8195**), they will provide you with free information about traveling with disabilities in New Mexico. The brochure "Art of Accessibility" lists hotels, restaurants, and attractions in Albuquerque that are accessible to disabled travelers. The **Directory of Recreational Activities for Children with Disabilities** is a list of accessible camps, national forest campgrounds, amusement parks, and individual city

CyberDeals for Net Surfers

It's possible to get some great deals on airfare, hotels, and car rentals via the Internet. So go grab your mouse and start surfing—you could save a bundle on your trip. The Web sites highlighted below are worth checking out, especially since all services are free (but don't forget that time is money when you're online).

Microsoft Expedia (**www.expedia.com**)   The best part of this multi-purpose travel site is the "Fare Tracker": You fill out a form on the screen indicating that you're interested in cheap flights to Albuquerque or Santa Fe from your home-town, and, once a week, they'll e-mail you the best airfare deals. The site's "Travel Agent" will steer you to bargains on hotels and car rentals, and you can book everything, including flights, right online. This site is even useful once you're booked: Before you go, log on to Expedia for oodles of up-to-date travel information, including weather reports and foreign exchange rates.

Preview Travel (**www.reservations.com** and **www.vacations.com**)   Another useful travel site, "Reservations.com" has a "Best Fare Finder," which will search the Apollo computer reservations system for the three lowest fares for any route on any days of the year. Say you want to go from Chicago to Albuquerque and back between December 6th and 13th: Just fill out the form on the screen with times, dates, and destinations; within minutes, Preview will show you the best deals. If you find an airfare you like, you can book your ticket right online—you can even reserve hotels and car rentals on this site. If you're in the pre-planning stage, head to Preview's "Vacations.com" site, where you can check out the latest package deals for Albuquerque and other destinations around the world by clicking on "Hot Deals."

Travelocity (**www.travelocity.com**)   This is one of the best travel sites out there. In addition to its "Personal Fare Watcher," which notifies you via e-mail of the lowest airfares for up to five different destinations, Travelocity will track the three lowest fares for any routes on any dates in minutes. You can book a flight right then and there, and if you need a rental car or hotel, Travelocity will find you the best deal via the SABRE computer reservations system (a huge database used by travel agents worldwide). Click on "Last Minute Deals" for the latest travel bargains, including a link to "H.O.T. Coupons" (**www.hot-coupons.com**), where you can print out electronic coupons for travel in the United States and Canada.

services throughout New Mexico. *Access Santa Fe* (☎ **505/827-6465**), lists accessible hotels, attractions, and restaurants in the state capital, and the Taos Chamber of Commerce will answer questions regarding accessibility in Taos. No matter what, it is advisable to call hotels, restaurants, and attractions in advance to be sure that they are fully accessible.

5 Getting There

BY PLANE   The gateway to Santa Fe, Taos, and other Northern New Mexico communities is the Albuquerque International Sunport (☎ **505/842-4366** for the administrative offices; call the individual airlines for flight information).

Airlines serving Albuquerque include American (☎ **800/433-7300**), America West (☎ **800/235-9292**), Continental (☎ **800/523-3273**), Delta (☎ **800/221-1212**),

Trip.Com (**www.thetrip.com**)   This site is really geared toward the business traveler, but vacationers-to-be can also use Trip.Com's valuable fare-finding engine, which will e-mail you every week with the best city-to-city airfare deals on your selected route or routes.

Discount Tickets (**www.discount-tickets.com**)   Operated by the ETN (European Travel Network), this site offers discounts on airfares, accommodations, car rentals, and tours. It deals in flights between the United States and other countries, not domestic U.S. flights, so it's most useful for travelers coming from abroad.

E-Savers Programs   Several major airlines offer a free e-mail service known as **E-Savers,** via which they'll send you their best bargain airfares on a weekly basis. Here's how it works: Once a week (usually Wednesday), subscribers receive a list of discounted flights to and from various destinations, both international and domestic. Now here's the catch: These fares are only available if you leave the very next Saturday (or sometimes Friday night) and return on the following Monday or Tuesday. It's really a service for the spontaneously inclined and travelers looking for a quick getaway. But the fares are cheap, so it's worth taking a look. If you have a preference for certain airlines (in other words, the ones you fly most frequently), sign up with them first. Another caveat: You'll get frequent-flier miles if you purchase one of these fares, but you can't use miles to buy the ticket.

Here's a list of airlines and their websites, where you can not only get on the e-mailing lists, but also book flights directly:

- **American Airlines:** www.americanair.com
- **Continental Airlines:** www.flycontinental.com
- **TWA:** www.twa.com
- **Northwest Airlines:** www.nwa.com
- **US Airways:** www.usairways.com

Epicurious Travel (**travel.epicurious.com**), another good travel site, allows you to sign up for all of these airline e-mail lists at once.

—Jeanette Foster

Frontier (☎ **800/432-1359**), Mesa (☎ **800/637-2247**), Northwest (☎ **800/ 225-2525**), Southwest (☎ **800/435-9792**), TWA (☎ **800/221-2000**), United (☎ **800/241-6522**), and US Airways (☎ **800/428-4322**).

BY TRAIN   Amtrak (☎ **800/USA-RAIL** or 505/842-9650) passes through Northern New Mexico twice daily. The *Southwest Chief,* which runs between Chicago and Los Angeles, stops once eastbound and once westbound in Gallup, Grants, Albuquerque, Lamy (for Santa Fe), Las Vegas, and Raton.

You can get a copy of Amtrak's National Timetable from any Amtrak station, from travel agents, or by writing Amtrak, 400 N. Capitol St. NW, Washington, DC 20001.

BY BUS   Because Santa Fe is only about 58 miles northeast of Albuquerque via I-40, most visitors to Santa Fe take the bus directly from the Albuquerque airport.

Shuttlejack buses (☎ **505/243-3244** in Albuquerque, **505/982-4311** in Santa Fe) make the 70-minute run between the airport and Santa Fe hotels 7 to 10 times daily each way, from 4:45am to 10:45pm (cost is $20 one-way, payable to the driver). Reservations are required. Three other bus services shuttle between Albuquerque and Taos (via Santa Fe) for $30 to $35 one-way, $55 to $65 round-trip: Pride of Taos Tours/Shuttles (☎ **505/758-8340**), Faust's Transportation (☎ **505/758-3410**), and Twin Heart Express & Transportation (☎ **505/751-1201**).

The public bus depot in Albuquerque is located on 2nd Street at Lead (300 2nd Street SW). Contact Texas, New Mexico, and Oklahoma (T.N.M.& O.; ☎ **505/242-4998**) for information and schedules. Fares run about $11 to Santa Fe and $22 to Taos. However, the bus stations in Santa Fe (858 St. Michael's Dr.; ☎ **505/471-0008**) and Taos (at the Chevron bypass station at the corner of US 64 and NM 68; ☎ **505/758-1144**) are several miles south of each city center. Because additional taxi or shuttle service is needed to reach most accommodations, travelers usually find it more convenient to pay a few extra dollars for an airport-to-hotel shuttle.

BY CAR   The most convenient way to get around the Santa Fe region is by private car. Auto and RV rentals are widely available for those who arrive without their own transportation, either at the Albuquerque airport or at locations around each city.

I have received good rates and service from Avis at the Albuquerque airport (☎ **800/831-2847,** 505/842-4080, or 505/982-4361 in Santa Fe); Thrifty, 2039 Yale Blvd. SE, Albuquerque (☎ **800/367-2277** or 505/842-8733); Hertz, Albuquerque International Airport (☎ **800/654-3131** or 505/842-4235); Dollar, Albuquerque International Airport (☎ **800/369-4226** or 505/842-4304); Budget, Albuquerque International Airport (☎ **505/768-5900**); Alamo, 2601 Yale SE, Albuquerque (☎ **800/327-9633**); and Rent-A-Wreck of Albuquerque, 500 Yale SE (☎ **800/247-9556** or 505/242-9556).

Drivers who need wheelchair-accessible transportation should call Wheelchair Getaways of New Mexico, 1015 Tramway Lane NE, Albuquerque (☎ **800/408-2626** or 505/247-2626); it rents vans by the day, week, or month.

If you're arriving by car from elsewhere in North America, Albuquerque is at the crossroads of two major interstate highways. I-40 runs from Wilmington, North Carolina (1,870 miles east), to Barstow, California (580 miles west). I-25 extends from Buffalo, Wyoming (850 miles north), to El Paso, Texas (265 miles south). I-25 skims past Santa Fe's southern city limits. To reach Taos, you'll have to leave I-25 at Santa Fe and travel north 74 miles via US 84/285 and NM 68, or exit I-25 9 miles south of Raton, near the Colorado border, and proceed 100 miles west on US 64.

The following table shows the approximate mileage to Santa Fe from various cities around the United States.

PACKAGE TOURS   Unfortunately, you may not find a package tour in New Mexico. The tour companies I spoke to said most visitors to New Mexico have such disparate interests it's difficult to create packages to please them. Still, a few tour companies can help you arrange a variety of day trips during your visit and can also secure lodging. Southwest Airlines has begun offering ski packages to Albuquerque, Santa Fe, Taos, Angel Fire, and Red River, and may soon expand to other New Mexico destinations. For information, call ☎ **800/423-5683.** Otherwise, you may want to contact the following inbound operators:

Destination Southwest, Inc., 20 First Plaza Galeria, Suite 603, Albuquerque, NM 87102 (☎ **800/999-3109** or 505/766-9068; fax 505/766-9065).

Distances to Santa Fe (in miles)

From	Distance	From	Distance
Atlanta	1,417	Minneapolis	1,199
Boston	2,190	New Orleans	1,181
Chicago	1,293	New York	1,971
Cleveland	1,558	Oklahoma City	533
Dallas	663	Phoenix	595
Denver	391	St. Louis	993
Detroit	1,514	Salt Lake City	634
Houston	900	San Francisco	1,149
Los Angeles	860	Seattle	1,477
Miami	2,011	Washington, D.C.	1,825

Gray Line Tours, 800 Rio Grande NW, Suite 22, Albuquerque, NM 87104 (☎ **800/256-8991** or 505/242-3880; fax 505/243-0692).

Rojotours & Services, P.O. Box 15744, Santa Fe, NM 87506-5744 (☎ **505/474-8333;** fax 505/474-2992).

Sun Tours, Ltd., 4300 San Mateo Blvd. NE, Suite B-155, Albuquerque, NM 87110 (☎ **505/889-8888;** fax 505/881-4119).

CWT-A to Z Travelink, 6020 Indian School Rd., Albuquerque, NM 87110 (☎ **800/366-0282** or 505/883-5865; fax 505/883-0038).

3 For Foreign Visitors

Howling coyotes and parched cow skulls, dusty cowboys and noble Native Americans—you've seen them in the movies, along with dreamy sunsets and pastel earth hues. Though the denizens and landscapes of the Southwestern United States may seem familiar, for most the reality is quite different. This chapter will help you prepare for some of the uniquely American situations you are likely to encounter.

1 Preparing for Your Trip

ENTRY REQUIREMENTS

DOCUMENT REQUIREMENTS Citizens of Canada and Bermuda may enter the United States without passports or visas; they need only proof of nationality, the most common and hassle-free form of which is a passport.

The U.S. State Department has a Visa Waiver Pilot Program allowing citizens of certain countries to enter the United States without a visa for stays of fewer than 90 days of holiday travel. At press time these included Andorra, Argentina, Australia, Austria, Belgium, Brunei, Denmark, Finland, France, Germany, Iceland, Ireland, Italy, Japan, Liechtenstein, Luxembourg, Monaco, the Netherlands, New Zealand, Norway, San Marino, Spain, Sweden, Switzerland, and the United Kingdom. (The program as applied to the United Kingdom refers to British citizens who have the "unrestricted right of permanent abode in the United Kingdom," that is, citizens from England, Scotland, Wales, Northern Ireland, the Channel Islands, and the Isle of Man; and not, for example, citizens of the British Commonwealth of Pakistan.)

Citizens from these countries need only a valid passport and a round-trip air or cruise ticket in their possession upon arrival. If they first enter the United States, they may then visit Mexico, Canada, Bermuda, and/or the Caribbean islands and return to the United States without needing a visa. Further information is available from any U.S. embassy or consulate.

Citizens of countries other than those specified above, or those traveling to the United States for reasons or length of time outside the restrictions of the Visa Waiver Program, or those who require waivers of inadmissability must have two documents: a valid passport, with an expiration date at least 6 months later than the scheduled end of the visit to the United States. (Some countries are exceptions to the 6-month validity rule.) Contact any U.S. embassy or consulate for complete information); and a tourist visa, available from the nearest U.S. consulate.

To obtain a visa, the traveler must submit a completed application form (either in person or by mail) with a 1½-inch square photo and the required application fee. There may also be an issuance fee, depending on the type of visa and other factors. Usually you can obtain a visa right away or within 24 hours, but it may take longer during the summer rush period (June to August). If you cannot go in person, contact the nearest U.S. embassy or consulate for directions on applying by mail. Your travel agent or airline office may also be able to provide you with visa applications and instructions. The U.S. consulate or embassy that issues your visa will determine whether you will be issued a multiple- or single-entry visa. The Immigration and Naturalization Service officers at the port-of-entry in the U.S. will make an admission decision and determine your length of stay.

MEDICAL REQUIREMENTS   No inoculations are needed to enter the United States unless you're coming from, or have stopped over in, areas known to be suffering from epidemics, particularly cholera or yellow fever.

If you have a disease that needs treatment with medications containing narcotics or drugs requiring a syringe, carry a valid signed prescription from your physician to allay any suspicions that you are smuggling drugs.

CUSTOMS REQUIREMENTS   Every adult visitor may bring in free of duty: 1 liter of wine or hard liquor; 200 cigarettes or 100 cigars (although no Cuban cigars) or 3 pounds of smoking tobacco; and $100 worth of gifts. These exemptions are offered to travelers who spend at least 72 hours in the United States and who have not claimed them within the preceding 6 months. It's strictly forbidden to bring into the country foodstuffs (particularly cheese, fruit, cooked meats, and canned goods) and plants (vegetables, seeds, tropical plants, and so on). Foreign tourists may bring in or take out up to $10,000 in U.S. or foreign currency with no formalities; larger sums must be declared to Customs on entering or leaving the country.

INSURANCE

Unlike in Canada and Europe, there is no national health-care system in the United States. Because the cost of medical care is extremely high, I strongly advise every traveler to secure health insurance coverage before setting out; check your home policy to verify its coverage, if any, while you are abroad.

You may want to take out a comprehensive travel policy that covers (for a relatively low premium) sickness or injury costs (medical, surgical, and hospital); loss or theft of your baggage; trip-cancellation costs; guarantee of bail in case you are arrested; and costs of accidents, repatriation, or death. Such packages (for example, "Europe Assistance Worldwide Services" in Europe) are sold by automobile clubs at attractive rates, as well as by insurance companies and travel agencies.

MONEY

CURRENCY & EXCHANGE   The U.S. monetary system has a decimal base: one American dollar ($1) = 100 cents (100¢).

Dollar bills commonly come in $1 ("a buck"), $5, $10, $20, $50, and $100 denominations (the last two are not welcome when paying for small purchases and are not accepted in taxis or at subway ticket booths). There are also $2 bills (though seldom encountered today).

There are six denominations of coins: 1¢ (one cent or "penny"), 5¢ (five cents or "nickel"), 10¢ (ten cents or "dime"), 25¢ (twenty-five cents or "quarter"), 50¢ (fifty cents or "half dollar"), and the rare $1 piece.

Note: The "foreign-exchange bureaus" so common in Europe are rare even at airports in the United States and nonexistent outside major cities. Try to avoid having to change foreign money (or traveler's checks denominated in a currency other than U.S. dollars) at a small-town bank or even a branch bank in a big city. In fact, you might want to leave any currency other than U.S. dollars at home—it may prove a greater nuisance to you than it's worth.

TRAVELER'S CHECKS Traveler's checks denominated in U.S. dollars are readily accepted at most hotels, motels, restaurants, and large stores. The best place to change traveler's checks is at a bank. Do not bring traveler's checks denominated in other currencies.

CREDIT & CHARGE CARDS The method of payment most widely used is credit and charge cards: Visa (BarclayCard in Britain), MasterCard (EuroCard in Europe, Access in Britain, Chargex in Canada), American Express, Diners Club, Discover, and Carte Blanche. You can save yourself trouble by using this plastic money rather than cash or traveler's checks in most hotels, motels, restaurants, and retail stores (a growing number of food and liquor stores now accept credit/charge cards). You must have a credit or charge card to rent a car. It can also be used as proof of identity (often carrying more weight than a passport) or as a cash card, enabling you to draw money from banks and automated-teller machines (ATMs) that accept it.

SAFETY

GENERAL Tourist areas as a rule are safe, but, despite recent reports of decreases in violent crime in many cities, it would be wise to check with the tourist offices in Santa Fe, Taos, and Albuquerque if you are in doubt about which neighborhoods are safe. (See the "Orientation" sections in chapters 4, 11, and 15 for the names and addresses of the specific tourist bureaus.)

Remember that hotels are open to the public, and in a large hotel, security may not be able to screen everyone who enters. Always lock your room door; don't assume that once inside your hotel you are automatically safe and no longer need to be aware of your surroundings.

Be aware that New Mexico has the 2nd highest reported incidence of rape in the United States, and Santa Fe has the 6th highest reported incidence per capita in cities nationwide, according to the New Mexico State Department of Health, as reported in the *Santa Fe New Mexican.* Women should not walk alone in isolated places, particularly at night.

DRIVING Question your rental agency about personal safety, or ask for a brochure of traveler safety tips when you pick up your car. Obtain written directions, or a map with the route clearly marked, from the agency to show you how to get to your destination. And, if possible, arrive and depart during daylight hours.

In recent years, "car-jacking," a crime that targets both cars and drivers, has been on the rise in all U.S. cities. Incidents involving German and other international tourists in Miami made news around the world. Rental cars are especially targeted. If you exit a highway into a questionable neighborhood, leave the area as quickly as possible. If you have an accident, even on the highway, stay in your car with the doors locked until you are able to assess the situation or until the police arrive. If you are bumped from behind by another car on the street or are involved in a minor accident with no injuries and the situation appears to be suspicious, motion to the other driver to follow you to the nearest police precinct, a well-lit service station, or an all-night store. Never get out of your car in such situations.

If you see someone on the road who indicates a need for help, do not stop. Take note of the location, drive to a well-lighted area, and telephone the police by dialing ☎ **911.**

Also, make sure that you have enough gasoline in your tank to reach your intended destination, so that you're not forced to look for a service station in an unfamiliar and possibly unsafe neighborhood—especially at night. These warnings cannot be overemphasized; failure to do any of these things could be exceedingly dangerous or even fatal.

2 Getting to the U.S.

Travelers from overseas can take advantage of the **APEX (Advance-Purchase Excursion)** fares offered by all the major international carriers. Aside from these, attractive values are offered by Icelandair on flights from Luxembourg to New York and by Virgin Atlantic Airways from London to New York/Newark and to Los Angeles. To reach Northern New Mexico from Europe, you'll probably have to stop at one of these airports anyway to make a connecting flight.

British travelers should check out British Airways (☎ **0345/222-111** in the U.K. or **800/247-9297** in the U.S.), which offers direct flights from London to New York and to Los Angeles, as does Virgin Atlantic Airways (☎ **0293/747-747** in the U.K. or **800/862-8621** in the U.S.). Canadian readers might book flights on Air Canada (☎ **800/268-7240** in Canada or **800/776-3000** in the U.S.), which offers service from Toronto, Montreal, and Calgary to New York and to Los Angeles. In addition, many other international carriers serve the New York and Los Angeles airports, including: Air France (☎ **800/237-2747**), Alitalia (☎ **800/ 223-5730**), Japan Airlines (☎ **800/525-3663**), Lufthansa (☎ **800/645-3880**), Quantas (☎ **008/177-767** in Australia), and Swissair (☎ **800/221-4750**). SAS (☎ **800/221-2350**) serves New York and Seattle, but not Los Angeles.

Visitors arriving by air, no matter the port of entry, should reserve patience and resignation before setting foot on U.S. soil. Getting through Immigration control may take as long as 2 hours on some days, especially summer weekends. Add the time it takes to clear Customs, and you'll see that you should allow extra time for delays when planning connections between international and domestic flights—an average of 2 to 3 hours at least.

In contrast, travelers arriving by car or by rail from Canada will find that the border-crossing formalities have been streamlined to the point that they are practically nonexistent. Air travelers from Canada, Bermuda, and some places in the Caribbean can sometimes go through Customs and Immigration at the point of departure, which is much quicker and less tedious.

For further information about transportation to Santa Fe, Taos, and Albuquerque, see "Orientation" in chapters 4, 11, and 15, respectively.

3 Getting Around the U.S.

BY PLANE   On transatlantic or transpacific flights, some prominent American airlines (for example, American Airlines, Delta, Northwest, TWA, and United) offer travelers special discount tickets under the name **Visit USA,** allowing travel between a number of U.S. destinations at minimum rates. These tickets are not for sale in the United States and must, therefore, be purchased before you leave your foreign point of departure. This system is the best, easiest, and fastest way to see the United States at low cost. You should obtain information well in advance from your travel agent or the office of the airline concerned, since the conditions attached to these discount tickets can be changed without advance notice.

BY TRAIN   Long-distance trains in the United States are operated by Amtrak, the national rail passenger corporation. International visitors can buy a USA Railpass, good for 15 or 30 days of unlimited travel on Amtrak (☎ **800/872-7245**). The pass is available through many foreign travel agents. In 1998, prices for a 15-day pass were $285 off-peak, $425 peak; a 30-day pass costs $375 off-peak, $535 peak. (June 1 through September 7 is considered peak season.) With a foreign passport, you can also buy passes at some Amtrak offices in the United States, including locations in Boston, Chicago, Los Angeles, Miami, New York, San Francisco, and Washington, D.C. Reservations are generally required and should be made for each part of your trip as early as possible. Even cheaper than the above are regional USA Railpasses, allowing unlimited travel through a specific section of the United States. Reservations are generally required and should be made for each part of your trip as early as possible.

Visitors should be aware of the limitations of long-distance rail travel in the United States. With a few notable exceptions, service is rarely up to European standards: Delays are common, routes are limited and often infrequently served, and fares are rarely much lower than discount airfares. Thus, cross-country train travel should be approached with caution.

BY BUS   The cheapest way to travel around the United States is by bus. Greyhound/Trailways (☎ **800/231-2222**), the sole nationwide bus line, offers an Ameripass for unlimited travel for 7 days (for $199), 15 days (for $299), 30 days (for $409), and 60 days (for $599). Bus travel in the United States can be both slow and uncomfortable, so this option is not for everyone. Furthermore, bus stations are often situated in undesirable neighborhoods.

BY CAR   Travel by car gives visitors the freedom to make—and alter—their itineraries to suit their own needs and interests. And it offers the opportunity to visit some of the off-the-beaten-path locations, places that cannot be reached easily by public transportation. For many foreign travelers, traveling the wide-open roads of the western United States by car is the stuff of legend. For information on renting cars in the United States, see "Automobile Organizations" and "Automobile Rentals" in "Fast Facts: For the Foreign Traveler," below; "By Car" in "Getting There," in chapter 2; and "By Car" in "Getting Around," in chapters 4, 11, and 15.

FAST FACTS: For the Foreign Traveler

Automobile Organizations   Auto clubs supply maps, suggested routes, guidebooks, accident and bail-bond insurance, and emergency road service. The major auto club in the United States, with 955 offices nationwide, is the **American Automobile Association (AAA).** Members of some foreign auto clubs have reciprocal arrangements with AAA and enjoy its services at no charge. If you belong to an auto club in your home country, inquire about AAA reciprocity before you leave. You may be able to join AAA even if you're not a member of a reciprocal club; to inquire, call AAA (☎ **800/881-7585**). AAA can provide you with an **International Driving Permit,** validating your foreign license.

In addition, some automobile-rental agencies now provide many of these same services. Inquire about their availability when you rent your car.

Automobile Rentals   To rent a car you will need a major credit or charge card and a valid drivers' license. In addition, you usually need to be at least 25 years old (some companies do rent to younger people but add a daily surcharge). Be sure to return your car with the same amount of gas you started with; rental companies charge excessive prices for gasoline. See "By Car" in "Getting Around," in chapters 4, 11, and 15, for the phone numbers of car-rental companies in Santa Fe, Taos, and Albuquerque, respectively.

Business Hours   See "Fast Facts," in chapters 4, 11, and 15.

Climate   See "When to Go," in chapter 2.

Currency Exchange   You'll find currency-exchange services at major airports with international service. Elsewhere, they may be quite difficult to come by. In the United States, a very reliable choice is **Thomas Cook Currency Services, Inc.** They sell commission-free foreign and U.S. traveler's checks, drafts, and wire transfers; they also do check collections (including Eurochecks). Their rates are competitive, and the service is excellent. Thomas Cook maintains several offices in New York City, including one at 511 Madison Ave., and another at the JFK Airport International Arrivals Terminal (☎ **718/656-8444**). For the locations and hours of offices nationwide, call ☎ **800/287-7362.**

For Santa Fe, Taos, and Albuquerque banks that handle foreign-currency exchange, see the "Fast Facts" sections in chapters 4, 11, and 15, respectively.

Drinking Laws   You must be 21 to purchase alcoholic beverages in New Mexico, as in the rest of the United States.

Electric Current   The United States uses 110–120 volts AC, 60 cycles, compared with 220–240 volts AC, 50 cycles, as in most of Europe. In addition to a 100-volt transformer, small appliances of non-American manufacture, such as hair dryers or shavers, will require a plug adapter, with two flat, parallel pins.

Embassies/Consulates   All embassies are located in the national capital, Washington, D.C.; some consulates are located in major U.S. cities, and most countries maintain a mission to the United Nations in New York City. The embassies and consulates of the major English-speaking countries—Australia, Canada, the Republic of Ireland, New Zealand, and the United Kingdom—are listed below. If you are from another country, you can get the telephone number of your embassy by calling "Information" in Washington, D.C. (☎ **202/555-1212**).

The embassy of **Australia** is at 1601 Massachusetts Ave. NW, Washington, DC 20036 (☎ 202/797-3000). There is an Australian consulate at Century Plaza Towers, 19th Floor, 2049 Century Park East, Los Angeles, CA 90067 (☎ 310/229-4800). The consulate in New York is located temporarily at 1 Liberty Plaza, 37th Floor, New York, NY 10006 (☎ 212/408-8400).

The embassy of **Canada** is at 501 Pennsylvania Ave. NW, Washington, DC 20001 (☎ 202/682-1740). There's a Canadian consulate in Los Angeles at 550 S. Hope St., 9th Floor, Los Angeles, CA 90071 (☎ 213/346-2700). The one in New York is located at 1251 Ave. of the Americas, New York, NY 10020 (☎ 212/596-1600).

The embassy of the **Republic of Ireland** is at 2234 Massachusetts Ave. NW, Washington, DC 20008 (☎ 202/462-3939). The consulate in New York is located at 345 Park Ave., 17th Floor, New York, NY 10022 (☎ 212/319-2555).

The consulate in San Francisco is at 44 Montgomery St., Suite 3830, San Francisco, CA 94104 (☎ 415/392-4214).

The embassy of **New Zealand** is at 37 Observatory Circle NW, Washington, DC 20008 (☎ 202/328-4800). The consulate in New York is located at 780 Third Ave., Suite 1904, New York, NY 10017-2024 (☎ 212/832-4038). The consulate in Los Angeles is located at 12400 Wilshire Blvd., Suite 1150, Los Angeles, CA 90025 (☎ 310/207-1605).

The embassy of the **United Kingdom** is at 3100 Massachusetts Ave. NW, Washington, DC 20008 (☎ 202/462-1340). The consulate in New York is located at 845 Third Ave., New York, NY 10022 (☎ 212/745-0200). The consulate in Los Angeles is located at 11766 Wilshire Blvd., Suite 400, Los Angeles, CA 90025 (☎ 310/477-3322).

Emergencies   Call ☎ **911** to report a fire, call the police, or get an ambulance. This is a toll-free call (no coins are required at a public telephone).

If you encounter traveler's problems, check the local telephone directory to find an office of the **Traveler's Aid Society,** a nationwide, nonprofit, social-service organization geared toward helping travelers in difficult straits. Their services might include reuniting families separated while traveling, providing food and/or shelter to people stranded without cash, assisting crime victims, or even offering emotional counseling. In New York, they have an office in JFK Airport's International Terminal (☎ **718/656-4870**). If you're in trouble, seek them out.

Gasoline (Petrol)   One U.S. gallon equals 3.8 liters or 0.83 Imperial gallons. There are usually several grades (and price levels) of gasoline available at most gas stations, and their names change from company to company. Unleaded gas with the highest octane ratings is the most expensive; however, most rental cars take the least expensive—"regular" unleaded gas. Sometimes, the price is lower if you pay in cash rather than by credit or charge card.

Most gas stations are essentially self-service, although a number of them now offer higher-priced full service as well. Late- or all-night stations are usually self-service only.

Holidays   On the following legal national holidays, banks, government offices, post offices, and many stores, restaurants, and museums are closed: January 1 (New Year's Day), the third Monday in January (Martin Luther King, Jr.'s, Birthday [observed]), the third Monday in February (Presidents' Day, Washington's Birthday), the last Monday in May (Memorial Day), July 4 (Independence Day), the first Monday in September (Labor Day), the second Monday in October (Columbus Day), November 11 (Veterans' Day/Armistice Day), the fourth Thursday in November (Thanksgiving Day), and December 25 (Christmas). Also, the Tuesday following the first Monday in November is Election Day and is a legal holiday in presidential-election years (next in 2000).

Legal Aid   The well-meaning foreign visitor will probably never become involved with the American legal system. However, there are a few things you should know just in case. If you are stopped for a minor infraction of the highway code (for example, speeding), never attempt to pay the fine directly to a police officer; you may wind up arrested on the much more serious charge of attempted bribery. Pay fines by mail or directly to the clerk of the court. If you're accused of a more serious offense, it's wise to say and do nothing before consulting a lawyer. Under U.S. law, an arrested person is allowed one telephone call to a party of his or her choice. Call your embassy or consulate.

Mail   If you want your mail to follow you on your vacation and you aren't sure of your address, your mail can be sent to you, in your name, **c/o General Delivery** (Poste Restante) at the main post office of the city or region where you expect to be. (For the addresses and telephone numbers in Santa Fe, Taos, and Albuquerque, see the "Fast Facts" sections in chapters 4, 11, and 15, respectively.) The addressee must pick up the mail in person and must produce proof of identity (driver's license, credit or charge card, passport, etc.).

Domestic **postage rates** are 20¢ for a postcard and 32¢ for a letter. Check with any local post office for current international postage rates to your home country.

Generally found at intersections, **mailboxes** are blue with a red-and-white stripe and carry the designation **U.S. MAIL.** If your mail is addressed to a U.S. destination, don't forget to add the five-digit **postal code,** or ZIP (Zone Improvement Plan) code, after the two-letter abbreviation of the state to which the mail is addressed (CA for California, NM for New Mexico, NY for New York, and so on).

Newspapers & Magazines   National newspapers include *The New York Times, USA Today,* and the *Wall Street Journal.* National news weeklies include *Newsweek, Time,* and *U.S. News and World Report.* In large cities, most newsstands offer a small selection of the most popular foreign periodicals and newspapers, such as the *Economist, Le Monde,* and *Der Spiegel.* For information on local publications, see the "Fast Facts" sections in chapters 4, 11, and 15.

Radio/Television   Audiovisual media, with six coast-to-coast networks—ABC, CBS, NBC, Fox, the Public Broadcasting System (PBS), and the cable network CNN—play a major part in American life. In big cities, viewers have a choice of several dozen channels (including basic cable), most of them transmitting 24 hours a day, not counting the pay-TV channels that show recent movies or sports events. All options are usually indicated on your hotel TV set. You'll also find a wide choice of local radio stations, both AM and FM, each broadcasting particular kinds of talk shows and/or music—classical, country, jazz, pop, gospel—punctuated by news broadcasts and frequent commercials.

Rest Rooms   Visitors can usually find a rest room in a bar, restaurant, hotel, museum, department store, service station, or train station. Along major highways are "rest stops," many with rest room facilities.

Safety   See "Safety" in "Preparing for Your Trip," earlier in this chapter.

Taxes   In the United States there is no VAT (value-added tax) or other indirect tax at a national level. Every state, and each county and city in it, has the right to levy its own local tax on purchases, including hotel and restaurant checks, airline tickets, and so on. Taxes are already included in the price of certain services, such as public transportation, cab fares, telephone calls, and gasoline. The amount of sales tax varies from about 4% to 12%, depending on the state and city, so when you're making major purchases, such as photographic equipment, clothing, or stereo components, it can be a significant part of the cost.

Telephone/Telegraph/Telex   The telephone system in the United States is run by private corporations, so rates, especially for long-distance service and operator-assisted calls, can vary widely—even on calls made from public telephones. Local calls in the United States usually cost 25¢ (they're 25¢ throughout New Mexico).

Generally, hotel surcharges on long-distance and local calls are astronomical. It's usually cheaper to call collect, use a telephone charge card, or use a public pay telephone, which you'll find clearly marked in most public buildings and private establishments as well as on the street. Outside metropolitan areas, public telephones are more difficult to find. Stores and gas stations are your best bet.

Most long-distance and international calls can be dialed directly from any phone (stock up on quarters if you're calling from a pay phone or use a telephone charge card). For calls to Canada and to other parts of the United States, dial 1 followed by the area code and the seven-digit number. For international calls, dial 011 followed by the country code (Australia, 61; Republic of Ireland, 353; New Zealand, 64; United Kingdom, 44), then the city code (for example, 171 or 181 for London, 121 for Birmingham) and the telephone number of the person you wish to call.

For reversed-charge (collect calls) and person-to-person calls, dial 0 (zero, not the letter "O") followed by the area code and number you want; an operator will then come on the line, and you should specify that you are calling collect, or person-to-person, or both. If your operator-assisted call is international, ask for the overseas operator.

For local directory assistance ("information"), dial **1-411;** for long-distance information, dial 1, then the appropriate area code and 555-1212.

Like the telephone system, telegraph and telex services are provided by private corporations such as ITT, MCI, and above all, Western Union, the most important. You can bring your telegram in to the nearest Western Union office (there are hundreds across the country) or dictate it over the phone (☎ **800/ 325-6000**). You can also telegraph money (using a major credit or charge card) or have it telegraphed to you, very quickly over the Western Union system. (Note, however, that this service can be very expensive—the charge can run as high as 15% to 25% of the amount sent.)

Most hotels have fax machines available for guest use (be sure to ask about the charge to use it), and many hotel rooms are even wired for guests' fax machines. You'll probably also see signs for public faxes in the windows of local shops.

Telephone Directory   There are two kinds of telephone directories available to you. The general directory is the so-called White Pages, in which private and business subscribers are listed in alphabetical order. The inside front cover lists the emergency numbers for police, fire, and ambulance, and other vital numbers (such as the poison-control center, crime-victims hotline, and so on). The first few pages are devoted to community-service numbers, including a guide to long-distance and international calling, complete with country codes and area codes.

The second directory, printed on yellow paper (hence its name, Yellow Pages), lists all local services, businesses, and industries by type of activity, with an index at the back. The listings cover not only such obvious items as automobile repairs by make of car or drugstores (pharmacies), often by geographical location, but also restaurants by type of cuisine and geographical location, bookstores by special subject and/or language, places of worship by religious denomination, and other information that the tourist might otherwise not readily find. The Yellow Pages also often include city plans or detailed area maps, often showing ZIP codes and public transportation routes.

Time   The United States is divided into six time zones: From east to west, Eastern standard time (EST), Central standard time (CST), Mountain standard time (MST), Pacific standard time (PST), Alaska standard time (AST), and

Hawaii standard time (HST). Always keep the changing time zones in mind if you are traveling (or even telephoning) long distances in the United States. For example, noon in New York City (EST) is 11am in Chicago (CST), 10am in Santa Fe (MST), 9am in Los Angeles (PST), 8am in Anchorage (AST), and 7am in Honolulu (HST).

New Mexico is on Mountain standard time (MST), 7 hours behind Greenwich Mean Time. Daylight saving time is in effect from the first Sunday in April through the last Saturday in October (actually, the change is made at 2am on Sunday), except in parts of Arizona (the Navajo reservation *does* observe daylight saving time; the rest of the state does not), Hawaii, part of Indiana, and Puerto Rico. Daylight saving time moves the clock 1 hour ahead of standard time. (Americans use the adage "Spring ahead, fall back" to remember which way to change their clocks and watches.)

Tipping   This is part of the American way of life, based on the principle that one should pay for any special service received. (Often service personnel receive little direct salary and depend almost entirely on tips for their income.) Here are some rules of thumb:

In hotels, tip bellhops $1 per piece of luggage carried, and tip the chamber staff $1 per day. Tip the doorman or concierge only if he or she has provided some additional service (for example, calling a cab for you or obtaining difficult-to-get theater tickets).

In restaurants, bars, and nightclubs, tip the service staff 15% to 20% of the check, tip bartenders 10% to 15%, tip checkroom attendants $1 per garment, and tip valet-parking attendants $1 per vehicle. Tipping is not expected in cafeterias and fast-food restaurants.

Tip cab drivers 15% of the fare.

As for other service personnel, tip redcaps at airports or railroad stations $1 per piece of luggage, and tip hairdressers and barbers 15% to 20%.

Tipping ushers in cinemas, movies, and theaters and gas-station attendants is not expected.

4 Getting to Know Santa Fe

After visiting Santa Fe, Will Rogers reportedly once said, "Whoever designed this town did so while riding on a jackass backwards and drunk." You, too, may find yourself perplexed when maneuvering through the city. The meandering lanes and one-way streets can frustrate your best intentions. That's why people call it a walking town. Truly, that is the best way to get a feel for the idiosyncrasies of the place.

Like most cities of Hispanic origin, Santa Fe contains a plaza in the center of the city. Here, you'll find tall shade trees and lots of grass, a nice place to sit and make travel plans. The area is full of restaurants, shops, art galleries, and museums, many within centuries-old buildings, and is dominated by the beautiful St. Francis Cathedral, a French Romanesque structure to the east.

On the Plaza, you'll notice the variety of people who inhabit and visit this city. Here, you'll see Native Americans selling jewelry under the portal of the Palace of the Governors, teenagers in souped-up low-riders cruising along, and people young and old hanging out in the ice cream parlor. Such diversity, coupled with the variety of architecture, prompted the tourism department here to begin calling Santa Fe "The City Different."

Not far away is the Canyon Road district, a narrow, mostly one-way street packed with galleries and shops. Once it was the home of many artists, and today you'll still find some who work within gallery studios. There are a number of fine restaurants in this district as well.

Farther to the east slopes the rugged Sangre de Cristo Range. Locals spend a lot of time in these mountains picnicking, hiking, and skiing; for many, these mountains are why they choose to live in the region. When you look up at the mountains you'll see the peak of Santa Fe Baldy (with an elevation of more than 12,600 feet) as well as other peaks more than 12,000 feet high. Back in town, to the south of the Plaza, is the Santa Fe River; it's a tiny tributary of the Rio Grande that is little more than a trickle for much of the year.

North is the Española Valley, and beyond that, the village of Taos, about 66 miles away. South of the city are ancient Native American turquoise mines in the Cerrillos Hills, and to the southwest is metropolitan Albuquerque, some 58 miles away. To the west, across the Caja del Rio Plateau, is the Rio Grande, and beyond that, the 11,000-foot Jemez Mountains and Valle Grande—an ancient and massive volcanic caldera. Pueblos dot the entire Rio Grande Valley, within an hour's drive in any direction.

1 Orientation

ARRIVING

BY PLANE   The **Santa Fe Municipal Airport** (☎ 505/473-7243), just outside the southwestern city limits on Airport Road off Cerrillos Road, has three paved runways, used primarily by private planes. In conjunction with United Airlines, commuter flights are offered by United Express, which is operated by **Great Lakes Aviation** (☎ 800/241-6522). There are four daily departures from Denver during the week and three on weekends. When departing from Santa Fe, passengers can connect to other United Airlines flights in Denver. **Aspen Mountain Air,** affiliated with American Airlines (☎ 800/433-7300), offers flights to Dallas/Ft. Worth. Call for schedules and fares.

Getting to and from the airport: Virtually all air travelers to Santa Fe arrive in Albuquerque, where they either rent a car or take one of the bus services. See "Getting There," in chapter 2, for details.

BY TRAIN & BUS   For detailed information about train and bus service to Santa Fe, see "Getting There," in chapter 2.

BY CAR   I-25 skims past Santa Fe's southern city limits, connecting it along one continuous highway from Billings, Montana, to El Paso, Texas. I-40, the state's major east–west thoroughfare, which bisects Albuquerque, affords coast-to-coast access to "The City Different." (From the west, motorists leave I-40 in Albuquerque and take I-25 north; from the east, travelers exit I-40 at Clines Corners and continue 52 miles to Santa Fe on US 285.) For those coming from the northwest, the most direct route is via Durango, Colorado, on US 160, entering Santa Fe on US 84.

For information on car rentals in Albuquerque, see "Getting There," in chapter 2; and for agencies in Santa Fe, see "Getting Around," later in this chapter.

VISITOR INFORMATION

The **Santa Fe Convention and Visitors Bureau** is located at 201 W. Marcy St., in Sweeney Center at the corner of Grant Street downtown (P.O. Box 909), Santa Fe, NM 87504-0909 (☎ 800/777-CITY or 505/984-6760). If you would like information before you leave home but don't want to wait for it to arrive by mail, try this web site address: **www.santafe.org.** It will take you directly to the Santa Fe Convention and Visitors Bureau's home page.

CITY LAYOUT

MAIN ARTERIES & STREETS   The limits of downtown Santa Fe are demarcated on three sides by the horseshoe-shaped Paseo de Peralta and on the west by St. Francis Drive, otherwise known as US 84/285. Alameda Street follows the north side of the Santa Fe River through downtown, with the State Capitol and other federal buildings on the south side of the river, and most buildings of historic and tourist interest on the north, east of Guadalupe Street.

The Plaza is Santa Fe's universally accepted point of orientation. Its four diagonal walkways meet at a central fountain, around which a strange and wonderful assortment of people of all ages, nationalities, and lifestyles can be found at nearly any hour of the day or night.

If you stand in the center of the Plaza looking north, you'll be gazing directly at the Palace of the Governors. In front of you is Palace Avenue; behind you, San Francisco Street. To your left is Lincoln Avenue and to your right is Washington Avenue, which divides the downtown avenues into "east" and "west." St. Francis

Santa Fe

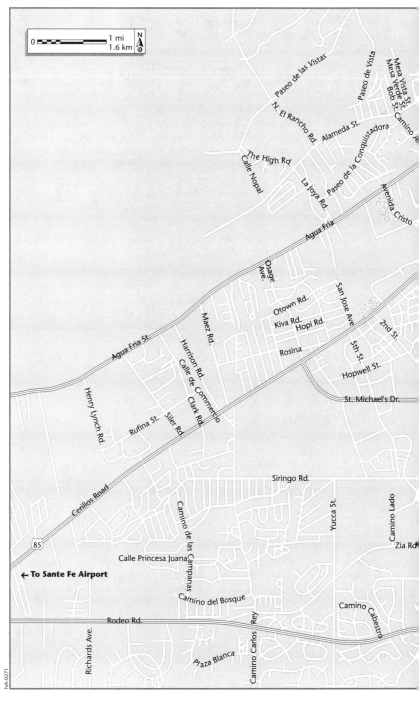

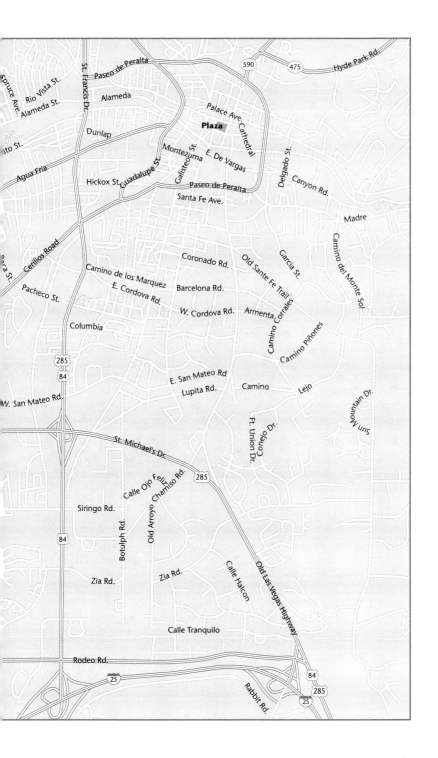

47

Cathedral is the massive Romanesque structure a block east, down San Francisco Street. Alameda Street is 2 full blocks behind you.

Near the intersection of Alameda Street and Paseo de Peralta, you'll find Canyon Road running east toward the mountains. Much of this street is one-way. The best way to see it is to walk up or down, taking time to explore shops and galleries and even have lunch or dinner.

Running to the southwest from the downtown area, beginning opposite the state office buildings on Galisteo Avenue, is Cerrillos Road. Once the main north–south highway connecting New Mexico's state capital with its largest city, it is now a 6-mile-long motel and fast-food strip. St. Francis Drive, which crosses Cerrillos Road 3 blocks south of Guadalupe Street, is a far less tawdry byway, linking Santa Fe with I-25, located 4 miles southeast of downtown. The Old Pecos Trail, on the east side of the city, also joins downtown and the freeway. St. Michael's Drive connects the three arteries.

FINDING AN ADDRESS   Because of the city's layout, it's often difficult to know exactly where to look for a particular street address. It's best to call ahead for directions.

MAPS   Free city and state maps can be obtained at tourist information offices. An excellent state highway map is published by the **New Mexico Department of Tourism,** 491 Old Santa Fe Trail (P.O. Box 20002), Santa Fe, NM 87504 (☎ **800/ 733-6396** or 505/827-7336). There's also a Santa Fe Visitors Center in the same building. More specific county and city maps are available from the **State Highway and Transportation Department,** 1120 Cerrillos Rd., Santa Fe, NM 87504 (☎ **505/ 827-5100**). Members of the **American Automobile Association,** 1644 St. Michael's Dr. (☎ **505/471-6620**), can obtain free maps from the AAA office. Other good regional maps can be purchased at area bookstores. Gousha publishes a laminated "FastMap" of Santa Fe and Taos that has proved indispensable during my travels.

2 Getting Around

BY BUS   In 1993, Santa Fe opened **Santa Fe Trails** (☎ **505/438-1464**), its first public bus system. There are seven routes, and visitors can pick up a map from the Convention and Visitors Bureau. Buses operate Monday through Friday from 6:30am to 10:30pm and Saturday from 8am to 8pm. There is no service on Sunday or holidays. Call for a current schedule and fare information.

BY CAR   Cars can be rented from any of the following firms in Santa Fe: Avis, Garrett's Desert Inn, 311 Old Santa Fe Trail (☎ **505/982-4361**); Budget, 1946 Cerrillos Rd. (☎ **505/984-8028**); Enterprise, 2641A Cerrillos Rd. and 4450 Cerrillos Rd. (☎ **505/473-3600**); and Hertz, Santa Fe Hilton, 100 Sandoval St. (☎ **505/982-1844**).

If Santa Fe is merely your base for an extended driving exploration of New Mexico, be sure to give the vehicle a thorough road check before starting out. There are a lot of wide-open desert and wilderness spaces in New Mexico, and if your car were to break down you could be stranded for hours in extreme heat or cold before someone might pass by.

Make sure your driver's license and auto club membership (if you're a member) are valid before you leave home. Check with your auto insurance company to make sure you're covered when out of state and/or when driving a rental car.

Street parking is difficult to find during summer months. There's a parking lot near the federal courthouse, 2 blocks north of the Plaza; another one behind Santa

Fe Village, a block south of the Plaza; and a third at Water and Sandoval streets. If you stop by the Santa Fe Convention and Visitors Bureau, at the corner of Grant and Marcy streets, you can pick up a wallet-size guide to Santa Fe parking areas. The map shows both street and lot parking.

Unless otherwise posted, the speed limit on freeways is 75 mph; on most other two-lane open roads it's 65 mph. The minimum age for drivers is 16. Seat belts are required for drivers and all passengers age 5 and over; children under 5 must use approved child seats.

Since Native American reservations enjoy a measure of self-rule, they can legally enforce certain designated laws. For instance, on the Navajo reservation (New Mexico's largest), it is forbidden to transport alcoholic beverages, leave established roadways, or go without a seat belt. Motorcyclists must wear helmets. If you are caught breaking reservation laws, you are subject to reservation punishment.

The **State Highway and Transportation Department** has a toll-free hotline (☎ **800/432-4269**) providing up-to-the-hour information on road closures and conditions.

A word of warning: According to the 1997 edition of *Accident Facts,* New Mexico has the third highest per capita rate of traffic deaths in the nation. Drive carefully!

BY TAXI   It's best to telephone for a cab, because they are difficult to flag from the street. Expect to pay a standard fee of $1.85 for the service and an average of about $1.50 per mile. **Capital City Cab** (☎ **505/438-0000**) is the main company in Santa Fe.

BY BICYCLE/ON FOOT   A bicycle is an excellent way to get around town. Check with **Palace Bike Rentals,** 409 E. Palace Ave. (☎ **505/986-0455**), or **Sun Mountain Bike Company,** 121 Sandoval St. (☎ **505/820-2902**) for rentals.

The best way to see downtown Santa Fe is on foot. Free walking-tour maps are available at the tourist information center in Sweeney Center, 201 W. Marcy St. (☎ **800/777-CITY** or 505/984-6760), and several walking tours are included in chapter 7.

FAST FACTS: Santa Fe

Airport   See "Orientation," above.

American Express   There is no office in Santa Fe; the nearest one is in Albuquerque (see "Fast Facts: Albuquerque," in chapter 15).

Area Code   All of New Mexico is in area code **505.**

Baby-sitters   Most hotels can arrange for sitters on request. Alternatively, call the **Santa Fe Kid Connection** at ☎ **505/471-3100.**

Business Hours   **Offices** and **stores** are generally open Monday through Friday from 9am to 5pm, with many stores also open Friday night, Saturday, and Sunday in the summer season. Most **banks** are open Monday through Thursday from 10am to 3pm and Friday from 10am to 6pm; drive-up windows may be open later. Some may also be open Saturday morning. Most branches have cash machines available 24 hours. See also "Liquor Laws," below.

Car Rentals   See "Getting Around," above.

Climate   Santa Fe is consistently 10°F cooler than the nearby desert but has the same sunny skies, averaging more than 300 days of sunshine out of 365. Midsummer (July and August) days are dry and sunny (around 80°F), often with brief afternoon thunderstorms; evenings are typically in the upper 50s. Winters are mild and fair, with occasional and short-lived snow (average annual snowfall is 32 inches, although the ski basin gets an average of 225 inches). The average annual rainfall is 14 inches, most of it in summer; the relative humidity is 45%. (See also "When to Go," in chapter 2.)

Currency Exchange   You can exchange foreign currency at two banks in Santa Fe: NationsBank, 1234 St. Michael's Dr. (☎ **505/471-1234**), and First Security Bank, 121 Sandoval St. (☎ **800/677-2962**).

Dentists   Located in the geographic center of the city is Dr. Leslie E. La Kind, at 400 Botulph Lane (☎ **505/988-3500**). Dr. La Kind offers emergency service.

Doctors   The Lovelace Alameda Clinic, 901 W. Alameda St. (☎ **505/995-2900**), is in the Solano Center near St. Francis Drive. It's open daily from 8am to 8pm. For Physicians and Surgeons Referral and Information Services, call the American Board of Medical Specialties at ☎ **800/776-2378.**

Embassies/Consulates   See "Fast Facts: For the Foreign Traveler," in chapter 3.

Emergencies   For police, fire, or ambulance emergency, dial ☎ **911.**

Eyeglass Repair   The **Quintana Optical Dispensary,** 109 E. Marcy St. (☎ **505/988-4234**), provides 2-hour prescription service Monday through Friday from 9am to 5pm and Saturday from 9am to noon. They will also repair your current glasses.

Hospitals   St. Vincent Hospital, 455 St. Michael's Dr. (☎ **505/983-3361**, or 505/820-5250 for emergency services), is a 268-bed regional health center. Patient services include urgent and emergency-room care and ambulatory surgery. Other health services include the Women's Health Services Family Care and Counseling Center (☎ **505/988-8869**). Lovelace Health Systems has a walk-in office at 901 W. Alameda St. (☎ **505/995-9773**).

Hot Lines   The following hot lines are available in Santa Fe: battered families (☎ **505/473-5200**), poison control (☎ **800/432-6866**), psychiatric emergencies (☎ **505/820-5242** or 505/982-2255), and sexual assault (☎ **505/986-9111**).

Information   See "Orientation," above.

Libraries   The Santa Fe Public Library is half a block from the Plaza at 145 Washington Ave. (☎ **505/984-6780**). There are branch libraries at Villa Linda Mall and at 1730 Llano St., just off St. Michael's Drive. The New Mexico State Library is at 325 Don Gaspar Ave. (☎ **505/827-3800**). Specialty libraries include the Archives of New Mexico, 1205 Camino Carlos Rey, and the New Mexico History Library, 120 Washington Ave.

Liquor Laws   The legal drinking age is 21 throughout New Mexico. Bars may remain open until 2am Monday through Saturday and until midnight on Sunday. Wine, beer, and spirits are sold at licensed supermarkets and liquor stores, but there are no package sales on election days until after 7pm. It is illegal to transport liquor through most Native American reservations.

Lost Property   Contact the city police at ☎ **505/473-5000.**

Newspapers & Magazines   *The New Mexican*—Santa Fe's daily paper—is the oldest newspaper in the West. Its offices are at 202 E. Marcy St. (☎ **505/983-3303**). The weekly *Santa Fe Reporter,* published on Wednesday, is often more willing to be controversial, and its entertainment listings are excellent.

Regional magazines published locally are *New Mexico Magazine* (monthly, statewide interest) and the *Santa Fean Magazine* (monthly, Southwestern lifestyles).

Pharmacies   The **R&R Professional Pharmacy,** at 1691 Galisteo St. (☎ **505/988-9797**), is open Monday through Friday from 9am to 6pm (8:30am to 5:30pm in summer) and Saturday from 9am to noon. Emergency and delivery service is available.

Photographic Needs   Everything from film purchases to minor camera repairs to 1-hour processing can be handled by the **Camera Shop,** 109 E. San Francisco St. (☎ **505/983-6591**). Twenty-four-hour processing is available at **Camera & Darkroom,** 216 Galisteo St. (☎ **505/983-2948**).

Police   In case of emergency, dial ☎ **911.**

Post Offices   The **Main Post Office** is at 120 S. Federal Place (☎ **505/988-6351**), 2 blocks north and 1 block west of the Plaza. It's open from 7:30am to 5:45pm. The Coronado Station branch is at 2071 S. Pacheco St. (☎ **505/438-8452**), and is open from 7:30am to 5pm. Some of the major hotels have stamp machines and mailboxes with twice-daily pickup. The ZIP code for central Santa Fe is 87501.

Radio   Santa Fe's radio stations include KSFR-FM 90.7 (classical and jazz), KNYN-FM 95.5 (country), KBAC-FM 98.1 (adult contemporary), KBOM-FM 106.7 (oldies), and KVSF 1260 AM (news and talk). Albuquerque stations are easily received in Santa Fe.

Safety   Though the tourist district appears very safe, Santa Fe is not on the whole a safe city; theft and the number of reported rapes have risen. The good news is that Santa Fe's overall crime statistics do appear to be falling. Still, when walking the city streets, guard your purse carefully, because there are many bag-grab thefts, particularly during the summer tourist months. Also, be as aware of your surroundings as you would in any other major city.

Taxes   A tax of 10.25% is added to all lodging bills.

Taxis   See "Getting Around," above.

Television   There are three Albuquerque network affiliates—KOB-TV (Channel 4, NBC), KOAT-TV (Channel 7, ABC), and KQRE-TV (Channel 13, CBS). The latter has an office at the State Capitol.

Time Zone   New Mexico is on Mountain standard time, 1 hour ahead of the West Coast and 2 hours behind the East Coast. When it's 10am in Santa Fe, it's noon in New York, 11am in Chicago, and 9am in San Francisco. Daylight saving time is in effect from early April to late October.

Useful Telephone Numbers   Information on **road conditions** in the Santa Fe area can be obtained by calling the State Highway and Transportation Department (☎ **800/432-4269**). For **time and temperature,** call ☎ **505/473-2211.**

Weather   For weather forecasts, call ☎ **505/988-5151.**

5

Where to Stay in Santa Fe

There may not be a bad place to stay in Santa Fe. From downtown hotels to Cerrillos Road motels, ranch-style resorts to quaint bed-and-breakfasts, the standard of accommodation is universally high.

You should be aware of the seasonal nature of the tourist industry in Santa Fe. Accommodations are often booked solid through the summer months, and most places raise their prices accordingly. Rates increase even more during Indian Market, the third weekend of August. During these periods it's essential to make reservations well in advance.

Still, there seems to be little agreement on what constitutes the tourist season; one hotel may raise its rates July 1 and lower them again in mid-September, while another may raise its rates from May to November. Some hotels raise their rates again over the Christmas holidays or recognize a shoulder season. It pays to shop around during the in-between seasons of May through June and September through October.

No matter the season, discounts are often available to seniors, affiliated groups, corporate employees, and others. If you have any questions about your eligibility for these lower rates, be sure to ask.

A combined city-state tax of 10.25% is added to every hotel bill in Santa Fe. And unless otherwise indicated, all recommended accommodations come with private bathroom. All hotels listed offer rooms for nonsmokers and for travelers with disabilities. For the B&Bs, I've indicated in the text whether they do this or not.

ACCOMMODATIONS CATEGORIES   In this chapter, hotels/motels are listed first by geographical area (downtown, Northside, or Southside) and then by price range, based on midsummer rates for doubles: **Very Expensive** refers to rooms that average $150 or more per night; **Expensive** rooms are those that go for $110 to $150; **Moderate** encompasses rooms that range from $75 to $110; and **Inexpensive,** those that cost up to $75.

Following the hotel/motel and bed-and-breakfast recommendations, you'll find suggestions for campgrounds and RV parks.

RESERVATIONS SERVICES   Although Santa Fe has more than 4,500 rooms in over 100 hotels, motels, bed-and-breakfast establishments, and other accommodations, it can still be difficult to find available rooms at the peak of the tourist season. Year-round assistance is available from **Santa Fe Central Reservations,** 320 Artist Rd., Suite 10 (☎ **800/776-7669** or 505/983-8200; fax 505/

984-8682). This service will also book tickets for the Santa Fe Opera, Chamber Music Festival, María Benitez Teatro Flamenco, and the Desert Chorale, as well as Jeep trips into the high country, white-water rafting, horseback riding, mountain bike tours, and golf packages. **Emergency Lodging Assistance**—especially during busy seasons—is available free after 4pm daily (☎ **505/986-0043**).

1 Best Bets

- **Best Historic Hotel: La Fonda,** 100 E. San Francisco St. (☎ **505/982-5511**), is the oldest hotel in Santa Fe. It has hosted a long list of notables, including Ulysses S. Grant and Kit Carson. Billy the Kid is rumored to have been a dishwasher there.
- **Best for a Romantic Getaway:** Bed-and-breakfast inns are always my first choice for a romantic getaway, and in Santa Fe I would recommend one of the new suites at the **Water Street Inn,** 427 Water St. Eclectic Southwestern decor and a private patio with a fountain make for an elegantly romantic stay (☎ **505/ 984-1193**).
- **Best for Families: Bishop's Lodge,** Bishop's Lodge Road (☎ **505/983-6377**), offers a wide variety of activities for children (pony ring, trail rides, pool, and day program) and is a good bet for families who can afford to spend a little extra money. Otherwise, **Villas de Santa Fe,** 400 Griffin St. (☎ **505/988-3000**), which offers units with full kitchens and has a convenience store and swimming pool, is a good choice for families.
- **Best Location:** There are a number of centrally located hotels. Among them, **La Fonda** (see address and telephone above) is the only hotel right on the Plaza; the **Inn of the Anasazi,** 113 Washington Ave. (☎ **505/988-3030**), is just a half block from the Plaza.
- **Best Fitness Facilities:** The **Eldorado Hotel,** 309 W. San Francisco St. (☎ **505/988-4455**), has a wonderful heated rooftop pool and Jacuzzi, exercise room with a view, professional massage therapist, and his-and-hers saunas.
- **Best Imaginative Bed-and-Breakfast:** If you want to stay in a bed-and-breakfast that reflects the unique style of its owner, try **Adobe Abode,** 202 Chapelle St. (☎ **505/983-3133**), which is within walking distance of the Plaza. Each of the rooms is individually and creatively decorated, with rich themes such as "Out of Africa" and "Texas Hill Country."
- **Best Southwestern Bed-and-Breakfast:** Recently remodeled with imaginative rooms, each named after a Northern New Mexico plant, the **Hacienda at Alexander's Inn,** 529 East Palace Ave. (☎ **888/321-5123** or 505/986-1431) is a great find, with prices that will probably go up as soon as word gets out.

2 Downtown

Everything within the horseshoe-shaped Paseo de Peralta and east a few blocks on either side of the Santa Fe River, is considered downtown Santa Fe. All of these accommodations are within walking distance of the Plaza.

VERY EXPENSIVE

Eldorado Hotel
309 W. San Francisco St., Santa Fe, NM 87501. ☎ **800/955-4455** or 505/988-4455. Fax 505/995-4544. 245 units. A/C MINIBAR TV TEL. High season $249–$359 double; low season $129–$279. Year-round $249–$975 suite. Ski and other package rates are available. AE, CB, DC, DISC, MC, V. 24-hour valet parking $9 per night. Pets are accepted.

Since its opening in 1986, the Eldorado has stood like a monolith at the center of town. Locals wonder how the five-story structure bypassed the two-story zoning restrictions. Still, the architects did manage to meld Pueblo Revival style with an interesting cathedral feel, inside and out. The lobby is grand, with a high ceiling that continues into the court area and the cafe.

Take your time while wandering through, since the place is adorned with well over a million dollars' worth of art, most of it from Northern New Mexico. Most notable in the entry to the court is an *olla,* or pot, made in the early 1920s by a Zia potter, and decorated with a parrot, a bird sacred to the Anasazi as well as the Pueblo people.

The rooms continue the artistic Southwestern motif. There's a warmth here, created in particular by the kiva fireplaces in many of the rooms as well as the tapestries supplied by Seret and Sons, a local antique dealer. This hotel and the Inn of the Anasazi are the establishments in town for those who desire consistency and fine service. The suites here come with a butler who will do "anything legal" for you, including walking your dog.

You'll find small families and businesspeople staying here, as well as conference-goers. Most of the rooms have views of downtown Santa Fe, many from balconies (request an east-facing room to be sure). The hotel rightfully prides itself on the spaciousness and quiet of its rooms, each with a hair dryer and Spectravision movie channels.

If you're really indulging, join the ranks of Mick Jagger, Geena Davis, and King Juan Carlos of Spain and try the penthouse five-room presidential suite. Just down the street from the main hotel is Zona Rosa, which houses two-, three-, and four-bedroom condo suites with full kitchens.

Dining: The innovative and elegant Old House restaurant was built on the preserved foundation of an early 1800s Santa Fe house. The viga-latilla (pine beam and cedar branch) ceiling, polished wood floor, pottery and *kachinas* (Pueblo Indian carved dolls) in niches give it a distinct regional touch, found also in its creative Southwestern cuisine. More casual meals are served in the spacious Eldorado Court. The lobby lounge offers low-key entertainment.

Amenities: Concierge, room service, butlers, dry cleaning and laundry service, nightly turndown, twice-daily maid service, safe-deposit boxes. There's also a heated rooftop swimming pool and Jacuzzi, medium-sized health club (with a view), his-and-hers saunas, professional massage therapist, business center, beauty salon, and boutiques.

Hilton of Santa Fe

100 Sandoval St. (P.O. Box 25104), Santa Fe, NM 87504-2387. ☎ **800/336-3676,** 800/HILTONS, or 505/988-2811. Fax 505/986-6439. 157 units. A/C TV TEL. $119–$299 double, $219–$549 suite, $299–$599 casita, depending on time of year. Call for rates. Extra person $20. AE, CB, DC, DISC, MC, V. Parking $5 per night.

With its landmark bell tower, the Hilton encompasses a full city block (a few-minutes' walk from the Plaza) and incorporates most of the historic landholdings of the 350-year-old Ortiz family estate. It's built around a central pool and patio area and is a fine blend of ancient and modern styles.

Rooms are fairly standard, not nearly as refined as those in the Eldorado, but many visitors like this hotel because it offers all the amenities of a fine hotel at a fairly reasonable price. It also has an intimacy that some of the other large downtown hotels lack. The lobby is cozy, with huge vigas and a big fireplace; it's decorated in a refined Southwestern style.

Downtown Santa Fe Accommodations

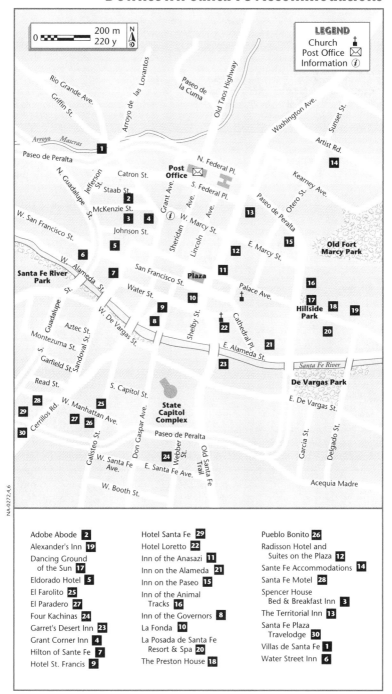

LEGEND
Church
Post Office
Information ⓘ

Adobe Abode **2**
Alexander's Inn **19**
Dancing Ground
  of the Sun **17**
Eldorado Hotel **5**
El Farolito **25**
El Paradero **27**
Four Kachinas **24**
Garret's Desert Inn **23**
Grant Corner Inn **4**
Hilton of Sante Fe **7**
Hotel St. Francis **9**

Hotel Santa Fe **29**
Hotel Loretto **22**
Inn of the Anasazi **11**
Inn on the Alameda **21**
Inn on the Paseo **15**
Inn of the Animal
  Tracks **16**
Inn of the Governors **8**
La Fonda **10**
La Posada de Santa Fe
  Resort & Spa **20**
The Preston House **18**

Pueblo Bonito **26**
Radisson Hotel and
  Suites on the Plaza **12**
Sante Fe Accommodations **14**
Santa Fe Motel **28**
Spencer House
  Bed & Breakfast Inn **3**
The Territorial Inn **13**
Santa Fe Plaza
  Travelodge **30**
Villas de Santa Fe **1**
Water Street Inn **6**

Remodeled in 1997 in a warm Aztec-Southwestern style, the guest rooms are large, most with a small patio or balcony. All rooms now have hair dryers, irons and ironing boards, robes, safes, VCRs, Spectravision movie channels, and coffeemakers.

In June 1994 the Hilton opened Casa Ortiz de Santa Fe, a small building adjacent to the main hotel, which houses three casitas. The building was once the coach house (ca. 1625) of Nicholas Ortiz III. Today, the thick adobe walls encompass elegant Southwestern-style suites. Each has a living room with kiva fireplace, fully stocked kitchenette (with microwave, stove, and minirefrigerator), and bathroom with whirlpool tub. All three have fireplaces.

Dining: Two restaurants occupy the premises of the early 18th-century Casa Ortiz. The Piñon Grill serves a variety of wood-fire grilled items in a casual atmosphere. The Chamisa Courtyard, which serves breakfast, features casual garden-style tables amid lush greenery under a large skylight; it's built on the home's enclosed patio. El Cañon Wine and Coffee Bar specializes in fine wines by the glass and gourmet coffees. El Cañon also serves breakfast, lunch, and dinner. Specialties include freshly baked breads and pastries as well as sandwiches.

Amenities: Concierge, room service, courtesy van, dry cleaning, laundry service, outdoor swimming pool, Jacuzzi, small health club, car-rental agency, travel agency, gift shop.

✪ Inn of the Anasazi

113 Washington Ave., Santa Fe, NM 87501. ☎ **800/688-8100** or 505/988-3030. Fax 505/988-3277. 59 units. A/C MINIBAR TV TEL. Nov–Mar $199–$345 double; Apr–Oct $235–$395 double. Holiday and festival rates may be higher. AE, CB, DC, DISC, MC, V. Valet parking $10 per day.

In an incredible feat, the designers of this fine luxury hotel have managed to create a feeling of grandness in a very limited space. Flagstone floors, vigas, and latillas are enhanced by oversized cacti that evoke the feeling of an Anasazi cliff dwelling and lend a warm and welcoming ambiance. Accents are appropriately Navajo, in a nod to the fact that the Navajo live in the area the Anasazi once inhabited. A half block off the Plaza, this hotel was built in 1991 to cater to travelers who know their hotels. Amenities include stereos and VCRs in all rooms, as well as private safes, coffeemakers with custom blended coffee beans, bathroom telephones, hair dryers, 100 percent cotton linens, and organic bath oils and shampoos, as well as organic food in the restaurant. On the ground floor are a living room and library with oversized furniture and replicas of Anasazi pottery and Navajo rugs.

Even the smallest rooms are spacious, with pearl-finished walls and decor in cream tones accented by novelties such as iron candle sconces, original art, four-poster beds, gaslit kiva fireplaces, and humidifiers. All the rooms are quiet and comfortable, though none have dramatic views.

Dining: See the Anasazi Restaurant in chapter 6 for a full description.

Amenities: Concierge, room service (6am to 11pm), laundry service, newspaper delivery, in-room massage, twice-daily maid service, tours of galleries and museums, stationary bicycles available for use in guest rooms, free coffee or refreshments in lobby. You'll also find video rentals, a library/boardroom, and audiovisual and communication equipment. Access to a nearby health club can be arranged.

✪ Inn on the Alameda

303 E. Alameda St., Santa Fe, NM 87501. ☎ **800/289-2122** or 505/984-2121. Fax 505/986-8325. 68 units. A/C TV TEL. Jan–Mar $147–$212 double, $227–$297 suite; Mar–June $162–$227 double, $241–$312 suite; July–Aug 22 $192–$257 double, $272–$342 suite; Aug 23–Oct $177–$242 double, $252–$327 suite; Nov–Dec $147–$212 double,

$227–$297 suite. Holidays and special events may be higher; rates subject to change. Rates include breakfast. AE, DC, DISC, MC, V. Free parking. Pets are welcome (the hotel offers a pet program that features pet amenities and a pet-walking map).

Just across the street from the bosque-shaded Santa Fe River and 3 blocks from the Plaza sits the Inn on the Alameda, a cozy stop for those who like the services of a hotel with the intimacy of an inn. Begun 10 years ago as a bed-and-breakfast, it now sprawls into four buildings. There are casita suites to the west, two 3-story buildings at the center, and another 1-story that contains suites. All are Pueblo-style adobe, ranging in age, but most were built in the late 1980s.

The owner, Joe Schepps, appreciates traditional Southwestern style; he's used red brick in the dining area and Mexican equipal furniture in the lobby. He went all out here in the construction, using thick vigas and shiny latillas set around a grand fireplace.

The rooms follow a similar good taste, though the decor is more standard Santa Fe style (boxy with pastel upholstery) than the lobby might lead you to expect. All rooms have VCRs and hair dryers. The newer deluxe rooms and suites in the easternmost building are in the best shape. The traditional rooms are quaint, some with interesting angled bed configurations. Beware of the casitas on the western corner of the property. After some recent tree trimming, they've tended to pick up traffic noise. Still, take note of the trees surrounding the inn—cottonwoods and aspens, which, when you step out on some balconies, make you feel as though you're in a tree house. If you're an art shopper this is an ideal spot because it's a quick walk to Canyon Road. Amenities include robes in all rooms and refrigerators and kiva fireplaces in some rooms.

Dining: An elaborate continental "Breakfast of Enchantment" is served each morning in the Agoyo Room, outdoor courtyard, or your own room. A full-service bar is open nightly.

Amenities: Concierge, limited room service, dry cleaning and self-serve laundry, newspaper delivery, baby-sitting can be arranged. There's also a medium-sized fitness facility, massage, and two open-air Jacuzzis.

Hotel Loretto

211 Old Santa Fe Trail (P.O. Box 1417), Santa Fe, NM 87501. ☎ **800/727-5531** or 505/988-5531. Fax 505/984-7988. 145 units. A/C TV TEL. Jan 1–April 30 $189–$259 double; May 1–Oct 31 $239–$379 double; Nov 1–Dec 20 $189–$259 double; Dec 21–Dec 31 $239–$379 double. Extra person $15. Children 17 and under stay free in parents' room. AE, CB, DC, DISC, MC, V. Free parking.

This much-photographed hotel, just 2 blocks from the Plaza, was built in 1975 to resemble the Taos Pueblo. Light and shadow dance upon the five-level structure as the sun crosses the sky. Two years ago it came under new ownership and is now undergoing a multi-million dollar makeover. The outdated decor has been replaced by a Southwest/Montana ranch style put into place by the same decorator used by Ted Turner and Jane Fonda. The new owners, Noble House Hotels and Resorts (owners of the Adolphus Hotel in Dallas and Little Palm in Key West), are determined to compete with other large hotels such as the Eldorado. With faux painted walls and an interesting and cozy new lobby lounge, they may just manage to catch up. Still, the hotel's rooms are pretty standard, a bit small, and the bathrooms are basic. With the renovation, the hotel hopes to attract more groups. Overall, it is fairly quiet and has nice views—especially on the northeast side, where you'll see both the historic St. Francis Cathedral and the Loretto Chapel (with its "miraculous" spiral staircase; see "More Attractions," in chapter 7). Each room has a coffeemaker, bottled water, and hair dryers.

Dining: Named for a carved wooden serpent above the bar, Nellie's (see chapter 6) serves fine nouveau Southwestern cuisine in a hip-folk-artsy environment. A coffee shop serves sandwiches, stews, muffins, and Starbucks Coffee.

Amenities: Concierge, room service, valet laundry, business center, and audio/visual conferencing equipment. There's also an outdoor heated swimming pool (mid-May to mid-October) and shopping arcade (with a fine-art gallery, boutiques, gift shops, sundries shop, and hair salon). Tennis and golf privileges nearby can be arranged.

✪ La Fonda

100 E. San Francisco St. (P.O. Box 1209), Santa Fe, NM 87501. ☎ **800/523-5002** or 505/982-5511. Fax 505/988-2952. 191 units. A/C TV TEL. $195 standard double, $205 deluxe double; $225–$550 suite. Extra person $15. Children under 12 stay free in parents' room. AE, CB, DC, DISC, MC, V. Parking $6 per day in a covered garage.

Whether you stay in this hotel on the southeast corner of the Plaza or elsewhere, it's worth strolling through, just to get a sense of how Santa Fe once was, and still in some ways is. This was the inn at the end of the Santa Fe Trail; it saw trappers, traders, and merchants, as well as notables such as President Rutherford B. Hayes and General Ulysses S. Grant. The original inn was dying of old age in 1920 when it was razed and replaced by the current La Fonda. Its architecture is Pueblo Revival: imitation adobe with wooden balconies and beam ends protruding over the tops of windows. Inside, the lobby is rich and slightly dark with people bustling about, drinking in the cafe and buying jewelry from Native Americans.

As you head farther into this 4-story building you may come across Ernesto Martinez, who wanders around finding things to paint. You'll see his colorful, playful designs throughout the hallways and in the rooms decorating tin mirror frames and carved wooden headboards.

The hotel has seen some renovation through the years, as well as a whole new wing recently completed to the east where you'll find deluxe suites and new meeting spaces. Overall, however, this hotel isn't the model of refinement. For that, you'd best go to the Hotel Santa Fe or other newer places. No room is the same here, and while each has its own funky touch, some are more kitsch than quaint. All rooms have hair dryers, Spectravision movie channels, irons, and ironing boards. Some have minirefrigerators, fireplaces, and private balconies. If you want a feel of the real Santa Fe, this is the place to stay.

Dining/Diversions: The French Pastry Shop is the place to get cappuccino and crêpes; La Fiesta Lounge draws many locals to their economical New Mexican food lunch buffet; and La Plazuela offers what some believe to be the best chile rellenos in town, in a skylit garden patio. The Bell Tower Bar, at the southwest corner of the hotel, is the highest point in downtown Santa Fe—a great place for a cocktail and a view of the city.

Amenities: Concierge, room service, dry cleaning and laundry service, tour desk, in-room massage, baby-sitting, express check-out, free coffee and refreshments in lobby. There's also an outdoor swimming pool, two indoor Jacuzzis, sundeck, cold plunge, massage room, ballroom, and shopping arcade.

La Posada de Santa Fe Resort and Spa

330 E. Palace Ave., Santa Fe, NM 87501. ☎ **800/727-5276** or 505/986-0000. Fax 505/982-6850. 159 units. A/C MINIBAR TV TEL. May–Oct plus the Thanksgiving and Christmas seasons, $189–$397 double; $289–$497 suite. Nov–Apr (except holidays), $159–$315 double; $225–$385 suite. Various packages available. AE, CB, DC, DISC, MC, V. Free parking.

If you're in the mood to stay in a little New Mexico adobe village, you'll enjoy this hotel just 3 blocks from the Plaza. The main building is an odd mix of architecture.

The original part was a Victorian mansion built in 1882 by Abraham Staab, a German immigrant, for his bride, Julia. Later it was adobeized—an adobe structure was literally built around it—so that now the Victorian presence is only within the charming bar and a half-dozen rooms, which still maintain the original brick, mahogany, and marble, as well as Italian paintings and French furniture and tapestries. It is said that Julia Staab, who died in 1896, continues to haunt the place. Mischievous but good-natured, she is Santa Fe's best-known and most frequently witnessed ghost.

The rest of the hotel follows in the Pueblo-style construction and is quaint, especially in the summer when surrounded by acres of green grass. Here, you get to experience squeaky maple floors, vigas and latillas, and, in many rooms, kiva fireplaces. Fortunately, the hotel has recently come under new ownership and major renovations are taking place in the common and guest rooms. At press time, these changes were just beginning with plans for completion in April 1999. The hotel attracts travelers and a fair number of families. Most rooms don't have views but have outdoor patios, and most are tucked back into the quiet compound. All have coffeemakers and hair dryers.

Dining/Diversions: The hotel has a restaurant, open for three meals daily, serving "food of the Americas." From spring to early fall, meals are also served outside on a big patio. The lounge has seasonal happy-hour entertainment (usually local musicians).

Amenities: Concierge, limited room service, dry cleaning and laundry service, in-room massage, twice-daily maid service, free coffee and refreshments in lobby. There's also a heated outdoor swimming pool and boutiques. After March 1999, the hotel also plans to have a Jacuzzi, sauna, sundeck, business center, and beauty salon.

Radisson Hotel and Suites on the Plaza

125 Washington Ave., Santa Fe, NM 87501. ☎ **800/333-3333** or 505/988-4900. Fax 505/983-9322. 100 units. A/C MINIBAR TV TEL. $149–$219 double, depending on time of year and type of room. Extra person $20. Children under 12 stay free in parents' room. Rates include breakfast. AE, CB, DC, DISC, MC, V. Parking $10 per day.

Recently purchased by the Radisson Hotel, I fear for the future of what was the Hotel Plaza Real. Already, the service of this New Orleans meets Santa Fe Territorial-style hotel built in 1990 has declined measurably. The construction and decor of the lobby is rustically elegant, built around a fireplace with balconies perched above. The rooms are clean and nicely decorated with Southwestern-style furniture and accent amenities such as *bancos* (adobe benches) and French doors opening onto balconies or terraces surrounding a quiet courtyard decorated with chile *ristras*. Most of the rooms are suites and cover guest needs well: coffeemaker, hair dryer, iron and ironing board in each. Try the bar for an afternoon drink or the veranda for coffee. Services include dry cleaning and laundry service, twice daily maid service, and access to a nearby health club. As for the service, you might expect to be ignored if you stay here. At least that was the case during the transition to new ownership.

EXPENSIVE

✪ Hotel St. Francis

210 Don Gaspar Ave., Santa Fe, NM 87501. ☎ **800/529-5700** or 505/983-5700. Fax 505/989-7690. 84 units. A/C TV TEL. May 1–Oct 31 plus the weeks of Dec 25 and Jan 1, $118–$208 double; $228–$353 suite. Nov–Feb $88–$158 double; $178–$278 suite. Mar–Apr $98–$173 double; $178–$278 suite. Children under 12 stay free in parents' room. AE, CB, DC, DISC, MC, V. Free parking.

If you long for the rich fabrics, fine antiques, and slow pace of a European Hotel, this is your place. One block from the Plaza, the building was first constructed in the 1880s and has seen a fire, countless government officials come to dine and drink, and finally dilapidation. It was renovated in 1986. Now elegantly redecorated, the lobby is crowned by a Victorian fireplace with hovering cherubs, a theme repeated throughout the hotel.

The rooms follow the European decor, each with its own unique bent. You'll find a fishing room, golf room, garden room, and music room, the motif evoked by the furnishings: a vintage set of golf clubs here, a sheet of music in a dry flower arrangement there. The hotel attracts individual travelers as well as families and many Europeans, well cared for by a concierge who speaks six languages. Request a room facing east and you'll wake each day to a view of the mountains, seen through lovely lace. All rooms have refrigerators and closet safes.

Dining/Diversions: A recent renovation has given the restaurant and bar a European gentlemen's club ambience. Breakfast, lunch, and dinner specials are served daily with prices worth checking out. The lobby and veranda are favorite spots for locals to take their afternoon tea. You'll eat scones, pastries, and tea sandwiches— all baked in-house—and drink tea, sherry, port, or champagne.

Amenities: Concierge, room service, dry cleaning and laundry service, free coffee or refreshments in lobby. You'll also find Spectravision movie channels and a guest membership at a nearby health club.

Hotel Santa Fe

1501 Paseo de Peralta, Santa Fe, NM 87501. ☎ **800/825-9876** or 505/982-1200. Fax 505/984-2211. 220 units. A/C MINIBAR TV TEL. Jan 4–Feb 11 $99 double; $129 suite. Feb 12–April 30 $119 double; $139 suite. May 1–June 24 $129 double; $159 suite. June 25–Aug 28 $149 double; $179 suite. Aug 29–Oct 31 $139 double; $169 suite. Nov 1–Dec 23 $109 double; $129 suite. Dec 24–Jan 3 $149 double; $179 suite. Extra person $10. Children 17 and under stay free in parents' room. AE, CB, DC, DISC, MC, V. Free parking.

About a 10-minute walk south of the Plaza you'll find this newer 3-story establishment, the only Native American–owned hotel in Santa Fe. The Picuris Pueblo is the majority stockholder here, and part of the pleasure of staying is the culture they bring to your visit. This is not to say that you'll get any sense of the rusticity of a pueblo in your accommodations—this sophisticated 6-year-old hotel is decorated in Southwestern style with a few novel aspects such as an Allan Houser bronze buffalo dancer watching over the front desk and a *horno*-shaped fireplace surrounded by comfortable furniture in the lobby.

The rooms are medium-sized with clean lines and comfortable beds, the decor accented with pine Taos-style furniture. You will get a strong sense of the Native American presence on the patio during the summer, when Picuris dancers come to perform and bread bakers uncover the *horno* and prepare loaves for sale.

Rooms on the north side get less street noise from Cerrillos Road and have better views of the mountains, but you won't have the sun shining onto your balcony.

Dining: The restaurant is another place where the hotel's origins are recognizable. The famed Corn Dance Cafe serves a standard breakfast, but for lunch and dinner you can dine on Native American food from all over the Americas. Expect buffalo and turkey instead of beef and chicken. Many of the dishes are accompanied by what chef Loretta Oden calls the three sisters: corn, beans, and squash.

Amenities: Concierge, limited room service, dry cleaning and laundry service, in-room massage, twice-daily maid service, baby-sitting, secretarial services, courtesy shuttle to the Plaza and Canyon Road. There's also a lovely outdoor heated pool, a Jacuzzi, conference rooms, Laundromat, car-rental desk, and Picuris Pueblo gift shop. Access to a nearby health club can be arranged.

Inn of the Governors

234 Don Gaspar Ave., Santa Fe, NM 87501. ☎ **800/234-4534** or 505/982-4333. Fax 505/989-9149. 100 units. A/C TV TEL. Jan–early Feb $129–$259 double. Feb–April $149–$279 double. May–June $169–$309 double. July–late Oct $179–$319 double. Late Oct–mid-Dec $149–$279 double. Late Dec–early Jan $179–$329 double. Extra person $10. Children under 18 stay free in parents' room. AE, CB, DC, MC, V. Free parking.

Tucked 2 blocks off the Plaza, this inn has an intimate feel despite its 100 rooms. The Southwestern decor lobby is accented with gray weathered wood; outside is a heated pool that steams through the winter. The building is Territorial style, the novelty of which is lost on people outside the compound, but once inside you can see the brick-trimmed roofline and distinctive portals. Built in 1965, it has been continuously renovated, leaving the rooms consistent.

The rooms are accented with Mexican furniture and headboards, wrought-iron lamps, and hand-painted tin mirror frames, which provide a softer feel than is found in some of the newer hotels. As its name would imply, the Governor's mansion used to rest on this spot. Winter sees a fair amount of legislative traffic, but the majority of the clientele are travelers. Rooms on the north side look toward downtown and the mountains, and many have balconies. All rooms have minirefrigerators, Spectravision movie channels, and hair dryers; many of the superior and deluxe rooms have fireplaces (wood provided daily), and some have balconies and stereos.

Dining/Diversions: The Mañana Bar and Restaurant serves three meals daily in a casual atmosphere. On warm days meals are served in an outdoor courtyard. The menu features light, healthy American cuisine. The adjacent bar is rustic, with cowhide chairs at a copper-topped bar beneath a viga ceiling; a pianist performs 6 nights a week.

Amenities: Concierge, room service, dry cleaning and laundry service, complimentary newspaper in lobby, in-room massage, twice-daily maid service, baby-sitting, express checkout, courtesy car, free coffee or refreshments in lobby. There is also an outdoor heated pool, access to a nearby health club, and conference rooms.

Villas de Santa Fe

400 Griffin St., Santa Fe, NM 87501. ☎ **800/869-6790** or 505/988-3000. Fax 505/988-4700. 90 suites. A/C TV TEL. $104–$155 1-bedroom suite with 1 or 2 beds, $124–$175 1-bedroom suite with gas fireplace; $185–$310 2-bedroom, 2-bathroom suite with gas fireplace. Rates include continental breakfast. AE, DC, DISC, MC, V. Free parking.

Formerly the Homewood Suites, this hotel is upscale practicality. Tucked within a residential neighborhood within walking distance from the Plaza, Villas is the place you go when you want a bit of luxury and the ability to cook and eat as you do at home. Built in 1994, its guest rooms on 3 stories are decorated in Southwestern style with a cold efficiency that marks the place. The rooms are consistently comfortable, with full kitchens that include microwaves, stoves, refrigerators, and dishwashers, as well as amenities such as pay movies and Nintendo, ironing boards and irons, recliners and sleeper sofas. Some have balconies and patios and some have gas fireplaces. There is a homey feel in the main room where an extended continental breakfast is served around a kitchen environment.

Amenities: Complimentary grocery shopping, local shuttle service, valet laundry service, year-round heated outdoor pool, two outdoor Jacuzzis, well-equipped health club, Laundromat, Suite Shop (with vending and beverages), and picnic area with gas grill.

MODERATE

Garrett's Desert Inn

311 Old Santa Fe Trail, Santa Fe, NM 87501. ☎ **800/888-2145** or 505/982-1851. Fax 505/989-1647. 82 units. A/C TV TEL. $69–$114 depending on season and type of room. AE, DC, DISC, MC, V. Free parking.

Completion of this hotel in 1957 prompted the Historic Design Review Board to implement zoning restrictions throughout downtown. Apparently, residents were appalled by the huge air conditioners adorning the roof. Though they're still unsightly, the hotel makes up for them in other ways. First, with all the focus today on retro fashions, this hotel 3 blocks from the Plaza is totally in. It's a clean, 2-story, concrete block building around a broad parking lot. The hotel underwent a complete remodeling in 1994; it managed to maintain some '50s touches, such as art deco colored tile in the bathrooms and plenty of space in the rooms, while enlarging the windows and putting in sturdy doors and wood accents. Rooms are equipped with tile vanities and hair dryers. Above all, it's centrally located, within walking distance from the Plaza and Canyon Road, but also far enough from busy streets to provide needed quiet. There is a concierge, limited room service, baby-sitting and express check-out. Locals frequent the hotel's Le Cafe on the Trail for crêpes and pancakes. There's a year-round heated pool.

Santa Fe Budget Inn

725 Cerrillos Rd., Santa Fe, NM 87501. ☎ **800/288-7600** or 505/982-5952. Fax 505/984-8879. 160 units. A/C TV TEL. July 4–Oct 25 and Dec 25–Jan 2 $75–$86 double ($10–$20 higher during Indian Market). Rest of the year $50–$58 double. A Sun–Thurs supersaver rate may apply in the off-season. AAA and AARP members receive $3 discounts. AE, CB, DC, MC, V. Free parking.

If you're looking for a convenient almost-downtown location at a reasonable price, this is one of your best bets. This 2-story stucco adobe motel with portals is spread through three buildings and is about a 10-minute walk from the Plaza. Built in 1985, it was remodeled in 1994. The rooms are plain, basic, and fairly small. Santa Fe Opera and Fiesta posters add a splash of color. The bathrooms and furniture could use some updating, but if you're a traveler who spends a lot of time out of the room this shouldn't matter because the place is clean and functional with comfortable (on the soft side) beds and good reading lights. Outside, there's a small park in back and an outdoor pool (open in summer) tucked away. To avoid street noise ask for a room at the back of the property. An adjacent restaurant serves American and New Mexican food.

INEXPENSIVE

Santa Fe Motel

510 Cerrillos Rd., Santa Fe, NM 87501. ☎ **800/745-9910** or 505/982-1039. Fax 505/986-1275. 21 units. A/C TV TEL. $54–$89 double; $69–$121 kitchenette; $89–$149 casita. Extra adult $10. Continental breakfast included with the price of the room. AE, DC, MC, V. Free parking.

If you like walking to the Plaza and restaurants but don't want to pay big bucks, this little compound is a good choice. Rooms here are larger than at the nearby Budget and have more personality than those at the Travelodge. Ask for one of the casitas in back—you'll pay more but get a little turn-of-the-century charm (when they were built), plus more quiet and privacy. Some have vigas, others skylights, fireplaces, and patios. The main part of the motel, built in 1955, is 2-story Territorial style, with upstairs rooms that open onto a portal with a bit of a view. Under new

---

ⓘ Family-Friendly Hotels

Bishop's Lodge *(see below)*   A children's pony ring, riding lessons, tennis courts with instruction, a pool with lifeguard, stocked trout pond just for kids, a summer daytime program, horseback trail trips, and more make this a veritable day camp for all ages.

El Rey Inn *(see page 68)*   Kids will enjoy the play area, table games, and pool; parents will appreciate the kitchenettes and laundry facilities.

Rancho Encantado *(see page 64)*   Horseback riding (on trails or pony ring), pool, tennis courts, and many indoor and outdoor games will keep kids happily busy here.

---

ownership in 1998, the hotel's rooms are, at press time, being renovated. They're decorated in a Southwest motif and have very basic furnishings, but nice firm beds. The bathrooms are supposed to be receiving much-needed updating. In the main building, kitchenettes are available and include refrigerator, microwave, stove, coffeemaker, and toaster. Fresh-brewed coffee is served each morning in the office, where a bulletin board lists Santa Fe activities.

Santa Fe Plaza Travelodge

646 Cerrillos Rd., Santa Fe, NM 87501. ☎ **800/578-7878** or 505/982-3551. Fax 505/983-8624. 48 units. A/C TV TEL. Nov–Apr $39–$75 double; May–Oct $65–$88 double. These rates subject to change. AE, CB, DC, DISC, MC, V. Free parking.

You can count on the motel next door to Hotel Santa Fe (6 blocks to the Plaza) on busy Cerrillos Road for comfort, convenience, and a no-frills stay. The rooms are very clean, nicely lit, and despite the busy location, relatively quiet. New mattresses and a pretty Southwestern ceiling border added to the decor make the rooms comfortable. Each room has a minirefrigerator, table and chairs, and a coffeemaker. The curbside pool, though basic, will definitely provide relief on hot summer days. A newspaper is delivered each morning.

3 Northside

Within easy reach of the Plaza, Northside encompasses the area that lies north of the loop of the Paseo de Peralta.

VERY EXPENSIVE

✪ Bishop's Lodge

Bishop's Lodge Rd. (P.O. Box 2367), Santa Fe, NM 87504. ☎ **505/983-6377.** Fax 505/989-8739. 88 units. A/C TV TEL. European Plan (meals not included), Jan 1–Mar 20 $105–$215 double; Mar 21–May 21 and Aug 30–Dec 31 $155–$305 double; May 22–June 30, $179–$349 double; July 1–Aug 29 $219–$389 double. Additional person $15. Children 3 and under stay free in parents' room. The summer American Plan package offers breakfast and choice of lunch or dinner as well as children's programs: May 22–June 30 $271–$441 double; July 1–Aug 29 $311–$481 double. Additional person $61. AE, DC, DISC, MC, V. Free parking.

This resort holds special significance for me, as my parents met in the lodge and were later married in the chapel. Years later, the whole family used to come here from Albuquerque so my parents could relax and we children could ride horses. It's a place rich with history. More than a century ago, when Bishop Jean-Baptiste Lamy was the spiritual leader of Northern New Mexico's Roman Catholic population, he often escaped clerical politics by hiking into this valley called Little Tesuque. He built a retreat and a humble chapel (now on the National Register of Historic Places) with high-vaulted ceilings and a hand-built altar. Today, Lamy's 1,000-acre getaway has become Bishop's Lodge.

Purchased in 1918 from the Pulitzer family (of publishing fame) by Denver mining executive James R. Thorpe, it remained in his family's hands until 1998, when the Australian real estate company ERE Yarmouth purchased it. The company plans an $11 million renovation over the next 3 years, including the addition of 56 guest rooms, a spa, and 10,000 square feet of meeting space as well as replacement of bedding and other furnishings. The lobby, lounge, and restaurant will also be renovated. We will have to wait to see what these changes mean to travelers.

The guest rooms, spread through 10 buildings, all feature handcrafted furniture and regional artwork. Guests receive a complimentary fruit basket upon arrival. Standard rooms are spacious and many have balconies, while deluxe rooms feature traditional kiva fireplaces, a combination bedroom/sitting room, and private decks or patios; some older units have flagstone floors and viga ceilings. All rooms have coffeemakers, robes, and in-room safes, and receive a morning newspaper. Deluxe suites are extremely spacious, with living rooms, separate bedrooms, private patios and decks, and artwork of near-museum quality. All deluxe units come with fireplaces, refrigerators, and in-room safes. The Lodge is an active resort three seasons of the year; in the winter, it takes on the character of a romantic country retreat.

Dining: Bishop's Lodge dining room features regional Southwestern cuisine. Attire is casual at breakfast and lunch, slightly more formal at dinner. There's a full vintage wine list, and El Rincon Bar serves before- and after-dinner drinks.

Amenities: Concierge, room service, laundry service, newspaper delivery, in-room massage, twice-daily maid service, baby-sitting, express check-out, courtesy shuttle three times daily, free coffee or refreshments in the lobby in the mornings, seasonal cookouts, and breakfast rides. There's a lovely outdoor pool with a seasonal lifeguard, small health club, aerobics classes, four tennis courts, pro shop and instruction, Jacuzzi, sauna, hiking and self-guided nature walk (the Lodge is a member of the Audubon Cooperative Sanctuary System), daily guided horseback rides, introductory riding lessons, a children's pony ring, supervised skeet and trap shooting, a stocked trout pond for children, Ping-Pong, and a summer daytime program with counselors for children.

Rancho Encantado

Route 4, Box 57C, Santa Fe, NM 87501. ☎ **800/722-9339** or 505/982-3537. Fax 505/983-8269. 45 units. A/C TV TEL. $125–$275 double; $130–$205 pueblo room; $210–$350 1-bedroom villa, $250–$420 2-bedroom villa, depending on the season. AE, DISC, DC, MC, V. Free parking.

Located 8 miles north of Santa Fe in the foothills of the Sangre de Cristo Mountains, Rancho Encantado, with its sweeping panoramic views, offers travelers luxury accommodations and plenty of wild Southwest activities. The resort was begun by Betty Egan, a former World War II captain in the Women's Army Corps, who purchased the property in the mid-1960s. Mrs. Egan, then recently widowed, was determined to begin a new and prosperous life with her family, and so in 1968 the 168-acre ranch became Rancho Encantado. The property came under new ownership in 1995, and with it came long-needed upgrades to sleeping rooms, the main lodge, and grounds.

The handsome main lodge is comfortable and unassuming, decorated in traditional Southwestern style with hand-painted tiles, ceiling vigas, tile floors, antique furnishings, Pueblo rugs, and Hispanic art objects hanging on stuccoed walls. The large fireplace in the living room/lounge is a focal point, especially on cold winter afternoons. In the main lodge and adjoining area the rooms are quite cozy with a hint of Victorian bed-and-breakfast feel. All rooms provide coffeemakers and minirefrigerators; most have fireplaces.

Surrounding the lodge are clusters of casitas the hotel calls villas. These are comfortable units with a homey feel, though they've needed a decorator's touch, and are, at press time, receiving it: new fabrics and soft goods, carpet, draperies, bedspreads, and some furnishings. Across the street from the main building are two-bedroom/two-bathroom villas. These newer split-level adobe units are equipped with fireplaces in the living room and master bedroom plus a full kitchen. Currently, the owners are breaking ground on 25 new Pueblo-style junior parlor suites, each with a kiva fireplace and private patio. Expected completion date is spring of 1999. Whichever you choose, you're sure to find the accommodations here more than adequate; satisfied guests have included Princess Anne, Robert Redford, Jimmy Stewart, Whoopi Goldberg, and John Wayne.

The new owners have expanded special programs at the resort. Watch for summer sunset margarita horseback rides, barbecues and chuck wagon breakfast cookouts, barn dances, and Native American and Hispanic storytelling and dancing, as well as a children's summer camp which includes music, art projects, hiking, basketball, swimming, and horse activities. In winter you can take a sleigh ride through the countryside.

Dining/Diversions: Rancho Encantado's restaurant is a favorite dinner spot for opera-goers. The food is good and the atmosphere relaxing. The west wall of the dining room has picture windows that overlook the Jemez Mountains, offering diners a first-rate view of the spectacular New Mexico sunset. Some of the traditional dishes remain, with an addition of some contemporary Western cuisine. You may enjoy tenderloin of beef, served with a Jack Daniels sauce, or a smoked salmon burrito. You can also get a good egg-salad sandwich. The Cantina, with its big-screen TV, is a popular gathering spot; there is also a snack bar on the premises.

Amenities: Laundry service, limited room service, baby-sitting, courtesy limo to Plaza. There's also an outdoor pool, small health club, Jacuzzi, tennis courts (tennis pro in summer), hiking trails, horseback riding, sand volleyball, basketball, horseshoes, pool table, bocce ball court (Italian lawn bowling), and library.

EXPENSIVE

Santa Fe Accommodations
320 Artist Rd., Santa Fe, NM 87501. ☎ **800/745-9910** or 505/982-6636. Fax 505/984-8682. 126 units. A/C. $89–$189 1-bedroom (up to 2 adults); $136–$236 2-bedroom (up to 4 adults); $144–$249 2-bedroom town house (up to 4 adults); $199–$339 3-bedroom town house (up to 6 adults). Extra person $20. Children 18 and under stay free in parents' room. Rates include extended continental breakfast. AE, DC, MC, V. Free on- and off-street parking.

Santa Fe Accommodations is not a hotel, but a company that manages a number of properties around Santa Fe. If you're interested in a condominium-type stay, they have a few options. The first is **Fort Marcy Hotel Suites.** Located about an 8-minute walk from the Plaza, these condominiums climb up a hill north of town. They are privately owned, so decor varies, although Santa Fe Accommodations gives incentives to encourage remodeling by owners. Logically, some are better decorated than others. All have full kitchens, with microwave ovens, stoves, ovens, and refrigerators, and most have dishwashers. They also have irons and ironing boards. The units have plenty of room, and the grounds are well kept, though some of the units are showing their age (built in 1975). The grounds have a rural feel with chamisa and pine trees. They've recently remodeled the clubhouse and meeting space. There's an indoor pool and Jacuzzi, nature trails, business center, conference rooms, and a Laundromat.

Two blocks from the Plaza, you'll find **Seret's 1001 Nights,** which offers a trip to a foreign land with the lush comforts of Middle Eastern decor. These one- and two-bedroom units in the historic Barrio de Analco have wonderful touches such as arched windows and doorways. They're filled with Middle Eastern antiques and tapestries. Each has a fully stocked kitchen with stove, refrigerator, and microwave. *Beware, however:* Parking is scarce in this part of town, though you can arrange to park at the supplier's store, Seret and Sons, 1 block away. These units don't have air-conditioning.

Rio Vista Suites, an apartment complex that's been converted to condominium units, has a convenient location near the Santa Fe River, just 2 blocks from Canyon Road and 6 blocks from the Plaza. For the price it's a good deal, each unit with a bedroom, living room, and kitchen/dining area, decorated in Southwest style and equipped with VCRs, stereos and CD players, and air conditioning. However, the rooms are small and the construction lacks character.

MODERATE

Radisson Deluxe Hotel Santa Fe

750 N. St. Francis Dr., Santa Fe, NM 87501. ☎ **800/333-3333** or 505/982-5591. Fax 505/988-2821. 128 units, 32 condos. A/C TV TEL. $89–$149 double, $218–$436 suite, $119–$209 condo, depending on time of year. AE, CB, DC, DISC, MC, V. Free parking.

Set on a hill as you head north toward the Santa Fe Opera, this 3-story hotel provides a decent stay. The lobby is unremarkable, with tile floors and aged wood trim. Previously remodeled in 1994, the hotel recently came under new ownership; more renovation is ongoing. In some ways it needs it: The rooms' door frames need repairs, and many hallways need repainting. I'd reserve a stay here for summer months when the country club–feeling pool is open. The rooms are decorated in blond furniture with a Southwestern motif, some with views of the mountains, others overlooking the pool. All are equipped with hair dryers, irons, and ironing boards. There's free drop-off and pick-up to the opera, Plaza, and elsewhere in town. Premium rooms are more spacious, some with large living rooms and private balconies. Each parlor suite has a Murphy bed and kiva fireplace in the living room, a big dining area, a wet bar and refrigerator, and a jetted bathtub. Cielo Grande condo units nearby come with fully equipped kitchens, fireplaces, and private decks.

4 Southside

Santa Fe's major strip, Cerrillos Road, is US 85, the main route to and from Albuquerque and the I-25 freeway. It's about 5¼ miles from the Plaza to the Villa Linda Mall, which marks the southern boundary of the city. Most motels are on this strip, although several of them are east, closer to St. Francis Drive (US 84) or the Las Vegas Highway.

EXPENSIVE

Residence Inn

1698 Galisteo St., Santa Fe, NM 87505. ☎ **800/331-3131** or 505/988-7300. Fax 505/988-3243. 120 suites. A/C TV TEL. $109–$199 studio suite; $119–$199 studio double suite;

$129–$239 penthouse suite. Rates vary according to season and include continental breakfast. AE, CB, DC, DISC, JCB, MC, V. Free parking.

Designed to look like a neighborhood, this inn provides the efficient stay that you'd expect from a Marriott. It's located about 10 minutes from the Plaza, a quiet drive through a few neighborhoods. The lobby and breakfast area are warmly decorated in red tile, with a fireplace and Southwest accents such as bancos and drums. There are three sizes of suites, each roomy, with fully equipped kitchens that include microwave, dishwasher, stove, oven, refrigerator, and coffeemaker. All rooms have fireplaces and balconies and are decorated in a Southwestern rose color. Outside, there is a sport court where guests can play basketball, tennis, and volleyball, as well as a grill, a pool that's open in summer, and three Jacuzzis. Access to a nearby health club can be arranged. A newspaper is delivered to your room and free coffee and refreshments are available in the lobby. Most who stay here are tourists, but you'll also encounter some government workers as well as business travelers and film crews.

Amenities include an outdoor swimming pool, three Jacuzzis, guest membership at nearby health club, sports court, jogging trail, Laundromat, barbecue grills on patio, dry cleaning and laundry service, complimentary local newspaper, grocery shopping service, and a social hour with complimentary hors d'oeuvres Monday through Thursday, 5 to 6:30pm.

MODERATE

Best Western Santa Fe

3650 Cerrillos Rd., Santa Fe, NM 87505. ☎ **800/528-1234** or 505/438-3822. Fax 505/438-3795. 116 units. A/C TV TEL. Jan 1–May 15 and Oct 16–Dec 31 $50–$75 double, $75–$95 suite; May 16–Oct 15 $60–$100 double, $85–$145 suite. Children 12 and under stay free in parents' room. Rates include continental breakfast. AE, CB, DC, DISC, MC, V. Free parking.

Previously the Days Inn, this 3-story pink hotel 15 minutes' drive from the Plaza offers clean cookie-cutter-type rooms at a reasonable price. It's a security-conscious hostelry; rooms can be entered only from interior corridors and there are private safes in each room. Built in 1990, its renovation is ongoing with new bedspreads and drapes in 1997. The lobby is decorated in light pastels, with nice little tables where guests can eat the continental breakfast. The indoor Jacuzzi and pool are very clean and sprightly decorated, a good family spot to relax between outings. Rooms are a bit narrow, with Aztec motif bedspreads and blonde furniture. Some doubles are more spacious, with a couch. All bathrooms are small but functional. Suites are larger, some with a Jacuzzi in the room itself; others have two rooms with a sleeper sofa in one. Amenities include a 24-hour desk, guest laundry and, in the lobby, coffee and tea throughout the day.

Doubletree

3347 Cerrillos Rd., Santa Fe, NM 87505. ☎ **800/777-3347** or 505/473-2800. Fax 505/473-4905. 213 units. AC TV TEL. $59–$249 double. AE, DC, DISC, MC, V. Free parking.

This is a good choice if you don't mind mixing business with pleasure. Since the Doubletree caters to a lot of conference traffic, there's a definite business feel to this hotel, built in 1986 and remodeled in 1996. The decor is tasteful Southwestern with rooms opening onto cavelike balconies or walkways bordered by grass. All rooms have hair dryers, vanity mirrors, irons and ironing boards, minirefrigerators, and coffeemakers. Though it's situated on busy Cerrillos Road, the rooms are placed so that they are quiet. A 24-hour business center provides fax, copy machine, and computer facilities. The cafe serves breakfast, lunch, and dinner. There are two Jacuzzis and a beautiful indoor pool, large enough for laps, as well as a small health club.

◐ El Rey Inn

1862 Cerrillos Rd. (P.O. Box 4759), Santa Fe, NM 87502. ☎ **800/521-1349** or 505/ 982-1931. Fax 505/989-9249. 94 units. A/C TV TEL. $60–$145 double; $95–$185 suite. Rates include continental breakfast. AE, CB, DC, DISC, MC, V. Free parking.

Staying at "The King" makes you feel like you're traveling the old Route 66 through the Southwest. The white stucco buildings of this court motel are decorated with bright trim around the doors and hand-painted Mexican tiles on the walls. Opened in the 1930s, it received additions in the 1950s and remodeling is ongoing. The lobby has vigas and tile floors decorated with Oriental rugs and dark Spanish furniture. No two rooms are alike. The oldest section, nearest the lobby, feels a bit cramped, though the rooms have style, with art deco tile in the bathrooms and vigas on the ceilings. Some have little patios. Be sure to request to be as far back as possible from Cerrillos Road.

The two stories of suites around the Spanish colonial courtyard are the sweetest deal I've seen in all of Santa Fe. These feel like a Spanish inn, with carved furniture and cozy couches. Some rooms have kitchenettes. The owners recently purchased the motel next door and have now added 10 deluxe units around the courtyard. The new rooms offer more upscale amenities and gas log fireplaces, as well as distinctive furnishings and artwork. Complimentary continental breakfast is served in a sunny room or on a terrace in the warmer months. There's also a sitting room with a library and games tables, outdoor swimming pool, Jacuzzi, sauna, picnic area, children's play area, and Laundromat. For its cheaper rooms, El Rey is Santa Fe's best moderately (and even inexpensively) priced accommodation.

Holiday Inn

4048 Cerrillos Rd., Santa Fe, NM 87505. ☎ **800/465-4329** or 505/473-4646. Fax 505/ 473-2186. 130 units. AC TV TEL. Jan 1–May 21 $79–$129 double; May 22–Sept 30 $99–$139 double; Oct 1–Dec 31 $79–$129 double. Minisuites are $10 more than regular rooms. AE, DC, DISC MC, V. Free parking.

Though the pastel decor is a bit cheesy for my taste, this is a good place to get a standard, reliable room. It's located about 5 miles from the historic district, about a 15-minute drive. Built in the early 1980s, the hotel was remodeled in 1996. The lobby has clean lines, though it's dominated by a cumbersome elevator shaft at the center. Judging by the number of pickup trucks in the parking lot, this seems to be the place where a lot of local ranchers and traders stay, as well as plenty of businesspeople. The sunny rooms are brightly wallpapered and have plenty of amenities: hair dryers, irons, and ironing boards; minisuites have refrigerators, wet bars, and microwaves. There's a small indoor/outdoor pool heated year-round as well as two saunas, a Jacuzzi, and a health club. Bobby Rubino's offers American cuisine. Room service is available, as are shuttles to and from the Santa Fe airport.

Super 8 Motel

3358 Cerrillos Rd., Santa Fe, NM 87501. ☎ **800/800-8000** or 505/471-8811. Fax 505/ 471-3239. 96 units. $82.90 double. AE, CB, DC, DISC, MC, V. Free parking.

It's nothing flashy, but this pink stucco, boxy motel attracts regulars who know precisely what to expect—a clean, comfortable room with standard furnishings: double beds, working desk, in-room safes, and free local phone calls. The motel has a 24-hour desk and continental breakfast is included.

Accommodations & Dining on Cerrillos Road

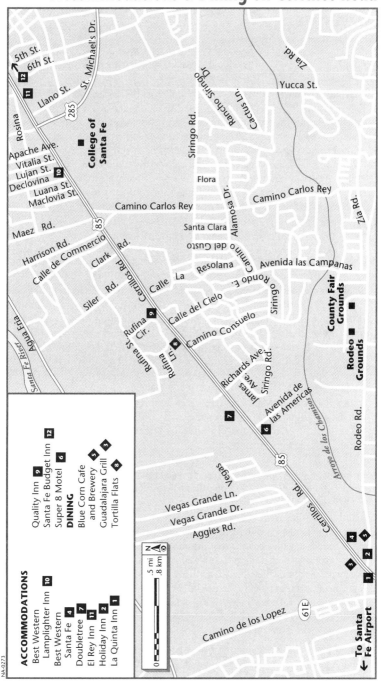

ACCOMMODATIONS

Best Western
Lamplighter Inn 10
Best Western
Santa Fe 4
Doubletree 7
El Rey Inn 11
Holiday Inn 2
La Quinta Inn 1

Quality Inn 9
Santa Fe Budget Inn 12
Super 8 Motel 6

DINING

Blue Corn Cafe
and Brewery 5
Guadalajara Grill 3
Tortilla Flats 8

To Santa
Fe Airport

NA-0273

INEXPENSIVE

Best Western Lamplighter Inn
2405 Cerrillos Rd., Santa Fe, NM 87505. ☎ **800/767-5267** or 505/471-8000. Fax 505/471-1397. 80 units. A/C TV TEL. $55–$99 double, depending on the season and type of room. AE, CB, DC, DISC, MC, V. Free parking.

This motel, built in the early 1970s, is doing its best to keep up with the times. Renovated in 1991–92, it comprises three buildings. The oldest faces busy Cerrillos Road and offers the smallest rooms and probably the most street noise. I recommend the back building where noise is diminished and rooms are larger with vaulted ceilings. In a third building are the suites with kitchenettes, each with a VCR and well-stocked kitchen with microwave, stove, and oven. All rooms are decorated in Southwestern-style decor and have coffeemakers, minirefrigerators, and movie channels. There's also a guest Laundromat. An indoor pool and Jacuzzi area has panels that open to let in sunlight in summer.

✪ La Quinta Inn
4298 Cerrillos Rd., Santa Fe, NM 87505. ☎ **800/531-5900** or 505/471-1142. Fax 505/438-7219. 130 units. A/C TV TEL. June to mid-Oct $80–$88 double; late Oct–May $60–$66 double. Children 18 and under stay free in parents' room. Large discount for AAA members. Rates include continental breakfast. AE, CB, DC, DISC, MC, V. Free parking. Pets stay free.

Though it's a good 15-minute drive from the Plaza, this is my choice of economical Cerrillos Road chain hotels. Built in 1986, it was just fully remodeled in a very comfortable and tasteful way. The rooms within the 3-story white brick buildings have an unexpectedly elegant feel, with lots of deep colors and art deco tile in the bathrooms. There's plenty of space in these rooms, and they're lit for mood as well as for reading. Each has a coffeemaker. A continental breakfast is served in the intimate lobby. The kidney-shaped pool has a nice lounging area, heated April to October. If you're a shopper or movie-goer, this hotel is just across a parking lot from the Villa Linda Mall. The Kettle, a 24-hour coffee shop, is adjacent. La Quinta also has a 24-hour desk, Laundromat (as well as valet laundry), and complimentary coffee at all times in the lobby. Continental breakfast includes fresh fruit, danish, cereal, bagels, coffee, tea, and juice.

Quality Inn
3011 Cerrillos Rd., Santa Fe, NM 87505. ☎ **800/228-5151** or 505/471-1211. Fax 505/438-9535. 99 units. A/C TV TEL. $55–$95 single or double. AE, CB, DC, DISC, ER, JCB, MC, V. Free parking. Pets are accepted

This hotel on the south end of town, about a 10-minute drive from the Plaza, provides good standard rooms at reasonable prices. Built in 1970, it's a 2-story white stucco building with a red-tile roof. Its most recent remodeling took place in 1996, mostly replacing carpet, drapes, and some furnishings. Expect nothing fancy here, even with the remodeling. Rooms are fairly quiet, with big windows to let in lots of light. Request a room looking in toward the courtyard and pool, and you'll get a bit of a resort feel. All rooms have coffeemakers and minirefrigerators; deluxe rooms have wet bars. There is limited room service and valet laundry. Baby-sitting is available. The coffee shop and dining room serve Mexican fare.

5 Bed & Breakfasts

If you prefer a homey, intimate setting to the sometimes impersonal ambience of a large hotel, one of Santa Fe's bed-and-breakfast inns may be right for you. All those listed here are located in or close to the downtown area and offer comfortable accommodations at expensive to inexpensive prices.

✪ Adobe Abode

202 Chapelle St., Santa Fe, NM 87501. ☎ **505/983-3133.** Fax 505/986-0972. E-mail: adobebnb@sprynet.com. 6 units. TV TEL. $115–$155 double. Rates include breakfast. DISC, MC, V. Free parking.

A short walk from the Plaza, in the same quiet residential neighborhood where the new Georgia O'Keeffe Museum resides, Adobe Abode is one of Santa Fe's most imaginative B&Bs. The living room is filled with everything from Mexican folk art and pottery to Buddhas and ethnic masks. The open kitchen features a country pine table as well as Balinese puppets. The creativity of the owner/innkeeper, Pat Harbour, shines in each of the guest rooms as well. The Out of Africa Room, in the main house, has elegant fabrics and tribal art. The Texas Hill Country Room features antiques and designer denim and plaid bedding. Both are in the main house, which was built in 1907 and renovated in 1989. In back are casitas occupying newer buildings, designed with flair. The Bronco Room is filled with cowboy paraphernal: hats, Pendleton blankets, pioneer chests, and my favorite—an entire shelf lined with children's cowboy boots. Finally, Pat has added a new two-room suite— the Provence Suite—which she decorated in sunny yellow and bright blue. Two rooms have fireplaces, while several have private patios. All rooms have coffeemakers and terry-cloth robes. Complimentary sherry, fruit, and Santa Fe cookies are served daily in the living room. Every morning a healthy breakfast of fresh-squeezed orange juice, fresh fruit, homemade muffins, scones or pastries, and a hot dish is served in the kitchen.

✪ Alexander's Inn

529 East Palace Ave., Santa Fe, NM 87501. ☎ **888/321-5123** or 505/986-1431. Fax 505/982-8572. 12 units (10 with bathroom), 4 cottages. A/C TV TEL. $75–$160 double. Rates include continental breakfast. MC, V. Free parking. Children and pets are accepted.

I'd fear my long-standing friendship with innkeeper Carolyn Lee biases my opinion about her inn, except that it receives outstanding recommendations from such publications as *Glamour* Magazine ("one of the most romantic inns in the Southwest") and *Southwest Art* ("101 reasons to visit Santa Fe"). Eleven years ago Carolyn had a dream of starting an inn and she put her whole self into this 1903 Victorian/New England–style house in a quiet residential area 6 blocks from the Plaza. Naming it after her son, she filled it with delicious antiques, bedding, and draperies. The rooms here have stenciling on the walls, hook and Oriental rugs, muted colors such as apricot and lilac, and white iron or four-poster queen-size beds (there are some king-size beds as well). Recently though, she's expanded into a new property even closer to the Plaza. The Hacienda offers guests a delightful Southwest stay in rooms gathered around a sunny patio and is an excellent deal. My favorite rooms here are the bright Cottonwood, with decor in muted tones, and the Sunflower, with French doors, maple floors, a kiva fireplace, and luxurious king bed. All have spacious bathrooms with Mexican tile. Separate from both properties are cottages complete with kitchens (equipped with stove, oven, and refrigerator, some with microwave) and living rooms with kiva fireplaces. Some of these don't have quite the charm of rooms in the main house and Hacienda; others have plenty of Southwestern charm, so discuss your desires when making reservations. Fresh flowers adorn all the rooms throughout the year, and all have robes, hair dryers, and makeup mirrors. Guests can enjoy privileges at El Gancho Tennis Club as well as the Jacuzzi in the back garden at the main inn. An extended continental breakfast of homemade baked goods is served on the veranda every morning, as well as afternoon tea and cookies.

Dancing Ground of the Sun
711 Paseo de Peralta, Santa Fe, NM 87501. ☎ **800/645-5673** or 505/986-9797. Fax 505/986-8082. www.dancingground.com. E-mail: innkeeper@dancingground.com. 8 units. AC TV TEL. Nov–Apr $75–$210 double; May–Oct and all holidays $95–$255 double. Rates include continental breakfast. MC, V. Free parking.

A great deal of thought and energy went into decorating these units, and it shows. Each of the eight rooms, five of which are casitas, has been outfitted with hand-crafted Santa Fe–style furnishings made by local artisans, and the decor of each room focuses on a mythological Native American figure, whose likeness has been hand-painted on the walls of that unit. There's Corn Dancer, who represents the anticipation of an abundant harvest; Kokopelli, a flute player believed to bring good fortune and abundance to the Native American people; and other themes. Many have ceiling vigas and all have nice touches, such as *nichos* (little niches) that come with an older adobe building such as this, constructed in the 1930s. Each of the five casitas has a fireplace and a fully equipped kitchen with microwave, refrigerator, stove, and coffeemaker. Two are equipped with washers and dryers. Spirit Dancer and Deer Dancer, completed in 1996, are the inn's newest rooms and both have kitchenettes. Each evening, the next day's breakfast of healthful, fresh-baked food is delivered to your door for you to enjoy at any hour. The two casitas closest to the street may have some street noise, but it should die down by bedtime.

✪ Dos Casas Viejas
610 Agua Fría St., Santa Fe, NM 87501. ☎ **505/983-1636.** Fax 505/983-1749. 8 units. TV TEL. $165–$245 single or double. Free off-street parking.

These two old houses (*dos casas viejas*), located not far from the Plaza in what some call the *barrio* on Agua Fría Street, offer the kind of luxury accommodations you'd expect from a fine hotel. Behind an old wooden security gate is a meandering brick lane along which are the elegant guest rooms. The innkeepers, Susan and Michael Strijek, maintain the place impeccably. The grounds are manicured, and the rooms, each with a patio and private entrance, are finely renovated and richly decorated. All rooms have Mexican-tile floors and kiva fireplaces; most have diamond-finished stucco walls and embedded vigas. They're furnished with Southwestern antiques and original art. Some have canopy beds and one has an imaginative sleigh bed; all are covered with fine linens and down comforters. Each room is supplied with robes, a hair dryer, and complimentary gourmet treats and refreshments. Valet laundry, newspaper delivery, and free coffee or refreshments in the lobby are avail-able. Guests can use the library and dining area (where a European breakfast is served each morning) in the main building. Breakfast can also be enjoyed on the patio alongside the elegant lap pool or (after you collect it in a basket) on your pri-vate patio. If you'd like a spa experience, Dos Casas now has in-room treatments, from massage to facials to salt glows.

El Farolito
514 Galisteo St., Santa Fe, NM 87501. ☎ **888/634-8782** or 505/988-1631. Fax 505/988-4589. 7 units. TV TEL. $95–$155 casita for two. Rates include expanded continental breakfast. AE, DISC, MC, V. Free parking. Children are welcome if a casita is available.

The new owners of this inn, within walking distance to the Plaza, have created an authentic theme experience for guests in each room. They've filled the common area with works by notable New Mexico artists. The themes include a Native American Room, decorated with rugs and pottery; a South-of-the-Border Room, decorated with Mexican folk art with a full-sized sofa sleeper; and an elegant Santa Fe–style Opera Room with handcarved, lavishly upholstered furniture. The walls of most of the rooms are stylishly rubbed with beeswax during plastering to give them a smooth, golden finish, and all have kiva fireplaces and private patios. Part of the inn was built before 1912 and the rest is new, but the old-world elegance carries through. For breakfast, the focus is on healthy food with a little decadence thrown in. You'll enjoy fresh-squeezed orange juice, apple-walnut bread or chile cornbread, 10 kinds of fresh fruit on a plate, and pastries from the French pastry shop in La Fonda.

El Paradero

220 W. Manhattan Ave., Santa Fe, NM 87501. ☎ **505/988-1177.** Fax 505/988-3577. E-mail: elpara@trail.com. 16 units (12 with bathroom). A/C TEL. May 15–Oct 31 $75–$140 double; Nov 1–May 14 $70–$125 double. Rates include full breakfast. MC, V. Free parking.

Located about a 10-minute walk from the Plaza, El Paradero (The Stopping Place) provides reliable, unpretentious accommodations and good service. It began in about 1810 as a Spanish adobe farmhouse. It doubled in size in 1878, when Territorial-style details were added; in 1912 Victorian touches were incorporated in the styling of its doors and windows. Innkeepers Ouida MacGregor and Thom Allen opened this as one of Santa Fe's first bed-and-breakfasts 16 years ago. They're deeply involved in the city and can direct visitors to unexpected sights and activities. Nine ground-level rooms surround a central courtyard and offer a clean, white decor, hardwood or brick floors, folk art, and handwoven textiles on the walls. Three more luxurious upstairs rooms feature tile floors and bathrooms as well as private balconies. Five rooms have fireplaces. Two suites occupying a brick 1912 coachman's house, a railroad-era Victorian building, are elegantly decorated with period antiques and provide living rooms with fireplaces, kitchen nooks, TVs, and phones. The ground floor of the main building has a parlor, a living room with a piano and fireplace, and a Mexican-style breakfast room where a full gourmet breakfast and afternoon tea are served daily. Also, if you'd like to take a trip up the mountain and have a picnic, they'll prepare a lunch for you.

Four Kachinas Inn

512 Webber St., Santa Fe, NM 87501. ☎ **800/397-2564** or 505/982-2550. Fax 505/989-1323. www.southwestern.com. E-mail: 4kachina@swcp.com. 6 units. TV TEL. $68–$132 double. Rates include continental breakfast and afternoon snacks. DISC, MC, V. Free parking.

Wild Kachinas and Navajo rugs stand out against clean and simple architectural lines at this quiet inn on a residential street within walking distance of downtown. The rooms are consistent, comfortable, and medium-sized. Each is named for a Hopi kachina: The Koyemsi Room is named for the "fun-loving, mudhead clown kachina"; the Poko Room, for the dog kachina that "represents the spirits of domestic animals"; the Hon Room, for the "powerful healing bear kachina"; and the Tawa Room, for the sun god kachina. Three of the rooms are on the ground floor. The upstairs room offers a view of the Sangre de Cristo Mountains. All have private patios. In a separate building, constructed of adobe bricks that were made on the property, is a lounge where guests can gather at any time of day to enjoy art and travel books and complimentary beverages and snacks. Be sure to try the coconut pound cake, a treat for which innkeeper John Daw consistently wins a blue ribbon at the county fair. An extended continental breakfast of juice, coffee or tea, pastries, yogurt, and fresh fruit is brought to guests' rooms each morning. One of the rooms here is completely accessible for travelers with disabilities.

✪ Grant Corner Inn

122 Grant Ave., Santa Fe, NM 87501. ☎ **800/964-9003** or 505/983-6678 for reservations, 505/984-9001 for guest rooms. Fax 505/983-1526. 12 units (10 with bathroom), 1 hacienda. A/C TV TEL. $80–$120 double without bathroom; $100–$155 double with bathroom.

Hacienda, $110–$130 guest rooms rented separately; $215–$255 for entire house. Rates include full gourmet breakfast. MC, V. Free parking. Certain rooms appropriate for children.

This early 20th-century manor, just 2 blocks west of the Plaza and next door to the new Georgia O'Keeffe Museum, offers a quiet stay in a fanciful Victorian ambience. Each room is furnished with antiques, from brass or four-poster beds to armoires and quilts, and monogrammed terry-cloth robes are available for those staying in rooms with shared bathrooms. All rooms have ceiling fans, and some are equipped with small refrigerators. Each room has its own character. For example, no. 3 has a hand-painted German wardrobe closet dating from 1772 and a washbasin with brass fittings in the shape of a fish; no. 8 has a private outdoor deck that catches the morning sun; and no. 11 has an antique collection of dolls and stuffed animals. Two rooms have kitchenettes, and two also have laundry facilities. The inn's office doubles as a library and gift shop. In addition to the rooms mentioned above, Grant Corner Inn now offers accommodations in their Hacienda, located at 604 Griffin St. It's a Southwestern-style condominium with two bedrooms, living and dining rooms, and a kitchen. It can be rented in its entirety or the rooms can be rented separately, depending on your needs.

Breakfast, for both the inn and the Hacienda, is served each morning in front of the living-room fireplace or on the front veranda in summer. The meals are so good that an enthusiastic public arrives for brunch here every Sunday (the inn is also open to the public for weekday breakfasts).

Inn of the Animal Tracks

707 Paseo de Peralta, Santa Fe, NM 87501. ☎ **505/988-1546.** www.santafe.org/animal-tracks. E-mail: animal@trail.com. 5 units. A/C TV TEL. $90–$130 double. Rates include a full breakfast. AE, MC, V. Free parking.

If you tend to miss your animals while you're away, this is the place to stay. The main sitting room is set around a kiva fireplace, and you may share the couch with a resident dog. Each room is decorated with pictures and memorabilia of animals such as an eagle, deer, otter, wolf, and rabbit. The rooms have a cozy feel and are well lit. I recommend the Otter Room with its old-fashioned tub, even though it is near the street (traffic noise throughout the day quiets down at night). Inhabiting a 90-year-old adobe home, this inn maintains that old character, with important renovations added in 1989. Guests tend to like the frequently served breakfast burrito, as well as other warm breakfasts and afternoon snacks such as apple pie and carrot cake. Since the inn is situated 2½ blocks from both the Plaza and Canyon Road, you'll hardly need a car.

Inn on the Paseo

630 Paseo de Peralta, Santa Fe, NM 87501. ☎ **800/457-9045** or 505/984-8200. Fax 505/989-3979. 20 units. A/C TV TEL. $85–$165 double. Rates include extended continental breakfast. AE, DC, MC, V. Free parking.

Located just a few blocks from the Plaza, this is a good choice for travelers who want to be able to walk to the shops, galleries, and restaurants but would rather not stay at a larger hotel. As you enter the inn you'll be welcomed by the warmth of the large fireplace in the foyer. Southwestern furnishings dot the spacious public areas and the work of local artists adorns the walls. The guest rooms are medium-sized, meticulously clean, and very comfortable with a hotel feel. The arrangements are fairly consistent from room to room, but the bathrooms are a bit stark (each with a hair dryer). Still, one room boasts a fireplace and many feature four-poster beds and private entrances. The focal point of each room is an original handmade patchwork quilt. The owner is a third-generation quilter, and she made all the quilts you'll see hanging throughout the inn (more than 25 of them). A breakfast buffet is served on the sundeck in warmer weather and indoors by the fire on cooler days. It consists of muffins, breads, granola, fresh fruit, and coffee or tea. Complimentary refreshments are served every afternoon.

Preston House

106 Faithway St., Santa Fe, NM 87501. ☎ **505/982-3465.** Fax 505/988-2397. www.prestonhouse.com/santafe. E-mail: prestonhouse@aol.com. 8 units (6 with bathroom), 2 cottages. A/C TV TEL. High season $75–$95 double without bathroom; $106–$175 double with bathroom; $150 cottage. Low season $55–$75 double without bathroom; $85–$105 double with bathroom; $125 cottage. Extra person $20. Rates include continental breakfast and afternoon tea. AE, MC, V. Free parking. Children 10 and over are welcome.

Lace, flowery upholstery and stained glass surround you at this quiet inn just 5 blocks east of the Plaza. A sky blue Queen Anne–style home built in 1886, it has that legendary simplicity of form. Amenities, however, are more elaborate. All rooms have terry-cloth robes, some offer fireplaces, and only two require sharing a bathroom. The house's owner, noted silk-screen artist and muralist Signe Bergman, exhibits her art throughout—dreamy works well suited to the inn. One of my favorite rooms is number 5, with a king bed, a corner fireplace, and lots of sun. An adjacent cottage built in 1987 received an award for compatible architecture from the Santa Fe Historical Association. These two rooms are larger, with king beds and bay windows. In winter, a quite extended continental breakfast (often includes quiche or French toast) is served family-style at a big pine table in the dining room. In summer, it's served under apricot trees on a brick patio surrounded by flowers.

Pueblo Bonito

138 W. Manhattan Ave., Santa Fe, NM 87501. ☎ **800/461-4599** or 505/984-8001. Fax 505/984-3155. 24 units. TV TEL. Jan–Feb $70–$110 double; March–April and Nov–Dec $80–$120 double. May–Oct, holidays, and special events, $100–$145 double. Rates include continental breakfast and afternoon tea. AE, DISC, MC, V. Free parking.

Private courtyards and narrow flagstone paths give a look of elegance to this 19th-century adobe hacienda and stables, located a few blocks south of the Santa Fe River. This is a good choice if you like more of an inn feel rather than a home feel in a B&B. Each guest room is named for a Pueblo tribe of the surrounding countryside. Every room—decorated with Native American rugs on wood or brick floors—has a queen-size bed and fireplace. A 1997 renovation added some new furniture and mirrors. Bathrooms are small but attractively tiled. Six rooms are suites, each with a fully stocked kitchen including microwave, refrigerator, stove, dishwasher, and coffeemaker as well as a living/dining room with fireside seating, and a bedroom. A couple of other rooms offer refrigerators and wet bars. The remainder are standard units with locally made willow headboards and couches, dining alcoves, and old Spanish-style lace curtains. Continental breakfast is served daily from 8 to 10am in the dining room or on the sundeck; if you prefer, there's room service. Afternoon tea is served daily from 4 to 6pm and includes complimentary margaritas and wine. There's also a Laundromat and an indoor Jacuzzi.

✪ Spencer House Bed & Breakfast Inn

222 McKenzie St., Santa Fe, NM 87501. ☎ **800/647-0530** (7am–6pm) or 505/988-3024. Fax 505/984-9862. 4 units, 1 cottage. A/C. $95–$175 double. Rates include breakfast. AE, MC, V. Free parking.

The Spencer House is unique among Santa Fe bed-and-breakfasts. Instead of Southwestern-style furnishings, you'll find beautiful antiques from England, Ireland, and colonial America. One guest room features an antique brass bed, another a pencil-post bed, yet another an English panel bed, and all rooms utilize Ralph Lauren fabrics and linens. Each room is outfitted with a fluffy down comforter and a hair dryer. All bathrooms are completely new, modern, and very spacious. Owner Jan McConnell takes great pride in the Spencer House and keeps it spotlessly clean. From the old Bissell carpet sweeper and drop-front desk in the reading nook to antique trunks in the bedrooms, no detail has been overlooked. In summer, a full breakfast—coffee, tea, yogurt, cereal, fresh fruit, and main course—is served on the outdoor patio. In winter, guests dine indoors by the wood-burning stove. Afternoon tea is served in the breakfast room. In 1995 two new rooms were added. One has a fireplace and private patio. The second is an 800-square-foot cottage with a living room, dining area, full kitchen and bathroom, private patio, and screened-in porch. Take note of the careful renovation of this 1920s adobe, as it received an award from the Santa Fe Historical Board.

Territorial Inn

215 Washington Ave., Santa Fe, NM 87501. ☎ **800/745-9910** or 505/989-7737. Fax 505/986-9212. 10 units (8 with bathroom). AC, TV TEL. $80–$165 double. Higher rates during special events. Extra person $20. Rates include continental breakfast. AE, DC, MC, V. Free parking.

This 2-story, Territorial-style building, which dates from the 1890s and is situated 1½ blocks from the Plaza, has a delightful Victorian feel with plenty of amenities. Constructed of stone and adobe with a pitched roof, it has 2 stories connected by a curving tiled stairway. Eight of its rooms, typically furnished with Early American antiques, offer private bathrooms; the remaining two share a bathroom. All rooms are equipped with ceiling fans and sitting areas, and two have fireplaces. Each room also has robes, hair dryers, and Spectravision movie channels. Free coffee and refreshments are available in the lobby, and an in-room massage as well as access to a nearby health club can be arranged. An extended continental breakfast is served in a sophisticated common area or in warm months in the back garden, which is shaded by large cottonwoods. There is also a rose garden and a gazebo-enclosed Jacuzzi.

✪ Water Street Inn

427 Water St., Santa Fe, NM 87501. ☎ **800/646-6752** or 505/984-1193. Fax 505/984-6235. 11 units. A/C TV TEL. $95–$200 double. Rates include continental breakfast and afternoon hors d'oeuvres and refreshments. AE, DISC, MC, V. Free parking. Children and pets are welcome with prior approval.

An award-winning adobe restoration to the west of the Hilton hotel and 4 blocks from the Plaza, this friendly inn features beautiful Mexican-tile bathrooms, several kiva fireplaces or wood stoves, and antique furnishings. Each room is packed with Southwestern art and books. A happy hour, with quesadillas and margaritas, is offered in the living room or on the upstairs portal in the afternoon, where an extended continental breakfast is also served. All rooms are decorated in a Moroccan/Southwestern style. Room 3 features a queen-size hideaway sofa to accommodate families. Room 4 provides special regional touches in its decor and boasts a chaise longue, fur rug, built-in seating, and corner fireplace. Four new suites have elegant contemporary Southwestern furnishings and outdoor private patios with fountains. There's also an outdoor Jacuzzi. All rooms have balconies or terraces, VCRs, and offer newspaper delivery and twice-daily maid service.

6 RV Parks & Campgrounds

RV PARKS

At least four private camping areas, mainly for recreational vehicles, are located within a few minutes' drive of downtown Santa Fe. Typical rates are $23 for full RV hookups, $18 for tents. Be sure to book ahead at busy times.

Babbitt's RV Resort
3574 Cerrillos Rd., Santa Fe, NM 87505. ☎ **505/473-1949.** Fax 505/471-9220. MC, V.

The resort has 95 spaces with full hookups, picnic tables, showers, rest rooms, laundry, and a soda and candy concession. It's just 5 miles south of the Plaza, so it's plenty convenient, but keep in mind that it is surrounded by the city.

Rancheros de Santa Fe Campground
736 Old Las Vegas Hwy. (exit 290 off I-25), Santa Fe, NM 87505. ☎ **800/426-9259** or 505/466-3482. www.rancheros.com. DISC, MC, V.

Tents, motor homes, and trailers requiring full hookups are welcome here. The park's 130 sites are situated on 22 acres of piñon and juniper forest. Facilities include tables, grills and fireplaces, hot showers, rest rooms, Laundromat, grocery store, nature trails, outdoor swimming pool, playground, games room, free nightly movies, public telephones, and propane. Cabins are also available. It's located about 6 miles southeast of Santa Fe and is open from March 15 to November 1.

Santa Fe KOA
934 Old Las Vegas Hwy. (exit 290 or 294 off I-25), Santa Fe, NM 87505. ☎ **505/466-1419** or 505/KOA-1514 for reservations. DISC, MC, V.

This campground about 11 miles northeast of Santa Fe sits among the foothills of the Sangre de Cristo Mountains. It offers full hookups, pull-through sites, tent sites, picnic tables, showers, rest rooms, laundry, store, Santa Fe–style gift shop, playground, recreation room, propane, and dumping station. Tent site $18.95. RV hookup $23.95.

CAMPGROUNDS
There are three forested sites along NM 475 going toward the Santa Fe Ski Basin. All are open from May to October. Overnight rates start at about $6, depending on the particular site.

Hyde Memorial State Park
740 Hyde Park Rd., Santa Fe, NM 87501. ☎ **505/983-7175.**

About 8 miles from the city, this pine-surrounded park offers a quiet retreat. Its campground includes shelters, water, tables, and pit toilets. Seven RV pads with electrical pedestals and an RV dump station are available. There are nature and hiking trails as well as a small winter skating pond.

Santa Fe National Forest
P.O. Box 1689 (NM 475), Santa Fe, NM 87504. ☎ **505/982-8674.** (This number only works seasonally; if you don't reach anyone, call 505/753-7331, and be patient; this is the number for the Española Ranger Station and they're not as helpful as they could be.)

Black Canyon campground, with 44 sites, is located just before you reach Hyde State Park. The sites sit within thick forest, with hiking trails nearby. It has potable water and sites for trailers up to 32 feet long. Big Tesuque, a first-come first-served campground, with 10 newly rehabilitated sites, is about 12 miles from town. The sites here are closer to the road and sit at the edge of aspen forests. Both Black Canyon and Big Tesuque campgrounds, located along the Santa Fe Scenic Byway, NM 475, are equipped with vault toilets.

6

Where to Dine in Santa Fe

Santa Fe may not be a major city, but it abounds in dining options with hundreds of restaurants of all categories. Competition among them is steep, and spots are continually opening and closing. Locals watch closely to see which ones will survive. Some chefs create dishes that incorporate traditional Southwestern foods with ingredients not indigenous to the region; their restaurants are referred to in the listings as "creative Southwestern." There is also standard regional New Mexican cuisine, and beyond that diners can opt for excellent steak and seafood, as well as continental, European, Asian, and, of course, Mexican menus.

Especially during peak tourist seasons, dinner reservations may be essential. Reservations are always recommended at better restaurants.

In the listings below, **Very Expensive** refers to restaurants where most dinner main courses are priced above $25; **Expensive** includes those where the main courses generally cost between $18 and $25; **Moderate** means those in the $12 to $18 range; and **Inexpensive** refers to those charging $12 and under.

1 Best Bets

- **Best Value:** If you're looking for good food and large portions for little money, you'll find it at **Tortilla Flats,** 3139 Cerrillos Rd. (☎ 505/471-8685). Portions are gigantic, and the atmosphere is quite friendly.
- **Best for Kids:** Without doubt, the **Cowgirl Hall of Fame,** 319 S. Guadalupe St. (☎ 505/982-2565), is great for children. The food on the kids' menu is simple enough to suit their tastes, and they'll be endlessly amused in the children's play area.
- **Best Continental: Bistro 315,** 315 Old Santa Fe Trail (☎ 505/986-9190), serves meticulously prepared French and European dishes on white tablecloths. It's also an excellent place for outdoor dining, spring through fall.
- **Best Creative American:** Decor, service, and cuisine are topnotch at **Santacafé,** 231 Washington Ave. (☎ 505/984-1788). The chef has a magical way of combining Asian and Southwestern spices.
- **Best Creative Southwestern: Anasazi Restaurant,** 113 Washington Ave. (☎ 505/988-3236), at the Inn of the Anasazi,

provides time-worn Southwestern atmosphere and eclectic food that melds such staples as tortilla soup and wontons into exquisite creations.

- **Best Italian:** There are other good Italian restaurants in town, but my favorite is **Il Piatto Cucina Italiano,** 96 West Marcy St. (☎ **505/984-1091**). Their Italian sausage is spicy, and their pastas are consistently good.
- **Best Spanish: El Farol,** 808 Canyon Rd. (☎ **505/988-9912**), offers great ambience and local color, not to mention the longest and best tapas menu in Santa Fe.
- **Best Northern New Mexico Enchilada: Guadalupe Cafe,** 422 Old Santa Fe Trail (☎ **505/982-9762**), serves its enchiladas flat, the way most New Mexicans like them. Corn tortillas are layered with chicken, beef, or cheese, and smothered with a fiery red or green chile sauce.
- **Best Outdoor Dining**: If you're longing to sit outside and enjoy a lazy New Mexico lunch, you can't beat **La Casa Sena,** 125 E. Palace Ave. (☎ **505/ 988-9232**). The restaurant's patio (open spring through fall) sits within an 1867 hacienda courtyard, with a fountain and lots of flowers.

2 Restaurants by Cuisine

AMERICAN
San Francisco Street Bar and Grill (Downtown, *I*)
Second Street Brewery (Southside, *I*)
Tesuque Village Market (Northside, *I*)
Zia Diner (Downtown, *I*)

ASIAN
Chows (Southside, *I*)
mu du noodles (Southside, *I*)
Peking Palace (Southside, *M*)

BARBECUE/CAJUN
Cowgirl Hall of Fame (Downtown, *I*)

CONTINENTAL
Geronimo (Downtown, *E*)
The Palace (Downtown, *M*)
Pink Adobe (Downtown, *E*)

CREATIVE SOUTHWESTERN
Anasazi Restaurant (Downtown, *E*)
Atomic Grill (Downtown, *M*)
Cafe Pasqual's (Downtown, *M*)
Coyote Cafe (Downtown, *E*)
La Casa Sena (Downtown, *E*)
Santacafé (Downtown, *E*)
Tesuque Village Market (Northside, *I*)

DELI/CAFE
Carlos' Gosp'l Cafe (Downtown, *I*)
Plaza Cafe (Downtown, *I*)
Sage Bakehouse (Downtown, *I*)

ECLECTIC
Paul's (Downtown, *M*)

FRENCH
Bistro 315 (Downtown, *M*)

INDIAN
India Palace (Downtown, *M*)

ITALIAN
Andiamo! (Downtown, *M*)
Il Piatto Cucina Italiano (Downtown, *M*)
Osteria d'Assisi (Downtown, *M*)
The Palace (Downtown, *M*)
Pranzo Italian Grill (Downtown, *M*)
Upper Crust Pizza (Downtown, *I*)

JAPANESE
Shohko-Cafe and Hiro Sushi (Downtown, *M*)

MEXICAN
El Paragua (North of town, *I*)
Felipe's Tacos (Southside, *I*)
Guadalajara Grill (Southside, *I*)
Marisco's La Playa (Southside, *M*)
Old Mexico Grill (Southside, *M*)

Key to abbreviations: *E* = Expensive, *I* = Inexpensive, *M* = Moderate

NEW AMERICAN

Celebrations (Downtown, *M*)
Jack's (Downtown, *E*)
Nellie's (Downtown, *E*)

NEW MEXICAN

Blue Corn Cafe (Downtown, *I*)
Green Onion (Southside, *I*)
Guadalupe Cafe (Downtown, *I*)
La Choza (Downtown, *I*)
La Tertulia (Downtown, *M*)
The Shed (Downtown, *I*)
Tecolote Cafe (Southside, *I*)
Tía Sophia's (Downtown, *I*)

Tomasita's Cafe (Downtown, *I*)
Tortilla Flats (Southside, *I*)

SPANISH

El Farol (Downtown, *M*)

STEAKS/SEAFOOD

Bobcat Bite (Southside, *I*)
Cowboy of Santa Fe (Downtown, *M*)
El Nido (Northside, *E*)
Ore House on the Plaza
   (Downtown, *M*)
Steaksmith at El Gancho
   (Southside, *M*)
Vanessie of Santa Fe (Downtown, M)

3 Downtown

This area includes the circle defined by the Paseo de Peralta and St. Francis Drive, as well as Canyon Road.

EXPENSIVE

✪ Anasazi Restaurant

113 Washington Ave. ☎ **505/988-3236.** Reservations recommended. Breakfast $5.25–$9.50; lunch $8–$11.75; dinner $17.50–$29. AE, CB, DC, DISC, MC, V. Daily 7–10:30am, 11:30am–2:30pm, and 5:30–10pm. CREATIVE SOUTHWESTERN/NATIVE AMERICAN.

This ranks right up there with Santacafé as one of Santa Fe's richest dining experiences. And though it's part of the Inn of the Anasazi (see chapter 5), it's a fine restaurant in its own right. You'll dine surrounded by diamond-finished walls decorated with petroglyph symbols. Stacked flagstone furthers the Anasazi feel of this restaurant named for the ancient people who once inhabited the area. There's no pretension here; the waitstaff is friendly but not overbearing, and tables are spaced nicely, making it a good place for a romantic dinner. All the food is inventive, and organic meats and vegetables are used whenever available.

For breakfast, try the breakfast burrito with homemade chorizo, green chile potatoes, and refried Anasazi beans. A must with lunch or dinner is the grilled corn tortilla soup with ginger-pork pot stickers. It's thick, served with tortilla strips and thinly sliced scallions, and a chile-spiced bread stick like a snake in the grass. For an entree, I enjoyed grilled swordfish with a roasted corn puree, light enough to enhance the fish flavor rather than diminish it. For dinner, I recommend the cinnamon chile–rubbed beef tenderloin with white-cheddar chipotle, chile mashed potatoes, and mango salsa. Desserts are thrilling; try the sour-cream chocolate cake, rich and moist. There are daily specials, as well as a nice list of wines by the glass and special wines of the day.

Bistro 315

315 Old Santa Fe Trail. ☎ **505/986-9190.** Reservations recommended. Main courses $17–$29 at dinner. AE, MC, V. Summer, daily 11:30am–2pm and 5:30–9:30pm; winter, Mon–Sat 11:30am–2pm and 5:30–9pm. FRENCH.

Bistro 315 has enjoyed instant success since it opened in 1995, and no wonder—heading it up are Matt Yohalem, a graduate of Johnson and Wales, and Chef Poissonier, formerly with Le Cirque under Chef Daniel Boulud. The restaurant has recently expanded and still fills up. The food is simply excellent. The menu changes seasonally; on my last visit there I started with croquettes of goat cheese and bell pepper coulis and moved on to a cassoulet, with lamb, sausage, chicken, and vegetables in a rich sauce. The grilled tomato soup was also excellent, and I was fortunate to be there on a night when grilled smoked chicken was on the menu. My favorite dessert here is the warm tarte tatin served with crème fraîche. Because the restaurant is so popular, reservations are an absolute must.

Cafe Pasqual's

121 Don Gaspar Ave. ☎ **505/983-9340.** Reservations recommended for dinner. Breakfast $4.75–$10.75; lunch $4.95–$10.75; dinner $17.95–$26.75. AE, MC, V. Mon–Sat 7am–3pm; Mon–Sun 6–10pm (until 10:30pm in summer). Brunch Sun 8am–3pm. CREATIVE SOUTHWESTERN.

"You have to become the food, erase the line between it as an object and you. You have to really examine its structure, its size, its color, its strength, its weakness, know who grew it, how long it's been out of the field," said Pasqual's owner Katharine Kagel. This attitude is completely apparent in this restaurant where the walls are lined with murals depicting voluptuous villagers playing guitars, drinking, and even flying. Needless to say it's a festive place, though it's also excellent for a romantic dinner. Service is jovial and professional. My favorite dish for breakfast or lunch is the huevos motuleños (two eggs over easy on blue-corn tortillas and black beans topped with sautéed bananas, feta cheese, salsa, and green chile). Soups and salads are also served for lunch, and there's a delectable grilled-salmon burrito with herbed goat cheese and cucumber salsa. The frequently changing dinner menu offers grilled meats and seafoods, plus vegetarian specials. Start with the vegetable pot stickers and move onto the chicken mole Puebla (chicken with a dark sauce made from chocolate), served with an Oaxacan tamale. Avoid the pollo pibil, since it isn't as interesting as most of the other dishes. There's a communal table for those who would like to meet new people over a meal. Pasqual's offers imported beers and wine by the bottle or glass. Try to go at an odd hour—late morning or afternoon—or make a reservation for dinner; otherwise, you'll have to wait. The restaurant also sells colorful calendars, T-shirts, and Kagel's cookbook.

Coyote Cafe

132 Water St. ☎ **505/983-1615.** Reservations recommended. Main courses $6.50–$15.95 (Rooftop Cantina); fixed-price dinner $39.50 (Coyote Cafe). AE, DC, DISC, MC, V. Cafe: Oct–Apr, daily 11:30am–2:30pm and 6–9pm; Apr–Oct, daily 6–9pm. Rooftop Cantina: daily 11:30am–9pm. CREATIVE SOUTHWESTERN.

World-renowned chef and cookbook author Mark Miller has been "charged with single-handedly elevating the chile to haute status." That statement from *New York Times Magazine* sums up for me the experience of eating at this trendy nouveau Southwest restaurant a block from the Plaza. The atmosphere is urban Southwest, with calfskin-covered chairs and a zoo of carved animals watching from a balcony. The exhibition kitchen shows lots of brass and tile, and the waitstaff is well-mannered, efficient, and friendly. It's the place to go for a fun night out, or you can sample the great food for lunch at a fraction of the price. Some complain that on a busy night the space is noisy, and I'm especially careful not to sit on the banco toward the northeastern corner where a fan rumbles always.

The menu changes seasonally, so if the food I mention isn't available, look for variations. An incredible lunch is the pork carnitas tamale appetizer ordered as an entree. It comes with chipotle-orange barbecue sauce and black bean–avocado relish. My mother loves the chicken enchilada, especially nice if you like to go light on the cheese—the red chile sauce is amazing. Dinners are three-course affairs, though diners can order à la carte at the counter and watch the chefs in action. The affair starts with Coyote cocktails that might include a Brazilian daiquiri or margarita del Maguey. For an appetizer you have a number of choices, including a chile-cured salmon gravlax salad with mango-habañero sauce or a Mexican garlic and scallop soup. You can't go wrong with the new rotisserie chicken recently added to the menu, served with sweet potato mash, though I like to go with something that allows the chef's talents to shine more, such as the seared Maine scallops with ancho-wild mushroom serape and pumpkin-cascabel sauce. You can order drinks from the full bar or wine by the glass. Smoking is not allowed.

The Coyote Cafe has two adjunct establishments. In summer, the place to be seen is the Rooftop Cantina, where light Mexican fare and cocktails are served upon a festively painted terrace (try the Yucatán taquitos). On the ground floor is the Coyote Cafe General Store, a retail gourmet Southwestern food market featuring the Coyote Cafe's own food line called Coyote Cocina (try the salsa), as well as hot sauces and salsas from all over the world.

Geronimo

724 Canyon Rd. ☎ **505/982-1500.** Reservations recommended. Lunch $8–$13; dinner $18–$30. AE, MC, V. Tues–Sun 11:30am–2:15pm; daily 6–10pm. CREATIVE CONTINENTAL.

When Geronimo opened in 1991, no one was sure if it would succeed since so many previous restaurants at this site had failed. But this elegant eatery has done more than just survive—it has flourished, and now, with a new chef, the food is better than ever. It occupies an old adobe structure known as the Borrego House, built by Geronimo Lopez in 1756 and now completely restored. Numerous small dining rooms help it retain the comfortable feel of an old Santa Fe home.

I especially recommend lunch here, because you can get a taste of this often complex food for a fraction of the dinner price. Reserve a spot on the porch and watch the action on Canyon Road. My favorite at lunch is the house smoked ruby trout salad, with crimson beluga lentils and organic grains with a sweet sesame dressing. The open-faced smoked salmon sandwich with herbed aïoli and homemade potato chips is also nice. And if you've never tried one, go for the buffalo burger—it's more flavorful than beef. For a dinner appetizer try the char-grilled cold-water lobster tail on herb-spun angel hair pasta. For an entree, the grilled black pepper elk tenderloin with scallion risotto is a bit exotic, while the grilled ahi tuna on braised shiitakes with wilted watercress is just delicious. For dessert, you won't be disappointed by the trio of brûlées—espresso chocolate, Chambord, and orange—or the Belgian chocolate Grand Marnier cake. The menu changes seasonally, and there is an excellent wine list.

La Casa Sena

125 E. Palace Ave. ☎ **505/988-9232.** Reservations recommended. Lunch $7.75–$10; dinner $18–$27. 5-course chef's tasting menu $42, with wine $57. La Cantina, main courses $12.50–$23. AE, CB, DC, DISC, MC, V. Mon–Sat 11:30am–3pm; daily 5:30–10pm. Brunch Sat–Sun 11am–3pm. CREATIVE SOUTHWESTERN.

Though this restaurant suffered a fire in 1996, it's been restored and reopened, and many believe the food is even better now. It sits within the Sena compound, a prime example of a Spanish hacienda, a Territorial-style adobe house built in 1867 by Civil War hero Maj. José Sena for his wife and 23 children. The house, which surrounds a garden courtyard, is today a veritable art gallery, with museum-quality landscapes on the walls and Taos-style handcrafted furniture. The cuisine in the main dining room might be described as Northern New Mexican with a continental flair. Lunches include Caribbean pork soft tacos and almond-encrusted

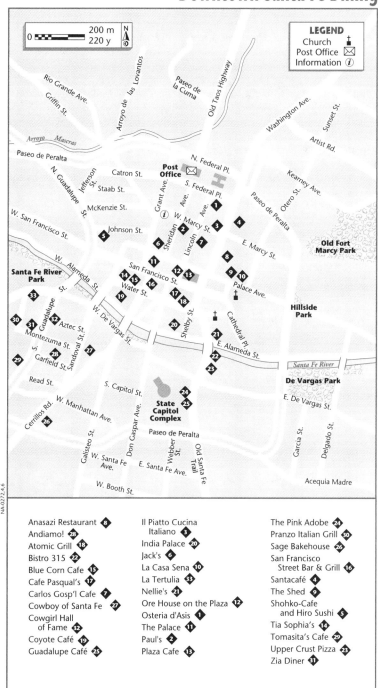

Anasazi Restaurant 8
Andiamo! 28
Atomic Grill 18
Bistro 315 22
Blue Corn Cafe 15
Cafe Pasqual's 17
Carlos Gosp'l Cafe 7
Cowboy of Santa Fe 27
Cowgirl Hall
  of Fame 32
Coyote Café 19
Guadalupe Café 25

Il Piatto Cucina
  Italiano 3
India Palace 20
Jack's 6
La Casa Sena 10
La Tertulia 33
Nellie's 21
Ore House on the Plaza 12
Osteria d'Asis 1
The Palace 11
Paul's 2
Plaza Cafe 13

The Pink Adobe 24
Pranzo Italian Grill 30
Sage Bakehouse 26
San Francisco
  Street Bar & Grill 16
Santacafé 4
The Shed 9
Shohko-Cafe
  and Hiro Sushi 5
Tia Sophia's 14
Tomasita's Cafe 29
Upper Crust Pizza 23
Zia Diner 31

salmon with gazpacho salsa. In the evening, diners might start with a salad of mixed organic greens, goat cheese, and a fresh herb vinaigrette, then move to American corn-fed lamb chops with habañero-papaya sauce, tropical fruit *ensalada,* and crispy root vegetables.

In the adjacent **La Cantina,** waiters and waitresses sing Broadway show tunes as they carry platters from the kitchen to the table. The more moderately priced Cantina menu offers the likes of blue-corn-crusted salmon or honey-glazed Mexican pork loin. Both restaurants have exquisite desserts. Try the black-and-white bittersweet chocolate terrine with raspberry sauce. The award-winning wine list features more than 850 wines. There's patio dining in summer.

Nellie's

211 Old Santa Fe Trail (at Hotel Loretto). ☎ **505/984-7915.** Reservations recommended. Breakfast and lunch $6.75–$9.25; dinner $16–$22. AE, DC, DISC, MC, V. Daily 7am–9:30pm. Winter closed from 2–5:30pm. NEW AMERICAN.

Named for a locally carved wooden snake that hangs over the bar, Nellie's is a creative new addition to Santa Fe's restaurant scene. Decorated in warm earth tones with brightly colored masks for accents, it's a nice place for a romantic meal or just a night out. For breakfast, I recommend the pecan brioche French toast, served with Chantilly cream and apricot-infused Vermont maple syrup. Lunch can be especially nice on the patio in summer. Try the Southwestern chicken salad (grilled breast with baby field greens, roasted peppers, and avocado, with buttermilk ranch dressing). For dinner, start with the lobster tortilla soup and move on to red chile raspberry pork tenderloin, with thyme and corn compote. Innovative desserts are offered nightly, such as vanilla bean crème brûlée with a caramel wall and a berry sauce. The service could have been faster and more attentive. A variety of fine wines is available by the glass or bottle.

Pink Adobe

406 Old Santa Fe Trail. ☎ **505/983-7712.** Reservations recommended. Lunch $4.75–$8.75; dinner $10.75–$23.25. AE, CB, DC, DISC, MC, V. Mon–Fri 11:30am–2pm; daily 5:30–10pm. CONTINENTAL/SOUTHWESTERN.

More show than flavor? Probably. This restaurant a few blocks off the Plaza offers a swirl of local old-timer gaiety, and food that is more imaginative than flavorful, but has remained popular since the restaurant opened in 1946. I remember eating my first lamb curry here, and my mother ate her first blue-corn enchilada, back in the '50s, and was taken aback by the odd colors. The restaurant occupies an adobe home believed to be at least 350 years old. Guests enter through a narrow side door into a series of quaint, informal dining rooms with tile or hardwood floors. Stuccoed walls display original modern art or Priscilla Hoback pottery on built-in shelves.

For lunch, I'll always have a chicken enchilada topped with an egg. The gypsy stew (chicken, green chile, tomatoes, and onions in sherry broth) sounds great but is on the bland side. At the dinner hour, the Pink Adobe offers the likes of escargot and shrimp rémoulade as appetizers. I recommend the lamb curry or the poulet marengo (chicken baked with brandy wine and mushrooms). You can't leave without trying the hot French apple pie.

Smoking is allowed only in the **Dragon Room,** the lounge across the alleyway from the restaurant. Under the same ownership, the charming bar (a real local scene) has its own menu offering traditional New Mexican food. Locals go there especially to eat hearty green chile stew. The full bar is open Monday through Friday from 11:30am to 2am, Saturday 5pm to 2am, and Sunday 5pm to midnight. There's live entertainment Tuesday, Thursday, and Saturday.

✪ Santacafé
231 Washington Ave. ☎ **505/984-1788.** Reservations recommended. Lunch $5–$10; dinner $17–$27. AE, MC, V. Mon–Sat 11:30am–2pm; daily 6–10pm. CREATIVE SOUTHWESTERN.

When you eat at this fine restaurant, be prepared for spectacular bursts of flavor. The food is Southwestern with an Asian flair, surrounded by a minimalist decor that accentuates the beautiful architecture of the 18th-century Padre Gallegos House, 2 blocks from the Plaza. The white walls are decorated only with deer antlers, and each room contains a fireplace. In warm months you can sit under elm trees in the charming courtyard. Beware that on busy nights the rooms are noisy.

The dishes change to take advantage of seasonal specialties, each served with precision. A simple starter such as miso soup is enriched with a lobster-mushroom roulade. One of my favorites is the seared chile-garlic prawns served with fresh pea (or lima) and mushroom risotto. A more adventurous eater might try the pan-seared achiote duck breast with raisin couscous, spiced pecans, and pineapple pasilla puree. There's an extensive wine list, with wine by the glass as well. Desserts are made in-house and are artistically presented. Some have criticized chef Ming Tsai for overdoing his recipes; others claim the prices are too steep. I just find the experience inventively delicious in all respects.

MODERATE

Andiamo!
322 Garfield St. ☎ **505/995-9595.** Reservations recommended. Main courses $7.50–$17.50. AE, DISC, MC, V. Wed–Mon 5:30–9pm and until 9:30pm on Fri and Sat. ITALIAN.

Quite a few new restaurants have sprung up in Santa Fe over the past few years, several of which were created by defectors of some of the city's most popular eateries. Andiamo! is one of those making a successful go of it. Chris Galvin, once the sous chef at Cafe Escalera, has joined forces with business partner Joan Gillcrist at this fine restaurant. They have created an authentically Tuscan atmosphere in which a daily changing menu features antipasto, pasta, and excellent desserts. Still, as with many of these little spinoffs, you tend to feel a bit cramped into the space, and noise levels can get out of hand. I enjoyed the Caesar salad and the penne with merguez, with a bit of musky flavor from the lamb sausage. For dessert, I'd recommend the polenta pound cake with lemon crème Anglaise. Beer and wine are served at this nonsmoking restaurant.

Celebrations Restaurant and Bar
613 Canyon Rd. ☎ **505/989-8904.** Reservations recommended. Breakfast/lunch up to $8.95, with daily specials; dinner main courses up to $14.95, with nightly specials. MC, V. Daily 8:30am–2pm; Wed–Sat 5:30–9pm; call for seasonal hours. AMERICAN BISTRO.

Housed in a former art gallery with beautiful stained-glass windows and a kiva fireplace, Celebrations boasts "the ambience of a bistro and the simple charm of another era." In summer, guests can dine on a brick patio facing Canyon Road. The meals here are a delicious melding of flavors, particularly those that cook awhile, such as the étouffée and stew. Three meals are served daily, starting with breakfast— an omelet with black beans or French toast with orange syrup, for example. Lunch choices include soup, salad, and pasta specials, Swiss raclette, sandwiches such as the oyster poor boy, and the ploughman's lunch. Casseroles, pot pies, and hearty soups are always available in winter. The dinner menu changes with the chef's whims, but recent specialties have included sautéed pecan trout, roasted rack of lamb, and my favorite, crawfish étouffée. All desserts (including the red chile piñon ice cream) are homemade. There is a full bar, as well as a choice of beers and wines by the bottle or glass.

Cowboy of Santa Fe

331 Sandoval St. ☎ **505/982-8999.** Reservations accepted. Main courses lunch $7.50–$18, dinner $12–$25. AE, MC, V. Daily 11:30am–2:30pm and 5:30–10pm. Bar menu served until midnight. WESTERN BARBECUE/STEAKS.

It was a big day on the dusty streets of Santa Fe when the head wrangler of Geronimo announced that he was going to take over the large, defunct Double A Restaurant space and put in this new Montana ranch-style eatery. Many are happy he did, and hope the place can survive. The ambience is luxury-barn, with a high ceiling adorned with a chandelier of tangled antlers. Stressed wooden tables and heavy, comfortable chairs surround a center stone fireplace. Service is excellent. The food appears to be basic fare upon first perusal, even a bit over-priced, but a sampling demonstrates that great imagination and care have gone into its planning and preparation. The buttery biscuits served with all meals are worth a visit on their own. If you're looking for a light lunch try the Cowboy cobb salad (butter lettuce with juicy grilled chicken, applewood-smoked bacon, avocado, and maytag blue cheese). For the heartier appetite I'd recommend the BBQ braised short ribs with shoestring potatoes and apple cole slaw. Another interesting item is a green chile macaroni and cheese. The dinner menu has a country-fried rainbow trout with cornmeal-fried okra, and a Cowboy T-bone steak with horseradish mashed potatoes and a pepper sauce that is very tasty (it's made with corn and Jack Daniels). There's a full bar and country-and-western dancing to live music Wednesday through Saturday nights.

El Farol

808 Canyon Rd. ☎ **505/983-9912.** Reservations recommended. Tapas $3.95–$8.95; main courses $10.95–$22.50. DC, DISC, MC, V. Daily 11:30am–4pm and 6–10pm. SPANISH.

This is the place to head for local ambience and old-fashioned flavor. El Farol (The Lantern) is the Canyon Road artists' quarter's original neighborhood bar. Recently it has become a center of controversy; some of the neighborhood folks resent the amplified music played into the night, and a recent arson incident burned part of the restaurant. At press time the owner was busy repairing the damage, and he was excited to say the fire led to a brightening of the rooms and upgrading of the front porch. The restaurant has cozy low ceilings and hand-smoothed adobe walls. Thirty-five varieties of tapas are offered, including such delicacies as *gambas al ajillo* (shrimp with a sherry-garlic sauce) and grilled cactus with romesco sauce. I like to order two or three tapas and have my companion do the same so that we can share. However, if you prefer a full dinner, try the paella or the marinated lamb chops with huckleberry, cranberry, or rosemary sauce. Jazz, folk, and ethnic musicians play almost every night beginning at 9:30pm. In summer, an outdoor patio seating 50 is open to diners.

Il Piatto Cucina Italiano

96 West Marcy St. ☎ **505/984-1091.** Reservations recommended. Main courses $8–$15. AE, MC, V. Mon–Fri 11:30am–2pm; Mon–Sat 5:30–9pm. TRADITIONAL NORTHERN ITALIAN.

This is a spinoff from a more expensive restaurant. A child of Bistro 315, Il Piatto brings executive chef Matt Yohalem's expertise to thinner wallets. It's an Italian cafe, simple and elegant, with contemporary art on the walls—nice for a romantic evening. Service is efficient, though on a busy night, overworked. The menu changes seasonally, complemented by a few perennial standards. For a starter, try the fresh arugula with pine nuts, raisins, shaved onions, and parmigiana. Among entrees, my favorite is the fettuccine carbonara (rich cream-and-egg sauce and

---

ⓘ Family-Friendly Restaurants

Bobcat Bite *(see page 97)*   The name and the ranch-style atmosphere will appeal to families that are looking for great steaks and huge hamburgers at low prices.

Cowgirl Hall of Fame *(see page 91)*   Kids love the Kid's Corral where, among other things, they can play a game of horseshoes.

Upper Crust Pizza *(see page 95)*   Many people feel they have the best pizza in town, and they'll deliver it to tired tots and their families at downtown hotels.

---

prosciutto), though you can't go wrong with the Italian sausage served over polenta. A full wine and beer menu is available.

India Palace

227 Don Gaspar Ave. (at the back of the Water St. parking compound.) ☎ **505/986-5859.** Reservations accepted. Main courses $7.95–$19.95, luncheon buffet $6.95. AE, DC, DISC, MC, V. Daily 11:30am–2:30pm and 5–10pm, 364 days a year, except Super Bowl Sunday. EAST INDIAN.

Once every few weeks I get a craving for the lamb *vindaloo* served at this restaurant in the center of downtown. A festive ambience, with pink walls painted with mosque shadows, makes this a nice place for a romantic meal. The service is efficient and most of the waiters are from India, as is chef Amarjit Behal. The tandoori chicken, fish, lamb, and shrimp are rich and flavorful, as is the *baingan bhartha* (eggplant in a delicious sauce). A luncheon buffet provides an excellent selection of vegetarian and non-vegetarian dishes at a reasonable price. Beer and wine are available, or you might want some *chai* tea.

Jack's

135 W. Palace. ☎ **505/983-7220.** Reservations recommended. Main courses $9–$12 at lunch; $12–$19 at dinner. AE, MC, V. Tues–Sun 11:30am–3pm and 5:30–9pm; same hours daily June–Sept. NEW AMERICAN.

Within 1 week, two friends told me their favorite new restaurant in Santa Fe was Jack's. My opinion? It's well worth a visit. Jack Shaab, the proprietor who was previously a partner in Bistro 315 and Il Piatto, both successful Santa Fe eateries, has covered major ground in a short while. He already has a strong following, so expect a crowd during high season. You won't find the stunning Southwestern decor of Santacafé here; this is an edgier, more citified ambience. It's decorated in black and brown, with butcher paper on the tables and crayons you can use for coloring while waiting to be served. The service is unpredictable—sometimes efficient, sometimes negligent.

If you don't feel like trying out this upstart for an expensive dinner, come for lunch. For an appetizer, I suggest the sautéed salmon cakes with wasabi aïoli, found on both the lunch and dinner menus. For lunch, I enjoyed the vegetable tart with goat cheese and roasted tomato sauce. If you like hearty flavors, order the cornmeal-crusted chicken breast, stuffed with feta, ricotta, and sundried tomatoes and served with a mushroom cream sauce. For dinner, you might try the sautéed Chilean sea bass with roasted sweet-pepper rice. You'll also find duck breast, pork tenderloin, and a mixed grill of lamb. The chocolate mousse I ordered for dessert at first seemed too frozen, but was in fact just extremely rich, almost chewy. It had its own identity, much like the entire dining experience here. There's a full bar, as well as a nice wine menu.

La Tertulia

416 Agua Fría St. ☎ **505/988-2769.** Reservations recommended. Lunch $5.50–$9; dinner $8–$22. AE, DC, DISC, MC, V. Tues–Sun 11:30am–2pm and 5–9pm. NEW MEXICAN.

This restaurant is the place Santa Feans go when they want good New Mexican food and a fancy atmosphere. Housed in a former 18th-century convent, La Tertulia's thick adobe walls separate six dining rooms, including the old chapel and a restored *sala* (living room) with a valuable Spanish colonial art collection. There's also an outside garden patio for summer dining. Dim lighting and viga-beamed ceilings, shuttered windows, wrought-iron chandeliers, lace tablecloths, and hand-carved santos in wall niches lend a feeling of historic authenticity. *La tertulia* means "gathering place" or "discussion," and the gourmet regional dishes here will give you something to talk about. They include filet y relleños (cheese stuffed chiles and a filet mignon) and *camarones con pimientos y tomates* (shrimp with peppers and tomatoes) as well as a variety of fresh fish dishes. My favorite, however, is the burrito plate, served with rice and posole. If you feel like dessert, try the chocolate piñon-nut truffle torte or natillas (custard). The full bar features homemade sangría.

Ore House on the Plaza

50 Lincoln Ave. ☎ **505/983-8687.** Reservations recommended. Main courses $12–$23. AE, MC, V. Mon–Sat 11:30am–2:30pm, Sun noon–2:30pm; daily 5:30–10pm. STEAKS/SEAFOOD AND NEW MEXICAN.

The Ore House's second-story balcony, at the southwest corner of the Plaza, is an ideal spot from which to watch the passing scene while you enjoy cocktails and hors d'oeuvres. In fact, it is *the* place to be between 4 and 6pm every afternoon. The decor is Southwestern, with plants and lanterns hanging amid white walls and booths. The menu, now presided over by Chef Eduardo Rios, has fresh seafood and steaks, as well as some interesting Nueva Latina dishes which incorporate some interesting sauces. Daily fresh fish specials include salmon and swordfish (poached, blackened, teriyaki, or lemon), rainbow trout, lobster, and shellfish. Steak Ore House (wrapped in bacon and topped with crabmeat and béarnaise sauce) and chicken Ore House (a grilled breast stuffed with ham, Swiss cheese, green chile, and béarnaise) are local favorites. The Ore House also caters to noncarnivores with vegetable platters.

The bar, with solo music Wednesday through Saturday nights, is proud of its 66 different custom margaritas. It offers a selection of domestic and imported beers and an excellent wine list. An appetizer menu is served from 2:30 to 5pm daily, and the bar stays open until midnight or later (on Sunday it closes at midnight).

The Palace

142 W. Palace Ave. ☎ **505/982-9891.** Reservations recommended. Lunch $5.25–$10.50; dinner $12.50–$23.95 AE, DISC, MC, V. Mon–Sat 11:30am–4pm; daily 5:45–10pm. ITALIAN/CONTINENTAL.

When the Burro Alley site of Doña Tules's 19th-century gambling hall was excavated in 1959, an unusual artifact was discovered: a brass door knocker, half shaped like a horseshoe, and the other half like a saloon girl's stockinged leg. That knocker has become the logo of The Palace, which maintains a Victorian flavor as well as a bit of a bordello flair with lots of plush red upholstery. The brothers Lino, Pietro, and Bruno Pertusini brought a long family tradition into the restaurant business: Their father was chef at the Villa d'Este on Lake Como, Italy. You'll find an older crowd here and fairly small portions. The Caesar salad—prepared tableside—is always good, as are the meat dishes such as the grilled Black Angus New York strip. Fish dishes are inventive and tasty. Try crab cakes with a sauce aurore for lunch or grilled cornmeal-dusted trout with crab filling for dinner. For a light meal, my father likes to order the spaghetti pomodoro; the cannelloni is also nice but much richer. They serve a variety of vegetarian dishes, and there are usually daily specials. The wine list is long and well considered. There is outdoor dining, and the bar is open Monday through Saturday from 11:30am to 2am and Sunday from 5:45pm to midnight, with nightly entertainment including dancing on Saturday after 9pm.

✪ Paul's

72 W. Marcy St. ☎ **505/982-8738.** Reservations recommended for dinner. Lunch $5.95–$7.95; dinner $14–$19. AE, DC, DISC, MC, V. Mon–Sat 11:30am–2pm; daily 5:30–9pm. ECLECTIC.

It would be easy to walk right by this little downtown cafe, but don't, or you'll miss one of Santa Fe's more delightful dining experiences. The lunch menu presents a nice selection of main courses, such as salad Niçoise, dill salmon cakes, and an incredible pumpkin bread stuffed with pine nuts, corn, green chile, red chile sauce, queso blanco, and caramelized apples. Sandwiches are also available at lunch. At dinner, the lights are dimmed and the bright Santa Fe interior (with folk art on the walls and colorfully painted screens that divide the restaurant into smaller, more intimate areas) becomes a great place for a romantic dinner. The menu might include red chile duck wontons in a soy ginger cream to start and pecan-herb-crusted baked salmon with sorrel sauce as an entree. The grilled ahi with roasted pepper, artichoke hearts, and green olive salsa is excellent. Every dish is artistically exquisite in its presentation. Paul's won the "Taste of Santa Fe" award for appetizer in 1997 (duck wontons), best main course in 1992 (the salmon), and best dessert in 1994 (strawberry cheesecake brûlée). The chocolate ganache is exquisite. A wine list is available. Smoking is not permitted in the restaurant.

✪ Pranzo Italian Grill

540 Montezuma St., Sanbusco Center. ☎ **505/984-2645.** Reservations recommended. Lunch $5.95–$9.95; dinner $5.95–$17.50. AE, DC, DISC, MC, V. Mon–Sat 11:30am–3pm; Nightly 5–11pm. REGIONAL ITALIAN.

Housed in a renovated warehouse and freshly redecorated in warm Tuscan colors, this sister of Albuquerque's redoubtable Scalo restaurant caters to local Santa Feans with a contemporary atmosphere of modern abstract art and food prepared on an open grill. Homemade soups, salads, creative thin-crust pizzas, and fresh pastas are among the less expensive menu items. *Bianchi e nere al capesante* (black-and-white linguine with bay scallops in a light seafood sauce) and *pizza pollo affumicato* (with smoked chicken, pesto, and roasted peppers) are consistent favorites. Steak, chicken, veal, and fresh seafood grills—heavy on the garlic—dominate the dinner menu. The bar offers the Southwest's largest collection of grappas, as well as a wide selection of wines and champagnes by the glass. The upstairs rooftop terrace is lovely for seasonal moon-watching over a glass of wine. **Portare Via Cafe,** adjacent to the restaurant, is a great place for a light breakfast or lunch. The cinnamon rolls and scones are particularly good, and cappuccino and pastries are served throughout the day. Sandwiches are available at lunch.

Shohko-Cafe and Hiro Sushi

321 Johnson St. ☎ **505/983-7288.** Reservations recommended. Lunch $4.25–$12.50; dinner $9–$18. AE, DISC, MC, V. Mon–Fri 11:30am–2pm; Mon–Thurs 5:30–9pm, Fri–Sat 5:30–9:30pm. JAPANESE SUSHI.

Santa Fe has two rivaling sushi restaurants, this one and the neighboring Sakura. It seems that each person in town swears one is better than the other. This is my choice, but if it's very busy you'll also find good food at Sakura (where there's patio dining during the warm months). Opened in 1976 as Santa Fe's first Japanese restaurant, in a 150-year-old adobe building that had been a bordello in the 19th century, Shohko celebrated its 20th anniversary in 1996. The atmosphere is sparse and comfortable, a blending of New Mexican decor (such as ceiling vigas and Mexican tile floors) with traditional Japanese decorative touches (rice paper screens, for instance). Up to 30 fresh varieties of raw seafood, including sushi and sashimi, are served at plain pine tables in cozy rooms or at the sushi bar. Request the sushi bar, as the atmosphere is coziest here and you can watch the chefs at work. My mother likes the tempura combination with veggies, shrimp, and scallops. On an odd night I'll order the Japanese chicken curry, but most nights I have sushi, particularly the anago and spicy tuna roll, though if you're daring you might try the Santa Fe Roll (with green chile, shrimp tempura, and masago). Wine, imported beers, and hot sake are available.

Vanessie of Santa Fe

434 W. San Francisco St. (Parking entrance is on Water St.) ☎ **505/982-9966.** Reservations recommended. Dinner $12.95–$19.95. AE, DC, DISC, MC, V. Daily 5:30–10:30pm (earlier in off-season). STEAKS/SEAFOOD.

Vanessie is as much a piano bar as it is a restaurant. The talented musicians Doug Montgomery and Charles Tichenor hold forth at the keyboard, caressing the ivories with a repertoire that ranges from Bach to Barry Manilow. A 10-item menu, served at large, round, wooden tables beneath hanging plants in the main dining room or on a covered patio, never varies: rotisserie chicken, fresh fish, New York sirloin, filet mignon, Australian rock lobster, grilled shrimp, and rack of lamb. I especially like the rotisserie chicken. Portions are large; however, they're served à la carte, which almost bumps this restaurant up into the expensive category. As sides you can order fresh vegetables, sautéed mushrooms, baked potato, or onion loaf (my mom raves about this). For dessert, the slice of cheesecake served is large enough for three diners. There's a short wine list.

INEXPENSIVE

Atomic Grill

103 E. Water St. ☎ **505/820-2866.** Most items under $8.50. Summer, daily 7am–3am; rest of year, Mon–Fri 11am–3am, Sat 7am–3am, Sun 7am–1am. AE, DISC, MC, V. CREATIVE MEXICAN/AMERICAN.

A block south of the Plaza, this cafe offers decent patio dining at reasonable prices. Of course, there's indoor dining as well. The whole place has a hip and comfortable feel, and the food is prepared imaginatively. This isn't my choice for downtown restaurants but it's great if you're dining at an odd hour, particularly late at night. For breakfast try the raspberry French toast made with home-baked challah bread, served with apricot butter and maple syrup. For lunch, the green chile stew is tasty, although made with not quite enough chicken habañero sausage. The fish tacos are also nice, if a little bland (ask for extra salsa), and the burgers are good. They've recently added wood-fired pizzas; try the grilled chicken pesto. For dessert, the carrot cake is big enough to share and quite tasty. Wine by the glass and 100 different beers are available. They also deliver to the downtown area from 11am to midnight.

Blue Corn Cafe

133 W. Water St. ☎ **505/984-1800.** Reservations accepted for parties of 6 or more. Main courses $6.25–$9.75. AE, DC, DISC, MC, V. Daily 11am–11pm. NEW MEXICAN.

If you're ready for a fun and inexpensive night out eating decent New Mexican food, this is your place. The decor is clean and breezy, with white walls, wooden tables (imprinted with chiles), and abstract art. The atmosphere is fun, though not quiet, so it's a good place for kids. The waitstaff is overworked, thus a bit slow, but friendly and well-intentioned. I recommend sampling dishes from the combination menu. You can get two to five items served with your choice of rice, beans, or posole (one of the best I've tasted). I had the chicken enchilada, which I recommend, and the chalupa, which I don't because it was soggy. You can have tacos, tamales, and relleños too. Every night there are specialties worth trying. The shrimp fajitas were tasty, served with a nice guacamole and the usual toppings. Recently, the Blue Corn opened a brewery and so you might also want to sample the High Altitude Pale Ale or the Plaza Porter. My choice is the prickly pear iced tea (black tea with enough cactus juice to give it a zing). The Spanish flan is tasty and large enough to share. The **Blue Corn Cafe & Brewery** (4056 Cerrillos Rd., Suite G. ☎ **505/438-1800**) at the corner of Cerrillos and Rodeo roads has similar fare and atmosphere and a southside location.

Carlos' Gosp'l Cafe

125 Lincoln Ave. ☎ **505/983-1841.** Menu items $2.75–$7. No credit cards. Mon–Sat 11am–3pm. DELI.

A visit may have you singing the praises of the "Say Amen" desserts at this cafe in the inner courtyard of the First Interstate Bank Building. First, though, try the tortilla or hangover (potato, corn, and green chile chowder with Monterey Jack cheese) soups (served with tasty cornbread) or the deli sandwiches. Service is friendly, though at times a little absent-minded. My favorite is the Gertrude Stein sandwich, with Swiss cheese, tomato, red onion, sprouts, and mayonnaise. It comes with a generous potato salad. Carlos's has outdoor tables set on a sunny patio, but many diners prefer to sit indoors, reading newspapers or chatting around the large common table. During the lunch hour it can be a busy, noisy place. Gospel and soul music play continually; paintings of churches and performers cover the walls.

✪ Cowgirl Hall of Fame

319 S. Guadalupe St. ☎ **505/982-2565.** Reservations recommended. Lunch $2.95–$9.95; Dinner $4.50–$14.95. AE, DC, DISC, MC, V. Mon–Thurs 11am–11pm, Fri 11am–midnight, Sat 8am–midnight, Sun 8am–10:30pm. The bar is open Mon–Sat until 2am, Sun until midnight. REGIONAL AMERICAN/BARBECUE/CAJUN.

Whenever I want to have lots of fun eating, I go to the Cowgirl. The main room is a bar—a hip hangout spot, and a good place to eat as well if you don't mind the smoke. The back room is quieter, with wood floors and tables and plenty of cowgirl memorabilia. Best of all is the warm season when you sit out on a brick patio lit with strings of white lights. The service here is fast and friendly and the food is always excellent. In wintertime, my favorite is a big bowl of gumbo or crawfish étoufée, and the rest of the time I order Jamaican jerk chicken or pork tenderloin when it's a special. Careful, both can be *hot*. The bunkhouse smoked brisket with potato salad, barbecue beans, and cole slaw is excellent, as is the cracker-fried catfish with jalapeño-tartar sauce. Recent specialties of the house included butternut squash casserole and grilled-salmon soft tacos (to die for). The daily blue plate special is a real buy, especially on Tuesday nights when they serve chile relleños for $4.95. There's even a special "kid's corral" that has horseshoes, a rocking horse, a horse-shaped rubber tire swing, hay bales, and a beanbag toss. Happy hour is from 3 to 6pm. There is live music almost every night.

A new restaurant at the same site caters to more refined tastes, with a Rocky Mountain lodge atmosphere. The **Mustang Grill** has natural beef, veal, lamb, fish, and vegetarian dishes at prices ranging from $15 to $22. You might start with an appetizer of mesquite-smoked duck breast and move on to pan-seared venison médaillons with wild mushroom ragout. Dishes are served with such delicacies as corn pancakes, blackened nopales, or risotto. Open Friday, Saturday, and Sunday from 5:30–10pm. Reservations are recommended.

✪ Guadalupe Cafe

422 Old Santa Fe Trail. ☎ **505/982-9762.** Breakfast $4.50–$8.75; lunch $6–$12; dinner $6.95–$15.95. DISC, MC, V. Mon–Fri 7am–2pm, Sat–Sun 8am–2pm; Mon–Sat 5:30–9pm. NEW MEXICAN.

When I want New Mexican food, I go to this restaurant, and like many Santa Feans, I go there often. This casually elegant cafe, recently featured in *Bon Appétit* magazine, is in a white stucco building that's warm and friendly and has a nice-sized patio for dining in warmer months. Service is generally friendly and conscientious. For breakfast, try the spinach-mushroom burritos or huevos rancheros, and for lunch, the chalupas or stuffed sopaipillas. Any other time, I'd start with fresh roasted ancho chiles (filled with a combination of Montrachet and Monterey Jack cheeses, piñon nuts, and topped with your choice of chile) and move on to the sour-cream chicken enchilada or any of their other Southwestern dishes. Order both red and green chile ("Christmas") so that you can sample some of the best sauces in town. To the menu they've recently added some delicious salads, such as a Caesar with chicken. For those who don't enjoy Mexican food, there are also *hamburguesas* (hamburgers) and a selection of traditional favorites such as chicken-fried steak, turkey piñon meatloaf, and chicken salad. Daily specials are available and don't miss the famous chocolate-amaretto adobe pie for dessert. Beer, wine, and margaritas are served.

La Choza

905 Alarid St. ☎ **505/982-0909.** Lunch or dinner $6.75–$8.75. DISC, MC, V. Summer, Mon–Sat 11am–9pm; winter, Mon–Thurs 11am–8pm, Fri–Sat 11am–9pm. NEW MEXICAN.

The sister restaurant of The Shed (see below) offers some of the best New Mexican food in town at a convenient location near the intersection of Cerrillos Road and St. Francis Drive. When other restaurants are packed, you may have to wait a little while here—although often you'll be seated quickly. It's a warm, casual eatery, the walls vividly painted with magical images, especially popular on cold days when diners gather around the wood-burning stove and fireplace. Service is friendly and efficient, starting with complimentary chips and salsa. The menu offers enchiladas, tacos, and burritos on blue-corn tortillas, as well as green chile stew, chile con carne, and carne adovada. The portions are medium-sized, so if you're hungry start with guacamole or nachos. For years, I've ordered the cheese or chicken enchilada, two dishes I will always recommend. My new favorite, though, is the blue-corn burritos (tortillas stuffed with beans and cheese) served with posole; the dish can be made vegetarian if you'd like. For dessert, you can't leave without trying the mocha cake (chocolate cake with a mocha pudding filling, served with whipped cream). This may be the best dessert you'll ever eat. Vegetarians and children have their own menus. Beer and wine are available.

Osteria d'Assisi

58 S. Federal Place. ☎ **505/986-5858.** Lunch $6.95–$9.50; dinner $9.95–$12.95, with specials up to $16.50. AE, DC, MC, V. Mon–Sat 11am–10pm. NORTHERN ITALIAN.

Here again, we have a less expensive spinoff of a more expensive restaurant. This one was opened by one of the brothers from The Palace restaurant; expect to get good food at a fraction of the price. However, you sacrifice fine service and consistency here. Located just a few blocks from the Plaza, this restaurant has a quaint country Italian atmosphere with sponge-painted walls, simple wooden furniture, and the sound of Italian from chef Bruno Pertusini, of Lago di Como, Italy, punctuating the air. For antipasto, I enjoyed the *caprese* (fresh mozzarella with tomatoes and basil, garnished with baby greens in a vinaigrette). For pasta, I recommend the lasagna, and for fish, try the delightful Italian seafood stew. There are daily specials such as the lamb osso buco served with mashed potatoes, which I enjoyed. All meals are served with homemade Italian bread, and there are a number of special desserts. Beer and wine are by the bottle or glass. There's also a small deli in front from which you can take home meats and cheeses, and a patio open during the warmer months.

Plaza Cafe

54 Lincoln Ave. (on the Plaza). ☎ **505/982-1664.** No reservations. Main courses $2.50–$10.25. AE, DISC, MC, V. Daily 10am–7pm. AMERICAN/NEW MEXICAN/GREEK.

Santa Fe's lone hold-out to diner-style eating, this cafe has excellent food in a bright and friendly atmosphere. I like to meet friends here, sit in a booth, eat, and laugh about life. A restaurant since the turn of the century, it's been owned by the Razatos family since 1947. The decor has changed only enough to stay comfortable and clean, with red upholstered banquettes, art deco tile, and a soda-fountain-style service counter. Service is always quick and conscientious, and only during the heavy tourist seasons will you have to wait long for a table. The hamburgers and sandwiches are good. I also like their soups and New Mexican dishes such as the green chile stew, or, if you're more adventurous, the pumpkin posole. The Greek dishes are also worth trying. Monday, Wednesday, and Friday there are Greek specials such as vegetable moussaka; beef and lamb gyros are offered every day. My assistant, Julia, loves their Italian sodas, which come in many flavors, from vanilla to Amaretto. Or you can have a shake, a piece of coconut cream pie, or their signature dessert, *cajeta* (apple and pecan pie with Mexican caramel). Beer and wine are available.

Sage Bakehouse

535-C, Cerrillos Rd. ☎ **505/820-SAGE.** All menu items under $6. Mon–Fri 7am–5pm, Sat 8am–3pm. DISC, MC, V. GOURMET CAFE.

Restaurants all over Santa Fe use elegantly sharp sourdough bread from this bakery on Cerrillos Road across from the Hotel Santa Fe. And whenever I'm going visiting I'll stop and pick up a peasant loaf or some rich olive bread. If you're a bread lover, you might want to stop in for breakfast or lunch. The atmosphere is quiet and hip, with lots of marble and metal, a rounded counter and a few small tables, as well as sidewalk seating during the warm months. Breakfasts include good espressos and mochas, and a bread basket which allows you to sample some of the splendid treats. There are also large blueberry muffins. Lunches are simple, only a few sandwiches from which to choose, but you can bet they're good. Try the black forest ham and gruyere on rye, or the roasted red bell pepper and goat cheese on olive. People all over town are talking about the chocolate chip cookies. Rumor has it there's more chocolate than cookie in them.

San Francisco St. Bar & Grill

114 W. San Francisco St. ☎ **505/982-2044.** E-mail: robday@earthlink.net. No reservations. Lunch $5.25–$6.75; dinner $5.25–$12.50. AE, DC, DISC, MC, V. Daily 11am–11pm. AMERICAN.

Your goal is food. Forget fancy atmosphere. Forget high prices. You're downtown. This is the place. Actually, this cafe-style restaurant has a pleasant simplicity that I often enjoy with buddies on a Friday night. We go to watch my artist friend Robert cover himself with ketchup while eating his hamburger, and to savor the thick, juicy delicacies ourselves. On nights when I'm looking for something lighter, there's a good selection of salads, though they tend to be heavy on the lettuce, light on the meats and cheeses. I've enjoyed a chicken breast with roasted red pepper aïoli as well as a number of daily specials that often include good soups and pasta dishes. Service is always fast, though, at times, a little forgetful. During busy months you'll have to wait for a table. The full bar service includes draft beers and daily wine specials.

✪ The Shed

113½ E. Palace Ave. ☎ **505/982-9030.** Reservations accepted at dinner. Lunch $4.75–$8; dinner $6.75–$13.95. DISC, MC, V. Mon–Sat 11am–2:30pm; Wed–Sat 5:30–9pm. NEW MEXICAN.

During lunch time lines often form outside The Shed, half a block east of the Palace of the Governors. A luncheon institution since 1953, it occupies several rooms and the patio of a rambling hacienda that was built in 1692. Festive folk art adorns the doorways and walls. The food is delicious, some of the best in the state, and a compliment to traditional Hispanic and Pueblo cooking. The chicken or cheese enchilada is renowned in Santa Fe. Tacos and burritos are good, too, all served on blue-corn tortillas with pinto beans and posole. The green chile soup is a local favorite. The Shed's Joshua Carswell has added vegetarian and low-fat Mexican foods to the menu, as well as a wider variety of soups and salads and grilled chicken and steak. Don't leave without trying the mocha cake, possibly the best dessert you'll ever eat. Beer and wine are available.

Tía Sophia's

210 W. San Francisco St. ☎ **505/983-9880.** Breakfast $1.65–$7.95; lunch $3.50–$8.50. MC, V. Mon–Sat 7am–2pm. NEW MEXICAN.

If you want to see how real Santa Fe locals look and eat, go to this friendly downtown restaurant, now in its 23rd year. You'll sit at big wooden booths and sip diner coffee. Daily breakfast specials include eggs with blue-corn enchiladas (Tuesday) and burritos with chorizo, potatoes, chile, and cheese (Saturday). My favorite is the breakfast burrito or huevos rancheros (eggs over corn tortillas, smothered with chile). Some like the Atrisco plate: two eggs, green chile stew, a cheese enchilada, beans, posole, and a sopaipilla. Beware of what you order because, as the menu states, Tía Sophia's is "not responsible for too hot chile." Because this is a popular place, be prepared to wait for a table.

Tomasita's Cafe

500 S. Guadalupe St. ☎ **505/983-5721.** No reservations. Lunch $4.25–$9.50; dinner $4.75–$9.95. MC, V. Mon–Sat 11am–10pm. NEW MEXICAN.

When I was in high school, I used to eat at Tomasita's, a little dive on a back street. I always ordered a burrito, and I think people used to bring liquor in bags. Recently, President Clinton ate here during a brief visit to Los Alamos. It's now in a new building near the train station, and of course its food has become renowned. The atmosphere is simple—hanging plants and wood accents—with lots of families sitting at booths or tables and a festive spillover from the bar, where many come to drink margaritas. Service is quick, if not a little rushed, which is my biggest gripe about the new Tomasita's. Sure the food is still tasty, but unless you go at some totally odd hour you'll wait for a table, and once you're seated, you may eat and be out again in less than an hour. The burritos are still excellent, though you may want to try the chile rellŸos, a house specialty. Vegetarian dishes, burgers, steaks, and daily specials are also offered. There's full bar service.

Upper Crust Pizza

329 Old Santa Fe Trail. ☎ **505/982-0000.** No reservations. Pizzas $4.95–$16.05. DISC, MC, V. Summer, daily 11am–11pm; winter, Mon–Thurs and Sun 11am–10pm, Fri–Sat 11am–11pm. PIZZA.

Santa Fe's best pizzas are found here, in an adobe house near the old San Miguel Mission. Meals-in-a-dish include the Grecian gourmet pizza (feta and olives) and the whole-wheat vegetarian pizza (topped with sesame seeds). You can either eat here (inside or in a street-side patio) or request free delivery (it takes about 30 minutes) to your downtown hotel. Beer and wine are available, as are salads, calzones, and stromboli.

Zia Diner

326 S. Guadalupe St. ☎ **505/988-7008.** Reservations accepted only for parties of 6 or more. Lunch $3.50–$8.95; dinner $5.25–$15.95. AE, MC, V. Daily 11:30am–10pm. INTERNATIONAL/AMERICAN.

Santa Fe's alternative weekly, *The Reporter,* awarded this local favorite the prize for the "Best Comfort Food" in town, and that phrase describes the place well. In a renovated 1880 coal warehouse, it's an art deco diner with a turquoise-and-mauve color scheme. It boasts a stainless-steel soda fountain and a shaded patio. Extended hours make it a convenient stopover after a movie or late outing; however, during key meals on weekends it can get crowded and the wait can be long. The varied menu features homemade soups, salads, fish-and-chips, scrumptious piñon meatloaf, and of course, enchiladas. Specials range from turkey pot pie to yankee pot roast to three-cheese calzone. I like their corn, green chile, and asiago pie, as well as their soup specials. There are fine wines, a full bar, great desserts (for example, tapioca pudding, apple pie, and strawberry rhubarb pie), an espresso bar, and of course, you can get malts, floats, and shakes anytime.

4 Northside

EXPENSIVE

El Nido

NM 22, Tesuque. ☎ **505/988-4340.** Reservations recommended. Main courses $13.95–$23.95. AE, MC, V. Tues–Thurs and Sun 5:30–9:30pm, Fri–Sat 5:30–10pm. STEAK/SEAFOOD.

This is my favorite place to eat when I'm with my friend Carla. Her family is old Santa Fe, as is this restaurant. In the warm atmosphere, decorated with bird cages and smooth adobe partitions and bancos, we always encounter interesting characters, and since Carla eats here weekly, she knows what to order. In fact, during our last visit she pointed to a corner of the front room (where two fires blaze in winter) and jokingly said she was born there. In the 1950s and 1960s her parents used to party and dance at El Nido into the wee hours of the morning. Indeed, El Nido (the Nest) has been a landmark for many years. Built as a residence in the 1920s, it was a dance hall and Ma Nelson's brothel before it became a restaurant in 1939.

The food here is fresh and well-prepared with just a touch of fusion (European and Cajun influences) added to the specials. I'd suggest coming here if you're a bit overloaded by the seasonings at restaurants such as Santacafé, Coyote Cafe, and the Anasazi. The place is roomy, and the service is friendly and informal. Carla insists on oysters Rockefeller for an appetizer, though you can also start with a lighter ceviche. For entrees, she always has the salmon, which comes broiled with a light dill sauce on the side. I enjoy the broiled lamb chops, served with a light and tasty spinach mint sauce. All meals come with salad and baked potato, rice, or french fries. For dessert, try the crème brûlée, or, if you're a chocolate lover, try the chocolate piñon torte. There's a full bar, including a good selection of wines and local microbrew beers.

INEXPENSIVE

Tesuque Village Market

NM 22, (P.O. Box 231) Tesuque, 87574. ☎ **505/988-8848.** Main courses $4.95–$12. MC, V. Summer, daily 6am–10pm; winter, daily 7am–9pm. AMERICAN/SOUTHWESTERN.

Parked in front of this charming market and restaurant you'll see Range Rovers and beat-up ranch trucks, an indication that the food here has broad appeal. Located under a canopy of cottonwoods at the center of this quaint village, the restaurant is so good it's worth the trip 15 minutes north of Santa Fe. During warmer months you can sit on the porch; in other seasons the interior is comfortable, with plain wooden tables next to a deli counter and upscale market. For me, this is a breakfast place, where blue-corn pancakes rule. Friends of mine like the breakfast burritos and huevos rancheros. Lunch and dinner are also popular, and there's always a crowd (though, if you have to wait for a table, the wait is usually brief). For lunch, I recommend the burgers, and for dinner, one of the hearty specials such as lasagna, or my favorite, pork chops verde (boneless pork chops with a green chile sauce). For dessert, there's a variety of housemade pastries and cakes at the deli counter, as well as fancy granola bars and oversized cookies in the market. A kids menu is available.

5 Southside

Santa Fe's motel strip and other streets south of the Paseo de Peralta have their share of good, reasonably priced restaurants.

MODERATE

✪ Old Mexico Grill

2434 Cerrillos Rd., College Plaza South. ☎ **505/473-0338.** Reservations recommended for large parties. Lunch $5.95–$9.95; dinner $8.75–$17.50. DISC, MC, V. Tues–Fri 11:30am–2:30pm; Sun–Thurs 5:30–9pm, Fri–Sat 5:30–9:30pm. MEXICAN.

Rethink Mexican food at this festive restaurant off Cerrillos Road at St. Michaels. Certainly you'll find tacos here, served the Mexican way on soft corn tortillas, with excellent salsas. But you'll also find tasty moles and pipians, with sauces of ground pumpkin seeds and the highest-quality chiles. On weekends this is a very busy place, with chefs in the exhibition cooking area working feverishly on the open mesquite grill, but other times you can find a cozy corner for a romantic meal. Service is usually cordial and efficient. I like to start with *ceviche de camarones y concha*s (shrimp and scallops cooked in lime juice with onions peppers and cilantro), then move onto a plate of *arrancheras de pollo* (chicken fajitas) or *de camarones* (shrimp fajitas). Or, if I'm feeling more daring, I might try the *carne asada a la tampiqueña* (beef tenderloin with a toasted pepita/avocado sauce, garnished with sundried tomatoes and roasted poblano peppers) served with a cheese enchilada, beans, and guacamole. There is a nice selection of soups and salads at lunch and dinner and a variety of homemade desserts. A full bar serves Mexican beers (10 in all) and margaritas.

Peking Palace

1710 Cerrillos Rd. ☎ **505/984-1212.** Main courses $7.95–$15.95. AE, MC, V. Mon–Thurs 11:30am–9:30pm, Fri 11:30am–10pm, Sat noon–10pm, Sun noon–9:30pm. CHINESE FROM MANY REGIONS.

Elegant subtlety defines both the food and decor of this recently reopened restaurant on Cerrillos not quite at St. Michaels Drive. Moody adobe, with vigas and lots of nichos, sets the tone where diners can choose booths or tables. With plenty of space, this is a good place for a quiet, romantic dinner or a more festive party. Service is friendly, though a little slow. The spring rolls taste delightful, light and crispy, but the hot and sour soup lacks zing. Look for daily specials such as shrimp with asparagus—delicious. I also enjoy the Szechwan chicken (chicken breast with vegetables in a piquin sauce). The food here is prepared carefully and healthily. Sometimes, Chinese food can leave me feeling lethargic, but this doesn't. The luncheon buffet is inexpensive and popular among locals.

Steaksmith at El Gancho

Old Las Vegas Hwy. ☎ **505/988-3333.** Reservations recommended. Main courses $8.95–$24.95. AE, CB, DC, DISC, MC, V. Daily 4–11pm. STEAKS/SEAFOOD.

Surrounded by piñon and juniper, and inside accented by raw wood, this steakhouse is a favorite for many Santa Fe locals, but not for me. In fact, my mother and her best friend eat here (15 minutes northeast on Old Pecos Trail) regularly. They like the food and the festive atmosphere (there's often a crowd). I find the service quite uneven, especially if you have a large party, and the food at times mediocre. I prefer El Nido, the Ore House, or Mustang Grill for my big meat nights. A creative appetizer menu of tapas ranges from ceviche to deep-fried avocado. My mother orders the grilled shrimp and her friend orders the baby back ribs. Broiled gulf shrimp and Alaskan King crab are other friends' favorites. There is also a choice of salads, homemade desserts, and bread, plus a full bar and lounge (serving a tapas menu from 4pm) that even caters to cappuccino lovers.

INEXPENSIVE

Chows

720 St. Michaels Dr. ☎ **505/471-7120.** Main courses $6.50–$14.95. MC, V. Mon–Fri 11:30am–2pm, Sat noon–3pm; daily 5–9pm. CREATIVE CHINESE.

This upscale but casual restaurant, near the intersection of St. Francis and St. Michaels, is Chinese with a touch of health-conscious Santa Fe. The decor is tasteful, with lots of wood and earth tones. The food is unconventional, cooked without MSG. You can get standard pot stickers and fried rice, but you may want to investigate imaginatively named dishes such as firecracker dumplings (carrots, onions, ground turkey, and chile in a Chinese pesto spinach sauce); nuts and birds (chicken, water chestnuts, and zucchini in a Szechuan sauce); or my favorite, Pearl River Splash (whole steamed boneless trout in a ginger onion sauce). For dessert, try the chocolate-dipped fortune cookies. Wine by the bottle or glass as well as beer are available.

Bobcat Bite

Old Las Vegas Hwy. ☎ **505/983-5319.** No reservations. Menu items $3.50–$11.95. No credit cards. Wed–Sat 11am–7:50pm. STEAKS/BURGERS.

This local classic (in business for more than 40 years), located about 5 miles southeast of Santa Fe, is famed for its high-quality steaks—such as the 13-ounce rib eye—and huge hamburgers, including a remarkable green chile cheeseburger. The ranch-style atmosphere and friendly service appeal to families.

Felipe's Tacos

1711-A Llano St., in St. Michael's Village. ☎ **505/473-9397.** All menu items under $6. No credit cards. Mon–Fri 8:30am–7pm, Sat 9am–4pm.

Locals buzz around the small rapid-food restaurant like *moscas en miel* (flies on honey), and it's no wonder—the food is *muy sabrosa* (very flavorful) and prepared with lean meats, no lard, and fresh ingredients. You order at a counter, and the food generally comes quickly, ready for you to apply your own choice of a variety of salsas. As far as I'm concerned there's one thing to order here, because it's so good, why bother with anything else. That's the original chicken burrito (charbroiled chicken with cheese, beans, avocado, and salsa). You can also get it with steak. I see plenty of quesadillas served as well, and during the morning hours, la Mexicana burrito (eggs, pico de gallo, potatoes, and beans) is popular. Avoid the tacos, which are bland. Non-alcoholic drinks are served.

Green Onion

1851 St. Michael's Dr. ☎ **505/983-5198.** Lunch $5–$8; dinner $5–$9.50. AE, DISC, MC, V. Mon–Sat 11am–2am, Sun 11am–midnight. NEW MEXICAN, BURGERS, SANDWICHES, PIZZA.

This isn't my choice for food, but on that odd occasion when I get a desire to down some beer and scream at a TV screen, this is where I go. Roast-beef burritos and chicken enchiladas highlight an established menu at this sports bar, which also features a choice of sandwiches and pizza. You can view sports on a big-screen TV, or play darts, foosball, and video games.

Guadalajara Grill

3877 Cerrillos Rd. ☎ **505/424-3544.** Main courses $2.50–$9.95. AE, DISC, MC, V. Sun–Thurs 10:30am–9pm, Fri–Sat 10:30am–10pm; closed on Tues in winter. MEXICAN.

A brother restaurant to the Guadalajara Grill in Taos, this is a good casual place to sample authentic Mexican, rather than *New* Mexican food. Seven brothers from the restaurant's namesake town own and run these restaurants and offer dishes with flavors a little more distinct, less melded than our own here. Next to a liquor store, the restaurant is set in a small strip mall just north of the Cerrillos/Rodeo Road intersection. The room is square with bright plastic-covered tables and a funky purple neon light on the ceiling. It's a festive atmosphere, the service friendly and efficient. To start, you can sample a frozen margarita or your choice of 12 Mexican beers. My favorite dish here is the tacos, served with soft, handmade corn tortillas, well-seasoned meat, and an excellent salsa. At lunch, the menu is à la carte; at dinner all entrees come with rice and beans. Other favorites for lunch are a variety of types of burritos, and for dinner, *camaron al mojo de ajo* (shrimp sautéed with garlic and lime juice). If you're really daring you can sample the *barbacoa lengua* (cow tongue), or *cachete* (cow cheek), cooked until tender.

Marisco's La Playa

537 Cordova Rd. ☎ **505/982-2790.** Main courses $6.95–$12.95. MC, V. Wed–Mon 11am–9pm. MEXICAN SEAFOOD.

What this Mexican seafood restaurant lacks in ambience, it makes up for in *comida sabrosa* (tasty food). Set in a small shopping mall not far from St. Francis Drive, it has a beach scene mural on one wall and stark luminescent lighting from above. It was opened by two cousins who wanted to bring good Mexican playa (beach) food to the drylands, and judging from the crowds here (you may have to wait 15 to 20 minutes, but it's worth it) they've succeeded. It features such dishes as shrimp or fish tacos and *pescado a la plancha* (trout seasoned with butter, garlic, and paprika). Some locals complain that the place is too pricey, but I say for good fish, it's moderate. My favorite dish, one my Chinese doctor friend, Michael, says is excellent for

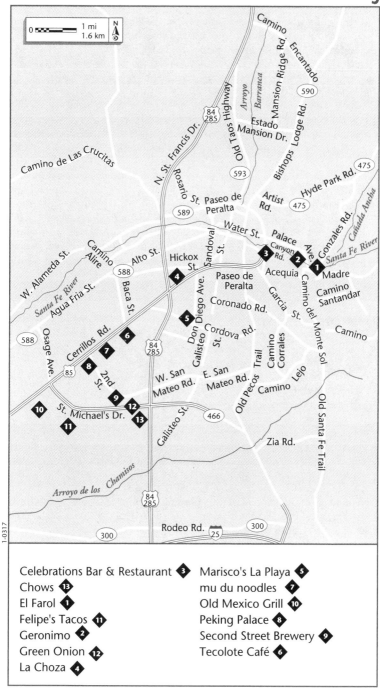

Celebrations Bar & Restaurant **3**
Chows **13**
El Farol **1**
Felipe's Tacos **11**
Geronimo **2**
Green Onion **12**
La Choza **4**

Marisco's La Playa **5**
mu du noodles **7**
Old Mexico Grill **10**
Peking Palace **8**
Second Street Brewery **9**
Tecolote Café **6**

my chi, is the *caldo vuelve a la vida* (come back to life soup)—a huge bowl, even if you order the small, of shrimp, octopus, scallops, clams, crab legs, and calamari in a tasty broth. Wash it down with a domestic or imported beer.

mu du noodles

1494 Cerrillos Rd. ☎ **505/983-1411.** Reservations for parties of 5 or larger only. Main courses lunch $6.75–$8.75; dinner $8.50–$11. Mon–Fri 11:30am–2:30pm; Mon–Sat 5:30–9pm (sometimes 10pm in summer); after 8:30pm always call to be sure. AE, DC, DISC, MC, V. PACIFIC RIM CUISINE.

If you're ready for a light, healthy meal with lots of flavor, head to this small restaurant about an 8-minute drive from downtown. There are two rooms, with plain pine tables and chairs and sparse Asian prints on the walls. The back room with carpet is cozier, and a woodsy-feeling patio is definitely worth requesting during the warmer months. The waitstaff is friendly and unimposing. Appetizers include duck pockets and turkey pot stickers, as well as specials daily. I almost always order the Malaysian laksa, thick rice noodles in a blend of coconut milk, hazel nuts, onions, and red curry, stir fried with chicken or tofu and julienned vegetables and sprouts. You may want to each order a different dish and share. The Pad Thai is lighter and spicier than most, served with a chile/vinegar sauce. Beers, wines, and sakes are available, termed "imported and hand crafted" which means they're tailored to meet the standards of the menu. I'm especially fond of the ginseng ginger ale and Way 2 Cool root beer they serve.

Second Street Brewery

1814 Second St. (at the railroad tracks). ☎ **505/982-3030.** Main courses $3.99–$12.99. AE, DC, DISC, MC, V. Mon–Sat 11:30am–midnight, Sun noon–11pm (call after 9:30pm to be sure). AMERICAN PUB FARE.

In a metal building, tucked back off Second Street, this new brewery has managed to create a lively pub scene and fairly warm atmosphere. Inside, the walls are painted gold hues with interesting contemporary art and wooden tables. It's a party type of place, especially during the warm months when diners and beer savorers sit out on the patio. The beers are quite tasty—I had a hearty cream stout and my friend enjoyed the amber ale. You can even get a 4-ounce sampler size for 75¢ and try a few different brews. The food isn't extremely memorable, but in winter it can warm a hearty appetite with such homestyle dishes as chicken pot pie and shepherd's pie (a little too tomatoey for my taste). The jerk chicken breast is tasty, though it could use more sauce. My assistant, Julia, enjoys the eggplant sandwich. The menu also offers lighter fare such as quiches, soups, and salads. There's a kid's menu and wines are available. Call to find out about special events. Recently they held a crawfish boil. Also look for their "Hoppy" Hour, when beer prices are reduced. There's also darts and live entertainment on Fridays, Saturdays, and most Wednesdays.

Tecolote Cafe

1203 Cerrillos Rd. ☎ **505/988-1362.** Main dishes $2.95–$9.25. AE, CB, DC, DISC, MC, V. Tues–Sun 7am–2pm. NEW MEXICAN/AMERICAN.

This is a local breakfast lovers' favorite. The decor is simple, but the food is elaborate: eggs any style, omelets, huevos rancheros—all served with fresh-baked muffins or biscuits and maple syrup. Try the atole piñon hotcakes (made with blue cornmeal) or the French toast made with house-baked bread, sliced thick. Luncheon specials include carne adovada burritos and green chile stew.

Tortilla Flats

3139 Cerrillos Rd. ☎ **505/471-8685.** Breakfast $1.75–$6.25; lunch $5.25–$9; dinner $6.25–$11. DISC, MC, V. Sun–Thurs 7am–9pm, 10pm in summer; Fri–Sat 7am–10pm. NEW MEXICAN.

This casual restaurant takes pride in its all-natural ingredients and vegetarian menu offerings (its vegetarian burrito is famous around town). The atmosphere is a bit like Denny's, but don't be fooled, the food is authentic. The blueberry pancakes are delicious, as are the fajitas and eggs with a side of black beans. I also like the blue-corn enchiladas and the chimichangas. The Santa Fe Trail steak (8 ounces of prime rib eye smothered with red or green chile and topped with grilled onions) will satisfy a big appetite. Above all, note the freshness of the tortillas and sopaipillas, made on the spot. You can even peek through a window into the kitchen and watch them being made. There's a full bar, with the legendary Ultimate Margarita, made with Grand Marnier and Cuervo Gold 1,800 Tequila. A children's menu and take-out service are available.

6 Out of Town

El Paragua

603 Santa Cruz Rd., Española (off the main drag; turn east at Long John Silver). ☎ **505/753-3211.** Reservations recommended. Main courses $6–$17. AE, DISC, MC, V. Summer, daily 11am–9:30pm; winter, daily 11am–9pm. NORTHERN NEW MEXICAN.

A half-hour drive north of Santa Fe in the town of Española, this is a great place to stop en route, though some Santa Feans make a special trip here. Every time I enter El Paragua (the umbrella) with its red tile floors and colorful saltillo-tile trimmings, I feel as though I've stepped into Mexico. The restaurant opened in 1958 as a small taco stand owned by two brothers, and through the years has flourished. It has received praise from many sources including *Gourmet Magazine* and N. Scott Momaday writing in *The New York Times.* You can't go wrong ordering the enchilada suprema, a chicken and cheese enchilada with onion and sour cream. Also on the menu are fajitas and a variety of seafood dishes and steaks including the *churrasco Argentino.* Served at your table in a hot brazier, it's cooked in a green herb *salsa chimichurri.* There's a full bar from which you may want to try Don Luis' Italian coffee, made with a coffee-flavored liquor called Tuaca.

7

What to See & Do in Santa Fe

One of the oldest cities in the United States, Santa Fe has long been a center for the creative and performing arts, so it's not surprising that most of the city's major sights are related to local history and the arts. The city's Museum of New Mexico, art galleries and studios, historic churches, and cultural sights associated with local Native American and Hispanic communities all merit a visit. It would be easy to spend a full week sightseeing in the city without ever heading out to any nearby attractions. Of special note is the Georgia O'Keeffe Museum opened just last summer.

SUGGESTED ITINERARIES

If You Have 2 Days

For an overview, start your first day at the Palace of the Governors; as you leave you might want to pick up a souvenir from the Native Americans selling crafts and jewelry beneath the portal facing the plaza. After lunch, take a self-guided walking tour of old Santa Fe, starting at the Plaza.

On Day 2, spend the morning at the Museum of Fine Arts and the afternoon browsing in the galleries on Canyon Road.

If You Have 3 Days

On the third day, visit the cluster of museums on Camino Lejo— the Museum of International Folk Art, the Museum of Indian Arts and Crafts, and the Wheelwright Museum of the American Indian. Then, wander through the historic Barrio de Analco and spend the rest of the afternoon shopping.

If You Have 4 Days or More

Devote your fourth day to exploring the pueblos, including San Juan Pueblo, headquarters of the Eight Northern Indian Pueblos Council, and Santa Clara Pueblo, with its Puye Cliff Dwellings.

On Day 5, go out along the High Road to Taos, with a stop at El Santuario de Chimayo, returning down the Rio Grande Valley. If you have more time, take a trip to Los Alamos, birthplace of the atomic bomb and home of the Bradbury Science Museum, and Bandelier National Monument.

If You're an Outdoorsperson

Start with the first day recommendation, just to get a feel for the culture of Santa Fe. Then, in spring or early summer, you might plan a raft trip down the Taos Box Canyon (a full-day event). During spring, summer, or fall, you could also contact one of the bicycle rental or touring companies and have them show you the way or take you to the Caja del Rio area or the West Rim of the Taos Box Canyon (See TK, below). If you go to one of these Taos destinations, plan to return via the "High Road" mentioned above.

On the following day, head up to the Windsor Trail for a hike in the Pecos Wilderness. A rigorous day-long trip will take you to the top of Santa Fe Baldy, where you'll have a 360° view of Northern New Mexico. Or perhaps you'd prefer to spend the day hiking and visiting ruins around Bandelier National Monument near Los Alamos. During winter, plan at least a day of skiing at the world-acclaimed Taos Ski Valley; however, you also might want to take skinny cross-country skis up to the Norski Trail near the Santa Fe Ski area, a pretty trek that meanders through an aspen forest. You can also snowshoe or backcountry ski on the Windsor Trail.

1 The Top Attractions

✪ Palace of the Governors

North Plaza. ☎ **505/827-6483.** Admission $5 adults, free for children under 16. 4-day passes good at all 4 branches of the Museum of New Mexico (and the Georgia O'Keeffe Museum) cost $10 for adults. Tues–Sun 10am–5pm. Closed Jan 1, Thanksgiving, Dec 25.

In order to fully appreciate this structure, it's important to know that this is where the only successful Native American uprising took place in 1680. Prior to the uprising, this was the local seat of power, and after De Vargas reconquered the natives it resumed that position. Built in 1610 as the original capitol of New Mexico, the Palace has been in continuous public use longer than any other structure in the United States. A watchful eye can find remnants of the conflicts this building has seen through the years. You'll want to begin out front, where Native Americans sell jewelry, pottery, and some weavings in the sun under the protection of the portal. This is a good place to buy, and it's a fun place to shop, especially if you take the time to visit with the artisans about their work. When you buy a piece you may learn its history, a treasure as valuable as the piece itself.

After entering the building, begin to the right, where a map illustrates 400 years of New Mexico history. Continue west and get a sense of that history, from the 16th-century Spanish explorations through the frontier era and modern times. Peek into a rickety stage coach and examine tools used by early Hispanic residents such as farm implements and kitchen utensils. There's a replica of a mid-19th century chapel, with a simple, bright-colored altarpiece made in 1830 for a Taos church by folk artist José Rafael Aragón. What I find most interesting are the period photos scattered throughout. The building's exterior seems elaborate now, but it was once a simple flat-topped adobe with thin posts. You can see a fireplace and chimney chiseled into the adobe wall, and, in the west section of the museum, a cutaway of the adobe floor. Farther in this direction, unearthed in a recent excavation, are storage pits where the Pueblo Indians kept corn, wheat, barley, and other goods during their reign at the palace. After the reconquest the pits were used to dispose of trash.

The museum focuses little on regional Native American culture (most Native American artifacts previously housed here have been moved to the Museum of

Indian Arts and Culture). However, recently a world-class collection of pre-Columbian art objects has been added. You'll see ceramics, gold, and stone work of South and Central America from 1500 B.C. to A.D. 1500. There's also an impressive 18th-century Segesser Hide painting collection, which documents events from America's Spanish Colonial past.

Governors' offices from the Mexican and 19th-century U.S. eras have been restored and preserved. My favorite display is a set of spurs ranging from the 16th to the late 19th centuries, including a spur with 5-inch rowels. There are two shops of particular interest. One is the bookstore, which has one of the finest selections of art, history, and anthropology books in the Southwest. The other is the print shop and bindery, where limited-edition works are produced on hand-operated presses.

The Palace is the flagship of the Museum of New Mexico system; the main office is at 113 Lincoln Ave. (☎ 505/827-6451, or 505/827-6463 for recorded information). The system comprises five state monuments and four Santa Fe museums: the Palace of the Governors, the Museum of Fine Arts, the Museum of International Folk Art, and the Museum of Indian Arts and Culture.

✪ Museum of Fine Arts

107 W. Palace (at Lincoln Ave.). ☎ 505/827-4455. Admission $5 adults, free for seniors on Wed, free for children under 17, free for all on Fri evening. 4-day passes are available ($10 for 5 museums). Tues–Sun 10am–5pm; Fri 5–8pm. Closed Jan 1, Easter, Thanksgiving, Dec 25.

Located catercorner from the Plaza and just opposite the Palace of the Governors, this was one of the first Pueblo Revival–style buildings constructed in Santa Fe (in 1917). As such, it was a major stimulus in Santa Fe's development as an art colony earlier in this century.

The museum's permanent collection of more than 8,000 works emphasizes regional art and includes landscapes and portraits by all the Taos masters and the contemporary artists R. C. Gorman, Amado Peña, Jr., and Georgia O'Keeffe, among others. The museum also has a collection of photographic works by such masters as Ansel Adams, Edward Weston, and Elliot Porter. Modern artists, many of them far from the mainstream of traditional Southwestern art, are featured in temporary exhibits throughout the year. Two sculpture gardens present a range of three-dimensional art from the traditional to the abstract.

Graceful St. Francis Auditorium, patterned after the interiors of traditional Hispanic mission churches, adjoins the art museum (see "The Performing Arts," in chapter 9). A museum shop sells books on Southwestern art, prints, and postcards of the collection.

✪ St. Francis Cathedral

Cathedral Place at San Francisco St. ☎ 505/982-5619. Donations appreciated. Open daily. Visitors may attend mass Mon–Sat at 7am and 5:15pm; Sun at 8 and 10am, noon, and 7pm.

Santa Fe's grandest religious structure is an architectural anomaly in Santa Fe because its design is French. Just a block east of the Plaza, it was built between 1869 and 1886 by Archbishop Jean-Baptiste Lamy in the style of the great cathedrals of Europe. French architects designed the Romanesque building—named after Santa Fe's patron saint—and Italian masons assisted with its construction. The small adobe Our Lady of the Rosary chapel on the northeast side of the cathedral has a Spanish look. Built in 1807, it's the only portion that remains from Our Lady of the Assumption Church, founded along with Santa Fe in 1610. The new cathedral was built over and around the old church.

A wooden icon set in a niche in the wall of the north chapel, Our Lady of Peace, is the oldest representation of the Madonna in the United States. Rescued from the

Downtown Santa Fe Attractions

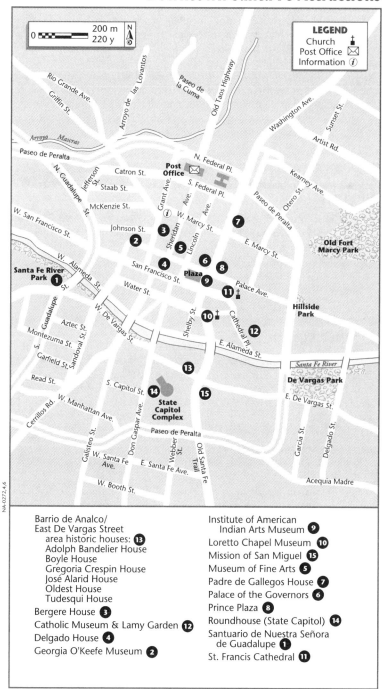

Barrio de Analco/
East De Vargas Street
  area historic houses: **13**
    Adolph Bandelier House
    Boyle House
    Gregoria Crespin House
    José Alarid House
    Oldest House
    Tudesqui House
Bergere House **3**
Catholic Museum & Lamy Garden **12**
Delgado House **4**
Georgia O'Keefe Museum **2**

Institute of American
  Indian Arts Museum **9**
Loretto Chapel Museum **10**
Mission of San Miguel **15**
Museum of Fine Arts **5**
Padre de Gallegos House **7**
Palace of the Governors **6**
Prince Plaza **8**
Roundhouse (State Capitol) **14**
Santuario de Nuestra Señora
  de Guadalupe **1**
St. Francis Cathedral **11**

old church during the 1680 Pueblo Rebellion, it was brought back by Don Diego de Vargas on his (mostly peaceful) reconquest 12 years later; thus, the name. Today, Our Lady of Peace plays an important part in the annual Feast of Corpus Christi in June and July.

During a $600,000 renovation in 1986, an early 18th-century wooden statue of St. Francis of Assisi was moved to the center of the altar screen. The cathedral's front doors feature 16 carved panels of historic note and a plaque memorializing the 38 Franciscan friars who were martyred during New Mexico's early years. There's also a large bronze statue of Bishop Lamy himself; his grave is under the main altar of the cathedral.

2 More Attractions

MUSEUMS

Catholic Museum and the Archbishop Lamy Commemorative Garden

223 Cathedral Place. ☎ **505/983-3811.** Donations appreciated. Mon–Fri 8:30am–4:30pm; Sat by appointment.

This museum will be especially interesting if you've read Willa Cather's *Death Comes for the Archbishop,* a fictional account of Archbishop Lamy's experience in Northern New Mexico. If you haven't read it, as you visit the St. Francis Cathedral, Bishop's Lodge, and other areas around Santa Fe, take special note of tales of the Archbishop, since he is central to the area's history. Though the exhibition changes every few years (and a new one should arrive right around press time), you are still likely to see a portrait of the determined, thin-lipped Frenchman—who resolutely battled what he felt was apostasy on the part of the Spanish clergy in New Mexico. You'll also see Lamy's boar hair trunk and the golden chalice given to him by Pope Pius IX in 1854. The next exhibit planned is called "400 Years of Faith" and will contain historic documents and artifacts from 400 years of Catholicism in New Mexico. The adjacent Lamy garden isn't much to see, but the gift shop in the museum has a nice collection of religious articles made locally.

✪ Georgia O'Keeffe Museum

217 Johnson St. ☎ **505/995-0785.** Admission $5 (4-day 5-museum passes to the Museum of New Mexico available). Tues–Sun 10am–5pm (Friday until 8pm).

For years, anxious visitors to Santa Fe asked, "Where are the O'Keeffes?" Locals flushed and were forced to answer: "The Metropolitan Museum of Art in New York and the National Gallery of Art in Washington, D.C." Although this East Coast artist is known the world over for her haunting depictions of the shapes and colors of Northern New Mexico, particularly the Abiquiu area, until now little of her work hung in the state. The local Museum of Fine Arts owns just 15 of her works.

The new museum, inaugurated in July 1997, contains the largest collection of O'Keeffes in the world: more than 80 oil paintings, drawings, watercolors, pastels, and sculptures. It is the only museum in the United States dedicated solely to one woman's work. You can see such "Killer O'Keeffes" as *Jimson Weed,* painted in 1932, and *Evening Star No. VII,* from 1917. The rich and varied collection adorns the walls of a cathedral-like, 10,000-square-foot space—a former Baptist church with adobe walls—downtown.

O'Keeffe's images and fame are, of course, tied inextricably to local desert landscapes. She first visited New Mexico in 1917 and returned for extended periods from the '20s through the '40s. The idea of bringing O'Keeffe's works together came from the private collector Anne Windfohr Marion. The Texas heiress heads the Burnett Foundation, which, along with the Georgia O'Keeffe Foundation, donated the initial 33 works. Ms. Marion and her husband, John L. Marion, a former chairman of Sotheby's North America, chose the designer of the Andy Warhol Museum in Pittsburgh, Richard Gluckman, to create the space for the O'Keeffe Museum.

Indian Arts Research Center

School of American Research, 660 Garcia St. (off Canyon Rd.). ☎ **505/954-7205.** E-mail: iarc@sarsf.org. Free admission for Native Americans and SAR members; $15 suggested donation for others. Public tours are given most Fri at 2pm (call for reservations). Group tours can also be arranged.

Having grown up in New Mexico surrounded by Native American arts, I had but a hodgepodge knowledge of whose work looked like what, and when it had been created. Then, I visited the vault here and was able to put my knowledge into an understandable framework. The School of American Research, of which this is a division, was established in 1907 as a center for advanced studies in anthropology and related fields. It sponsors scholarship, academic research, publications, and educational programs, all in the name of keeping traditional arts alive.

The school has collected over 10,000 objects, in the process compiling one of the world's finest collections of Southwest Indian pottery, jewelry, weavings, Kachinas, paintings, baskets, and other arts that span from the prehistoric era (around 300 to A.D. 500) to the present. You'll be led through temperature- and humidity-controlled rooms filled with work separated by tribe. Here, you can see the unique styles of each pueblo's pottery, from the Zia's swirling rainbow patterns full of birds and animal life to the San Ildefonso black-on-black that María Martínez made worldfamous. You'll also see the transformation of Navajo weavings from the muted Phase I, when they used all natural dyes, through the bold Phase III, when German dyes predominated creating near-neon intensity. Above all, you'll get a sense of the importance of preserving ancient art, a fount from which contemporary Native Americans can always draw and the rest of us can learn. Admission, however, is restricted; see above for details.

Institute of American Indian Arts Museum

108 Cathedral Place. ☎ **505/988-6211.** Admission (2-day pass) $4 adults, $2 seniors and students, free for children 16 and under. Mon–Sat 10am–5pm, Sun noon–5pm.

A visit to this museum (the most comprehensive collection of contemporary Native American art in the world), offers a profound look into the lives of a people trapped between two worlds: traditional and contemporary. Here, you'll see cutting-edge art that pushes the limits of many media, from creative writing to textile manufacturing to painting. One young artist says in a video, "I feel like if I see one more warrior riding off into the sunset, I'm going to throw up." Rather than clichéd images, you are more likely to see a series of clay canteens demonstrating the evolution of an art form from traditional and utilitarian (spherical shape) to a creative concept (tubular). Much of the work originates from artists from The Institute of American Indian Arts (IAIA), the nation's only congressionally chartered institute of higher education devoted solely to the study and practice of the artistic and cultural traditions of all American Indian and Alaska native peoples.

Exhibits change periodically. Two upcoming shows include "Native American Quilts" and "Savage Truths," work from some young artists bent on attacking the status quo. The museum store has a broad collection of contemporary jewelry, pottery, and other crafts, as well as books and cards.

✪ Museum of Indian Arts and Culture

710 Camino Lejo. ☎ **505/827-6344.** Admission $5 adults, free for children 16 and under. Tues–Sun 10am–5pm.

A new interactive permanent exhibit here has made this one of the most exciting Native American museum experiences in the Southwest. "Here, Now and Always" takes visitors through thousands of years of Native American history. More than 70,000 pieces of basketry, pottery, clothing, carpets, and jewelry—much of it quite old—are on continual rotating display. You begin in the new exhibit by entering through a tunnel that symbolizes the *sipapu,* the Anasazi entrance into the upper worlds; you are greeted by the sounds of trickling water, drums, and Native American music. Videos show Native Americans telling creation stories. The rest of the exhibit is just as innovatively presented. The exhibit allows visitors to reflect on the lives of modern-day Native Americans by juxtaposing a traditional Pueblo kitchen with a modern kitchen. You can step into a Navajo hogan and stroll through a trading post. The rest of the museum houses a lovely pottery collection as well as changing exhibits. There's always a contemporary show.

Look for demonstrations of traditional skills by tribal artisans and regular programs in a 70-seat multimedia theater. Call for information on year-round lectures and classes on native traditions and arts, as well as regular performances of Native American music and dancing by tribal groups. In February, look for an annual fiber show, and in June, a presentation on oral traditions.

The laboratory, founded in 1931 by John D. Rockefeller, Jr., is itself a point of interest. Designed by the well-known Santa Fe architect John Gaw Meem, it is an exquisite example of Pueblo Revival architecture.

✪ Museum of International Folk Art

706 Camino Lejo. ☎ **505/827-6350.** Admission $5 adults, free for children under 17. Wed free for seniors. ($10 for 5-museum pass available.) Tues–Sun 10am–5pm. The museum is located about 2 miles south of the Plaza, in the Sangre de Cristo foothills. Drive southeast on Old Santa Fe Trail, which becomes Old Pecos Trail, and look for signs pointing left onto Camino Lejo.

This branch of the Museum of New Mexico may not seem quite as typically Southwestern as other Santa Fe museums, but it's the largest of its kind in the world. With a collection of some 130,000 objects from more than 100 countries, it's my favorite city museum. It was founded in 1953 by the Chicago collector Florence Dibell Bartlett, who said: "If peoples of different countries could have the opportunity to study each other's cultures, it would be one avenue for a closer understanding between men." That's the basis on which the museum operates today.

The special collections include Spanish colonial silver, traditional and contemporary New Mexican religious art, Mexican tribal costumes, Mexican majolica ceramics, Brazilian folk art, European glass, African sculptures, East Indian textiles, and the marvelous Morris Miniature Circus. Particularly delightful are numerous dioramas—all done with colorful miniatures—of people around the world at work and play in typical town, village, and home settings. Recent acquisitions include American weather vanes and quilts, Palestinian costume jewelry and amulets, and Bhutanese and Indonesian textiles.

Children love to look at the hundreds of toys on display throughout the museum. Many of them are housed in a wing built especially to hold part of a collection donated in 1982 by Alexander and Susan Girard. Alexander Girard, a notable architect and interior designer, and his wife, Susan, spent their lives traveling the world collecting dolls, animals, fabrics, masks, and dioramas. They had a

Fetishes: Gifts of Power

According to Zuni lore, in the early years of man's existence, the Sun sent down his two children to assist humans, who were under siege from earthly predators. The Sun's sons, as it were, shot lightning bolts from their shields and destroyed the predators. For generations, Zunis, traveling across their lands in western New Mexico, have found stones shaped like particular animals. The Zunis believe the stones to be the remains of those long-lost predators, still containing their soul or last breath.

Today, in many shops in Santa Fe you too can pick up a carved animal figure, called a fetish. According to belief, the owner of the fetish is able to absorb the power of that creature, whatever it may be. Many fetishes were long ago used for protection and might in the hunt. Today, people own fetishes for many reasons. One might carry a bear for health and strength, or an eagle for keen perspective. A mole might be placed in a home's foundation for protection from elements underground, a frog buried with crops for fertility and rain, a ram carried in the purse for prosperity. For love, some locals recommend pairs of fetishes—often foxes or coyotes carved from a single piece of stone.

Many fetishes, arranged with bundles on top and attached with sinew, serve as an offering to the animal spirit that resides within the stone. Fetishes are still carved by many of the pueblos. Shop around for a little while until you begin to appreciate the difference between clumsily carved ones and more gracefully executed ones. A good fetish is not necessarily one that is meticulously carved. Some fetishes are barely carved at all, since the original shape of the stone already contains the form of the animal. Once you have a sense of the quality and elegance available, decide which animal (and power) suits you best. Native Americans caution, however, that the fetish cannot be expected to impart an attribute you don't already possess. Instead, it will help elicit the power that already resides within you. Good sources for fetishes are **Dewey Galleries Limited,** 53 Old Santa Fe Trail, 2nd floor (on the Plaza; ☎ 505/982-8632); **Keshi,** 227 Don Gaspar (☎ 505/989-8728); and **Morning Star Gallery,** 513 Canyon Rd. (☎ 505/982-8187).

home in Santa Fe, where they spent many years before they died. Their donation included over 100,000 pieces, 10,000 of which are exhibited at the museum.

The Hispanic Heritage Wing houses the country's finest collection of Spanish colonial and Hispanic folk art. Folk-art demonstrations, performances, and workshops are often presented here. The 80,000-square-foot museum also has a lecture room, a research library, and a gift shop where a variety of folk art is available for purchase.

Wheelwright Museum of the American Indian

704 Camino Lejo. ☎ **800/607-4636** or 505/982-4636. Donations appreciated. Mon–Sat 10am–5pm, Sun 1–5pm. Closed Jan 1, Thanksgiving, Dec 25.

Next door to the Folk Art, this museum offers an esoteric collection of living arts of all Native American cultures. The building resembles a Navajo hogan, with its doorway facing east (toward the rising sun) and its ceiling formed in the interlocking "whirling log" style. It was founded in 1937 by Boston scholar Mary Cabot Wheelwright in collaboration with a Navajo medicine man, Hastiin Klah, to preserve and document Navajo ritual beliefs and practices. Klah took the designs of sand paintings used in healing ceremonies and adapted them into the woven pictographs that are a major part of the museum's treasure. In 1976, the museum's focus was altered to include the living arts of all Native American cultures. The museum offers three to four exhibits per year. You may see a basketry exhibit or mixed-media Navajo toys, or amazing contemporary Navajo rugs. An added treat here is the Case Trading Post, an arts-and-crafts shop built to resemble the typical turn-of-the-century trading post found on the Navajo reservation, with vigas and a squeaky wood floor. Whole cases are devoted to a particular artist's work, so you get a sense of the scope of a silversmith's work or whimsical nature of a wood carver's. Many pieces are reasonably priced. Storyteller Joe Hayes holds the attention of listeners outside a tepee at dusk on certain days in July and August. The museum has excellent access for people with disabilities.

CHURCHES

Cristo Rey
Upper Canyon Rd., at Camino Cabra. ☎ **505/983-8528.** Free admission. Open most days, but call for hours.

This Catholic church ("Christ the King" in Spanish), a huge adobe structure, was built in 1940 to commemorate the 400th anniversary of Coronado's exploration of the Southwest. Parishioners did most of the construction work, even making adobe bricks from the earth where the church stands. The local architect John Gaw Meem designed the building, in missionary style, as a place to keep some magnificent stone *reredos* (altar screens) created by the Spanish during the colonial era and recovered and restored in the 20th century.

✪ Loretto Chapel Museum
207 Old Santa Fe Trail (between Alameda and Water sts.). ☎ **505/984-7971.** Admission $2 adults, $1 children 7–13, free for children 6 and under. Mon–Sat 9:30am–4:30pm, Sun 10:30am–4:30pm.

Though no longer consecrated for worship, the Loretto Chapel is an important site in Santa Fe. Patterned after the famous Sainte-Chapelle church in Paris, it was constructed in 1873—by the same French architects and Italian masons who were building Archbishop Lamy's cathedral—as a chapel for the Sisters of Loretto, who had established a school for young women in Santa Fe in 1852.

The chapel is especially notable for its remarkable spiral staircase: It makes two complete 360° turns with no central or other visible support! (A railing was added later.) The structure is steeped in legend. The building was nearly finished in 1878 when workers realized the stairs to the choir loft wouldn't fit. Hoping for a solution more attractive than a ladder, the sisters made a novena to St. Joseph—and were rewarded when a mysterious carpenter appeared astride a donkey and offered to build a staircase. Armed with only a saw, a hammer, and a T-square, the master constructed this work of genius by soaking slats of wood in tubs of water to curve them and holding them together with wooden pegs. Then he disappeared without bothering to collect his fee.

Mission of San Miguel
401 Old Santa Fe Trail (at E. De Vargas St.). ☎ **505/983-3974.** Admission $1 for adults, free for children 6 and under. Mon–Sat 10am–4pm, Sun 2:30–4:30pm. Summer hours start earlier. Mass daily at 5pm.

If you really want to get the feel of colonial Catholicism, visit this church. Better yet, attend Mass here. You won't be disappointed. Built in 1610, the church has massive adobe walls, high windows, an elegant altar screen (erected in 1798) and a 780-pound San José Bell (now found inside), which was cast in Spain in 1356. If that doesn't impress you, perhaps the buffalo hide and deerskin Bible paintings used in 1630 by Franciscan Missionaries to teach the Native Americans will. Anthropologists have excavated near the altar, down to the original floor that some claim to be part of a 12th-century pueblo. A small store just off the sanctuary sells religious articles.

Santuario de Nuestra Señora de Guadalupe

100 S. Guadalupe St. ☎ **505/988-2027.** Donations appreciated. Mon–Sat 9am–4pm. Closed weekends Nov–Apr.

At press time, this church with poetic lines and a chimerical history is embroiled in controversy. The Archdiocese of Santa Fe has asked the Guadalupe Historic Foundation—which renovated the *santuario* and now leases it from the archdiocese as a community building—to voluntarily terminate its lease so that the sanctuary may be used as a place of perpetual adoration. At least one priest and a few parishioners didn't approve of the space being used for chamber music concerts, flamenco dance programs, dramas, lectures, and art shows. After some conflict, during which the priest was fired from his post, the Foundation complied.

Built between 1795 and 1800 at the end of El Camino Real by Franciscan missionaries, this is believed to be the oldest shrine in the United States honoring the Virgin of Guadalupe, the patron saint of Mexico. Better known as Santuario de Guadalupe, the shrine's adobe walls are almost 3-feet thick, and the deep-red plaster wall behind the altar was dyed with oxblood in traditional fashion when the church was restored earlier in this century.

It is well worth a visit to see photographs of the transformation of the building over time; its styles have ranged from flat-topped Pueblo to New England town meeting and today's Northern New Mexico style. On one wall is a famous oil painting, *Our Lady of Guadalupe,* created in 1783 by the renowned Mexican artist José de Alzibar. Painted expressly for this church, it was brought from Mexico City by mule caravan.

PARKS & REFUGES

Arroyo de los Chamisos Trail

Begin at Santa Fe High School on Yucca St. or on Rodeo Rd. near Sam's Club. ☎ **505/473-7228.**

This trail, which meanders through the southwestern part of town, is of special interest to those staying in hotels along Cerrillos Road. The new 2.5-mile paved path follows a chamisa-lined *arroyo* (stream) and has mountain views. Great for walking or bicycling; dogs must be kept on a leash.

Old Fort Marcy Park

617 Paseo de Peralta (also access it by traveling 3 blocks up Artist Rd. and turning right).

Marking the 1846 site of the first U.S. military reservation in the Southwest, this park overlooks the northeast corner of downtown. Only a few mounds remain from the fort, but the Cross of the Martyrs, at the top of a winding brick walkway from Paseo de Peralta near Otero Street, is a popular spot for bird's-eye photographs. The cross was erected in 1920 by the Knights of Columbus and the Historical Society of New Mexico to commemorate the Franciscans killed during the Pueblo Rebellion of 1680. It has since played a role in numerous religious processions. Open daily 24 hours.

Greater Santa Fe

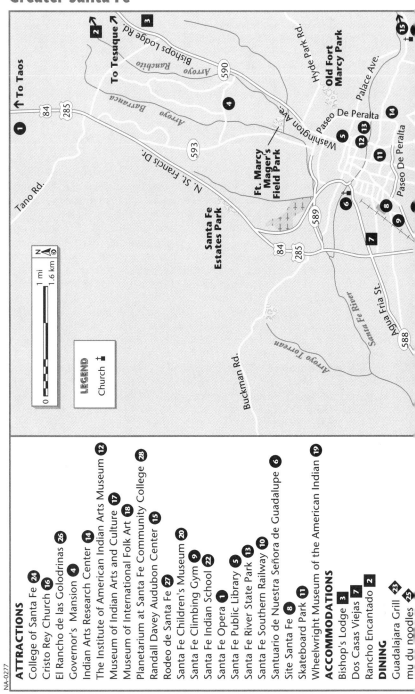

ATTRACTIONS
College of Santa Fe 24
Cristo Rey Church 16
El Rancho de las Golodrinas 26
Governor's Mansion 4
Indian Arts Research Center 14
The Institute of American Indian Arts Museum 12
Museum of Indian Arts and Culture 17
Museum of International Folk Art 18
Planetarium at Santa Fe Community College 28
Randall Davey Audubon Center 15
Rodeo de Santa Fe 27
Santa Fe Children's Museum 20
Santa Fe Climbing Gym 9
Santa Fe Indian School 22
Santa Fe Opera 1
Santa Fe Public Library 5
Santa Fe River State Park 13
Santa Fe Southern Railway 10
Santuario de Nuestra Señora de Guadalupe 6
Site Santa Fe 8
Skateboard Park 11
Wheelwright Museum of the American Indian 19

ACCOMMODATIONS
Bishop's Lodge 3
Dos Casas Viejas 7
Rancho Encantado 2

DINING
Guadalajara Grill 23
mu du noodles 25

NA-0277

112

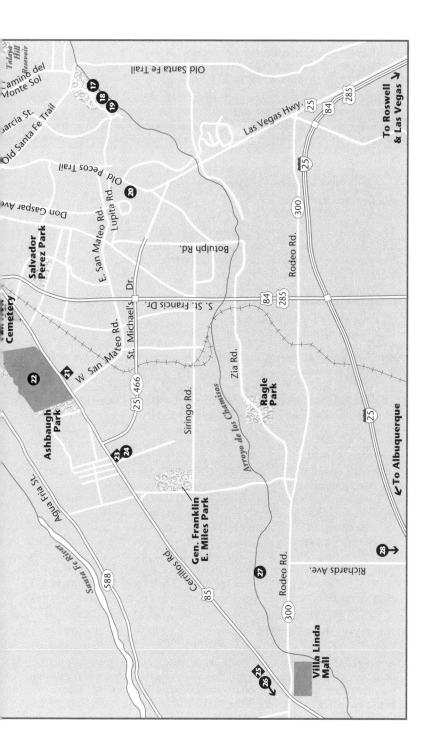

Randall Davey Audubon Center

Upper Canyon Rd. ☎ **505/983-4609.** Trail admission $1. Daily 9am–5pm. House tours conducted sporadically during the summer for $3 per person; call for hours.

Named for the late Santa Fe artist who willed his home to the National Audubon Society, this wildlife refuge occupies 135 acres at the mouth of Santa Fe Canyon. Just a few minutes' drive from the Plaza, it's an excellent escape. More than 100 species of birds and 120 types of plants live here, and varied mammals have been spotted—including black bears, mule deer, mountain lions, bobcats, raccoons, and coyotes. Trails winding through more than 100 acres of the nature sanctuary are open to day hikers, but not to dogs. There's also a natural-history bookstore on site.

Santa Fe River Park

Alameda St. ☎ **505/473-7236.**

This is a lovely spot for an early morning jog, a midday walk beneath the trees, or perhaps a sack lunch at a picnic table. The green strip, which does not close, follows the midtown stream for about 4 miles as it meanders along the Alameda from St. Francis Drive upstream beyond Camino Cabra, near its source.

OTHER ATTRACTIONS

✪ El Rancho de las Golondrinas

334 Los Pinos Rd. ☎ **505/471-2261.** Admission $4 adults, $3 seniors and teens, $1.50 children 5–12, free for children under 5. Festival weekends $6 adults, $4 seniors and teens, $2.50 children 5–12. June–Sept Wed–Sun 10am–4pm; Apr–May and Oct, open by advance arrangement. Closed Nov–Mar.

This 200-acre ranch, about 15 miles south of the Santa Fe Plaza via I-25 (take exit 276), was once the last stopping place on the 1,000-mile El Camino Real from Mexico City to Santa Fe. Today, it's a living 18th- and 19th-century Spanish village, comprising a hacienda, a village store, a schoolhouse, and several chapels and kitchens. There's also a working molasses mill, wheelwright and blacksmith shops, shearing and weaving rooms, a threshing ground, a winery and vineyard, and four water mills, as well as dozens of farm animals. A walk around the entire property is 1¾ miles in length.

The Spring Festival (the first weekend of June) and the Harvest Festival (the first weekend of October) are the year's highlights at Las Golondrinas ("The Swallows"). On these festival Sundays the museum opens with a procession and mass dedicated to San Ysidro, patron saint of farmers. Other festivals and theme weekends are held throughout the year. Volunteers in authentic costume demonstrate shearing, spinning, weaving, embroidery, wood carving, grain milling, blacksmithing, tinsmithing, soap making, and other activities. There's an exciting atmosphere of Spanish folk dancing, music, theater, and food. When driving from Albuquerque, the exit is no. 276B.

Roundhouse (State Capitol)

Paseo de Peralta and Old Santa Fe Trail. ☎ **505/986-4589.**

Some are surprised to learn that this is the only round capitol building in America. Built in 1966, it's designed in the shape of a Zia Pueblo emblem (or sun sign, which is also the state symbol). It symbolizes the Circle of Life: four winds, four seasons, four directions, and four sacred obligations. Surrounding the capitol is a lush 6½-acre garden boasting more than 100 varieties of plants, including roses, plums, almonds, nectarines, Russian olive trees, and sequoias. Benches and sculptures (by notable artists) have been placed around the grounds for the enjoyment of visitors.

Inside you'll find standard functional offices. The walls are hung with New Mexican art. Call the number above for information for tours.

Santa Fe Southern Railway

410 S. Guadalupe St. ☎ **888/929-8600** or 505/989-8600. Fax 505/983-7620. Tickets range from $5 for children to $21 for adults; $45 for Friday sunset ride includes dinner (May through Oct). Depending on the season, trains depart the Santa Fe Depot on various days (call to check) at 10:30am and return by 3pm. The sunset ride departs a half hour before sunset and returns 4 hours later.

"Riding the old Santa Fe" always referred to riding the Atchison, Topeka & Santa Fe Railroad. Ironically, the main route of the AT&SF bypassed Santa Fe, which probably forestalled some development for the capital city. Still, a spur was run off the main line to Santa Fe in 1880, and today, an 18-mile ride along that spur offers views of some of New Mexico's most spectacular scenery and a glimpse of railroad history.

The Santa Fe Depot is a well-preserved tribute to the Mission architecture that the railroad brought to the West in the early 1900s. Characterized by light-colored stuccoed walls, arched openings, and tile roofs, this style was part of an architectural revolution in Santa Fe at a time that builders snubbed the traditional Pueblo style. Standing on the brick platform, you'll hear a bell ring and a whistle blow; the train is ready to roll.

Inside the restored coach, passengers are surrounded by aged mahogany and faded velvet seats. The train snakes through crowded Santa Fe intersections onto the New Mexico plains, broad landscapes spotted with piñon and chamisa, with views of the Sandia and Ortiz mountains. Arriving in the small track town of Lamy, you get another glimpse of a Mission-style station, this one surrounded by spacious lawns where passengers picnic. Others choose to eat new American food at the historic Legal Tender Restaurant. Friday night, May through October, passengers can take an evening train and watch bold New Mexico sunsets while eating a buffet prepared by a local caterer. There's live music at a campfire during layover where coffee and dessert are served. There's also a cash bar selling beer, wine, and margaritas. Recently, they've added specialty trains at various times during the year, including a Santa Train, Halloween Mystery Train, Romantic Valentines Day Train, and Rodeo Train.

COOKING, ART & PHOTOGRAPHY CLASSES

If you are looking for something to do that's a little off the beaten tourist path, you might consider taking a class.

You can master the flavors of Santa Fe with an entertaining 3-hour demonstration cooking class at the ✪ **Santa Fe School of Cooking and Market,** on the upper level of the Plaza Mercado, 116 W. San Francisco St. (☎ **505/983-4511;** fax 505/983-7540). The class teaches about the flavors and history of traditional New Mexican and contemporary Southwestern cuisines. "Cooking Light" classes are offered for those who prefer to cook with less fat. Prices range from $35 to $60 and include a meal; call for a class schedule. The adjoining market offers a variety of regional foods and cookbooks, with gift baskets available.

If Southwestern art has you hooked, you can take a drawing and painting class led by Santa Fe artist Jane Shoenfeld. Students sketch such outdoor subjects as the Santa Fe landscape and adobe architecture. In case of inclement weather, classes are held in the studio. Each class lasts for 3 hours, and art materials are included in the fee, which ranges from $68 to $95. All levels of experience are welcome. Children's classes can be arranged. Contact Jane at **Sketching Santa Fe,** P.O. Box 5912,

Santa Fe, NM 87502 (☎ **505/986-1108;** fax 505/986-3845. www.Sfol. com.shoenfeld). Shoenfeld also holds 5-day workshops in Abiquiu at the Ghost Ranch. Call or refer to her Web page for dates.

Some of the world's most outstanding photographers convene in Santa Fe at various times during the year for the **Santa Fe Photography & Digital Workshops,** P.O. Box 9916, Santa Fe, 87504-5916, at a delightful campus in the hills on the east side of town (☎ **505/983-1400.** www.sfworkshop.com. E-mail:sfworkkshop@ aol.com). Most courses are full-time, lasting a week; however, others are shorter. I took one from the *National Geographic* photographer Michael "Nick" Nichols and greatly advanced my work. Courses range from Nevada Wier's Travel Photography class to Sam Abell's Project Workshop, in which photographers with ongoing projects work to find cohesion. Best of all, the teachers hold free slide lectures each Wednesday night at 8pm. Call for specific dates and prices. These courses aren't cheap, but they're worth it. Most include food and lodging packages.

WINE TASTINGS

If you enjoy sampling regional wines, consider visiting the wineries within easy driving distance of Santa Fe: **Balagna Winery/Il Santo Cellars,** 223 Rio Bravo Dr., in Los Alamos (☎ **505/672-3678**), north on US 84/285 and then west on NM 502; **Santa Fe Vineyards** (Route 1, Box 216A), about 20 miles north of Santa Fe on US 84/285 (☎ **505/753-8100**); **Madison Vineyards & Winery,** in Ribera (☎ **505/421-8028**), about 45 miles east of Santa Fe on I-25 North; and the Black Mesa Winery, 1502 NM 68, in Velarde (☎ **800/852-6372**), north on US 84/285 to NM 68.

Be sure to call in advance to find out when the wineries are open for tastings and to get specific directions.

3 Especially for Kids

Don't miss taking the kids to the **Museum of International Folk Art,** where they'll love the international dioramas and the toys (discussed earlier in this chapter). Also visit the tepee at the **Wheelwright Museum of the American Indian** (discussed earlier in this chapter), where storyteller Joe Hayes spins traditional Spanish *cuentos,* Native American folk tales, and Wild West tall tales on weekend evenings. **Bishop's Lodge** and **Rancho Encantado** both have extensive children's programs during the summer. These include horseback riding, swimming, arts-and-crafts programs, as well as special activities such as archery and tennis. Kids are sure to enjoy ✪ **El Rancho de las Golondrinas** (discussed above), a 200-acre ranch 15 miles south of Santa Fe, today a living 18th- and 19th-century Spanish village comprising a hacienda, a village store, a schoolhouse, and several chapels and kitchens.

Aerial's Gym
720 St. Michaels Dr. (near St. Francis) ☎ **505/424-6741.**

This gym provides kids with a fun adventure while allowing parents time to explore Santa Fe. In a huge air-conditioned space, kids can play on tumbling mats, balance beams, and bars. They can swirl their hands on a sand table and slide on a zip line. The "Parent's Night Out" program is on Friday and Saturday nights from 6 to 10pm; it costs $6 per hour. The gym has a summer program every afternoon from noon to 4pm, Monday to Friday. Kids ages 4 and up can do gymnastics, art projects, play games, and eat a snack for $20/day, or $85/week. Weekday mornings from 8:30am to noon there's a similar program for 2 to 4 year olds at the same price.

Be sure to make advance reservations. Regular gymnastics classes are also available; call for times.

Planetarium at Santa Fe Community College

6401 Richards Ave. (south of Rodeo Rd.). ☎ **505/428-1677** or 505/428-1777 for the information line. Admission $3.50 adults, $2 seniors and children 12 and under. Wed adult and family show 7–8pm; Sat children's show 10:30–11:30am; Celestial Highlights, a live program mapping the night sky for that particular month, is on the first Thurs of the month from 7–8pm.

The Planetarium offers imaginative programs, combining star shows with storytelling and other interactive techniques. Some of the titles reveal the inventiveness of the programs: Rusty Rocket's Last Blast, in which kids launch a model rocket; Planet Patrol; and the Solar System Stakeout, in which kids build a solar system. There's also a 10-minute segment on the current night sky. Programs vary, from those designed for preschoolers to ones for high school kids.

Rockin' Rollers Event Arena

2915 Agua Fría St. ☎ **505/473-7755.**

This roller rink offers public-skating sessions and lessons as well as rentals. There's a concession area where kids can get snacks. It's open at odd times, so call first. Admission is $3; rentals are just 50¢. Roller blades are allowed.

Rodeo de Santa Fe

2801 Rodeo Rd. ☎ **505/471-4300.**

The rodeo is held annually the weekend following the Fourth of July. It is a colorful and fun Southwestern event for kids, teens, and adults. (See "Northern New Mexico Calendar of Events" in chapter 2 for details.)

Santa Fe Children's Museum

1050 Old Pecos Trail. ☎ **505/989-8359.** www.sfchildmuseum.org. Admission $3 adults, $2 children under 12. Thurs and Sat 10am–5pm, Fri 9am–5pm, Sun noon–5pm. June–Aug, also open Wed 10am–5pm.

Designed for the whole family to experience, this museum offers interactive exhibits and hands-on activities in the arts, humanities, science, and technology. Most notable is a 16-foot climbing wall that kids—outfitted with helmets and harnesses—can scale. Special performances and hands-on sessions with artists and scientists are regularly scheduled. Recently *Family Life* magazine named this as one of the 10 hottest children's museums in the nation.

Santa Fe Climbing Gym

825 Early St. ☎ **505/986-8944.**

The walls and ceiling of this 2-story, cavernous gym are covered with foot and hand holds. A number of programs appeal to kids. Year-round, you'll find "Kid's Climb," supervised indoor climbing for ages 7 to 14. It takes place Friday afternoons and Saturday mornings from September through May and on Saturday mornings during the summer. The cost of $15 to $20 includes instruction, activities, and equipment. No experience is needed, but reservations are a must. In summer, there is also Kids's Rock, a fully supervised outdoor climbing experience in which transportation and equipment are included in the price of $65 to $75. Kids ages 7 and up can attend. In summer, group instruction is also available on Tuesday evenings. These are small classes, good for beginners and younger kids.

Santa Fe Public Library

145 Washington Ave. ☎ **505/984-6780.** Mon–Thurs 10am–9pm, Fri and Sat 10am–6pm, Sun 1–5pm. Call for additional information.

Special programs, such as storytelling and magic shows, can be found here weekly. The library is located in the center of town, 1 block from the Plaza. Call for additional information.

Skateboard Park

De Vargas St. ☎ **505/473-7236** or 505/438-1485. Free admission. Open 24 hours.

Split-level ramps for daredevils, park benches for onlookers, and climbing structures for youngsters are located at this park near downtown.

4 Santa Fe Strolls

Santa Fe, with its intricate streets and resonant historical architecture, lends itself to walking. The city's downtown core extends only a few blocks in any direction from the Plaza, and the ancient Barrio de Analco and the Canyon Road artists' colony are a mere stone's-throw away.

WALKING TOUR 1
The Plaza Area

Start: The Plaza.
Finish: Loretto Chapel.
Time: 1 to 5 hours, depending on the length of visits to the museums and churches.
Best Times: Any morning after breakfast (before the afternoon heat), but after the Native American traders have spread out their wares.

1. **The Plaza.** This square has been the heart and soul of Santa Fe, as well as its literal center, since its concurrent establishment with the city in 1610. Originally designed as a meeting place, it has been the site of innumerable festivals and other historical, cultural, and social events. Long ago the Plaza was a dusty hive of activity as the staging ground and terminus of the Santa Fe Trail. Today, those who congregate around the central fountain enjoy the best people-watching in New Mexico. Santa Feans understandably feel nostalgic for the days when the Plaza, now the hub of the tourist trade, still belonged to locals rather than outside commercial interests.

   Facing the Plaza on its north side is the:

2. **Palace of the Governors.** Today, the flagship of the New Mexico State Museum system (see "The Top Attractions," above), the Palace has functioned continually as a public building since it was erected in 1610 as the capitol of Nuevo Mexico. Every day, Native American artisans spread out their crafts for sale beneath its portal.

   Even though you are just two stops into it, you might want to fortify your strength for the rest of the walk. I recommend the *carnitas* (fajitas—grilled meat and chile in a tortilla) or tamales from the street vendor immediately opposite the Palace, at Lincoln and Palace avenues, in front of the:

3. **Museum of Fine Arts.** With its renowned St. Francis Auditorium (see "The Top Attractions," above, and "The Performing Arts," in chapter 9), the museum holds works by Georgia O'Keeffe and other famed 20th-century Taos and Santa Fe artists. The building is a fine example of Pueblo Revival–style architecture.

   Virtually across the street is the:

4. **Delgado House,** 124 W. Palace Ave. This Victorian mansion is an excellent example of local adobe construction modified by late 19th-century architectural

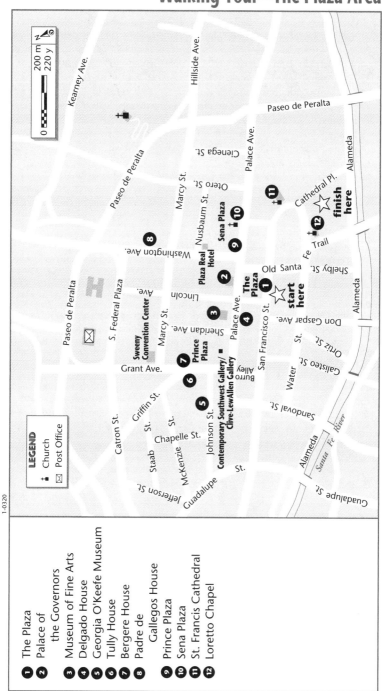

LEGEND
✝ Church
⊠ Post Office

1. The Plaza
2. Palace of
   the Governors
3. Museum of Fine Arts
4. Delgado House
5. Georgia O'Keefe Museum
6. Tully House
7. Bergere House
8. Padre de
   Gallegos House
9. Prince Plaza
10. Sena Plaza
11. St. Francis Cathedral
12. Loretto Chapel

1-0320

119

detail. It was built in 1890 by Felipe B. Delgado, a merchant most known for his business of running mule and ox freight trains over the Santa Fe Trail to Independence and the Camino Real to Chihuahua. The home remained in the Delgado family until 1970. It now belongs to the Historic Santa Fe Foundation.

If you continue west on Palace Avenue you'll come to two galleries worth perusing. The first is the **Contemporary Southwest Gallery,** where you'll find lots of vivid landscapes, but little that extends the limits of the genre. Next door, however, you'll come to **LewAllen Contemporary,** where you'll find an array of paintings, sculpture, ceramics, and work in other media that may indeed make you stop and ponder.

Nearby, you'll see a narrow lane—Burro Alley—jutting south toward San Francisco Street. You may want to head down the lane and peek into **Down and Outdoors** in Santa Fe, where you'll find a selection of comforters, pillows, outerwear, and fine sweaters. Head back to Palace and make your way north on Grant Street, turning left on Johnson Street to the:

5. **Georgia O'Keeffe Museum,** 217 Johnson St. Just opened in 1997, it houses the largest collection of O'Keeffe works in the world. The 10,000-square-foot space is the only museum in the United States dedicated solely to one woman's work.

Head back to Grant Street where you'll find the:

6. **Tully House,** 136 Grant Ave. Built in 1851 in Territorial style, this faux-brick adobe is unique because it has undergone no major exterior changes since its original nine rooms were constructed. It was built by a family of traders, most notably Pinckney R. Tully, who became a leading Confederate sympathizer during the Civil War.

Across the street is the:

7. **Bergere House,** 135 Grant Ave. Built around 1870, this house hosted U.S. president Ulysses S. Grant and his wife Julia during their 1880 visit to Santa Fe.

Proceed north on Grant, turning right on Marcy. On the north side of this corner is the **Sweeney Convention Center,** host of major exhibitions and home of the Santa Fe Convention and Visitors Bureau.

Three blocks farther east, through a residential, office, and restaurant district, turn left on Washington Avenue. A short distance along on your right, note the:

8. **Padre de Gallegos House,** 227–237 Washington Ave. The house was built in 1857 in the Territorial style. Padre de Gallegos was a priest who, in the eyes of newly arrived Archbishop Jean-Baptiste Lamy, kept too high a social profile and was therefore defrocked in 1852. Gallegos later represented the territory in Congress and eventually became the federal superintendent of Native American affairs.

Reverse course and turn south again on Washington Avenue, passing en route the public library and some handsomely renovated accommodations such as the Territorial Inn. This is a good time to stop for refreshments at a little cart in front of the Radisson Hotel and Suites on the Plaza; during summer, you'll find a variety of drinks served on the veranda, and in winter, the small bar inside can be quite cozy. When you leave there, you'll notice across the street the entrance to the Palace of the Governors archives. As you approach the Plaza, turn left (east) on Palace Avenue. A short distance farther on your left is:

9. **Prince Plaza,** 113 E. Palace Ave. A former governor's home, this Territorial-style structure, which now houses The Shed restaurant, had huge wooden gates to keep out tribal attacks.

Next door is:

Walking Tour—Barrio de Analco/Canyon Road

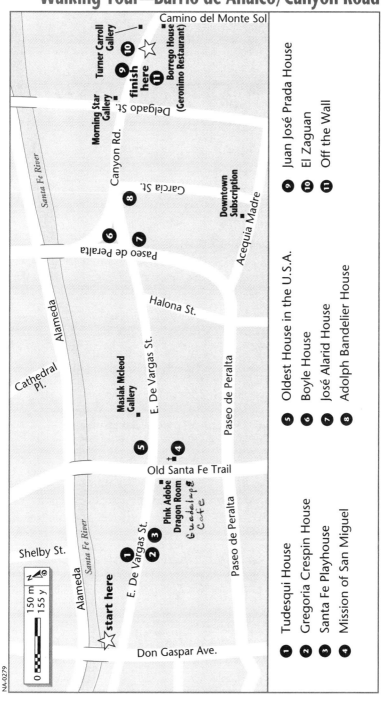

Camino del Monte Sol

Turner Carroll Gallery

finish here

Borrego House (Geronimo Restaurant)

Morning Star Gallery

Delgado St.

Canyon Rd.

Santa Fe River

Garcia St.

Downtown Subscription

Acequia Madre

Paseo de Peralta

Halona St.

Alameda

E. De Vargas St.

Cathedral Pl.

Maslak Mcleod Gallery

Paseo de Peralta

Old Santa Fe Trail

Santa Fe River

Pink Adobe Dragon Room

Guadalupe Cafe

Shelby St.

E. De Vargas St.

Alameda

start here

Don Gaspar Ave.

Paseo de Peralta

150 m
155 y
0

① Tudesqui House
② Gregoria Crespin House
③ Santa Fe Playhouse
④ Mission of San Miguel

⑤ Oldest House in the U.S.A.
⑥ Boyle House
⑦ José Alarid House
⑧ Adolph Bandelier House

⑨ Juan José Prada House
⑩ El Zaguan
⑪ Off the Wall

NA-0279

123

for centuries to irrigate gardens in the area. A 30- to 45-minute walk will bring you to **Downtown Subscription,** where you can have some excellent coffee and baked goods. From there, you can take Garcia Street north back to the base of Canyon Road.

5 Organized Tours

BUS, CAR & TRAM TOURS

Gray Line Tours
1330 Hickox St. ☎ **505/983-9491.**

The trolley-like Roadrunner departs several times daily in summer (less often in winter) from the La Fonda Hotel on the Plaza, beginning at 10am, for 1½-hour city tours. Buy tickets as you board. Daily tours to Taos, Chimayo, and Bandelier National Monument are also offered.

LorettoLine
At the Inn at Loretto, 211 Old Santa Fe Trail. ☎ **505/983-3701.**

For an open-air tour of the city, contact LorettoLine. Tours last 1½ hours and are offered daily from April to October. Tour times are every hour on the hour during the day from 10am to 3pm. Tickets are $9 for adults, $4 for children.

WALKING TOURS

As with the above independent strolls, these are the best way to get an appreciable feel for Santa Fe's history and culture.

A foot in Santa Fe
At the Inn at Loretto, 211 Old Santa Fe Trail. ☎ **505/983-3701.**

Personalized 2½-hour tours are offered twice daily (9:30am and 1:30pm) from the Inn at Loretto at a cost of $10. Reservations are not required.

Storytellers and the Southwest: A Literary Walking Tour
985 Agua Fría #110. ☎ **505/989-4561.** $10 per person; 2-person minimum.

Barbara Harrelson, a former Smithsonian museum docent and avid reader, takes you on a 2-hour literary walking tour of downtown, exploring the history, legends, characters, and authors of the region through its landmarks and historic sites. It's a great way to absorb the unique character of Santa Fe. Tours take place by appointment.

Walking Tour of Santa Fe
54½ East San Francisco St. (tour meets at 107 Washington Ave.) ☎ **800/338-6877** or 505/983-6565.

One of Santa Fe's best walking tours begins under the T-shirt tree at Tees & Skis, 107 Washington Ave., near the northeast corner of the Plaza (at 9:30am and 1:30pm) and lasts about 2½ hours. The tour costs $10 for adults. Children under 12 are free.

MISCELLANEOUS TOURS

Pathways Customized Tours
161-F Calle Ojo Feliz. ☎ **505/982-5382.** Tours range from $50–$200 per couple.

Don Dietz offers several planned tours, including a downtown Santa Fe walking tour, a full city tour, a trip to the cliff dwellings and native pueblos, a "Taos adventure," and a trip to Georgia O'Keeffe country (with a focus on the landscape that inspired the art now possible to view in the new O'Keeffe Museum). He will try to accommodate any special requests you might have. These tours last anywhere from 1½ to 9 hours, depending on the one you choose. Don has extensive knowledge of the area's culture, history, geology, and flora and fauna and will help you make the most of your precious vacation time.

Rain Parrish

704 Kathryn St. ☎ **505/984-8236.** Prices average approximately $125 per couple.

A Navajo (Diné) anthropologist, artist, and curator, offers custom guide services focusing on cultural anthropology, Native American arts, and the history of the Native Americans of the Southwest. Some of these are true adventures to insider locations. Ms. Parrish includes visits to local Pueblo villages.

Recursos de Santa Fe

826 Camino de Monte Rey. ☎ **505/982-9301.**

This organization is a full-service destination management company, emphasizing custom-designed itineraries to meet the interests of any group. They specialize in the archaeology, art, literature, spirituality, architecture, environment, food, and history of the Southwest. Call for a calendar and information about their annual writers' conferences.

Rojo Tours & Services, Inc.

P.O. Box 15744. 87506-5744 ☎ **505/474-8333.** Fax 505/474-2992.

Customized private tours are arranged to pueblos, cliff dwellings, and ruins, as well as art tours with studio visits.

Santa Fe Detours

107 Washington Ave. ☎ **800/338-6877** or 505/983-6565.

Santa Fe's most extensive tour-booking agency accommodates almost all travelers' tastes, from bus and rail tours to river rafting, backpacking, and cross-country skiing.

✪ Southwest Safaris

P.O. Box 945, Santa Fe, NM 87504. ☎ **800/842-4246** or 505/988-4246.

This tour is one of the most interesting Southwest experiences I've had. We flew in a small plane at 500 feet off the ground from Santa Fe to the Grand Canyon while experienced pilot Bruce Adams explained 300 million years of geologic history. We passed over the ancient ruins of Chaco Canyon and the vivid colors of the Painted Desert, as well as over many land formations on Navajo Nation land so remote they remain nameless. Then, of course, there was the spectacular Grand Canyon, where we landed for a Jeep tour and lunch on a canyon-side bench. Trips to many Southwest destinations are available, including Monument Valley, Mesa Verde, Canyon de Chelly, Arches/Canyonlands, as well as the ruins at Aztec, New Mexico. Recently, Adams has added local 1- and 2-hour scenic flights to places such as the Valle Grande, Acoma Pueblo, or following the canyons of the Rio Grande north. Prices range from $99 to $449.

6 Outdoor Activities

Note: In addition to all the activities and recreation centers listed below, there will be a new full-service family recreation center on the southside of Santa Fe by early to mid-1999. The complex will include a 50-meter pool, an ice-skating rink, three gyms, a workout room, racquetball courts, and an indoor running track. Contact the **Santa Fe Convention and Visitors Bureau** for more information.

BALLOONING   New Mexico is renowned for its spectacular Balloon Fiesta, which takes place annually in Albuquerque. If you want to take a ride, you'll probably have to go to Albuquerque or Taos, but you can book your trip in Santa Fe through **Santa Fe Detours,** 54½ East San Francisco St. (Tour desk for summer, 107 Washington Ave.) ☎ **800/338-6877** or 505/983-6565. Flights take place early in the day. Rates begin at around $135 a flight. If you've got your heart set on a balloon flight, I would suggest that you make your reservations early because flights are sometimes canceled due to bad weather. That way, if you have to reschedule, you'll have enough time to do so.

BIKING   You can cycle along main roadways and paved country roads year-round in Santa Fe, but be aware that traffic is particularly heavy around the Plaza, and all over town, motorists are not especially attentive to bicyclists, so you need to be especially alert. Mountain biking has exploded here and is especially popular in the spring, summer, and fall; the high-desert terrain is rugged and challenging, but mountain bikers of all levels can find exhilarating rides. The Santa Fe Convention and Visitors Bureau can supply you with bike maps.

I recommend the following trails: West of Santa Fe, the **Caja del Rio** area has nice dirt roads and some light technical biking; **Bland Canyon** in the Jemez Mountains to the south near Cochiti Pueblo is an exciting ride with views and stream crossings; the **railroad tracks south of Santa Fe** provide wide-open biking on beginner to intermediate technical trails; and the **Borrego Trail** up toward the Santa Fe Ski Area is a very challenging technical ride.

In Santa Fe bookstores, look for *Mountain Biking in Northern New Mexico: Historical and Natural History Rides* by Craig Martin and *The New Mexican Mountain Bike Guide* by Brant Hayengand and Chris Shaw. Both are excellent guides to trails in Santa Fe, Taos, and Albuquerque. The books outline tours for beginner, intermediate, and advanced riders. **Palace Bike Rentals,** 409 E. Palace Ave. (☎ **505/986-0455**), rents high-quality regular mountain bikes for $15/half day and $20/full day (until sunset) or front-suspension bikes for $20/half day and $25/full day (until sunset). They also have multiple-day rates. Children's bikes are available, as are child seats and child trailers. **Sun Mountain Bike Company,** 121 Sandoval St. (☎ **505/820-2902**), rents quality front-suspension and full-suspension mountain bikes for $20 to $27/half day and $30 to $40/full day. Add $10 and they'll deliver to and pickup from your hotel. Weekly rentals can be arranged. Both shops supply accessories such as helmets, locks, water, maps, and trail information. My buddy Louie Gonzales, a native New Mexican, owns **Sun Mountain Bike Company,** listed above, and he recently began running bike tours from April through October to some of the most spectacular spots in Northern New Mexico. Trips range from an easy Glorieta Mesa tour to my favorite, the West Rim Trail, which snakes along the Taos Gorge, to the technical Glorieta Baldy, with prices from $60 to $109. All tours include bikes, transportation, and a New Mexican meal or snack.

FISHING   In the lakes and waterways around Santa Fe, anglers typically catch trout (there are five varieties in the area). Other local fish include bass, perch, and kokanee salmon. The most popular fishing holes are Cochiti and Abiquiu lakes as well as the Rio Chama, Pecos River, and the Rio Grande. A world-renowned fly-fishing destination, the **San Juan River,** near Farmington, is worth a visit and can make for an exciting 2-day trip in combination with a tour around **Chaco Culture National Historic Park** (see chapter 10). Check with the New Mexico Game and Fish Department (☎ **505/827-7911**) for information (including maps of area waters), licenses, and fishing proclamations. **High Desert Angler,** 435 S. Guadalupe St. (☎ **505/988-7688**), specializes in fly-fishing gear and guide services.

GOLF   There are three courses in the Santa Fe area: the 18-hole **Santa Fe Country Club,** on Airport Road (☎ **505/471-2626**); and the often-praised, 18-hole **Cochiti Lake Golf Course,** 5200 Cochiti Hwy., Cochiti Lake, about 35 miles southwest of Santa Fe via I-25 and NM 16 and 22 (☎ **505/465-2239**). A new 18-hole municipal course on the south side of Santa Fe will open sometime in 1998. For information, call the **City Recreation Department** (☎ **505/438-1485**). **Santa Fe Golf and Driving Range,** 4680 Wagon Rd. (☎ **505/474-4680**), is also open to the public throughout the year. They have 42 practice tees, golf merchandise, and rental clubs, and will provide instruction.

HIKING   It's hard to decide which of the 1,000 miles of nearby national forest trails to challenge. Four wilderness areas are especially attractive: **Pecos Wilderness,** with 223,000 acres east of Santa Fe; **Chama River Canyon Wilderness,** 50,300 acres west of Ghost Ranch Museum; **Dome Wilderness,** 5,200 acres of rugged canyonland adjacent to Bandelier National Monument; and **San Pedro Parks Wilderness,** 41,000 acres west of Los Alamos. Also visit the 58,000-acre **Jemez Mountain National Recreation Area.** Information on these and other wilderness areas is available from the **Santa Fe National Forest,** P.O. Box 1689 (NM 475), Santa Fe, NM 87504 (☎ **505/438-7840**). If you're looking for company on your trek, contact the Santa Fe branch of the **Sierra Club,** 621 Old Santa Fe Trail, Suite 10 (☎ **505/983-2703**). You can pick up a hiking schedule in the local newsletter outside the office. Some people enjoy taking a chairlift ride to the summit of the **Santa Fe Ski Area** (☎ **505/982-4429**) and hiking around up there in the spring and summer months. You might also consider purchasing *The Hiker's Guide to New Mexico* (Falcon Press Publishing Co., Inc.) by Laurence Parent; it outlines 70 hikes throughout the state. Another title, *75 Hikes in New Mexico* by Craig Martin (The Mountaineers, Publisher) is also fun and useful.

HORSEBACK RIDING   Trips ranging in length from a few hours to overnight can be arranged by **Santa Fe Detours,** 54½ East San Francisco St. (Summer tour desk, 107 Washington Ave. ☎ **800/338-6877** or 505/983-6565.) You'll ride with "experienced wranglers" and can even arrange a trip that includes a cookout or brunch. Rides are also major activities at two local guest ranches: **The Bishop's Lodge** and **Rancho Encantado** (see "Where to Stay in Santa Fe," in chapter 5). In addition, **Rocky Mountain Tours,** 217 W. Manhattan St., Santa Fe, NM 87501 (☎ **505/984-1684**), arranges escorted rides for individuals of all ability as well as families. Trips can run from 90 minutes to a full day. Special packages such as "Raft and Ride," and "Design Your Own Ride" are also available.

HUNTING   Mule, deer, and elk are taken by hunters in the Pecos Wilderness and Jemez Mountains, as are occasional black bears and bighorn sheep. Wild turkeys and grouse are frequently bagged in the uplands, geese and ducks at lower elevations. Check with the **New Mexico Game and Fish Department** (☎ **505/827-7911**) for information and licenses.

RIVER RAFTING & KAYAKING   Although Taos is the real rafting center of New Mexico, several companies serve Santa Fe during the April-to-October white-water season. They include **Southwest Wilderness Adventures,** P.O. Box 9380, Santa Fe, NM 87501 (☎ **800/869-7238** or 505/983-7262); **New Wave Rafting,** 103 E Water St. (upstairs; ☎ **800/984-1444** or 505/984-1444); and **Santa Fe**

Rafting Co., 1000 Cerrillos Rd. (☎ **800/467-RAFT** or 505/988-4914). You can expect the cost of a full-day trip to range from about $70 to $90 before tax and the 3% federal land use fee. The day of the week (weekdays are less expensive) and group size may also affect the price. The companies listed above each offer 2- and 3-day trips as well. If you're a kayaker or would like to become one, the center for the sport is **Wild River Sports,** 1303 Cerrillos Rd. (☎ **505/982-7040**). Owners Brian and Heather Dudney can set you up with rental equipment and an ACA-certified instructor, or sell you any gear you may need, as well as give you directions to the best boating spots in the area. Beginner lessons cost $45 for a 2-hour pool class, $185 for a pool/river class, and $245 for a more extensive pool/lake/river class. All prices include equipment and boat rental. Canoes, inflatable kayaks, paddles, life vests, flotation, helmets, and wet suits are all rentable here. First-timer classes take place each Tuesday night, except for a few months mid-winter. Call for location and times.

RUNNING   Despite its elevation, Santa Fe is popular with runners and hosts numerous competitions, including the annual **Old Santa Fe Trail Run** on Labor Day. Each Wednesday, Santa Fe runners gather at 6pm at the Plaza and set out on foot for runs in the surrounding area. This is a great opportunity for travelers to find their way and to meet some locals. **Santa Fe Striders** (☎ 505/983-2144) sponsors various runs during the year. Call for information.

ROCK CLIMBING   During long winter evenings, while some go to the gym and pump iron, I like to go to **Santa Fe Climbing Gym,** 825 Early St. (☎ **505/986-8944**) and pump my own weight. Throughout the year there's open climbing nightly, though you do need to know how to climb and belay yourself, skills you can easily learn by taking an introductory class offered every week. Call for the particular day. On Sunday afternoons, the gym provides belays, a good way for a first-timer to check out the sport. There are also ongoing classes and clinics focusing on a variety of skills, from lead climbing to outdoor climbing. You can also hire a private outdoor guide. Adults $12 to $15 a day; introductory class $40; outdoor private $75 to $175. (See "Especially for Kids," above for Kids' programs and prices.)

SKIING   There's something available for every ability level at Ski Santa Fe, about 16 miles northeast of Santa Fe via Hyde Park (Ski Basin) Road. Lots of locals ski here, particularly on weekends; if you can, go on weekdays. It's a good family area and fairly small, so it's easy to split off from and later reconnect with your party. Built on the upper reaches of 12,000-foot Tesuque Peak, the area has an average annual snowfall of 225 inches and a vertical drop of 1,650 feet. Seven lifts, including a 5,000-foot triple chair and a new quad chair, serve 39 runs and 590 acres of terrain, with a total capacity of 7,800 riders an hour. Base facilities, at 10,350 feet, center around **La Casa Mall,** with a cafeteria, lounge, ski shop, and boutique. Another restaurant, Totemoff's, has a midmountain patio.

The ski area is open daily from 9am to 4pm; the season often runs from Thanksgiving to early April, depending on snow conditions. Rates for all lifts are $40 for adults, $27 for children and seniors, free for kids less than 46 inches tall (in their ski boots), and free for seniors 72 and older. For more information, contact **Ski Santa Fe,** 1210 Luisa St., Suite 5, Santa Fe, NM 87505 (☎ **505/982-4429**). For 24-hour reports on snow conditions, call ☎ **505/983-9155.** The **New Mexico Snow Phone** (☎ **505/984-0606**) gives statewide reports. Ski packages are available through **Santa Fe Central Reservations** (☎ **800/776-7669** outside New Mexico or 505/983-8200 within New Mexico).

Cross-country skiers find seemingly endless miles of snow to track in the **Santa Fe National Forest** (☎ 505/438-7840). A favorite place to start is at the Black Canyon campground, about 9 miles from downtown en route to the Santa Fe Ski Area. In the same area are the **Borrego Trail** (high intermediate) and the **Norski Trail,** 7 miles up from Black Canyon. Other popular activities at the ski area in winter include snowshoeing, snowboarding, sledding, and innertubing. Snowshoe and snowboard rentals are available at a number of downtown shops and the ski area.

SOARING   Soaring is available for those who don't believe the sky is the limit. There are two types of soaring. In one, you and the pilot are in a propless and motorless plane that generally seats only two people. A powered plane tows you up and you glide about catching updrafts to stay afloat for hours. In the other, the plane is equipped with a retractable prop. This allows you to take off without use of a tow plane. Once at altitude, the prop retracts, leaving you to glide. Either type allows for plenty of scenic viewing and the thrill of free birdlike flight. For information and rates, call **Santa Fe Soaring** (☎ **505/424-1928**).

SPAS   If traveling, skiing, or other activities have left you weary, a great place to treat your body and mind is **Ten Thousand Waves,** a Japanese-style health spa about 3 miles northeast of Santa Fe on Hyde Park Road (☎ **505/982-9304**). This serene retreat, nestled in a grove of piñon, offers hot tubs, saunas, and cold plunges, plus a variety of massage and other bodywork techniques. Bathing suits are optional in the 10-foot communal hot tub, where you can stay as long as you want for $13. Nine private hot tubs cost $18 to $25 an hour, with discounts for seniors and children. You can also arrange therapeutic massage, hot-oil massage, in-water watsu massage, herbal wraps, salt glows, and facials. New in 1996 were four treatment rooms that feature dry brush aromatherapy treatments and Ayurvedic treatments; a women's communal tub; and lodging at the **Houses of the Moon,** a six-room Japanese-style inn. The spa is open on Sunday, Monday, Wednesday, and Thursday from 10am to 9:30pm; Tuesday from 4:30 to 9:30pm; and Friday and Saturday from 10am to midnight (winter hours are shorter, so be sure to call). Reservations are recommended, especially on weekends.

Another option is a stay at a spa. **Vista Clara Ranch Resort and Spa** is still finding its way after recently opening 25 minutes south of Santa Fe, just outside Galisteo (☎ **888/663-9772** or 505/466-4772; www.vistaclara.com). This resort/ spa has a stunning setting and some fine amenities. In 1998, the new owner Kaye Sandford and her crew were busy rescuing the buildings from nature. Now, the 2-story structure, built in 1987, shows the gloss of a major renovation. Rooms are tastefully austere with wood floors, viga ceilings, and handcarved furniture. The baths are ample, all with tub/shower and pretty Mexican tile. The pool is large and ozone-cleaned as is the hot tub (with an amazing sunset view); the whole experience is odorless. Facilities include a large underground *kiva* where fitness classes take place, and a charming therapy center where guests can have a steam bath, sauna, massage, and body treatments such as masks and salt glows, as well as beauty treatments—even astrological readings. Guided nature hikes up to a stone dike covered with petroglyphs, art classes, and horseback riding occupy visitors' days. Best of all is the food. Three meals daily are prepared by Steven and Kirstin Jarret, light healthy food, what Kirstin calls ìrustic and sophisticated flavors of the Southwest and beyond. Spa packages are available for 5 nights, $1,380, and 7 nights, $1,950. Overnight lodging, spa treatments, and activities are also available on an à la carte basis.

SWIMMING   The City of Santa Fe operates four indoor pools and one outdoor pool. The pool closest to downtown is found at the **Fort Marcy Complex** (☎ **505/984-6725**) on Camino Santiago, off Bishop's Lodge Road. Admission to the pool is $1.25 for adults, $1 for students, and 50¢ for children 8 to 13. Call the Santa Fe Convention and Visitors Bureau for information about the other area pools.

TENNIS   Santa Fe has 44 public tennis courts and 4 major private facilities. The **City Recreation Department** (☎ **505/438-1485**) can help you locate indoor, outdoor, and lighted public courts.

7 Spectator Sports

HORSE RACING   The ponies generally run from Memorial Day through September at **The Downs at Santa Fe** (☎ **505/471-3311**), about 11 miles south of Santa Fe off US 85, near La Cienega. However, in 1997, San Ildefonso Pueblo purchased the track, and, at press time, there's rumor they will not open this year. Call to be sure. General admission if there are horses is free. A closed-circuit TV system shows instant replays of each race's final-stretch run and transmits out-of-state races for legal betting.

RODEO   The Rodeo de Santa Fe, 2801 Rodeo Rd. (☎ **505/471-4300**), is held annually the weekend following the Fourth of July. (See "Northern New Mexico Calendar of Events," in chapter 2, for details.)

Santa Fe Shopping

8

Each time I head out to shop in Northern New Mexico I'm amazed by the treasures in the forms of handcrafts, art, and artifacts that I find. There's a broad range of work, from very traditional Native American crafts and Hispanic folk art to extremely innovative contemporary work. The cultures here are so alive and changing, the work transforms constantly, with traditional themes always at the heart of it. Some call Santa Fe one of the top art markets in the world, and it's no wonder. Galleries speckle the downtown area, and as an artists' thoroughfare, Canyon Road is preeminent. Still, the greatest concentration of Native American crafts is displayed beneath the portal of the Palace of the Governors. Any serious arts aficionado should try to attend one or more of the city's great arts festivals—the Spring Festival of the Arts in May, the Spanish Market in July, the Indian Market in August, and the Fall Festival of the Arts in October.

1 The Shopping Scene

Few visitors to Santa Fe leave the city without acquiring at least one item from the Native American artisans at the Palace of the Governors. When you are thinking of making such a purchase, keep the following pointers in mind:

Silver jewelry should have a harmony of design, clean lines, and neatly executed soldering. Navajo jewelry typically features large stones, with designs shaped around the stone. Zuni jewelry usually has patterns of small or inlaid stones. Hopi jewelry rarely uses stones; it usually has a motif incised into the top layer of silver and darkened.

Turquoise of a deeper color is usually higher quality, so long as it hasn't been color treated (undesirable because the process adds false color to the stone). Often, turquoise is "stabilized," which means it is soaked in resin, and then the resin is baked into the stone. This makes the stone less fragile, but also prevents it from changing color with age and contact with body oils. Many people find the aging effect desirable. Beware of "reconstituted turquoise." In this process the stone is disassembled and reassembled; it usually has a uniformly blue color that looks very unnatural.

Pottery is traditionally hand-coiled and of natural clay, not thrown on a potter's wheel using commercial clay. It is hand-polished with a stone, hand-painted, and fired in an outdoor oven (usually an open firepit) rather than an electric kiln. Look for an even shape; clean, accurate painting; a high polish (if it is a polished piece); and an artist's signature.

Navajo rugs are appraised according to tightness and evenness of weave, symmetry of design, and whether natural (preferred) or commercial dyes have been used.

Kachina dolls are more highly valued according to the detail of their carving: fingers, toes, muscles, rib cages, feathers, etc. Elaborate costumes are also desirable. Oil staining is preferred to the use of bright acrylic paints.

Sand paintings should display clean, narrow lines, even colors, balance, an intricacy of design, and smooth craftsmanship.

Local museums, particularly the Wheelwright Museum and the Institute of American Indian Art, can provide a good orientation to contemporary craftsmanship.

Contemporary artists are mainly painters, sculptors, ceramists, and fiber artists, including weavers. Peruse one of the outstanding **gallery catalogs** for an introduction to local dealers—*The Collector's Guide to Santa Fe and Taos* by Wingspread Incorporated (P.O. Box 13566-L, Albuquerque, NM 87192), *The Santa Fe Catalogue* by Modell Associates (P.O. Box 1007, Aspen, CO 81612), or *Performance de Santa Fe* by Cynthia Stearns (P.O. Box 8932, Santa Fe, NM 87504-8932). They're widely available at shops or can be ordered directly from the publishers. For a current listing of gallery openings, with recommendations on which ones to attend, purchase a copy of the monthly magazine the *Santa Fean* by Santa Fean, LLC (444 Galisteo, Santa Fe, NM 87501).

Business hours vary quite a bit among establishments, but most are open at least Monday through Friday from 10am to 5pm, with mall stores open until 8 or 9pm. Most shops are open similar hours on Saturday, and many also open on Sunday afternoon during the summer. Winter hours tend to be more limited.

After the high-rolling 1980s, during which art markets around the country soared, came the penny-pinching 1990s. Many galleries in Santa Fe were forced to shut their doors. Those that remained tended to specialize in particular types of art, a refinement process that has improved the gallery scene here. Still, some worry that the lack of serious art buyers in the area leads to fewer good galleries and more T-shirt and trinket stores. The Plaza has its share of those, but still has a good number of serious galleries, appealing to those buyers whose interests run to accessible art—Southwestern landscapes and the like. On Canyon Road, the art is often more experimental and more diverse, from contemporary sculpture to eastern European portraiture.

2 The Top Galleries

CONTEMPORARY ART

Adieb Khadoure Fine Art
610 Canyon Rd. ☎ **505/820-2666.**

This is a working artists' studio featuring contemporary artists Jeff Uffelman and Hal Larsen and Santa Fe artist Phyllis Kapp. Their works are shown in the gallery daily from 10am to 6pm, and Adieb Khadoure also sells elegant rugs, furniture, and pottery from around the world.

Canyon Road Contemporary Art
403 Canyon Rd. ☎ **505/983-0433.**

This gallery represents some of the finest emerging U.S. contemporary artists as well as internationally known artists. You'll find figurative, landscape, and abstract paintings, as well as raku pottery.

Hahn Ross Gallery
409 Canyon Rd. ☎ **505/984-8434.**

Owner Tom Ross, a children's book illustrator, specializes in representing artists who create colorful, fantasy-oriented works. I'm especially fond of the wild party scenes by Susan Contreras. Check out the new sculpture garden here.

La Mesa of Santa Fe
225 Canyon Rd. ☎ **505/984-1688.**

Step into this gallery and let your senses dance. Dramatically colored ceramic plates, bowls, and other kitchen items fill one room. Contemporary kachinas by Gregory Lomayesva—a real buy—line the walls, accented by steel lamps and rag rugs. An adventure.

Leslie Muth Gallery
131 W. Palace Ave. ☎ **505/989-4620.**

Here, you'll find "Outsider Art," wild works made by untrained artists in a bizarre variety of media, from sculptures fashioned from pop-bottle lids to portraits painted on flattened beer cans. Much of it is extraordinary and affordable.

✪ LewAllen Contemporary
129 W. Palace Ave. ☎ **505/988-8997.**

This is one of my favorite galleries. You'll find bizarre and beautiful contemporary works in a range of mediums from granite to clay to twigs. There are always exciting works on canvas as well.

✪ Shidoni Foundry, Gallery, and Sculpture Gardens
Bishop's Lodge Rd., Tesuque. ☎ **505/988-8001.**

Shidoni Foundry is one of the area's most exciting spots for sculptors and sculpture enthusiasts. At the foundry, visitors may take a tour through the facilities to view casting processes. In addition, there is a 5,000-square-foot contemporary gallery, a bronze gallery, and a wonderful sculpture garden.

NATIVE AMERICAN & OTHER INDIGENOUS ART

Frank Howell Gallery
103 Washington Ave. ☎ **505/984-1074.**

If you've never seen the wonderful illustrative hand of (sadly, the late) Frank Howell, you'll want to visit this gallery. You'll find a variety of contemporary American and American Indian art. There's sculpture by award-winner Tim Nicola, as well as fine art, jewelry, and graphics.

Glenn Green Galleries
50 E. San Francisco St. ☎ **505/988-4168.**

This gallery, which maintains exclusive representation for Allan Houser's bronze and stone sculptures, also exhibits paintings, prints, photographs, and jewelry by other important artists.

✪ Joshua Baer & Company
116½ E. Palace Ave. ☎ **505/988-8944.**

This is a great place to explore. You'll find 19th-century Navajo blankets, pottery, jewelry, as well as primitive art from around the world.

Maslak-Mcleod

225 E. de Vargas. ☎ **505/820-6389.**

Enter a world of strange creatures from the north in this gallery that specializes in Inuit and other Native Canadian art. Here, you'll find seals carved from bone and native myths emerging from stone.

✪ Morning Star Gallery

513 Canyon Rd. ☎ **505/982-8187.**

This is one of my favorite places to browse. Throughout the rambling gallery are American Indian art masterpieces elegantly displayed. You'll see a broad range of works, from late-19th-century Navajo blankets to 1920s Zuni needlepoint jewelry.

✪ Ortega's on the Plaza

101 West San Francisco St. ☎ **800/874-9297** or 505/988-1866.

A hearty shopper could spend hours here, perusing inventive turquoise and silver jewelry and especially fine strung bead work, as well as rugs and pottery. In an adjacent room is a wide array of clothing, all with a hip Southwestern flair.

PHOTOGRAPHY

Andrew Smith Gallery

203 W. San Francisco St. ☎ **505/984-1234.**

I'm always amazed when I enter this gallery and see works I've seen reprinted in major magazines for years. There they are, photographic prints, large and beautiful, hanging on the wall. Here, you'll see famous works by Edward Curtis, Eliot Porter, Ansel Adams, Annie Leibovitz, and others.

Photo-eye Gallery

370 Garcia St. ☎ **505/988-5152.**

You're bound to be surprised each time you step into this new gallery a few blocks off Canyon Road. Dealing in contemporary photography, the gallery represents 40 renowned, as well as emerging, artists. The company has also taken on the Platinum Gallery collection, from the notable Santa Fe gallery that closed in 1996.

SPANISH & HISPANIC ART

Montez Gallery

Sena Plaza Courtyard, 125 E Palace Ave., Suite 33. ☎ **505/982-1828.**

This shop is rich with Hispanic art, decorations, and furnishings such as *santos* (saints), *retablos* (paintings), *bultos* (sculptures), and *trasteros* (armoires).

Santos of New Mexico

2712 Paseo de Tularosa. ☎ **505/473-7941.**

Here, you'll find the work of award-winning *Santero* Charles M. Carillo: Traditional New Mexican *santos* crafted out of cottonwood root and decorated with homemade pigments, as well as hand-*adzed* panels. By appointment only.

TRADITIONAL ART

Altermann & Morris Galleries

225 Canyon Rd. ☎ **505/983-1590.**

This is a well of interesting traditional art, mostly 19th- and 20th-century American paintings and sculpture. The gallery represents Remington and Russell, in addition to Taos founders, Santa Fe artists, and members of the Cowboy Artists of America and National Academy of Western Art. Stroll through the sculpture garden and meet whimsical bronzes of children and dogs.

✪ Gerald Peters Gallery
1011 Paseo de Peralta (P.O. Box 908). ☎ **505/988-8961.**

By fall of 1998, Gerald Peters plans to be moved into a new 2-story Pueblo-style building. The works displayed here are so fine you'll feel as though you're in a museum. You'll find 19th- and 20th-century American painting and sculpture, featuring art of Georgia O'Keeffe, William Wegman, and the founders of the Santa Fe and Taos artist colonies.

The Mayans Gallery Ltd.
601 Canyon Rd. ☎ **505/983-8068** www.artnet.com/mayans.html. E-mail: arte2@aol.com.

Established in 1977, this is one of the oldest galleries in Santa Fe; you'll find 20th-century American and Latin American paintings, photography, prints, and sculpture.

✪ Nedra Matteucci Galleries
1075 Paseo de Peralta. ☎ **505/982-4631.**

As you approach this gallery, note the elaborately crafted stone and adobe wall that surrounds it, merely a taste of what's to come. The gallery specializes in 19th- and 20th-century American art. Inside, you'll find a lot of high-ticket works such as those of early Taos and Santa Fe painters, as well as classic American impressionism, historical Western modernism, and contemporary Southwestern landscapes and sculpture, including monumental pieces displayed in the sculpture garden.

✪ Owings-Dewey Fine Art
76 E. San Francisco St., upstairs. ☎ **505/982-6244.**

These are treasure-filled rooms. You'll find 19th- and 20th-century American painting and sculpture including works by Georgia O'Keeffe, Robert Henri, Maynard Dixon, Fremont Ellis, and Andrew Dasburg, as well as antique works such as Spanish colonial *retablos, bultos,* and tin works. Don't miss the Day of the Dead exhibition around Halloween.

3 More Shopping A to Z

ANTIQUES

El Paso Import Company
418 Sandoval St. ☎ **505/982-5698.**

Whenever I'm in the vicinity of this shop, I always browse through. It's packed—and I mean packed—with colorful, weathered colonial and ranchero furniture. The home furnishings and folk art here are imported from Mexico and have a primitive feel.

Jackalope
2820 Cerrillos Rd. ☎ **505/471-8539.**

Spread over 7 acres of land, this is a wild place to spend a morning browsing through exotic furnishings from India and Mexico, as well as imported textiles, pottery, jewelry, and clothing. A great place to find gifts.

BELTS

Caballo
727 Canyon Rd. ☎ **505/984-0971.**

The craftspeople at Caballo fashion "one of a kind, one at a time" custom-made belts. Everything is hand-tooled, hand-carved, and hand-stamped. The remarkable buckles are themselves worthy of special attention. This shop merits a stop.

BOOKS

Collected Works Bookstore
208-B W. San Francisco St. ☎ **505/988-4226.**

This is a good downtown book source, with a carefully chosen selection of books up front, in case you're not sure what you want, and shelves of Southwest, travel, nature, and other books.

Horizons–The Discovery Store
328 S. Guadalupe St. ☎ **505/983-1554.**

Here, you'll find adult and children's books, science-oriented games and toys, telescopes, binoculars, and a variety of unusual educational items. I always find interesting gifts for my little nieces in this store.

Nicholas Potter, Bookseller
211 E. Palace Ave. ☎ **505/983-5434.**

This bookstore handles rare and used hardcover books, as well as tickets to many local events.

CRAFTS

Davis Mather Folk Art Gallery
141 Lincoln Ave. ☎ **505/983-1660.**

This small shop is a wild animal adventure. You'll find New Mexican animal wood carvings in shapes of lions, tigers, and bears—even chickens—as well as other folk and Hispanic arts.

Gallery 10
225 Canyon Rd. ☎ **505/983-9707.**

"Important art by native peoples" is how this gallery dubs its offerings, and they're right. This is definitely museum-quality Native American pottery, weavings, basketry, and contemporary paintings and photography. My favorite potter, Tammy Garcia, has work here when she's not sold out of it.

✪ Nambe Foundry Outlets
924 Paseo de Peralta (at Canyon Rd.). ☎ **505/988-5528.**

Here, you'll find cooking, serving, and decorating pieces, fashioned from an exquisite sand-cast and handcrafted alloy. Also available at their stores at 104 W. San Francisco St. (☎ **505/988-3574**), and 216A Paseo del Pueblo Norte (Yucca Plaza), Taos (☎ **505/758-8221**).

FASHIONS

Dewey Trading Company
53 Old Santa Fe Trail. ☎ **505/983-5855.**

Look for Native American trade blankets and men's and women's apparel here.

Jane Smith Ltd.
550 Canyon Rd. ☎ **505/988-4775.**

This is the place for flashy Western-style clothing. You'll find boots with more colors on them than there are Crayolas and jackets made by Elvis's very own designer. There are also flamboyant takes on household goods such as bedding and furniture.

Judy's Unique Apparel
714 Canyon Rd. ☎ **505/988-5746.**

Judy's has eclectic separates made locally or imported from around the globe. You'll find a wide variety of items here, many at surprisingly reasonable prices.

Origins
135 W. San Francisco St. ☎ **505/988-2323.**

A little like a Guatemalan or Turkish marketplace, this store is packed with wearable art, folk art, and work of local designers. Look for good buys on ethnic jewelry. Throughout the summer there are trunk shows, with a chance to meet the artists.

Overland Sheepskin Company
217 Galisteo St. ☎ **505/983-4727.**

The rich smell of leather will draw you in the door, and possibly hold onto you until you purchase a coat, blazer, hat, or other finely made leather item.

FOOD

The Chile Shop
109 E. Water St. ☎ **505/983-6080.**

This store has too many cheap trinketlike items for me. But many find novelty items to take back home. You'll find everything from salsas to cornmeal and tortilla chips. The shop also stocks cookbooks and pottery items.

Cookworks
322 S. Guadalupe St. ☎ **505/988-7676.**

For the chef or merely the wannabe, this is a fun place for browsing. You'll find inventive food products and cooking items spread across three shops. There's also gourmet food and cooking classes.

Coyote Cafe General Store
132 W. Water St. ☎ **505/982-2454.**

This store is an adjunct to one of Santa Fe's most popular restaurants. The big thing here is the enormous selection of hot sauces; however, you can also get a wide variety of Southwestern food items, T-shirts, and aprons.

Señor Murphy Candy Maker
100 E. San Francisco St. (La Fonda Hotel). ☎ **505/982-0461.**

This candy store is unlike any you'll find in other parts of the country—everything here is made with local ingredients. The chile piñon-nut brittle is a taste sensation! Señor Murphy has another shop at 223 Canyon Rd. (☎ **505/983-9243**).

FURNITURE

Southwest Spanish Craftsmen
328 S. Guadalupe St. ☎ **505/982-1767.**

The Spanish colonial and Spanish provincial furniture, doors, and home accessories in this store are a bit too elaborate for my tastes, but if you find yourself dreaming of carved wood, this is your place.

Taos Furniture
1807 Second St. (P.O. Box 5555). ☎ **505/988-1229.**

Prices are a little better away from downtown at this shop where you'll find classic Southwestern furnishings handcrafted in solid Ponderosa pine—both contemporary and traditional.

GIFTS & SOUVENIRS

El Nicho
227 Don Gaspar Ave. ☎ **505/984-2830.**

For the thrifty art shopper this is the place to be. Inside the funky Santa Fe village, you'll find handcrafted Navajo and Oaxacan folk art as well as carvings, jewelry, and other items by local artisans.

Thea
612A Agua Fría St. ☎ **505/995-9618.**

This new shop is so rich and enticing that you won't want to leave. Owned by Svetlana Britt, an exotic Russian woman, it features candles, scents, and aromatherapy. These are excellent gift items, colorfully and elaborately packaged. Named for the goddess of light, the whole store has a luminous quality.

JEWELRY

Packards
61 Old Santa Fe Trail. ☎ **505/983-9241.**

Opened by a notable trader, Al Packard, and later sold to new owners, this store on the Plaza is worth checking out to see some of the best jewelry available. You'll also find exquisite rugs and pottery.

Tresa Vorenberg Goldsmiths
656 Canyon Rd. ☎ **505/988-7215.**

You'll find some wildly imaginative designs in this jewelry store where more than 30 artisans are represented. All items are handcrafted and custom commissions are welcomed.

MALLS & SHOPPING CENTERS

De Vargas Center Mall
N. Guadalupe St. and Paseo de Peralta. ☎ **505/982-2655.**

There are more than 55 merchants and restaurants in this mall just northwest of downtown. This is Santa Fe's small, struggling mall. Though there are fewer shops than Villa Linda, this is where I shop because I don't tend to get the mall phobia I get in the more massive places. Open Monday through Thursday from 10am to 7pm, Friday from 10am to 9pm (may change to earlier), Saturday from 10am to 6pm, and Sunday from noon to 5pm.

Sanbusco Market Center
500 Montezuma St. ☎ **505/989-9390.**

Unique shops and restaurants occupy this remodeled warehouse near the old Santa Fe Railroad Yard. Though most of the shops in this little mall are overpriced, it's a fun place to window-shop. There's a farmers' market in the adjacent railyard next to the Santa Fe Clay building, open from 7am to noon on Tuesday and Saturday in the summer.

Villa Linda Mall
4250 Cerrillos Rd. (at Rodeo Rd.). ☎ **505/473-4253.**

Santa Fe's largest mall (including department stores) is near the southwestern city limits, not far from the I-25 on-ramp. If you're from a major city, you'll probably find shopping here very provincial. Anchors include JCPenney, Sears, Dillard's, and Mervyn's. Open Monday through Saturday from 10am to 9pm, Sunday from noon to 6pm.

MARKETS

Farmers' Market

In the railyard adjacent to Sanbusco Market Center, 500 Montezuma St. ☎ **505/ 983-4098.**

Every Saturday and Tuesday from 7am to noon, you'll find a farmers' market with everything from fruits, vegetables, and flowers to cheeses, cider, and salsas. Great local treats!

Trader Jack's Flea Market

US 84/285 (about 8 miles north of Santa Fe). No phone.

If you're a flea-market hound, you'll be happy to find Trader Jack's. More than 500 vendors here sell everything from used cowboy boots (you might find some real beauties) to clothing, jewelry, books, and furniture, all against a big Northern New Mexico view. The flea market is open from mid-April to late November on Friday, Saturday, and Sunday.

NATURAL ART

Mineral & Fossil Gallery of Santa Fe

127 W. San Francisco St. ☎ **800/762-9777** or 505/984-1682.

You'll find ancient artwork here, from fossils to geodes in all sizes and shapes. There's also natural mineral jewelry and decorative items for the home, including lamps, wall clocks, furniture, art glass, and carvings. Mineral & Fossil also has galleries in Scottsdale, Sedona, and Denver.

POTTERY & TILES

Artesanos Imports Company

222 Galisteo St. ☎ **505/983-1743** or 505/982-0860.

This is like a trip south of the border, with all the scents and colors you'd expect on such a journey. You'll find a wide selection of Talavera tile and pottery, as well as light fixtures and many other accessories for the home. There's even an outdoor market where you can buy fountains and chile ristras.

Santa Fe Pottery

323 S. Guadalupe St. ☎ **505/989-3363.**

The work of more than 50 master potters from New Mexico and the Southwest is on display here. You'll find everything from mugs to lamps.

RUGS

Seret & Sons Rugs, Furnishings, and Architectural Pieces

149 E. Alameda St. and 232 Galisteo St. ☎ **505/988-9151** or 505/983-5008.

If you're like me and find Middle Eastern decor irresistible, you need to wander through either of these shops. You'll find kilims and Persian and Turkish rugs, as well as some of the Moorish-style ancient doors and furnishings that you see around Santa Fe.

WINES & BEERS

Kokoman Circus
301 Garfield St. ☎ **505/983-7770.**

> Specialty wines, beers, and gourmet foods abound at this new shop/cafe not far from some of the close-to-town hotels. Beware: the deli has delicious, but *expensive* food.

Santa Fe After Dark   9

Santa Fe is a city committed to the arts. Its night scene is dominated by highbrow cultural events, beginning with the world-famous Santa Fe Opera; the club and popular music scene run a distant second.

Complete information on all major cultural events can be obtained from the **Santa Fe Convention and Visitors Bureau** (☎ **800/777-CITY** or 505/984-6760) or from the **City of Santa Fe Arts Commission** (☎ **505/984-6707**). Current listings are published each Friday in the "Pasatiempo" section of *The New Mexican,* the city's daily newspaper, and in the *Santa Fe Reporter,* published every Wednesday.

Nicholas Potter, Bookseller, 211 E. Palace Ave. (☎ **505/ 983-5434**), carries tickets to select events. You can also order by phone from TicketMaster (☎ **505/842-5387** for information, 505/884-0999 to order). Discount tickets may be available on the night of a performance; the opera, for example, offers standing-room tickets on the day of the performance. Sales start at 10am.

A variety of free concerts, lectures, and other events are presented in the summer, cosponsored by the City of Santa Fe and the Chamber of Commerce. The **El Corazón de Santa Fe** ("the heart of Santa Fe") program has featured Saturday night musical and cultural events on the Plaza, and the city hopes to continue the program, though, with a new mayoral administration, there was no confirmation of plans for 1999.

The **Santa Fe Summer Concert Series** (☎ **505/256-1777**), at the Paolo Soleri Outdoor Amphitheatre on the campus of the Santa Fe Indian School (Cerrillos Road), has brought such name performers as B. B. King, Frank Zappa, and Kenny Loggins to the city. More than two dozen concerts and special events are scheduled each summer.

Note: Many companies noted here perform at locations other than their listed addresses, so check the site of the performance you plan to attend.

1 The Performing Arts

No fewer than 24 performing-arts groups flourish in this city of 60,000. Many of them perform year-round, but others are seasonal. The acclaimed Santa Fe Opera, for instance, has just a 2-month summer season: July and August.

MAJOR PERFORMING ARTS COMPANIES
OPERA & CLASSICAL MUSIC

✪ Santa Fe Opera

P.O. Box 2408, Santa Fe, NM 87504-2408. ☎ **800/280-4654** or 505/986-5900 for tickets. Tickets $20–$110 Mon–Thurs; $28–$118 Fri–Sat. Wheelchair seating $14 Mon–Thurs; $20 Fri–Sat. Standing room (sold on day of performance beginning at 10am) $6 Mon–Thurs; $8 Fri–Sat; $15 Opening Night Gala. Backstage tours: First Mon in July to last Fri in Aug, Mon–Sat at 1pm; $6 adults, free for children 15 and under.

Opera fans are talking about the new theater, just completed for the 1998 season. Like the old one, it's located on a wooded hilltop 7 miles north of the city off US 84/285, and is still partially open-air, now with open sides only (the original theater had a partially open ceiling). A controversial structure, this new one replaced the original built in 1968, known for its sweeping curves attuned to the contour of the surrounding terrain. At night, the lights of Los Alamos could be seen in the distance under clear skies. Planners assure that such novelties are found in the new structure as well.

Many rank the Santa Fe Opera second only to the Metropolitan Opera of New York as the finest company in the United States today. Established in 1957 by John Crosby—still the opera's artistic director—it consistently attracts famed conductors, directors, and singers (the list has included Igor Stravinsky). At the height of the season the company is 500 strong, including the skilled craftspeople and designers who work on the sets. The opera company is noted for its performances of the classics, little-known works by classical European composers, and American premieres of 20th-century works.

The 9-week, 40-performance opera season runs from early June through late August. In 1999, you can see such classics as *Carmen* by Bizet and *Idomeneo* by Mozart. Usually there is a Strauss opera; in 1999, it will be *Ariadne Auf Naxos*. And for the less traditional-minded, there's *Countess Maritza* by Kalman and *Dialogues of the Carmelites* by Poulenc. All performances begin at 9pm, until the last 2 weeks of the season when performances begin at 8:30pm.

A gift shop has been added, as well as additional parking. The entire theater is now wheelchair accessible.

ORCHESTRAL & CHAMBER MUSIC

Oncydium Haydn Orchestra

369 Montezuma Ave., Suite 405, Santa Fe, NM 87501-2626. ☎ **505/988-0703.**

This New York– and Santa Fe–based chamber ensemble presents one classical concert per year in mid-August at the Fort Marcy Complex. Call for information and a schedule.

Santa Fe Pro Musica Chamber Orchestra & Ensemble

320 Galisteo, Suite 502 (P.O. Box 2091), Santa Fe, NM 87504-2091. ☎ **505/988-4640.** Tickets $15–$35.

This chamber ensemble performs everything from Bach to Vivaldi to contemporary masters. During Holy Week, the Santa Fe Pro Musica presents its annual Baroque Festival Concert. Christmas brings candlelight chamber ensemble concerts. Pro Musica's season runs October through April.

✪ Santa Fe Symphony Orchestra and Chorus

P.O. Box 9692, Santa Fe, NM 87504. ☎ **800/480-1319** or 505/983-1414. Tickets $8–$35 (6 seating categories).

This 60-piece professional symphony orchestra has grown rapidly in stature since its founding in 1984. Matinee and evening performances of classical and popular works are presented in a subscription series at Sweeney Center (Grant Avenue at Marcy Street) from August to May. There's a preconcert lecture before each performance. During the spring there are music festivals (call for details).

Serenata of Santa Fe

P.O. Box 8410, Santa Fe, NM 87504. ☎ **505/989-7988.** Tickets $12 general admission, $15 reserved seats.

This professional chamber-music group specializes in bringing lesser-known works of the masters to the concert stage. Concerts are presented from September to May. Call the number above for location, dates, and details.

CHORAL GROUPS

Desert Chorale

219 Shelby St. (P.O. Box 2813), Santa Fe, NM 87504. ☎ **800/905-3315** (ProTix) or 505/988-7505. Tickets $22–$35 adults, half price for students.

This 24- to 30-member vocal ensemble, New Mexico's only professional choral group, recruits members from all over the country. It's nationally recognized for its eclectic blend of both Renaissance melodies and modern avant-garde compositions. During summer months the chorale performs classic concerts at various locations, including the Loretto Chapel, as well as smaller cameo concerts at more intimate settings throughout Santa Fe and Albuquerque. The chorale also performs a popular series of Christmas concerts during December. Most concerts begin at 8pm (3 or 6pm on Sunday).

Sangre de Cristo Chorale

P.O. Box 4462, Santa Fe, NM 87502. ☎ **505/662-9717.** Tickets $10–$40 depending on the season.

This 34-member ensemble has a repertoire ranging from classical, baroque, and Renaissance works to more recent folk music and spirituals, much of it presented a cappella. The group gives concerts in Santa Fe, Los Alamos, and Albuquerque. The Christmas dinner concerts are extremely popular.

Santa Fe Women's Ensemble

424 Kathryn Place, Santa Fe, NM 87501. ☎ **505/983-2137.** Tickets $13 and $16 adults, $8 and $12 students.

This choral group of 12 semiprofessional singers offers classical works sung a cappella as well as with varied instrumental accompaniment during April and December. Both the "Spring Offering" concerts (in mid-April) and the "Christmas Offering" concerts (in mid-December) are held in the Loretto Chapel (Old Santa Fe Trail at Water Street). Call for tickets.

MUSIC FESTIVALS & CONCERT SERIES

Santa Fe Chamber Music Festival

239 Johnson St., Suite. B (P.O. Box 853), Santa Fe, NM 87504. ☎ **505/983-2075** or 505/982-1890 for the box office (after June 22). Tickets $15–$40.

This festival brings an extraordinary group of international artists to Santa Fe every summer. Its 6-week season of some 50 concerts runs from mid-July through mid-August and is held in the beautiful St. Francis Auditorium. Each festival season features chamber-music masterpieces, new music by a composer in residence, jazz, free youth concerts, preconcert lectures, and open rehearsals. Performances are Monday,

Tuesday, Thursday, and Friday at 8pm; Saturday at various evening times; and Sunday at 6pm. Open rehearsals, youth concerts, and preconcert lectures are free to the public.

Santa Fe Concert Association

P.O. Box 4626, Santa Fe, NM 87502. ☎ **800/905-3315** (ProTix) or 505/984-8759 for tickets. Tickets $15–$65.

Founded in 1938, the oldest musical organization in Northern New Mexico has a September-to-May season that includes approximately 15 annual events. Among them are a distinguished artists' series featuring renowned instrumental and vocal soloists and chamber ensembles, special Christmas Eve and New Year's Eve concerts, and sponsored performances by local artists. All performances are held at the St. Francis Auditorium; tickets are sold by the association or ProTix.

THEATER COMPANIES

Greer Garson Theater Center

College of Santa Fe, 1600 St. Michael's Dr., Santa Fe, NM 87505. ☎ **505/473-6511.** Tickets $8–$17 adults, $5 students ($22–$35 for summer-season Santa Fe Stages performances; see below for details).

In this graceful, intimate theater, the college's Performing Arts Department produces four plays annually, with five presentations of each, given between October and May. Usually, the season consists of a comedy, a drama, a musical, and a classic. The college also sponsors studio productions and 10 contemporary music concerts.

✪ Santa Fe Playhouse

142 E. de Vargas St., Santa Fe, NM 87501. ☎ **505/988-4262.** Tickets $10 adults, $8 students and seniors; on Sun, people are asked to "pay what you wish."

Founded in the 1920s, this is the oldest extant theater group in New Mexico. Still performing in a historic adobe theater in the Barrio de Analco, it attracts thousands for its dramas, avant-garde theater, and musical comedy. Its popular one-act melodramas call on the public to boo the sneering villain and swoon for the damsel in distress.

✪ Santa Fe Stages

105 E. Marcy St., Suite 107, Santa Fe, NM 87501. ☎ **505/982-6683.** Tickets $25–$40.

Most locals couldn't imagine international theater and dance troupes coming to Santa Fe, but it happened beginning in 1994 when artistic director Martin Platt founded this theater. He recently left Santa Fe for London to expand a theater business of which he is part owner, and locals hope the offerings will continue to be outstanding here. Staged at two theaters on the College of Santa Fe campus, and at times at the St. Francis Auditorium downtown, the gatherings are small and intimate, adding to the audience's enjoyment.

Shakespeare in Santa Fe

355 E. Palace Ave. (box office only), Santa Fe, NM 87501. ☎ **505/982-2910.** Reserved seating is available for various prices; lawn and surrounding area is available with a suggested donation of $5.

Every Friday, Saturday, and Sunday during July and August, in the library courtyard of St. John's College (southeast of downtown—off Camino del Monte Sol), Shakespeare in Santa Fe presents Shakespeare in the Park. Sunset picnic suppers are sold by Wild Oats Market, or you can bring your own.

DANCE COMPANIES

✪ María Benitez Teatro Flamenco

Institute for Spanish Arts, P.O. Box 8418, Santa Fe, NM 87501. ☎ **800/905-3315** or 505/ 982-1237 for tickets. Tickets $18–$29.50 (subject to change).

This is a performance you won't want to miss. True flamenco is one of the most thrilling of dance forms, displaying the inner spirit and verve of the gypsies of Spanish Andalusia, and María Benitez, trained in Spain, is a fabulous performer. The Benitez Company's "Estampa Flamenca" summer series is performed nightly except Tuesday from July through early September. With a recent remodel, the María Benitez Theater at the Radisson Hotel is modern and showy.

MAJOR CONCERT HALLS & ALL-PURPOSE AUDITORIUMS

Plan B Evolving Arts

1050 Old Pecos Trail. ☎ **505/982-1338.** Tickets for films $6.

Plan B Evolving Arts presents the work of internationally, nationally, and region-ally known contemporary artists in art exhibitions, dance, new music concerts, poetry readings, performance-art events, theater, and video screenings. The Cinématique screens films from around the world nightly, with special series pre-sented regularly. Plan B also runs the Warehouse/Teen Project, a unique program designed to encourage creativity, individuality, and free expression by giving teens a safe, free place to create programs and events, including workshops, art exhibi-tions, a radio show and publication, theater ensemble, cafe (with open-mike oppor-tunities), and concerts featuring local teen bands. Plan B's galleries are open daily noon to 7pm.

Paolo Soleri Amphitheatre

At the Santa Fe Indian School, 1501 Cerrillos Rd. ☎ **505/989-6318.** Call for tickets or con-tact TicketMaster at 505/884-0999.

I'm not much of a rock concert–goer because they're always too loud, smokey, and crowded. That's why this is practically the only place I'll go, and it's an incredible experience. Out under the stars, this amphitheater offers plenty of room, excellent views of the stage from any seat, and good acoustics. Concerts are presented during summer months. In recent years the facility has attracted such big-name acts as Joan Armatrading, the Grateful Dead, B. B. King, Kenny Loggins, Anne Murray, Suzanne Vega, Ziggy Marley, Lyle Lovett, Dave Matthews, Allan Parsons Project, the Reggae Sunsplash, and, my favorite, Big Head Todd and the Monsters. For information on scheduled performers while you're in Santa Fe, contact **Big River Corporation,** P.O. Box 8036, Albuquerque, NM 87198 (☎ **505/256-1777**). Be sure to take a blanket to sit on, as the bench-type seats are made of poured concrete.

✪ St. Francis Auditorium

In the Museum of Fine Arts, Lincoln and Palace aves. ☎ **505/827-4455.** Ticket prices vary; see above for specific performing-arts companies.

This atmospheric music hall, patterned after the interiors of traditional Hispanic mission churches, is noted for its excellent acoustics. The hall hosts a wide variety of musical events, including the Santa Fe Chamber Music Festival in July and August. The Santa Fe Symphony Festival Series, the Santa Fe Concert Associ-ation, the Santa Fe Women's Ensemble, and various other programs are also held here.

Sweeney Convention Center
201 W. Marcy St. ☎ **800/777-2489** or 505/984-6760. Tickets $10–$30, depending on seating and performances. Tickets are never sold at Sweeney Convention Center; event sponsors handle ticket sales.

Santa Fe's largest indoor arena hosts a wide variety of trade expositions and other events during the year. It's also the home of the Santa Fe Symphony Orchestra and the New Mexico Symphony Orchestra's annual Santa Fe Series.

2 The Club & Music Scene

In addition to the clubs and bars listed below, there are a number of hotels whose bars and lounges feature some type of entertainment. (See chapter 5, "Where to Stay in Santa Fe.")

COUNTRY, JAZZ & FOLK

Cowgirl Hall of Fame
319 S Guadalupe St. ☎ **505/982-2565.** No cover for music in the main restaurant, except on Tues when it's $2. Other performances $2–$8.

It's difficult to categorize what goes on in this bar and restaurant, but there's live entertainment nightly. Some nights there's blues guitar, others there's comedy, and others there's flamenco music and dance. You might also find something called cowboy poetry or an acoustic open microphone night. In the summer, this is a great place to sit under the stars and listen to music or see some fun entertainment inside.

✪ El Farol
808 Canyon Rd. ☎ **505/983-9912.** Cover $4–$10.

The original neighborhood bar of the Canyon Road artists' quarter (its name means "the lantern") is the place to head for local ambience. Its low ceilings and dark brown walls are home to Santa Fe's largest and most unusual selection of *tapas* (bar snacks and appetizers). Jazz, folk, and ethnic musicians—some of national note—perform most nights.

Fiesta Lounge
In La Fonda Hotel, 110 E. San Francisco St. ☎ **505/982-5511.** No cover.

This lively lobby bar offers cocktails and live entertainment nightly.

Rodeo Nites
2911 Cerrillos Rd. ☎ **505/473-4138.** No cover Mon–Wed, $2.50 Thurs, $3 Fri–Sat. Closed Sun.

There's live country dance music nightly at this popular club.

ROCK & DISCO

Catamount Bar and Grille
125 E. Water St. ☎ **505/988-7222.**

The post-college crowd hangs out at this bar where there's live rock and blues music on weekends and some weeknights.

The Drama Club
125 N. Guadalupe St. ☎ **505/988-4374.**

This place is doing its best to present Santa Fe with a club scene. Some nights work better than others. On nights when there's a deejay, it can be quite dull, but other nights there are live performances by jazz, rock-and-roll, and world music groups, and the place lights up. There are also stage acts ranging from drag shows to nationally known comedy acts. You'll find pool tables up front. Though the crowd here varies greatly, it's mostly a gay and lesbian club.

3 The Bar Scene

Dana's After Dark
222 N. Guadalupe. ☎ **505/982-5225.** No cover.

This after-hours club caters to late-night lesbian and gay crowds, but it's such a cool place I'd recommend it for anyone. Opened in the spring of 1997, it's in an old adobe house that has been painted inside with wild colors like summer-squash orange and lime green. Open nightly from 6:30pm to "late," which could mean anywhere from 1am to 4am (in summer, usually until 4am), it's the place for late-night food, fine coffee, and carefully prepared desserts. You can listen to a variety of types of music from ultra-lounge music to cha-cha and mambo. Or, you can go into the music room and play piano or conga drums, or into the game room and play retro-board games from the '60s. No alcoholic beverages are served.

Evangelo's
200 W. San Francisco St. ☎ **505/982-9014.** No cover.

A popular downtown hang-out, this bar can get raucous at times. It's an interesting place, with tropical decor and a mahogany bar. More than 250 varieties of imported beer are available, and pool tables are an added attraction. On Friday and Saturday nights starting at 9pm, live bands play; some nights there's jazz, others rock, and others reggae. Evangelo's is extremely popular with the local crowd. You'll find your share of business people, artists, and even bikers here. Open daily from noon until 1 or 2am.

Vanessie of Santa Fe
434 W. San Francisco St. ☎ **505/982-9966.** No cover.

This is unquestionably Santa Fe's most popular piano bar. The talented Doug Montgomery and Charles Tichenor have a loyal local following. Their repertoire ranges from Bach to Billy Joel, Gershwin to Barry Manilow. They play nightly from 8pm until closing, which could be from midnight to 2am. There's an extra microphone, so if you're daring (or drunk), you can stand up and accompany the piano and vocals (though this is *not* a Karaoke scene). National celebrities have even joined in—including Harry Connick, Jr. (and he wasn't even drunk). Vanessie's offers a great bar menu.

10 Excursions from Santa Fe

Native American pueblos and ruins, a national monument and national park, Los Alamos (the A-bomb capital of the United States), and the scenic and fascinating High Road to Taos are all easy day trips from Santa Fe. A longer drive will take you to Chaco Culture National Historic Park (well worth the time).

1 Exploring the Northern Pueblos

Of the eight northern pueblos, Tesuque, Pojoaque, Nambe, San Ildefonso, San Juan, and Santa Clara are within about 30 miles of Santa Fe. Picuris (San Lorenzo) is on the High Road to Taos (see section 3, below), and Taos Pueblo is just outside the town of Taos.

The six pueblos described in this section can easily be visited in a single day's round-trip from Santa Fe, though I suggest visiting just those few that really give a feel of the ancient lifestyle. Plan to focus most of your attention on San Juan, Santa Clara, and San Ildefonso, including San Juan's arts cooperative, Santa Clara's Puye Cliff Dwellings, and San Ildefonso's broad plaza. If you're in the area at a time when you can catch certain rituals, that's when to see some of the others.

Certain **rules of etiquette** should be observed in visiting the pueblos. These are personal dwellings and/or important historic sites, and must be respected as such. Don't climb on the buildings or peek into doors or windows. Don't enter sacred grounds, such as cemeteries and kivas. If you attend a dance or ceremony, remain silent while it is taking place and refrain from applause when it's over. Many pueblos prohibit photography or sketches; others require you to pay a fee for a permit. If you don't respect the privacy of the Native Americans who live at the pueblo, you'll be asked to leave.

TESUQUE PUEBLO

Tesuque (Te-*soo*-keh) Pueblo is located about 9 miles north of Santa Fe on US 84/285. You will know that you are approaching the pueblo when you see a carpet outlet store. If you're driving north and you get to the unusual Camel Rock and a large roadside casino, you've missed the entrance. The 400 pueblo dwellers at Tesuque are faithful to their traditional religion, rituals, and ceremonies. Excavations confirm that a pueblo has existed here at least since the year

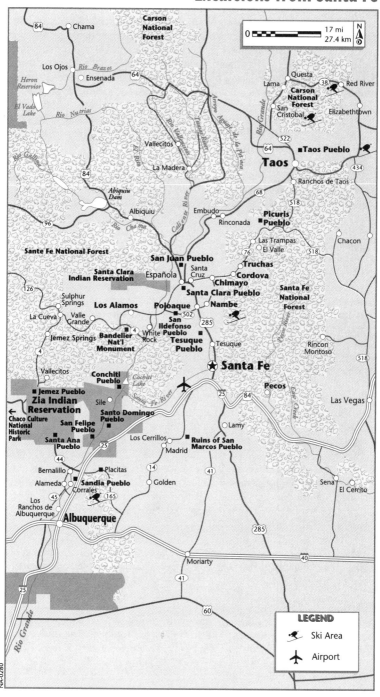

0 17 mi
   27.4 km

N

84 Chama

Carson National Forest

Los Ojos   Rio Brazos
Ensenada

Heron Reservoir

El Vado Lake

Rio Nutrias

64

Rio Gallina

84

Sante Fe National Forest

126

Questa

Lama   38 Red River

Carson National Forest

San Cristobal   Elizabethtown

522

64   Taos Pueblo

Taos

Ranchos de Taos   434

68   518

Picuris Pueblo

Embudo

Rinconada

Chacon

Las Trampas

76   El Valle   518

San Juan Pueblo   Truchas

Santa Cruz   Cordova

Española   Chimayo

Santa Clara Indian Reservation   Santa Clara Pueblo

Sulphur Springs

La Cueva   Valle Grande

Los Alamos   Pojoaque

Nambe

502

285

Santa Fe National Forest

Jemez Springs

Bandelier Nat'l Monument

4

San Ildefonso Pueblo

White Rock

Tesuque Pueblo

Tesuque

Rincon Montoso

518

4

Vallecitos

Conchiti Pueblo   Cochiti Lake

★ Santa Fe

Jemez Pueblo

Zia Indian Reservation

Chaco Culture National Historic Park

Sile

Santo Domingo Pueblo

San Felipe Pueblo

Santa Ana Pueblo

44

Bernalillo

Alameda

Los Ranchos de Albuquerque

45

Sandia Pueblo

Corrales   165

Albuquerque

25

Placitas

Los Cerrillos

Madrid

14

Golden

Lamy

Ruins of San Marcos Pueblo

41

Pecos

Las Vegas

Santa Fe River   84

Galisteo Creek   25

Sena

El Cerrito

Moriarty

285

41

40

60

25

Rio Grande

LEGEND

Ski Area

Airport

NA-0280

Albiquiu

Abiquiu Dam

La Madera

Vallecitos

Rio Chama

96

El Rito

Caliente River

Arroyo Hondo de la Presa

Rio Grande

Rio Vallecitos

A.D. 1200; accordingly, this pueblo is now on the National Register of Historic Places. When you come to the welcome sign at the pueblo, turn right, go a block, and park on the right. You'll see the Plaza off to the left. There's not a lot to see; to the south are some very old homes with exposed adobe walls. There's a big open area where dances are held and the church, which is simple sculpted adobe with a small bell and wooden cross on top. Visitors are asked to remain in this area.

Some Tesuque women are skilled potters; Ignacia Duran's black-and-white and red micaceous pottery and Teresa Tapia's miniatures and pots with animal figures are especially noteworthy. The **San Diego Feast Day,** which may feature buffalo, deer, flag, or Comanche dances, is November 12.

The Tesuque Pueblo address is Route 5, Box 360-T, Santa Fe, NM 87501 (☎ 505/983-2667). Admission to the pueblo is free; however, there is a $20 charge for still cameras; special permission is required for movie cameras, sketching, and painting. The pueblo is open daily from 9am to 5pm. Camel Rock Casino (☎ **505/984-8414**) is open daily 7am to 4am and has a snack bar on the premises.

POJOAQUE PUEBLO

About 6 miles farther north on US 84/285, at the junction of NM 502, is Pojoaque (Po-*hwa*-keh). Though small (population 200) and without a definable village (more modern dwellings exist now), Pojoaque is important as a center for traveler services; in fact, Pojoaque, in its Tewa form, means "water-drinking place." The historical accounts of the Pojoaque people are sketchy, but we do know that in 1890 smallpox took its toll on the Pojoaque population, forcing most of the Pueblo residents to abandon their village. Since the 1930s, the population has gradually increased, and in 1990 a war chief and two war captains were appointed. Today, visitors won't find much to look at, but the Poeh Center, operated by the pueblo, features a museum and crafts store. Indigenous pottery, embroidery, silverwork, and beadwork are available for sale at the Pojoaque Pueblo Tourist Center.

You'll want to leave US 84/285 and travel on the frontage road back to where the Pueblo actually was. There, you'll encounter lovely orchards and alfalfa fields backed by desert and mountains. A modern community center is located near the site of the old Pueblo and church. On December 12, the annual feast day of **Our Lady of Guadalupe** features a bow-and-arrow or buffalo dance. Continue on this frontage road until you come to a fork, where the road turns to dirt. This little hidden route crosses the Nambe River, then meanders by orchards and through the village of Nambe. You'll want to get to the church at Nambe, which is where this road meets NM 503.

The pueblo's address is Route 11, Box 71, Santa Fe, NM 87501 (☎ **505/ 455-2278**). Admission is free. Contact the Governor's Office at the number above for information about sketching and camera fees. The Pueblo is open every day during daylight hours.

NAMBE PUEBLO

If you're still on US 84/285, continue north from Pojoaque about 3 miles until you come to NM 503; turn right and travel until you see the Bureau of Reclamation sign for Nambe Falls; turn right on NP 101. Approximately 2 miles farther is Nambe ("mound of earth in the corner"), a 700-year-old Tewa-speaking pueblo (population 450), with a solar-powered tribal headquarters, at the foot of the Sangre de Cristo Range. Only a few original pueblo buildings remain, including a large round kiva, used today in ceremonies. Pueblo artisans make woven belts, beadwork, and brown micaceous pottery. One of my favorite reasons for visiting this Pueblo is to see the herd of 36 bison that roam on 179 acres set aside for them.

Nambe Falls make a stunning three-tier drop through a cleft in a rock face about 4 miles beyond the pueblo, tumbling into Nambe Reservoir. A recreational site at the reservoir offers fishing, boating (nonmotor boats only), hiking, camping, and picnicking. The **Waterfall Dances** on July 4 and the **Saint Francis of Assisi Feast Day** on October 4, which has an elk dance ceremony, are observed at the sacred falls.

The address is Route 1, Box 117-BB, Santa Fe, NM 87501 (☎ **505/455-2036** or 505/455-2304 for the Ranger Station). Admission to the pueblo is free, but there is a $7 charge for still cameras, $10 for movie cameras, and $15 for sketching. At the recreational site, the charge for fishing is $10 per day for adults, $6 per day for children; for camping it is $10 per night. The pueblo is open daily from 8am to 5pm. The recreational site is open March, September, and October from 7am to 7pm, April and May from 7am to 8pm, and June through August from 6am to 8pm.

SAN ILDEFONSO PUEBLO

Pox Oge, as this pueblo is called in its own Tewa language, means "place where the water cuts down through," possibly named for the way the Rio Grande cuts through the mountains nearby. Turn left on NM 502 at Pojoaque, and drive about 6 miles to the turnoff. This pueblo has a broad, dusty plaza, with a kiva on one side, ancient dwellings on the other, and a church at the far end. It's nationally famous for its matte-finish black-on-black pottery, developed by tribeswoman María Martinez in the 1920s. One of the most-visited pueblos in Northern New Mexico, San Ildefonso attracts more than 20,000 visitors a year.

The San Ildefonsos could best be described as rebellious, since they were one of the last pueblos to succumb to the reconquest spearheaded by Don Diego de Vargas in 1692. Within view of the pueblo is the volcanic Black Mesa, a symbol of their strength. Through the years, each time San Ildefonso felt itself threatened by enemy forces, the residents, along with members of other pueblos, would hide out up on the butte, returning to the valley only when starvation set in. Today, a visit to the pueblo is valuable mainly in order to see or buy rich black pottery. A few shops surround the plaza, and there's the **San Ildefonso Pueblo Museum** tucked away in the governor's office beyond the plaza. I especially recommend visiting during ceremonial days. **San Ildefonso Feast Day** is January 23, and features the buffalo and Comanche dances in alternate years. **Corn Dances,** held in early September, commemorate a basic element in pueblo life, the importance of fertility in all creatures—humans as well as animals—and plants.

The pueblo has a 4½-acre fishing lake that is surrounded by bosque, open April through October. Picnicking is encouraged, though you may want to look at the sites before you decide to stay; some are nicer than others. Camping is not allowed.

The pueblo's address is Route 5, Box 315A, Santa Fe, NM 87501 (☎ **505/455-3549**). The admission charge is $3 for a noncommercial vehicle and $10 for a commercial vehicle, plus 50¢ per passenger. The charge for using a still camera is $5; $15 for a video camera or sketching. If you plan to fish, the charge is $7 for adults, $3 for seniors and children under 12 years of age. The pueblo is open in the summer, daily from 8am to 5pm; call for weekend hours. In the winter, it is open Monday through Friday from 8am to 4:30pm. It is closed for major holidays and tribal events.

SAN JUAN PUEBLO

If you continue north on US 84/285, you will reach the pueblo via NM 74, a mile off NM 68, about 4 miles north of Española.

The largest (population 1,950) and northernmost of the Tewa-speaking pueblos and headquarters of the Eight Northern Indian Pueblos Council, San Juan is located on the east side of the Rio Grande—opposite the 1598 site of San Gabriel, the first Spanish settlement west of the Mississippi River and the first capital of New Spain. In 1598, the Spanish, impressed with the openness and helpfulness of the people of San Juan, decided to establish a capital there (it was moved to Santa Fe 10 years later)—making San Juan Pueblo the first to be subjected to Spanish colonization. The Indians were generous, providing food, clothing, shelter, and fuel—they even helped sustain the settlement when its leader Conquistador Juan de Oñate became preoccupied with his search for gold and neglected the needs of his people. Unfortunately, the Spanish subjugation of the Indians left them virtual slaves, forced to provide the Spanish with corn, venison, cloth, and labor. They were compelled to participate in Spanish religious ceremonies and to abandon their own religious practices. Under no circumstances were Indian ceremonies allowed; those caught participating in them were punished. In 1676, several Indians were accused of sorcery and jailed in Santa Fe. Later they were led to the Plaza, where they were flogged or hanged. This despicable incident became a turning point in Indian-Spanish relations, generating an overwhelming feeling of rage in the Indian community. One of the accused, a San Juan Pueblo Indian named Po'Pay, became a leader in the Great Pueblo Revolt, which led to freedom from Spanish rule for 12 years.

The past and present cohabit here. Though Roman Catholics, members of the San Juan tribe still practice traditional religious rituals. Thus, two rectangular kivas flank the church in the main plaza, and *caciques* (pueblo priests) share power with civil authorities. The annual **San Juan Fiesta** is held June 23 and 24, and features buffalo and Comanche dances. Another annual ceremony is the **turtle dance** on December 26. The **matachine dance,** performed here Christmas day, vividly depicts the subjugation of the Native Americans by the Catholic Spaniards.

The address of the pueblo is P.O. Box 1099, San Juan Pueblo, NM 87566 (☎ 505/852-4400). Admission is free. Photography or sketching may be allowed with prior permission from the Governor's Office. For information, call the number above. The charge for fishing is $8 for adults and $5 for children and seniors. The pueblo is open every day during daylight hours.

The **Eight Northern Indian Pueblos Council** (☎ 505/852-4265) is a sort of chamber of commerce and social-service agency. Each year, the council publishes a guide to the Northern Pueblos, which contains descriptions of each and a calendar of dances and other events. It can be obtained by calling the number above.

A crafts shop, **Oke Oweenge Arts and Crafts Cooperative** (☎ 505/852-2372), specializes in local wares. This is a fine place to seek out San Juan's distinctive red pottery, a lustrous ceramic incised with traditional geometric symbols. Also displayed for sale are seed, turquoise, and silver jewelry; wood and stone carvings; indigenous clothing and weavings; embroidery; and paintings. Artisans often work on the premises and visitors can watch. The co-op is open Monday through Saturday from 9am to 5pm (but is closed San Juan Feast Day). **Sunrise Crafts,** another crafts shop, is located to the right of the co-op. There, you'll find one-of-a-kind handcrafted pipes, beadwork, and burned and painted gourds.

Right on the main road that goes through the pueblo is the **Tewa Indian Restaurant,** serving traditional pueblo chile stews, breads, blue-corn dishes, posole, teas,

Indian Pueblos & Ancient Cultures

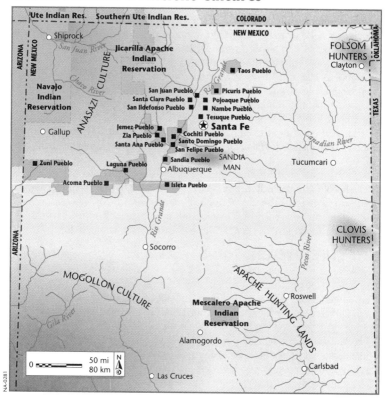

and desserts. It's open Monday through Friday from 9am to 2:30pm; closed holidays and feast days.

Fishing and picnicking are encouraged at the San Juan Tribal Lakes, open year-round. **Ohkay Casino** (☎ 505/747-0700) offers table games and slot machines, as well as live music every Friday night. It's open Monday through Thursday 6am to 2am and Friday through Sunday 24 hours.

SANTA CLARA PUEBLO

Close to Española (on NM 5), Santa Clara, with a population of about 1,600, is one of the largest pueblos, and the one most special to me. I've spent a good bit of time here writing about the Santa Clara people. You'll see the village sprawling across the river basin near the beautiful Black Mesa, rows of tract homes surrounding an adobe central area. An incredible setting, the pueblo itself is not much to see; however, a trip through it will give a real feel for the contemporary lives of these people. Though stories vary, the Santa Clarans teach their children that their ancestors once lived at Puye and migrated down to the river bottom. At one time I wrote a story about a language program at Santa Clara. Artisan/elders were working with children to teach them their native Tewa language, on the brink of extinction because so many now speak English. These elder artists helped the children paint a mural depicting the Santa Claran's migration from Puye in the 13th century. I've also written about noted potter Nancy Youngblood, who comes from a long line of famous potters, and now does alluring contemporary work.

One stunning sight here is the cemetery. Stop on the west side of the church and look over a 4-foot wall. It's a primitive site, with plain wooden crosses, as well as others adorned with plastic flowers. Within the village there are lots of little pottery and craft shops. If you write to the pueblo (address below) well in advance, you may be able to take one of the driving and walking tours offered Monday through Friday, including visits to the pueblo's historic church and artists' studios. Visitors can enter specified studios to watch artists making baskets and highly polished red-and-black pottery. Follow up your letter with a phone call.

There are corn and harvest dances on **Santa Clara Feast Day** (August 12); other special days include buffalo and deer dances (early February) and children's dances (December 28).

The famed **Puye Cliff Dwellings** (see below) are on the Santa Clara reservation. The pueblo's address is P.O. Box 580, Española, NM 87532 (☎ **505/753-7326**). Admission is free. The charge for still cameras is $5; for movie cameras and sketching, the charge is $15. The pueblo is open every day during daylight hours; the visitor center is open Monday through Friday from 8am to 4:30pm.

PUYE CLIFF DWELLINGS

Well worth visiting, the Puye Cliff Dwellings offer a view of centuries of culture so well preserved you can almost hear ancient life clamoring around you. First, you encounter dwellings believed to have been built around 1450. Above on a 200-foot tuft cliff face are dwellings dating from 1200. By 1540 this dwelling's population was at its height and Puye was the center for a number of villages of the Pajarito Plateau. Today, this settlement, which typifies Pajaritan culture in the placement of its houses and its symbolic decorations, is a series of rooms and caves reached by sturdy ladders and steps which visitors can climb up and down, clambering in and out of the homes. Petroglyphs are evident in many of the rocky cliff walls. Make your way to the 7,000 foot mesa top and you'll find on the cliff's edge ceremonial kivas as well as a labyrinth of dwellings representing four huge terraced community houses built around a court.

About 6 miles farther west is the **Santa Clara Canyon Recreational Area,** a sylvan setting for camping that is open year-round for picnicking, hiking, and fishing in ponds and Santa Clara Creek.

If you would like to visit the cliff dwellings, call ☎ **505/753-7326.** The admission is $5 for adults, $4 for children and seniors. The dwellings are open daily in the summer from 8am to 8pm; daily in the winter from 8am to 4:30pm.

2 Los Alamos & the Ancient Cliff Dwellings of Bandelier National Monument

Pueblo tribes lived in this rugged area for well over 1,000 years, and an exclusive boys' school operated atop the 7,300-foot plateau from 1918 to 1943. Then, the **Los Alamos National Laboratory** was established here in secrecy—Project Y of the Manhattan Engineer District, the hush-hush wartime program that developed the world's first nuclear weapons.

Project director J. Robert Oppenheimer, later succeeded by Norris E. Bradbury, worked with a team of 30 to 100 scientists in research, development, and production of the weapons. Today, more than 10,000 people work at the Los Alamos National Laboratory, making it the largest employer in Northern New Mexico. Still operated by the University of California for the federal Department of Energy, its 32 technical areas occupy 43 square miles of mesa-top land.

The laboratory is known today as one of the world's foremost scientific institutions. It's still oriented primarily toward defense research—the Trident and Minuteman strategic warheads were designed here, for example—but it has many other research programs, including international nuclear safeguards and nonproliferation, space and atmospheric studies, supercomputing, theoretical physics, biomedical and materials science, and environmental restoration.

In 1995, workers at Los Alamos began preparation to build replacement plutonium pits for weapons in the enduring U.S. nuclear weapons stopckpile. Los Alamos has become the only plutonium-handling facility in the United States capable of producing these pits. The Laboratory produced its first demonstration war-reserve pit in 1997 and will soon be able to produce up to 50 pits per year if needed.

ORIENTATION/USEFUL INFORMATION

Los Alamos is located about 35 miles west of Santa Fe and about 65 miles southwest of Taos. From Santa Fe, take US 84/285 north approximately 16 miles to the Pojoaque junction, then turn west on NM 502. Driving time is only about 50 minutes.

Los Alamos is a town of 18,000 spread over the colorful, fingerlike mesas of the Pajarito Plateau, between the Jemez Mountains and the Rio Grande Valley. As NM 502 enters Los Alamos from Santa Fe, it follows Trinity Drive, where accommodations, restaurants, and other services are located. Central Avenue parallels Trinity Drive and has restaurants, galleries, and shops, as well as the Los Alamos Historical Museum (free) and the Bradbury Science Museum (free).

The **Los Alamos Chamber of Commerce,** P.O. Box 460, Los Alamos, NM 87544 (☎ **505/662-8105;** fax 505/662-8399; e-mail: lacoc@unix.nets.com), runs a visitor center that is open Monday through Friday from 9am to 4pm and Saturday from 10am to 4pm.

EVENTS

The Los Alamos events schedule includes a **Sports Skiesta** in mid-March; **arts-and-crafts fairs** in May, August, and November; a **county fair, rodeo, and arts festival** in August; and a **triathlon** in August/September.

WHAT TO SEE & DO

Aside from the sights described below, Los Alamos offers the **Pajarito Mountain ski area,** Camp May Road (P.O. Box 155), Los Alamos, NM 87544 (☎ **505/ 662-5725**), with five chairlifts—it's only open on Saturday, Sunday, Wednesday, and federal holidays. It's an outstanding ski area that rarely gets crowded; many trails are steep with moguls. Los Alamos also offers the **Los Alamos Golf Course,** 4250 Diamond Dr. (☎ **505/662-8139**), at the edge of town; and the **Larry R. Walkup Aquatic Center,** 2760 Canyon Rd. (☎ **505/662-8170**), the highest-altitude indoor Olympic-size swimming pool in the United States. There's even an outdoor ice-skating rink, with a snack bar and skate rentals, open from Thanksgiving through late February (☎ **505/662-8174**). There are no outstanding restaurants in Los Alamos, but if you get hungry you can stop at the **Blue Window,** 800 Trinity Dr. (☎ **505/662-6305**), a country-style restaurant serving pasta, sandwiches, and salads with a view of the Sangre de Cristo Mountains. The Chamber of Commerce has maps for self-guided historical walking tours, and LANL has self-guided driving-tour tapes available in stores and at hotels around town.

Black Hole

4015 Arkansas, Los Alamos, 87544. ☎ **505/662-5053.** http://members.aol.blkholela/
home/index.htm. Free admission. Mon–Fri 9am–5pm, Sat 11am–5pm.

This store/museum is an engineer's dream world, a creative photographer's heaven, and a Felix Unger nightmare. Owned and run by Edward Grothus, it's an old grocery store packed to the ceiling with the remains of the nuclear age, from geiger counters to giant Waring blenders. If you go, be sure to visit with Grothus. He'll point out an A-frame building next door that he's christened the "First Church of High Technology," where he says a "critical mass" each Sunday. In this business for 47 years, Grothus has been written about in *Wired Magazine* and has supplied props for the movies *Silkwood, Earth II,* and the *Manhattan Project.* He's so concerned about the effects of the nuclear age, he made the news when he sent a can of Organic Plutonium (really soup) to President Clinton, a gift about which he said, "the secret service was not amused." Bring a jacket; it's dark and 40° cold in the hole.

✪ Bradbury Science Museum

At the Los Alamos National Laboratory, 15th St. and Central Ave. ☎ **505/667-4444.** Free admission. Tues–Fri 9am–5pm, Sat–Mon 1–5pm. Closed major holidays.

This is a great place to get acquainted with what goes on at a weapons production facility *after* nuclear proliferation. Though the museum is run by Los Alamos National Laboratory, which definitely puts a positive spin on the business of producing weapons, it's a fascinating place to explore and includes more than 35 hands-on exhibits. Begin in the History Gallery where you'll learn of the evolution of the site from the Los Alamos Ranch School days through the Manhattan Project to the present, including a 1939 letter from Albert Einstein to President Franklin D. Roosevelt suggesting research into uranium as a new and important source of energy. Next, move into the Research and Technology Gallery, where you can see work that's been done on the Human Genome Project and see a computer map of human DNA. You can try out a laser and learn about the workings of a particle accelerator. Meanwhile, listen for announcement of the film "The Town that Never Was," an 18-minute presentation on this community that grew up shrouded in secrecy (shown in the Auditorium). Further exploration will take you to the Defense Gallery where you can test the heaviness of plutonium against other substances, see an actual 5-ton Little Boy nuclear bomb (like the one dropped on Hiroshima), and see first-hand how Los Alamos conducts worldwide surveillance of nuclear explosions.

Fuller Lodge Art Center

2132 Central Ave. ☎ **505/662-9331.** Free admission. Mon–Sat 10am–4pm.

This is a public showcase for work by visual artists from Northern New Mexico and the surrounding region. Two annual arts-and-crafts fairs are also held here—in August and October. The gallery shop sells local crafts at good prices.

In the same building is the **Los Alamos Arts Council** (☎ **505/662-8403**), a multidisciplinary organization that sponsors two art fairs (May and November), as well as evening and noontime cultural programs.

Los Alamos Historical Museum

2132 Central Ave. ☎ **505/662-4493.** Free admission. Summer, Mon–Sat 9:30am–4:30pm, Sun 11am–5pm; winter, Mon–Sat 10am–4pm, Sun 1–4pm. Closed Jan 1, Thanksgiving, and Dec 25.

Fuller Lodge, a massive vertical-log building built by John Gaw Meem in 1928, is well worth the visit. The log work is intricate and artistic, and the feel of the old place is warm and majestic. It once housed the dining and recreation hall for the Los Alamos Ranch School for boys and is now a National Historic Landmark. It is accessible to people with disabilities. Its current occupants include the museum office and research archives and the Fuller Lodge Art Center (see above). The museum, located in the small log-and-stone building to the north of Fuller Lodge, depicts area history, from prehistoric cliff dwellers to the present. Exhibits range from Native American artifacts to school memorabilia and an excellent new permanent Manhattan Project exhibit that offers a more realistic view of the devastation resulting from use of atomic bombs than is offered at the Bradbury Science Museum. Most interesting is a quote from physicist Philip Morrison comparing the destruction by fire bombs of cities such as Osaka, Kobe, and Nagoya with destruction by nuclear bombs of Hiroshima and Nagasaki. One wall has three panoramic photographs of Hiroshima after the bomb. The museum sponsors guest speakers and operates a tax-free bookstore. Now, you can even visit the museum, albeit somewhat vicariously, on the World Wide Web at **www.vla.com/lahistory** or **www.losalamos.com/lahistory.**

NEARBY

✪ Bandelier National Monument

NM 4 (HCR 1, Box 1, Suite 15, Los Alamos, NM 87544). ☎ **505/672-3861** ext 517. Admission $10 per vehicle. Open every day during daylight hours. Closed Jan 1 and Dec 25.

Less than 15 miles south of Los Alamos along NM 4, this National Park Service area contains both extensive ruins of the ancient cliff-dwelling Anasazi Pueblo culture and 46 square miles of canyon-and-mesa wilderness. During busy summer months head out early, as there can be a waiting line for cars to park.

After an orientation stop at the visitor center and museum to learn about the culture that flourished here between 1100 and 1550, most visitors follow a trail along Frijoles Creek to the principal ruins. The pueblo site, including an underground kiva, has been stabilized. The biggest thrill for most folks, though, is climbing hardy ponderosa pine ladders to visit an alcove—140 feet above the canyon floor—that was once home to prehistoric people. Tours are self-guided or led by a National Park Service ranger. Be aware that dogs are not allowed on trails.

On summer nights, rangers offer campfire talks about the history, culture, and geology of the area. Some summer evenings, the guided night walks reveal a different, spooky aspect of the ruins and cave houses, outlined in the two-dimensional chiaroscuro of the thin cold light from the starry sky. During the day, nature programs are sometimes offered for adults and children. The small museum at the visitor center displays artifacts found in the area.

Elsewhere in the monument area, 70 miles of maintained trails lead to more tribal ruins, waterfalls, and wildlife habitats. However, a recent fire has decimated parts of this area, so periodic closings will take place in order to allow the land to reforest.

The separate **Tsankawi** section, reached by an ancient 2-mile trail close to **White Rock,** has a large unexcavated ruin on a high mesa overlooking the Rio Grande Valley. The town of White Rock, about 10 miles southeast of Los Alamos on NM 4, offers spectacular panoramas of the river valley in the direction of Santa Fe; the White Rock Overlook is a great picnic spot.

Within Bandelier, areas have been set aside for picnicking and camping. The national monument is named after the Swiss-American archaeologist Adolph Bandelier, who explored here in the 1880s.

Past Bandelier National Monument on NM 4, beginning about 15 miles from Los Alamos, is **Valle Grande,** a vast meadow 16 miles in area—all that remains of a volcanic caldera created by a collapse after eruptions nearly a million years ago. When the mountain spewed ashes and dust as far away as Kansas and Nebraska, its underground magma chambers collapsed, forming this great valley—one of the largest volcanic calderas in the world. However, lava domes that pushed up after the collapse obstruct a full view across the expanse. Valle Grande is now privately owned land, though negotiations are currently underway with the U.S. government to purchase the property, possibly to turn it into a park.

3 Along the High Road to Taos

Unless you're in a hurry to get from Santa Fe to Taos, the High Road—also called the Mountain Road or the King's Road—is by far the most fascinating route. It runs through tiny ridgetop villages where Hispanic traditions and way of life continue much as they did a century ago.

CHIMAYO

About 28 miles north of Santa Fe on NM 84/285 is the historic weaving center of Chimayo. It's approximately 16 miles past the Pojoaque junction, at the junction of NM 520 and NM 76 via NM 503. In this small village, families still maintain the tradition of crafting handwoven textiles initiated by their ancestors seven generations ago, in the early 1800s. One such family is the Ortegas, and both **Ortega's Weaving Shop** and **Galeria Ortega** are fine places to take a close look at this ancient craft.

Today, however, many more people come to Chimayo to visit ✪ **El Santuario de Nuestro Señor de Esquipulas** (the Shrine of Our Lord of Esquipulas), better known simply as "El Santuario de Chimayo." Ascribed with miraculous powers of healing, this church has attracted thousands of pilgrims since its construction in 1814–16. Up to 30,000 people participate in the annual Good Friday pilgrimage, many of them walking from as far away as Albuquerque.

Although only the earth in the anteroom beside the altar is presumed to have the gift of healing powers, the entire shrine radiates true serenity. It's quite moving to peruse the written testimonies of rapid recovery from illness or injury on the walls of the anteroom, and equally poignant to read the as-yet-unanswered entreaties made on behalf of loved ones.

A National Historic Landmark, the church has five beautiful *reredos,* or panels of sacred paintings, one behind the main altar and two on each side of the nave. Each year during the fourth weekend in July, the military exploits of the 9th-century Spanish saint Santiago are celebrated in a weekend fiesta, including the historic play **Los Moros y Los Cristianos** (Moors and Christians).

Lovely **Santa Cruz Lake** has a dual purpose: This artificial lake provides water for Chimayo Valley farms and also offers a recreation site for trout fishing and camping at the edge of the Pecos Wilderness. To reach it, turn south 4 miles on NM 503, about 2 miles east of Chimayo.

WHERE TO DINE

✪ Restaurante Rancho de Chimayo

P.O. Box 11, Chimayo, NM, 87522 (CTR 98). ☎ **505/351-4444.** Reservations recommended. Lunch $7.50–$13; dinner $10–$15. AE, DC, DISC, MC, V. Daily 11:30am–9pm; Sat and Sun breakfast 8:30–11am. Closed Mon from Oct–May. NEW MEXICAN.

For as long as I can remember, my family and all my friends' families have scheduled trips into Northern New Mexico to coincide with lunch- or dinner-time at this fun restaurant. Located in an adobe home built by Hermenegildo Jaramillo in the 1880s, it is now run as a restaurant by his descendants. Unfortunately, over the years the restaurant has become so famous that tour buses now stop here. However, the food has suffered only a little. In the warmer months request the terraced patio. During winter, you'll be seated in one of a number of cozy rooms with thick viga ceilings. The food is Native New Mexican, prepared from generations-old Jaramillo family recipes. You can't go wrong with the enchiladas, served layered, Northern New Mexico style, rather than rolled. For variety you might want to try the combinación picante (carne adovada, tamale, enchilada, beans, and posole). Each plate comes with two sopaipillas. With a little honey, who needs dessert? Margaritas from the full bar are delicious.

CORDOVA

Just as Chimayo is famous for its weaving, the village of Cordova, about 7 miles east on NM 76, is noted for its wood-carvers. Small shops and studios along the highway display *santos* (carved saints) and various decorative items carved from aspen and cedar.

TRUCHAS

Robert Redford's 1988 movie, *The Milagro Beanfield War,* featured the town of Truchas (which means "trout"). A former Spanish colonial outpost built on top of an 8,000-foot mesa, 4 miles east of Cordova, it was chosen as the site for the film in part because traditional Hispanic culture is still very much in evidence. Subsistence farming is prevalent here. The scenery is spectacular: 13,101-foot Truchas Peak dominates one side of the mesa, and the broad Rio Grande Valley dominates the other.

About 6 miles east of Truchas on NM 76 is the small town of **Las Trampas,** noted for its San José Church, which some call the most beautiful of all churches built during the Spanish colonial period.

PICURIS (SAN LORENZO) PUEBLO

Near the regional education center of Peñasco, about 24 miles from Chimayo near the intersection of NM 75 and NM 76, is the Picuris (San Lorenzo) Pueblo (☎ **505/587-2519** or 505/587-2957). The 375 citizens of this 15,000-acre mountain pueblo, native Tiwa speakers, consider themselves a sovereign nation: Their forebears never made a treaty with any foreign country, including the United States. Thus, they observe a traditional form of tribal council government. A few of the original mud-and-stone houses still stand and are home to tribal elders. A striking above-ground ceremonial kiva called "the Roundhouse," built at least 700 years ago, and some historic excavated kivas and storerooms are open to visitors. The **annual feast day** at San Lorenzo Church is August 10.

Still, the people here are modern enough to have fully computerized their public showcase operations as Picuris Tribal Enterprises. Besides running the Hotel Santa Fe in the state capital, they own the **Picuris Pueblo Museum and Visitor's Center,** where weaving, beadwork, and distinctive reddish-brown clay cooking pottery are exhibited daily from 9am to 6pm. Self-guided tours through the old village ruins begin at the museum and cost $1.75; the camera fee is $5 (includes entrance fee); sketching and video camera fees are $10. There's also an information center, crafts shop, and grocery store. Fishing permits ($6 for adults and children) are available, as are permits to camp at Pu-Na and Tu-Tah Lakes, regularly stocked with trout.

About a mile east of Peñasco on NM 75 is **Vadito,** the former center for a conservative Catholic brotherhood, the Penitentes, earlier in this century.

DIXON & EMBUDO

Taos is about 24 miles north of Peñasco via NM 518. But day-trippers from Santa Fe can loop back to the capital by taking NM 75 west from Picuris Pueblo. Dixon, approximately 12 miles west of Picuris, and its twin village Embudo, a mile farther on NM 68 at the Rio Grande, are home to many artists and craftspeople who exhibit their works during the annual **autumn show** sponsored by the Dixon Arts Association. For a taste of the local grape, you can follow signs to **La Chiripada Winery** (☎ **505/579-4437**), whose product is surprisingly good, especially to those who don't know that New Mexico has a long wine-making history. Local pottery is also sold in the tasting room. The winery is open Monday through Saturday from 10am to 5pm.

Two more small villages lie in the Rio Grande Valley at 6-mile intervals south of Embudo on NM 68. **Velarde** is a fruit-growing center; in season, the road here is lined with stands selling fresh fruit or crimson chile ristras and wreaths of native plants. **Alcalde** is the site of Los Luceros, an early-17th-century home that is to be refurbished as an arts and history center. The unique **Dance of the Matachines,** a Moorish-style ritual brought from Spain by the conquistadors, is performed here on holidays and feast days.

ESPAÑOLA

The commercial center of Española (population 7,000) no longer has the railroad that led to its establishment in the 1880s, but it may have New Mexico's greatest concentration of **low riders.** These late-model customized cars, so called because their suspension leaves them sitting quite close to the ground, are definitely their owners' objects of affection. The cars have inspired a unique auto subculture. You can't miss the cars—they cruise the main streets of town, especially on weekend evenings.

Sights of interest in Española include the **Bond House Museum,** a Victorian-era adobe home that exhibits local history and art; and the **Santa Cruz Church,** built in 1733 and renovated in 1979, which houses many fine examples of Spanish colonial religious art. The new **Convento,** built to resemble a colonial cathedral, on the Española Plaza (at the junction of NM 30 and US 84), will house an office of the Chamber of Commerce, restaurants, and shops. Major events include the July **Fiesta de Oñate,** commemorating the valley's founding in 1596; the October **Tri-Cultural Art Festival** on the Northern New Mexico Community College campus; and the weeklong **Summer Solstice** celebration staged in June by the nearby Ram Das Puri ashram of the Sikhs (☎ **888/346-2420** or 505/753-4988).

Complete information on Española and the vicinity can be obtained from the **Española Valley Chamber of Commerce,** 417 Big Rock Center, Española, NM 87532 (☎ **505/753-2831**).

If you admire the work of Georgia O'Keeffe, try to plan a short trip to **Abiquiu,** a tiny town at a bend of the Rio Chama, 14 miles south of Ghost Ranch and 22 miles north of Española on US 84. Once you see the surrounding terrain, it will be clear that this was the inspiration for many of her startling landscapes. Since March 1995, **O'Keeffe's adobe home** (where she lived and painted) has been open for public tours. However, a reservation must be made in advance; the charge is $20 for

Georgia O'Keeffe & New Mexico: A Desert Romance

In June 1917, during a short visit to the Southwest, the painter Georgia O'Keeffe (born 1887) visited New Mexico for the first time. She was immediately enchanted by the stark scenery; even after her return to the energy and chaos of New York City, her mind wandered frequently to New Mexico's arid land and undulating mesas. However, not until coaxed by the arts patron and "collector of people" Mabel Dodge Luhan 12 years later did O'Keeffe return to the multi-hued desert of her daydreams.

O'Keeffe was reportedly ill when she arrived in Santa Fe in April 1929, both physically and emotionally. New Mexico seemed to soothe her spirit and heal her physical ailments almost magically. Two days after her arrival, Mabel Dodge Luhan persuaded O'Keeffe to move into her home in Taos. There, she would be free to paint and socialize as she liked.

In Taos, O'Keeffe began painting what would become some of her best-known canvases—close-ups of desert flowers and objects such as cow and horse skulls. "The color up there is different . . . the blue-green of the sage and the mountains, the wildflowers in bloom," O'Keeffe once said of Taos. "It's a different kind of color from any I've ever seen—there's nothing like that in north Texas or even in Colorado." Taos transformed not only her art, but her personality as well. She bought a car and learned to drive. Sometimes, on warm days, she ran stark naked through the sage fields. That August, a new, rejuvenated O'Keeffe rejoined her husband, photographer Alfred Stieglitz, in New York.

The artist returned to New Mexico year after year, spending time with Mabel Dodge Luhan as well as staying at the isolated Ghost Ranch. She drove through the countryside in her snappy Ford, stopping to paint in her favorite spots along the way. Up until 1949, O'Keeffe always returned to New York in the fall. Three years after Stieglitz's death, though, she relocated permanently to New Mexico, spending each winter and spring in Abiquiu and each summer and fall at Ghost Ranch. Georgia O'Keeffe died in Santa Fe in 1986.

a 1-hour tour. A number of tours are given each week—on Tuesday, Thursday, and Friday—and a limited number of people are accepted per tour. Visitors are not permitted to take pictures. Fortunately, O'Keeffe's home remains as it was when she lived there (until 1986). Call several months in advance for reservations (☎ **505/685-4539**).

A GREAT NEARBY PLACE TO STAY & DINE

✪ Rancho de San Juan

U.S. Highway 285 (en route to Ojo Caliente), P.O. Box 4140, Fairview Station, Española, NM 87533. ☎ **505/753-6818.** 9 units. TEL. $175–$350 double. Full breakfast included. AE, DISC, MC, V.

This inn provides an authentic Northern New Mexico desert experience with the comfort of a luxury hotel. Opened 4 years ago, it's the passion of architect and chef John Johnson, responsible for the design and cuisine, and interior designer David Heath, responsible for the elegant interiors. The original part of the inn comprises four rooms around a central courtyard. Five additional casitas have been added in the outlying hills. The original rooms are a bit small but very elegant, with European antiques and spectacular views of desert scapes and distant, snow-capped peaks. All units have fireplaces, private portals, makeup mirrors, hair dryers, Italian robes and sheets, and Caswell Massey soaps in the bath. My favorite room in the main part is the Black Mesa, though all are consistently nice. Of the casitas—all quite roomy—my favorite is the Anasazi. It has lots of light, a raised sleeping area, and a jet tub with a view. The Kiva suite has a round bedroom and a skylight just above the bed, perfect for star-gazing.

Each morning, John serves an elaborate full breakfast. In the evenings, a prix-fixe dinner is served, and includes four courses, the meal ranging in price from $45 to $95, depending on the wine. The food is eclectic French/Italian/American; such specialties as breast of African pheasant and/or sautéed Alaskan halibut are served in the cozy dining room with a sunset view.

A few minutes' hike from the inn is the **Grand Chamber,** an impressive shrine which the innkeepers commissioned to be carved into a sandstone outcropping, where weddings and other festivities are held.

Many locals from the area like to rejuvenate at **Ojo Caliente Mineral Springs,** Ojo Caliente, NM 87549 (☎ **800/222-9162** or 505/583-2233). It's on US 285, 50 miles (a 1-hour drive) northwest of Santa Fe and 50 miles southwest of Taos. This National Historic Site was considered sacred by prehistoric tribes. When Spanish explorer Cabeza de Vaca discovered and named the springs in the 16th century, he called them "the greatest treasure that I found these strange people to possess." No other hot spring in the world has Ojo Caliente's combination of iron, soda, lithium, sodium, and arsenic. The dressing rooms are fairly new and in good shape; however, the whole place could use sprucing up. If you're a fastidious type you won't be comfortable here. The resort offers herbal wraps and massages, lodging, and meals. It's open daily from 8am to 8pm (9pm Friday and Saturday).

4 Pecos National Monument

About 15 miles east of Santa Fe, I-25 meanders through **Glorieta Pass,** site of an important Civil War skirmish. In March 1862, volunteers from Colorado and New Mexico, along with Fort Union regulars, defeated a Confederate force marching on Santa Fe, thereby turning the tide of Southern encroachment in the West.

Take NM 50 east to **Pecos,** a distance of about 7 miles. This quaint town, well off the beaten track since the interstate was constructed, is the site of a noted **Benedictine monastery.** About 26 miles north of here on NM 63 is the village of **Cowles,** gateway to the natural wonderland of the Pecos Wilderness. There are many camping, picnicking, and fishing locales en route.

Pecos National Historical Park (☎ **505/757-6414**), about 2 miles south of the town of Pecos off NM 63, contains the ruins of a 15th-century pueblo and 17th- and 18th-century missions. Coronado mentioned Pecos Pueblo in 1540: "It is feared through the land," he wrote. With a population of about 2,000, the Native Americans farmed in irrigated fields and hunted wild game. Their pueblo had 660 rooms and many kivas. By 1620, Franciscan monks had established a church and convent. Military and natural disasters took their toll on the pueblo, and in 1838, the 20 surviving Pecos went to live with relatives at the Jemez Pueblo.

The **E. E. Fogelson Visitor Center** tells the history of the Pecos people in a well-done, chronologically organized exhibit, complete with dioramas. A 1½-mile loop trail begins at the center and continues through Pecos Pueblo and the **Misión de Nuestra Señora de Los Angeles de Porciuncula** (as the church was formerly called). This excavated structure—170 feet long and 90 feet wide at the transept— was once the most magnificent church north of Mexico City.

Pecos National Historical Park is open Memorial Day to Labor Day, daily from 8am to 6pm; the rest of the year, daily from 8am to 5pm; closed January 1 and December 25. Admission is $2 per person; $4 per carload.

5 Chaco Culture National Historic Park

A combination of a stunning setting and well-preserved ruins makes the long drive to Chaco Canyon worth the trip. Whether you come from the north or south, you drive in on a dusty (and sometimes muddy) road that seems to add to the authenticity and adventure of this remote New Mexico experience.

When you finally arrive, you walk through stark desert country that seems perhaps ill-suited as a center of culture. However, the ancient Anasazi people successfully farmed the lowlands and built great masonry towns, which connected with other towns over a wide-ranging network of roads crossing this desolate place.

What's most interesting here is how changes in architecture—beginning in the mid-800s when the Anasazi started building on a larger scale than they had previously—chart the area's cultural progress. They used the same masonry techniques that tribes had used in smaller villages in the region, walls one stone thick with generous use of mud mortar, but they built stone villages of multiple stories with rooms several times larger than in the previous stage of their culture. Within a century, six large pueblos were underway. This pattern of a single large pueblo with oversized rooms, surrounded by conventional villages, caught on throughout the region. New communities built along these lines sprang up. Old villages built similarly large pueblos. Eventually there were more than 75 such towns, most of them closely tied to Chaco by an extensive system of roads.

This progress led to Chaco becoming the economic center of the San Juan Basin by A.D. 1000. As many as 5,000 people may have lived in some 400 settlements in and around Chaco. As masonry techniques advanced through the years, walls rose more than 4 stories in height. Some of these are still visible today.

You may want to focus your energy on seeing **Pueblo Bonito,** the largest prehistoric Southwest Native American dwelling ever excavated. It contains giant kivas and 800 rooms covering more than 3 acres. Also, the **Pueblo Alto Trail** is a nice hike that takes you up on the canyon rim so you can see the ruins from above. In the afternoon, with thunderheads building, the views are spectacular. If you're a cyclist, there's a special map with trails outlined, an excellent way to traverse the vast expanse while experiencing the quiet of these ancient dwellings.

This trip involves some 380 miles of driving. You may want to call ahead to inquire about road conditions because the roads can get extremely muddy. To get to Chaco from Santa Fe, take I-25 south to Bernalillo, then NM 44 northwest through Cuba to Nageezi. Turn left onto a dirt road that runs almost 30 miles south to the park's boundary. The trip takes about 3½ to 4 hours. Overnight camping is permitted year-round. Or, a nice stop on the way back is the **Riverdancer Inn** off State Highway 44, 16 miles on Highway 4 in Jemez Springs (☎ **800/809-3262** or 505/829-3262).

The park's address is Star NM 4, Box 6500, Bloomfield, NM 87413 (☎ **505/786-7014**). Admission is $8 per car, campsite extra. The visitor center is open Memorial Day through Labor Day, daily from 8am to 6pm; the rest of the year, daily from 8am to 5pm. Trails are open from sunrise to sunset. Ranger-guided walks and campfire talks are available in the summer.

11 Getting to Know Taos

Wedged between the western flank of the Sangre de Cristo Range and the semi-arid high desert of the upper Rio Grande Valley, Taos combines nature and culture, history and progress. There's considerably less commercialization here than in the state capital.

Located just 40 miles south of the Colorado border, about 70 miles north of Santa Fe and 135 miles from Albuquerque, Taos is best known for its thriving art colony, its historic Native American pueblo, and the nearby ski area, one of the most highly regarded in the Rockies. Taos also has several fine museums (including a brand-new one that opened in 1995) and a wide choice of accommodations and restaurants.

About 5,000 people consider themselves Taoseños (permanent residents of Taos) today. This area may have been inhabited for 5,000 years; throughout the Taos valley there are ruins that date back more than 1,000 years.

The Spanish first visited this area in 1540, colonizing it in 1598. In the last 2 decades of the 17th century, they put down three rebellions at the Taos Pueblo. During the 18th and 19th centuries Taos was an important trade center: New Mexico's annual caravan to Chihuahua, Mexico, couldn't leave until after the annual midsummer Taos Fair. French trappers began attending the fair in 1739. Even though the Plains tribes often attacked the pueblos at other times, they would attend the market festival under a temporary annual truce. By the early 1800s, Taos had become a meeting place for American mountain men, the most famous of whom, Kit Carson, made his home in Taos from 1826 to 1868.

Thoroughly Hispanic, Taos remained loyal to Mexico during the Mexican War of 1846. The town rebelled against its new U.S. landlord in 1847, even killing newly appointed Governor Charles Bent in his Taos home. Nevertheless, the town was eventually incorporated into the Territory of New Mexico in 1850. During the Civil War, Taos fell into Confederate hands for 6 weeks; afterward, Carson and two other men raised the Union flag over Taos Plaza and guarded it day and night. Since that time, Taos has had the honor of flying the flag 24 hours a day.

Taos's population declined when the railroad bypassed it in favor of Santa Fe. In 1898 two East Coast artists—Ernest Blumenschein and Bert Phillips—discovered the dramatic, varied effects of

Taos Downtown & Area

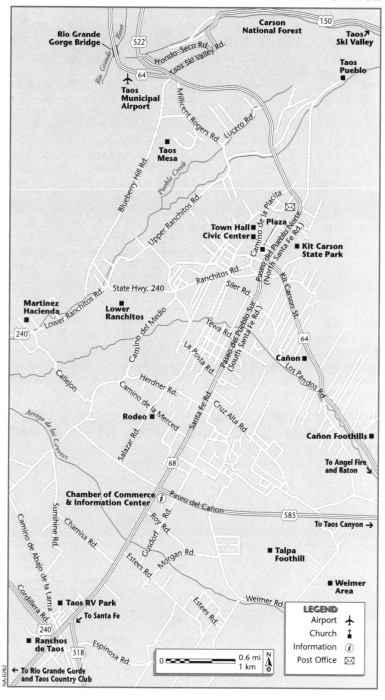

sunlight on the natural environment of the Taos valley and depicted them on canvas. By 1912, thanks to the growing influence of the **Taos Society of Artists,** the town had gained a worldwide reputation as a cultural center. Today, it is estimated that more than 15% of the population are painters, sculptors, writers, musicians, or otherwise earn their income from artistic pursuits.

The town of Taos is merely the focal point of the rugged 2,200-square-mile Taos County. Two features dominate this sparsely populated region: the high desert mesa, split in two by the 650-foot-deep chasm of the Rio Grande; and the Sangre de Cristo Range, which tops out at 13,161-foot Wheeler Peak, New Mexico's highest mountain. From the forested uplands to the sage-carpeted mesa, the county is home to a large variety of wildlife. The human element includes Native Americans who are still living in ancient pueblos and Hispanic farmers who continue to irrigate their farmlands by centuries-old methods.

Taos is also inhabited by many people who have chosen to retreat from, or altogether drop out of, mainstream society. There's a laid-back attitude here, even more pronounced than the general *mañana* attitude for which New Mexico is known. Most Taoseños live here to play here—and that means outdoors. Many work at the ski area all winter (skiing whenever they can) and work for raft companies in the summer (to get on the river as much as they can). Others are into rock climbing, mountain biking, and backpacking. That's not to say that Taos is just a resort town. With the Hispanic and Native American populations' histories in the area, there's a richness and depth here that most resort towns lack.

Taos's biggest task these days is to try to stem the tide of overdevelopment that is flooding Northern New Mexico. In the "Northern New Mexico Today" section of chapter 1, I addressed the city's success in battling back airport expansion and some housing developments. A grassroots community program has been implemented recently that will give all neighborhoods a say in how their area is developed.

1 Orientation

ARRIVING

BY PLANE   The **Taos Airport** (☎ 505/758-4995) is about 8 miles northwest of town on US 64. Call for information on local charter services. It's easiest to fly into Albuquerque International Airport, rent a car, and drive up to Taos from there. The drive will take you approximately 2½ hours. If you'd rather be picked up at Albuquerque International Airport, call **Pride of Taos** (☎ 505/758-8340). They offer charter bus service to Taos town and the Taos Ski Valley daily. **Faust's Transportation, Inc.** (☎ 505/758-3410) offers a similar service.

BY BUS   The Taos Bus Center, Paseo del Pueblo Sur at the Chevron station (☎ 505/758-1144), is not far from the Plaza. **Greyhound/Trailways** and **TNM&O Coaches** arrive and depart from this depot several times a day. For more information on these and other local bus services to and from Albuquerque and Santa Fe, see "Getting There," in chapter 2.

BY CAR   Most visitors arrive in Taos via either NM 68 or US 64. Northbound travelers should exit I-25 at Santa Fe, follow US 285 as far as San Juan Pueblo, and then continue on the divided highway when it becomes NM 68. Taos is about 79 miles from the I-25 junction. Southbound travelers from Denver on I-25 should exit about 6 miles south of Raton at US 64 and then follow it about 95 miles to Taos. Another major route is US 64 from the west (214 miles from Farmington).

VISITOR INFORMATION

The **Taos County Chamber of Commerce,** at the junction of US 64 and NM 68 (P.O. Drawer I), Taos, NM 87571 (☎ **800/732-TAOS** or 505/758-3873), is open year-round, daily from 9am to 5pm. It's closed on major holidays. **Carson National Forest** also has an information center in the same building. On the Internet you can access information about Taos at http://taoswebb.com. The e-mail address for the Taos County Chamber of Commerce is taos@taoswebb.com.

CITY LAYOUT

The Plaza is a short block west of Taos's major intersection—where US 64 (Kit Carson Road) from the east joins NM 68, **Paseo del Pueblo Sur** (also known as South Pueblo Road or South Santa Fe Road). US 64 proceeds north from the intersection as **Paseo del Pueblo Norte** (North Pueblo Road). **Camino de la Placita** (Placitas Road) circles the west side of downtown, passing within a block of the other side of the Plaza. Many of the streets that join these thoroughfares are winding lanes lined by traditional adobe homes, many of them over 100 years old.

Most of the art galleries are located on or near the Plaza, which was paved over with bricks several years ago, and along neighboring streets. Others are located in the **Ranchos de Taos** area a few miles south of the Plaza.

MAPS   To find your way around town, pick up a free copy of the Taos map from the **Chamber of Commerce at Taos Visitor Center,** 1139 Paseo del Pueblo Sur (☎ **505/758-3873**). Good, detailed city maps can be found at area bookstores as well (see "Shopping," in chapter 14).

2 Getting Around

BY BUS & TAXI

If you're in Taos without a car, you're in luck because there is now a local bus service, provided by **Taos Transit** (☎ **505/737-2606**). It operates Monday through Saturday from 7am to 9pm. The route runs from Kachina Lodge on Paseo del Pueblo Norte and ends at the Ranchos Post Office on the south side of town, with buses reaching each stop about every 45 minutes. They also go to Taos Pueblo. Bus fares are 50¢ one-way, $1 all day, and $5 for a 7-day pass.

In addition, Taos has two private bus companies. **Faust's Transportation** (☎ **505/758-3410**) has a shuttle bus service linking town hotels and Taos Ski Valley; they run three times a day for $10 round-trip.

Faust's Transportation also offers town taxi service daily from 7am to 9pm, with fares of about $7 anywhere within the city limits for up to two people ($2 per additional person), $40 to Albuquerque International Airport, and $35 to Taos Ski Valley from Taos town.

BY CAR

With offices at the Taos airport, **Dollar** (☎ **800/369-4226** or 505/758-9501) is reliable and efficient. Other car-rental agencies are available out of Albuquerque. See "Getting Around," chapter 15 for details.

PARKING   Parking can be difficult during the summer rush, when the stream of tourists' cars moving north and south through town never ceases. If you can't find parking on the street or in the Plaza, check out some of the nearby roads (Kit Carson Road, for instance) because there are plenty of metered and unmetered lots in Taos town.

WARNING FOR DRIVERS Reliable paved roads lead to starting points for side trips up poorer forest roads to many recreation sites. Once you get off the main roads, you won't find gas stations or cafes. Four-wheel-drive vehicles are recommended on snow and much of the otherwise unpaved terrain of the region. If you're doing some off-road adventuring, it's wise to go with a full gas tank, extra food and water, and warm clothing—just in case. At the higher-than-10,000-foot elevations of Northern New Mexico, sudden summer snowstorms are not unheard of.

ROAD CONDITIONS Information on road conditions in the Taos area can be obtained free from the **State Police** (☎ **505/758-8878** within New Mexico). Also, for highway conditions throughout the state, call the **State Highway Department** (☎ **800/432-4269**).

BY BICYCLE/ON FOOT

Bicycle rentals are available from **Gearing Up Bicycle Shop,** 129 Paseo del Pueblo Sur (☎ **505/751-0365**); daily rentals run $20 for a mountain bike with front suspension. **Hot Tracks Cyclery & Ski Touring Service,** 214 Paseo del Pueblo Sur (☎ **505/751-0949**), rents front-suspension mountain bikes and full-suspension bikes for $9/hour, $15/half day, and $20/full day. **Native Sons Adventures,** 1033 Paseo del Pueblo Sur (☎ **800/753-7559** or 505/758-9342), rents unsuspended bikes for $15/half day and $20/full day, front-suspension bikes for $25/half day and $35/full day, and full-suspension bikes for $35/half day and $45/full day; they also rent car racks for $5. Each shop supplies helmets and water bottles with rentals.

Most of Taos's attractions can easily be reached by foot since they are within a few blocks of the Plaza.

FAST FACTS: Taos

Airport See "Orientation," above.

Area Code The telephone area code for all of New Mexico is 505.

Business Hours Most businesses are open Monday through Friday from 10am to 5pm, though some may open an hour earlier and close an hour later. Many tourist-oriented shops are also open on Saturday morning, and some art galleries are open all day Saturday and Sunday, especially during peak tourist seasons. Banks are generally open Monday through Thursday from 9am to 3pm and often for longer hours on Friday. Call establishments for specific hours.

Car Rentals See "Getting Around," above.

Climate Taos's climate is similar to that of Santa Fe. Summer days are dry and sunny, except for frequent afternoon thunderstorms. Winter days are often bracing, with snowfalls common but rarely lasting too long. Average summer temperatures range from 50°F to 87°F. Winter temperatures vary between 9°F and 40°F. Annual rainfall is 12 inches; annual snowfall is 35 inches in town and 300 inches at Taos Ski Valley, where the elevation is 9,207 feet. (A foot of snow is equal to an inch of rain.)

Currency Exchange Foreign currency can be exchanged at the Centinel Bank of Taos, 512 Paseo del Pueblo Sur (☎ **505/758-6700**).

Dentists If you need dental work, try Dr. Walter Jakiela, 536 Paseo del Pueblo Norte (☎ **505/758-8654**); Dr. Michael Rivera, 107 Plaza Garcia, Suite. E (☎ **505/758-0531**); or Dr. Tom Simms, 923-B Paseo del Pueblo Sur (☎ **505/758-8303**).

Doctors   Members of the Taos Medical Group, on Weimer Road (☎ 505/758-2224), are highly respected. Also recommended are Family Practice Associates of Taos, at 630 Paseo del Pueblo Sur, Suite 150 (☎ **505/758-3005**).

Driving Rules   See "Getting Around," above.

Drugstores   See "Pharmacies," below.

Embassies/Consulates   See chapter 3, "Fast Facts: For the Foreign Traveler."

Emergencies   Dial ☎ **911** for police, fire, and ambulance.

Eyeglasses   Taos Eyewear, in Cruz Alta Plaza (☎ **505/758-8758**), handles most needs Monday through Friday between 8:30am and 5pm. It also has emergency service.

Hospital   Holy Cross Hospital, 1397 Weimer Rd., off Paseo del Canyon (☎ **505/758-8883**), has 24-hour emergency service. Serious cases are transferred to Santa Fe or Albuquerque.

Hot Lines   The crisis hot line (☎ **505/758-9888**) is available for emergency counseling.

Information   See "Visitor Information," above.

Library   The Taos Public Library, 402 Camino de la Placita (☎ 505/758-3063), has a general collection for Taos residents, a children's library, and special collections on the Southwest and Taos art.

Liquor Laws   The legal drinking age is 21 in New Mexico, as it is throughout the United States. Bars may remain open until 2am Monday through Saturday and until midnight on Sunday. Wine, beer, and spirits are sold at licensed supermarkets and liquor stores, but there are no package sales on election days until after 7pm. It is illegal to transport liquor through most Native American reservations.

Lost Property   Check with the city police (☎ **505/758-2216**).

Newspapers & Magazines   *The Taos News* (☎ **505/758-2241**) and the *Sangre de Cristo Chronicle* (☎ **505/377-2358**) are published every Thursday. *Taos Magazine* is also a good source of local information. The *Albuquerque Journal* and the *New Mexican* from Santa Fe are easily obtained at the Fernandez de Taos Bookstore on the Plaza.

Pharmacies   There are several full-service pharmacies in Taos. Furr's Pharmacy (☎ **505/758-1203**), Smith's Pharmacy (☎ **505/758-4824**), and Wal-Mart Pharmacy (☎ **505/758-2743**) are all located on Pueblo Sur and are easily seen from the road.

Photographic Needs   Check Plaza Photo, Taos Main Plaza (☎ **505/758-3420**). Minor camera repairs can be done the same day, but major repairs must be sent to Santa Fe and usually require several days. Plaza Photo offers a full line of photo accessories and 1-hour processing. April's 1-Hour Photos, at 613E N. Pueblo Rd. (☎ **505/758-0515**), is another good choice.

Police   In case of emergency, dial ☎ **911.** All other inquiries should be directed to Taos Police, Civic Plaza Drive (☎ **505/758-2216**). The Taos County Sheriff, with jurisdiction outside the city limits, is located in the county courthouse on Paseo del Pueblo Sur (☎ **505/758-3361**).

Post Offices   The main Taos Post Office is at 318 Paseo del Pueblo Norte, Taos, NM 87571 (☎ **505/758-2081**), a few blocks north of the Plaza traffic light. There are smaller offices in Ranchos de Taos (☎ **505/758-3944**) and at El Prado (☎ **505/758-4810**). The ZIP code for Taos is 87571.

Radio   Local stations are KTAO-FM (101.7), which broadcasts an entertainment calendar daily (☎ **505/758-1017**); the National Public Radio Stations—KUNM-FM (98.5) from Albuquerque and KRZA-FM (88.7) from Alamosa—for news, sports, and weather; and KAFR-FM (99.1) from Angel Fire.

Taxes   Gross receipts tax for Taos town is 6.8125%, and for Taos County it's 6.3125%. There is an additional local bed tax of 3.5% in Taos town and 3% on hotel rooms in Taos County.

Television   Channel 2, the local access station, is available in most hostelries. For a few hours a day there is local programming. Cable networks carry Santa Fe and Albuquerque stations.

Time   As is true throughout New Mexico, Taos is in the Mountain time zone. It's 2 hours earlier than New York, 1 hour earlier than Chicago, and 1 hour later than Los Angeles. Daylight saving time is in effect from early April to late October.

Useful Telephone Numbers   For information on road conditions in the Taos area, call the state police at ☎ **505/758-8878** or dial ☎ 800/432-4269 (within New Mexico) for the state highway department. Taos County offices are at ☎ **505/758-8834.**

Where to Stay in Taos

A tiny town with a big tourist market, Taos has some 2,200 rooms in 88 hotels, motels, condominiums, and bed-and-breakfasts. Many new properties have recently opened, turning this into a buyer's market. In the slower season, you may even want to try bargaining your room rate down, because competition for travelers is steep. Most of the hotels and motels are located on Paseo del Pueblo Sur and Norte, with a few scattered just east of the town center along Kit Carson Road. The condos and bed-and-breakfasts are generally scattered throughout Taos's back streets.

During peak seasons, visitors without reservations may have difficulty finding a vacant room. **Taos Central Reservations,** P.O. Box 1713, Taos, NM 87571 (☎ **800/821-2437** or 505/758-9767), might be able to help.

Fifteen hundred or so of Taos County's beds are in condominiums and lodges at or near the Taos Ski Valley. The **Taos Valley Resort Association,** P.O. Box 85, Taos Ski Valley, NM 87525 (☎ **800/776-1111** or 505/776-2233; fax 505/776-8842), can book these as well as rooms in Taos and all of Northern New Mexico, and can broker private home rentals. The World Wide Web address for Taos Valley Resort Association is http://taoswebb.com/nmresv. If you'd rather e-mail for a reservation, the address is res@taoswebb.com.

Some three dozen bed-and-breakfasts are listed with the Taos Chamber of Commerce. The **Taos Bed and Breakfast Association** (☎ **800/876-7857** or 505/758-4747) and the **Traditional Taos Inns Bed and Breakfast Association** (☎ **800/939-2215** or 505/776-8840), both with strict guidelines for membership, will provide information and make reservations for member inns.

Accommodations and Tours of Taos, 1033-A Paseo del Pueblo Sur, Taos, NM 87571 (☎ **800/290-5384** or 505/751-1292), will help you find accommodations from bed-and-breakfasts to home rentals, hotels, and cabins throughout Taos and Northern New Mexico. They'll also help you arrange rental cars and package prices for outdoor activities such as white-water rafting, horseback riding, snowmobiling, fishing trips, and ski packages.

Unlike in Santa Fe, there are two high seasons in Taos: winter (the Christmas-to-Easter ski season, except for January, which is notoriously slow) and summer. Spring and fall are shoulder seasons, often with lower rates. The period between Easter and Memorial

Day is notoriously slow in the tourist industry here, and many restaurants and other businesses take their annual vacations at this time. Book well ahead for ski holiday periods (especially Christmas) and for the annual arts festivals (late May to mid-June and late September to early October).

In these listings, the following categories have been used to describe peak-season prices for a double: **Expensive** applies to accommodations that charge over $100 per night; **Moderate** refers to $75 to $100; and **Inexpensive** indicates $75 and under. A tax of 11.38% in Taos town and 11.1325% in Taos County will be added to every hotel bill.

1 Best Bets

- **Best Historic Hotel:** The **Historic Taos Inn,** 125 Paseo del Pueblo Norte (☎ 800-TAOS-INN or 505/758-2233), dates from the mid-1800s and was once home to Taos's first doctor. It was also the first place in town to install indoor plumbing. Today, though the inn maintains much of its historic detail, it is equipped with all modern conveniences. It appears on both the State and National Registers of Historic Places.
- **Best for Families:** Without a doubt, Taos's best full-service hotel for families is the **Best Western Kachina Lodge and Meeting Center,** 413 Paseo del Pueblo Norte (☎ 800/522-4462 or 505/758-2275). The room prices are manageable, the location is excellent, there's an outdoor pool where kids can cool off during the summer, snack machines are helpful when Mom and Dad just don't feel like taking the car out again, and there are laundry facilities on the premises.
- **Best Moderately Priced Hotel:** For rooms in this category (that are not bed-and-breakfasts), you're best off with the **Sun God,** 919 Paseo del Pueblo Sur (5513 NDCBU), Taos, NM 87571 (☎ 800/821-2437 or 505/758-3162). You'll get clean rooms with a Southwestern feel on nice, grassy grounds.
- **Best Bed-and-Breakfast:** The best bed-and-breakfast in Taos is the **Adobe and Pines Inn,** P.O. Box 837, Ranchos de Taos, NM 87557 (☎ 800/723-8267 or 505/751-0947). The rooms are creatively decorated, hosts Chuck and Charil Fulkerson are gracious, and the setting is lush and peaceful.
- **Best Modern Adobe Architecture:** While you'll find many bed-and-breakfasts in New Mexico in historic or old buildings that were constructed of true adobe bricks, you'd be hardpressed to find new, modern buildings using the same materials. **Little Tree Bed and Breakfast,** P.O. Drawer II, Taos, NM 87571 (☎ 505/776-8467) is a beautiful adobe inn. Even inside, you can see pieces of straw and mica in the walls.
- **Best Romantic Getaway: Alma del Monte–Spirit of the Mountain,** 372 Hondo Seco Rd., P.O. Box 1434, Taos, NM 87571. (☎ 800/273-7203, 505/776-2721, or 505/776-8888) is completely charming and has all the amenities for romance in each room: expensive bedding, fireplaces, and jet bathtubs with views.
- **Best Spa Retreat: Casa de las Chimeneas,** 405 Cordoba Lane, P.O Box 5303, Taos, NM 87571. ☎ 505/758-4777. For years, this inn has been known for its luxury accommodations. Now, an added spa—Mountain Massage and Spa Treatments—offers a sauna, massages, steam tents, salt glows, and facials, inches from your door.
- **Best Location for Skiers:** The **Inn at Snakedance,** P.O. Box 89, Taos Ski Valley, NM 87525 (☎ 800/322-9815 or 505/776-2277), is a modern hotel with ski-in/ski-out privileges.

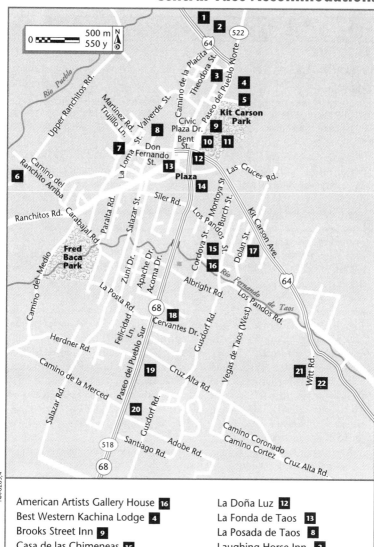

Central Taos Accommodations

500 m
550 y

American Artists Gallery House **16**
Best Western Kachina Lodge **4**
Brooks Street Inn **9**
Casa de las Chimeneas **15**
Casa Europa **6**
El Pueblo Lodge **3**
Fechin Inn **5**
Hacienda del Sol **1**
The Historic Taos Inn **10**
Indian Hills Inn **14**
Inn on La Loma Plaza **7**

La Doña Luz **12**
La Fonda de Taos **13**
La Posada de Taos **8**
Laughing Horse Inn **2**
Mabel Dodge Luhan House **11**
Old Taos Guesthouse **21**
Quality Inn **20**
Ramada Inn **19**
San Geronimo Lodge **22**
Sun God Lodge **18**
The Willows Inn **17**

2 The Taos Area

EXPENSIVE
HOTELS/MOTELS

Fechin Inn
227 Paseo del Pueblo Norte, Taos, NM 87571. ☎ **800/811-2933** or 505/751-1000. Fax 505/751-7338. www.fechin-inn.com. 99 units. AC TV TEL. $109–$179 double; $199–$319 suite. Rates vary according to season. AE, CB, DC, DISC, MC, V. Free parking. Pets are welcome.

When this luxury hotel opened in the summer of 1996, word quickly spread that it hadn't lived up to expectations, and it's no wonder. People who hoped it would replicate the house built next door by Russian artist Nicolai Fechin in 1927 (see discussion of the Fechin Institute in chapter 14) were living in the wrong century. The new hotel certainly doesn't have the refined warmth of the Inn of the Anasazi in Santa Fe. It's closer in style to the Eldorado, and considering that it's a large hotel, I would call it a qualified success.

Its main feature is the carved wood by Jeremy Morelli of Santa Fe. In line with the carving in the Fechin House, much of it is beveled and then waxed, giving it the fine texture of skin. The two-story lobby is airy, with a bank of windows and French doors looking south to a portal where *ristras* hang and diners can eat breakfast in the warmer months. The rooms are spacious and have a Southwestern decor with nice touches such as hickory furniture and flagstone-topped tables, all rooms have balconies or patios, guest robes, hair dryers, and minirefrigerators. All the suites have kiva fireplaces. What's notable here is the quiet. Surrounded on three sides by rural land, mostly you'll hear birds, though Kit Carson Park next door does send some sounds your way if you're on the south side of the hotel. The bathrooms are delightful, with gray saltillo tile and warm, adjustable lighting. There's a library where you can play chess or backgammon. For an additional cost you can eat an elaborate continental breakfast. In the evenings drinks are served, often to the sound of live entertainment.

Amenities: Concierge, limited room service, dry cleaning and laundry service. There's also a medium-sized health club, Jacuzzi, conference rooms, and Laundromat.

✪ Historic Taos Inn
125 Paseo del Pueblo Norte, Taos, NM 87571. ☎ **800/TAOS-INN** or 505/758-2233. Fax 505/758-5776. 36 units. AC TV TEL. $75–$225, depending on the type of room and season (Memorial Day to mid-Oct, and Christmas and spring break are high season). Rates include discounted breakfast. AE, DC, MC, V.

It's rare to see a hotel that has withstood the years with grace. The Historic Taos Inn has. Never do you forget that you're within the thick walls of a number of 19th-century Southwestern homes, and yet surrounded by 20th-century luxury. Dr. Thomas Paul Martin, the town's first (and for many years only) physician, purchased the complex in 1895. In 1936, a year after the doctor's death, his widow, Helen, enclosed the plaza—now the inn's darling two-story lobby—and turned it into a hotel. In 1981–82 the inn was restored; it's now listed on both the State and National Registers of Historic Places.

The lobby doubles as the **Adobe Bar,** a real local gathering place, with adobe *bancos* (benches) and a sunken fireplace, all surrounding a wishing well that was once the old town well. A number of rooms open onto a balcony that overlooks this area. If you like community and don't mind the sound of jazz and flamenco drifting up toward your room, these rooms are for you. However, if you appreciate solitude and silence, request one of the courtyard rooms downstairs. All the rooms are unique and comfortable, decorated with Spanish colonial art, Taos-style furniture, and interesting touches such as handwoven Oaxacan bedspreads and little *nichos* often decorated with Mexican pottery; many rooms have fireplaces and all have hair dryers and irons and ironing boards.

Dining/Diversions: Doc Martin's, with good nouveau Southwestern cuisine and a hint of Asia, is one of Taos's leading dining establishments (see chapter 13). The Adobe Bar, popular among Taos artists and other locals, offers live entertainment on certain weeknights as well as a full bar menu for light lunch or dinner, snacks, margaritas, and an espresso-dessert menu.

Amenities: Room service, baby-sitting can be arranged, free coffee or refreshments in lobby, VCRs on request, seasonal outdoor swimming pool, year-round Jacuzzi in a greenhouse.

Quail Ridge Inn

Ski Valley Rd. (P.O. Box 707), Taos, NM 87571. ☎ **800/624-4448** or 505/776-2211. Fax 505/776-2949. http://taoswebb.com/hotel/quailridge. E-mail: quail@taoswebb.com. 110 units. TV TEL. $69–$165 single or double; $160–$395 suite. A 3% gratuity is added to all rates. Rates include full breakfast. Extra person $10. Children under 18 stay free with parent. DC, MC, V.

Pueblo-style adobe condominiums surround tennis courts at this sports resort, a place for those who spend more time out of their rooms than in them. Located 4 miles north of Taos en route to Ski Valley 14 miles distant, it was built over a period of time between 1977 and 1982. The resort is receiving at press time a needed $300,000 interior and exterior renovation. These privately owned and thus individually decorated units come with some standard features but with varying degrees of taste. Families and ski pals tend to stay here. Rooms range in size from standard hotel rooms, to one- and two-bedroom condominiums, to large two-bedroom casitas, all decorated in some form of Southwest style. All condo and casita units have fully stocked kitchens with refrigerator, microwave, stove/oven, coffeemaker, toaster, and dishwasher. Every room features a fireplace and full shower/bathrooms.

With its two indoor tennis courts, nice-sized outdoor pool (heated year-round), and hot tub, and its surroundings among the sage, this is a nice stopping place, though don't expect luxury accommodations. As with most of the condo accommodations in New Mexico, the walls here are thin and sound travels. During the summer the resort is home to the University of New Mexico Lobo Tennis Camp. Two and three-day clinics are available.

Dining: The resort's Taos Kangaroo Restaurant serves three meals a day. Breakfast is standard fare, while lunch and dinner include pizza and Thai food, a natural combination, says the proprietor, an Aussie; there's a strong Asian influence in Australian cuisine.

Amenities: Coin-operated laundry, year-round heated swimming pool, hot tub and sauna, six outdoor and two indoor tennis courts, racquetball/squash courts, summer volleyball pit, small fitness center with weights and exercise room.

BED & BREAKFASTS

✪ Adobe and Pines Inn

NM 68 (P.O. Box 837), Ranchos de Taos, NM 87557. ☎ **800/723-8267** or 505/751-0947. Fax 505/758-8423. www.toasnet.com/adobepines/. 5 units, 3 casitas. TV. $95–$185 double. Rates include breakfast. AE, DC, DISC, MC, V.

With this inn, owners Chuck and Charil Fulkerson wanted to create a magical escape. They succeeded. Much of it is located in a 150-year-old adobe directly off NM 68, less than half a mile south of St. Francis Plaza.

The inn is set around a courtyard marked by an 80-foot-long grand portal. It's surrounded by pine and fruit trees on what's believed to be sacred land. Each room has a private entrance and fireplace (three even have a fireplace in the bathroom), and is uniquely decorated. The theme here is the use of colors, which are richly displayed on the walls and in the furnishings. There's Puerta Azul, a cozy blue room; Puerta Verde, done in deep greens; and Puerta Turquese, a separate turquoise-painted guest cottage with a full kitchen. The two newest rooms, completed in 1996, have bold maroon and copper-yellow themes. The walls have hand prints and petroglyph motifs, and each room is furnished with rich and comfortable couches. Both have large Jacuzzis supplied with bubble bath and candles.

Morning brings a delicious full gourmet breakfast in front of the fire (in winter) in the glassed-in breakfast room. You can expect such delights as bansoufflé pancakes or apple caramel bread pudding, or their specialty, *migas*, a mixture of eggs, tortilla chips, chile, and cheese, served with salsa, turkey sausage, and a citrus fruit compote. Chuck and Charil are most gracious hosts; they will help you plan activities and make dinner reservations.

Adobe and Stars Bed and Breakfast Inn

At the corner of State Hwy. 150 and Valdez Rim Rd. (P.O. Box 2285), Taos, NM 87571. ☎ **800/211-7076** or 505/776-2776. 8 units. TEL. $95–$180 double. Rates include full breakfast and hors d'oeuvres. AE, DISC, MC, V. Free parking.

On first appearance, this brand-new inn looks stark, sitting on the mesa between Taos town and Taos Ski Valley. However, once inside, it's apparent that innkeeper Judy Salathiel has an eye for detail. The breakfast area and common room are sunny, with large windows facing the mountains. A few rooms are upstairs, such as La Luna, my favorite, with views in every direction and a heart-shaped Jacuzzi tub for two. All rooms have kiva fireplaces and private decks or patios. Most of the downstairs rooms open onto a portal. All are decorated with handcrafted Southwestern-style furniture, and many have Jacuzzi tubs. The full breakfast may vary from New Mexican dishes (such as breakfast burritos served with green chile stew) to baked goods (apple and strawberry turnovers). In the afternoons, New Mexico wines are served with the inn's special salsa and blue-corn chips, as are sweets such as chocolate cake and piñon lemon bars.

✪ Alma del Monte–Spirit of the Mountain

372 Hondo Seco Rd. (P.O. Box 1434), Taos, NM 87571. ☎ **800/273-7203,** 505/776-2721, or 505/776-8888. 5 units. $125–$150 single or double; prices vary with seasons and holidays. Rates include full breakfast. AE, MC, V.

For a real Taos experience I highly recommend this bed-and-breakfast recently built on sage-covered lands bordered by fast-rising mountains and on the way to the ski area. The house is a new horseshoe-shaped, Pueblo-style adobe; each room opens onto the courtyard outfitted with a fountain and hammocks hanging in the warm months. Proprietor Suzanne Head has designed and decorated the place impeccably; the living/dining room provides excellent sunrise and sunset views, and the house has saltillo-tile floors and traditional antiques, as well as elegant Ralph Lauren bedding. Each room has a jet tub and kiva-style fireplace. Many have picture-window views and skylights while others have private gardens. Above all, the rooms are quiet, since no roads border the property. Breakfasts are equally unique: Specialties such as a deep-dish baked apple pancake or French toast stuffed with fruit and cream cheese are served on china with real silverware.

✪ Casa de las Chimeneas

405 Cordoba Lane, at Los Pandos Rd. (P.O. Box 5303), Taos, NM 87571. ☎ **505/758-4777.**
Fax 505/758-3976. www.taoswebb.com/hotel/chimneyhouse. E-mail: casa@newmex.com.
7 units. AC TV TEL. $130–$160 double; $160 suite (for 2). Rates include breakfast and hors
d'oeuvres. AE, MC, V.

This 80-year-old adobe home has, since its opening in 1988, been a model of
Southwestern elegance. Now, with a new addition, it has become a full-service
luxury inn as well. The addition includes a spa with a small fitness room and sauna,
as well as complete massage and facial treatments given by Mountain Massage and
Spa Treatments, for an additional charge. If I had a choice to stay in any room in
New Mexico, my first would be the Rio Grande Room here and the second would
be the Territorial Room. Both of these new rooms have heated saltillo-tile floors, gas
kiva fireplaces, and jetted tubs. If you prefer a more antique-feeling room, the older
section is delightful. Each room in the inn is decorated with original works of art
and has elegant bedding, a private entrance, and minirefrigerators stocked with
complimentary soft drinks, juices, and mineral water. You'll also find bathrobes,
ironing boards, irons, and hair dryers, as well as a self-service Laundromat on the
premises. All rooms have kiva fireplaces and most look out on flower and herb gardens. My favorite in the older section is the Blue Room, with handmade quilts and
saltillo tile decorated with grapes. Breakfasts are complete and delicious. Specialties
include an artichoke heart and mushroom baked omelet or ricotta cream-cheese
blintz, as well as innkeeper Susan Vernon's special fruit frappé. In the evenings, hors
d'oeuvres are elaborate. During one evening I had canapés with avocado, cheese,
and tomato; a spicy broccoli soup; and moonshine cake. End the day at the large
hot tub in the courtyard. Smoking is not permitted.

Inn on La Loma Plaza

315 Ranchitos Rd. (P.O. Box 4159), Taos, NM 87571. ☎ **800/530-3040** or 505/758-1717.
Fax 505/751-0155. 7 units. TV TEL. $95–$150 standard double; $170–$195 artist's studio;
$320–$330 suite. Extra person $20. Children 12 and under $10 in parents' room. Discounts
available. Rates include breakfast. AE, MC, V.

You may just pass by the most wonderful thing about this place if you don't look
for it. The inn (formerly the Hacienda Inn) is located on a historic neighborhood
plaza, complete with dirt streets and a tiny central park. It doesn't look like much,
but it's a chance to glimpse a neighborhood stronghold—adobe homes built around
a square, with thick outer walls to fend off marauders. The inn is made from a 200-
year-old home, complete with aged vigas and maple floors, decorated tastefully with
comfortable furniture and Middle Eastern rugs. Each room is unique, most with
sponge-painted walls, willow shutters, and Talavera tile in the bathrooms to provide
an eclectic ambience. All have fireplaces, and most have balconies or terraces and
views. Some have special touches, such as the Happy Trails Room, with knotty pine
paneling, a brass bed, old chaps, and decorative hanging spurs. Some rooms have
kitchenettes. This 2-story building, a 10-minute walk from the Plaza, has a large
front lawn lined with bulbs and perennials blooming in the warmer months, as well
as a brick patio and Jacuzzi. Breakfast burritos and other delicacies are served in a
sunroom filled with plants or on the patio.

MODERATE
HOTELS

✪ Best Western Kachina Lodge & Meeting Center

413 Paseo del Pueblo Norte (P.O. Box NN), Taos, NM 87571. ☎ **800/522-4462** or
505/758-2275. Fax 505/758-9207. www.kachinalodge.com. E-mail: sales@kachinalodge.

⊕ Family-Friendly Hotels

Best Western Kachina Lodge & Meeting Center *(see page 177)*   An outdoor swimming pool and snack machines in the summer make a great late-afternoon diversion for hot, tired, and cranky kids.

El Pueblo Lodge *(see page 185)*   A slide, year-round swimming pool, and hot tub set on 3½ acres of land will please the kids; a barbecue, some minikitchens with microwave ovens, laundry facilities, and the rates will please their parents.

Quail Ridge Inn *(see page 175)*   The year-round swimming pool and tennis courts will keep active kids busy during the day when it's time for a parent's siesta.

---

com. 118 units. A/C TV TEL. $49–$150 double, depending on the season (Memorial Day to mid-Oct, and Christmas and spring break are high season) and total hotel occupancy. Extra person $10. Children under 12 stay free in parents' room. AE, DC, DISC, MC, V. No pets are allowed.

This lodge on the north end of town is an ideal spot for families and travelers. Built in the early 1960s, it has a lot of charm despite the fact that it's really a motor hotel. Rooms are placed around a grassy courtyard studded with huge blue spruce trees. In the center is a stage where a family from Taos Pueblo builds a bonfire and dances nightly in the summer and explains the significance of the dances—a real treat for anyone baffled by the Pueblo rituals.

Remodeling is ongoing in the Southwest-style rooms—some have couches and most have little Taos-style *trasteros* (armoires) that hold the TVs. The rooms are solidly built and quiet, and there's plenty of outdoor space for the kids to run, as well as a Jacuzzi and a large pool area which management assures me will get needed new tile by our publication date (but they assured me of that last year too, so. . .). A few rooms have kitchenettes. A Laundromat, beauty salon, and shopping arcade are also on the premises, and a courtesy limo is available.

The lodge has a number of eating and entertainment options: The **Hopi Dining Room** offers a family-style menu; the **Kiva Coffee Shop** is kiva shaped (round), making it a unique Southwestern diner; and the **Zuni Lounge** is open nightly.

Comfort Suites

1500 Paseo del Pueblo Sur (P.O. Box 1268), Taos, NM 87571. ☎ **888/751-1555** or 505/751-1555. http://taoswebb.com/taoshotels/comfortsuites/. E-mail: comfort@taos. newmex.com. 62 units. AC TV TEL. $69–$129 double. Rates include continental breakfast. AE, CB, DC, DISC, MC, V. Free parking.

New, clean, predictable. That's what you'll get in this recent addition to the Taos accommodation scene. Each room has a small living/dining area, with a sleeper/ sofa, microwave, minirefrigerator, and coffee maker, and a bedroom with hand-crafted wood furniture and a comfortable king and queen bed. If you have kids, you might want a ground floor poolside room. Though the pool isn't landscaped, it's roomy and is accompanied by a hot tub.

Ramada Inn

615 Paseo del Pueblo Sur, Taos, NM 87571. ☎ **800/659-TAOS** or 505/758-2900. Fax 505/758-1662. 124 units. A/C TV TEL. $69–$120 double. Rollaway $15 extra. Children under 18 stay free in parents' room. Rates include extended continental breakfast. AE, CB, DC, DISC, MC, V. Free parking.

This recently remodeled adobe-style hotel, a 10-minute walk from the Plaza, gives you what you'd expect from a chain hotel and that's why its very popular for travelers as well as tour groups. Built in 1995, it came under new ownership in 1996 and underwent a remodeling that gives it a warm, Southwestern feel. The rooms have new mattresses, box springs, TVs, carpet, drapes, and floral bedspreads. Though a little dark, the units are well constructed and quiet.

The hotel offers dry cleaning and laundry service (Monday through Friday), an indoor swimming pool, Jacuzzi, and sundeck.

Sagebrush Inn

Paseo del Pueblo Sur (P.O. Box 557), Taos, NM 87571. ☎ **800/428-3626** or 505/758-2254. Fax 505/758-5077. 100 units. A/C TV TEL. $70–$95 standard double; $90–$110 deluxe double; $95–$115 minisuite; $105–$140 executive suite. Extra person $10. Children under 12 stay free in parents' room. Rates include breakfast. AE, CB, DC, DISC, MC, V. Free parking.

Three miles south of Taos, surrounded by acres of sage, this inn is a strong example of the life of an adobe building, added onto decade after decade, creating an interesting mix of accommodations. The edifice was built in 1929 as a stagecoach stop. The original structure had 3 floors and 12 rooms hand-sculpted from adobe; the roof was held in place with hand-hewn vigas. This part still remains, and the rooms are small and cozy and have the feel of old Taos—in fact, Georgia O'Keeffe lived and worked here for 10 months in the late 1930s. But for those more accustomed to refined style, it might feel dated.

The treasure of this place is the large grass courtyard dotted with elm trees, where visitors sit and read in the warm months. Beware that some of the rooms added in the '50s through '70s have a tackiness not overcome by the vigas and tile work. More recent additions (to the west) are more skillful; these suites away from the hotel proper are spacious and full of amenities, but have noisy plumbing. All rooms have coffeemakers and minirefrigerators.

The lobby-cum-cantina has an Old West feel that livens at night with country-western dancing. Traditionally this has been a family hotel, but with a new convention center and an addition of a Comfort Suites hotel on the property, they're working to appeal to convention guests as well. With this addition there are now two outdoor pools, three Jacuzzis, tennis courts, and a business center.

The Los Vaqueros Room is open for dinner daily. A complimentary full breakfast is served to guests daily in the Sagebrush Dining Room. The lobby bar is one of Taos's most active nightspots for live music and dancing (see "Taos After Dark," in chapter 14).

The hotel provides valet laundry and a courtesy van.

BED & BREAKFASTS

American Artists Gallery House

132 Frontier Lane (P.O. Box 584), Taos, NM 87571. ☎ **800/532-2041** or 505/758-4446. Fax 505/758-0497. 10 units. $75–$150 double. Rates include full breakfast and afternoon snack and refreshments.

Though the exterior of this bed-and-breakfast about a 5-minute drive from the Plaza isn't much, innkeepers LeAn and Charles Clamurro make up for it on the interior, both in terms of hospitality and accommodations. Situated in a modest house, an additional small building, and a historic barn, the inn offers a variety of types of rooms. Some of the rooms, such as Gallery Rose, have rounded archways, pine floors, kiva fireplaces, and the charm only an older building can lend. The newer rooms, called Gallery A, B, and C (in the historic barn), are in much more of a new Southwestern style, with saltillo-tile floors and very high ceilings. Each has a corner kiva fireplace and a Jacuzzi tub. These newer rooms don't provide the privacy I like, because the tub area is not separate from the bedroom, but instead sits up on a raised level. However, the decor is tasteful and each has a minirefrigerator and wet bar. Breakfasts are a delight here. Charles cooks up specialties such as blue-corn pancakes with blueberry sauce or a variety of egg dishes.

The Brooks Street Inn

119 Brooks St. (P.O. Box 4954), Taos, NM 87571. ☎ **800/758-1489** or 505/758-1489. Fax 505/758-7525. 6 units (all with bathroom). $75–$105 double. AE, MC, V.

If you like the feel of staying in someone's home, this is a good choice. It's not fancy, but the hospitality is excellent. On a quiet street within walking distance from the Plaza, this pink and green stucco home has a cutesy Southwestern style, with comfortable furniture in the common area and a big pine table where guests eat breakfast family-style. The more homestyle rooms are in this main house, while the more inn-style rooms are across a courtyard. All have coffeemakers, and some have kiva fireplaces. The Piñon Room is cute and very Southwestern, though it would be too small to house more than one person. The Juniper is larger as is the Birch. Unfortunately, the innkeepers have skimped on the bedding; I found the sheets to be rough. Breakfast is delicious, including specialties such as stuffed French toast with apricot topping and espresso from their espresso bar. Innkeeper Carol Frank offers plenty of good direction about where to go and what to do, especially to those touring on two wheels; she and her husband Randy are avid Harley Davidson riders.

Casa Europa

840 Upper Ranchitos Rd. (HC 68, Box 3F), Taos, NM 87571. ☎ **800/758-9798** or 505/ 758-9798. 6 units. $70–$165 double. Extra person $20. Rates include full breakfast and evening hors d'oeuvres or European pastries. MC, V.

This cream-colored Territorial-style adobe (just 1¾ miles west of the Plaza) under giant cottonwoods is surrounded by open pastures dotted with grazing horses and offers lovely views of the mountains in the distance. Some rooms here date from the 1700s; however, a 1983 renovation made this a contemporary 2-story luxury inn. Elegant rooms, all with fireplaces, each with a sitting area and full bathroom (two have two-person Jacuzzis), are furnished with interesting antiques. The regional artwork in the rooms can be purchased. There's a sitting area with a TV upstairs and a common sitting room for reading and/or conversation downstairs, where coffee and pastries are offered each day between 3 and 4pm; during ski season hors d'oeuvres are served from 5 to 6pm. A full gourmet breakfast (specialties include cheese blintzes with a warm strawberry sauce and vegetarian eggs Benedict) is served each morning in the formal dining room. There's also an outdoor hot tub as well as a Swedish dry sauna. In-room massages are available at an extra charge. Smoking is not permitted.

Cottonwood Inn

2 State Rd. 230 (HCR 74, Box 24609), El Prado–Taos, NM 87529. ☎ **800/324-7120** or 505/776-5826. Fax 505/776-1141. 7 units. $85–$165 double. Rates include full breakfast and afternoon snack. MC, V.

This inn provides cozy comfort in a rural setting. Built in 1947 by a flamboyant artist, it has high ceilings with vigas and almost every room has a kiva fireplace. Renovated in 1996, the inn has new owners, Kit and Bill Owen. They have made the place luxurious, using thick carpeting in many of the rooms and saltillo tile in the bathrooms, as well as adding Jacuzzi tubs and steam baths to some rooms. The rooms have down pillows and comforters on the beds and are decorated in a subtle, Southwestern style. The inn's location halfway between Taos and the ski area lends a pastoral quality to your stay, with a herd of sheep wandering in a meadow to the west. My favorite rooms are the ones that open into the main part of the house, but if you prefer a private entrance, you have that option too. Rooms for nonsmokers and people with disabilities are available.

Hacienda del Sol

109 Mabel Dodge Lane (P.O. Box 177), Taos, NM 87571. ☎ **505/758-0287.** Fax 505/758-5895. 10 units. $78–$145 double. Rates include full breakfast. MC, V. Children welcome.

What's most unique about this bed-and-breakfast is its completely unobstructed view of Taos Mountain. The 1.2-acre property borders the Taos Pueblo. The land is pristine and the inn has a rich history. It was once owned by arts patron Mabel Dodge Luhan, and it was here that author Frank Waters wrote *The People of the Valley.* Innkeeper Marcine Landon considers herself somewhat of a gypsy in her use of bold splashes of color throughout the place, from the gardens, where in summer tulips, pansies, and flax grow, to the rooms themselves, where bold woven bedspreads and original art lend a Mexican feel. The main house is 190 years old, so it has the wonderful curves of adobe as well as thick vigas and deep windowsills. Some guest rooms are in this section. Others range from 2 to 8 years in age. These are finely constructed and I almost recommend them over the others since they're a little more private and the bathrooms more refined. All rooms have robes and books on New Mexico. Some have minirefrigerators and cassette players. Breakfast includes specialties such as blue-corn pancakes with blueberry sauce and eggs del sol, a crustless quiche with corn and salsa, as well as wild plum piñon-nut bread baked at Taos Pueblo. The Jacuzzi has a mountain view and is available for private guest use in half-hour segments.

La Doña Luz

114 Kit Carson Rd., Taos, NM 87571. ☎ **800/758-9187** or 505/758-4874. Fax 505/758-4541. 16 units. TV. $59–$125 double. Rates include extended continental breakfast. AE, DISC, MC, V.

There's a real artisan quality to this inn (formerly El Rincón Inn) just off the Plaza. The innkeepers, Nina Meyers and her son Paul "Paco" Castillo, have made it that way: Nina painted murals on doors and walls and Paco carved wood and set tile. The 200-year-old structure was once home to 19th-century cultural leader La Doña Luz Lucero de Martinez, who was most known for her hospitality. These innkeepers carry on her legacy. The inn comprises two dwellings separated by a flower-filled courtyard, where breakfast is served in warm weather. Fine art and hand-carved furnishings representing the three cultures of Taos (Indian, Spanish, and Anglo) are scattered through both houses, some of which are heirloom quality, reminiscent of the museum in the inn's adjacent store, **El Rincón** (see chapter 14).

Renovation is ongoing throughout the place. For now, I recommend rooms in the main 3-story house rather than the adjacent property connected to the store. The main-house rooms are up-to-date, all with VCRs, some with stereos and Jacuzzis, and two with full kitchens with amenities (stove, microwave, dishwasher [only one has this], as well as blender, crock pot, and a full-sized washer and dryer).

La Posada de Taos

309 Juanita Lane (P.O. Box 1118), Taos, NM 87571. ☎ **800/645-4803** or 505/758-8164. www.taosnet.com/laposada/. E-mail: laposada@taos.newmex.com. 5 units, 1 cottage. $85–$120 double. Winter discounts available except during holidays. Extra person $15. Rates include full breakfast. No credit cards. Children 13 and over welcome. No pets.

Martha Stewart would be very comfortable at this B&B situated in the La Loma Historic District just 2½ blocks from the Plaza, and though I have little in common with her, I was too. Full of Americana (and European antiques) collected by proprietor Nancy Brooks-Swan, it rests within thick and cozy adobe walls; the combination of Mexican tile and New England quilts is elegant. It's difficult to select a favorite room here, though I'd say the three off the common area are the coziest. All the rooms except one have fireplaces and private patios. El Solecito and the Beutler Room have Jacuzzi tubs. Most delightful of all is that Nancy and Bill Swan sit down with guests for breakfast, and they'll keep you laughing while regaling you with tales of the Inn and their adventures in Taos. The food is excellent. We had a fluffy egg pie with salsa and to-die-for home-baked pecan rolls. The inn provides a free pass to Taos Spa.

✪ Little Tree Bed & Breakfast

P.O. Drawer II, Taos, NM 87571. ☎ **505/776-8467.** 4 units. $80–$105 double. Rates include breakfast and afternoon snack. AE, DISC, MC, V.

Little Tree is one of my favorite Taos bed-and-breakfasts, partly because it's located in a beautiful, secluded setting, and partly because it's constructed with real adobe that's been left in its raw state, lending the place an authentic hacienda feel. Located 2 miles down a country road about midway between Taos and the ski area, it's surrounded by sage and piñon.

The rooms are charming and very cozy. They all have adobe floors, which are warm in the winter because radiant heat has been installed here. All rooms feature queen-size beds, private bathrooms, and access to the portal and courtyard garden, at the center of which is the little tree for which the inn is named. The Piñon (my favorite) and Juniper rooms are equipped with fireplaces and private entrances. The Piñon and Aspen rooms offer sunset views. The Spruce Room, Western in feeling, is decorated with beautiful quilts. All but one have a TV and VCR.

In the main building, the living room has a traditional viga-and-latilla ceiling and tierra blanca adobe (adobe that's naturally white; if you look closely at it you can see little pieces of mica and straw). Two cats entertain, and the visiting hummingbirds enchant guests as they enjoy a healthy breakfast on the portal during warmer months. On arrival, guests are treated to refreshments.

Mabel Dodge Luhan House

240 Morada Lane (P.O. Box 558), Taos, NM 87571. ☎ **800/84-MABEL** or 505/751-9686. 18 units (13 with bathroom). $75–$150 double. Extra person $17.50. Rates include full breakfast. MC, V.

This inn is also called "Las Palomas de Taos" because of the throngs of doves (palomas; actually, they looked like pigeons to me) that live in enchanting weathered birdhouses on the property. Like so many other free spirits, they were attracted by the flamboyant Mabel Dodge (1879–1962), who came to Taos in 1916. A familiar name in these parts, she and her fourth husband, a full-blooded Pueblo named Tony Luhan, enlarged this 200-year-old home to its present size of 22 rooms in the 1920s. If you like history, and don't mind the curves and undulations it brings to a building, this is a good choice. The place has a mansion feel, evoking images of the glitterati of the 1920s—writers, artists, adventurers—sitting on the terrace under the cottonwoods drinking margaritas. The entrance is marked by a Spanish colonial–style portal.

Recently under new ownership, badly needed repairs are being made. All main rooms have thick vigas, arched Pueblo-style doorways, hand-carved doors, kiva fireplaces, and dark hardwood floors. Guest rooms in the main building feature antique furnishings and six have fireplaces. Some rooms have private bathrooms and others must share. Eight more guest rooms were recently added with the completion of a second building. All new accommodations are equipped with fireplaces. Many educational workshops are held here throughout the year; the rooms are often reserved for participants. The Mabel Dodge Luhan House is now a National Historic Landmark.

Old Taos Guesthouse

1028 Witt Rd. (P.O. Box 6552), Taos, NM 87571. ☎ **800/758-5448** or 505/758-5448. www.taoswebb.com/hotel/oldtaoshouse/. 9 units. $70–$125 double. MC, V. Children are welcome.

Less than 2 miles from the Plaza, this 150-year-old adobe hacienda sits on 7.5 acres and provides a cozy Northern New Mexico rural experience. Once a farmer's home and later an artist's estate, it's recently been restored by owners Tim and Leslie Reeves, who have carefully maintained the country charm: Mexican tile in the bathrooms, vigas on the ceilings, and kiva-style fireplaces in most of the rooms. Each room enters from the outside, some off the broad portal that shades the front of the hacienda, some from a grassy lawn in the back, with a view toward the mountains. Some rooms are more utilitarian, some more quaint, so make a request depending on your needs. One of my favorites is the Taos Suite, with a king bed, a big picture window, and a full kitchen that includes an oven, stove, minirefrigerator, and microwave. I also like the charming room (no name) that opens out toward the back; it's cozy with a low ceiling and vigas, though the bathroom is small. There's a grass-surrounded hot tub (scheduled on the half hour) with an amazing view. If you're lucky like I was, you might get to soak while big snowflakes fall. Also in back is a nature and history path, recently completed, where guests can read brief quips about chamisa bushes and acequia systems (ditch systems), and see some too. The Reeves pride themselves on their healthy breakfasts. They serve a pot of hot organic oatmeal, homemade granola (Leslie's grandmother's recipe), and baked breads and muffins, all worth lingering over in the big common room where the sun shines through wide windows. If you're lucky, Tim will pull out some of his wild skiing videos. Smoking outside only.

Salsa del Salto

P.O. Box 1468, El Prado, NM 87529. ☎ **800/530-3097** or 505/776-2422. Fax 505/776-5734. 10 units. $85–$160 double. Extra person $20. MC, V.

Situated between Taos town and the Taos Ski Valley, Salsa del Salto is a good choice for those seeking a secluded retreat equipped like a country club. The main house was built in 1971 and has the openness of that era's architecture. The rooms here are tastefully decorated with pastel shades in a Southwestern motif and the beds are covered with cozy down comforters. Each room offers views of the mountains or mesas of Taos, and the private bathrooms are modern and spacious, each with a hair dryer. Two new rooms (my favorites) are well designed, decorated in a whimsical Southwestern style, and each includes two queen beds, a minirefrigerator, fireplace, TV, VCR, and Jacuzzi tub.

The focus here is on relaxation and outdoor activities. Salsa del Salto is the only bed-and-breakfast in Taos with a pool, Jacuzzi, and private tennis courts. Innkeeper Mary Hockett, a native New Mexican and avid sportswoman, is eager to share information about her favorite activities with her guests. Mary's husband, Dadou Mayer, who was born and raised in Nice, France, is an accomplished chef (and the author of *Cuisine à Taos,* a French cookbook). Dadou has also been a member of the French National Ski Team, and was named "The Fastest Chef in the United

States" when he won the Grand Marnier Ski Race. During the winter, you'll get the added bonus of an early morning briefing about ski conditions.

San Geronimo Lodge

1101 Witt Rd. (216M Paseo del Pueblo Norte #167), Taos, NM 87571. ☎ **800/894-4119** or 505/751-3776. Fax 505/751-1493. 17 units. TV TEL. $90–$120 double. Rates include full breakfast and afternoon snack. AE, DC, DISC, MC, V.

Built in 1925 in the style of a grand old lodge, this inn has high ceilings and rambling verandas, all situated on 2½ acres of grounds with views of Taos Mountain, yet it's a 5-minute drive from the Plaza. The owners—two sisters and another partner escaping the rigors of life on the East Coast—bought the lodge and did a major renovation in 1994. The only drawback here is that the structure is so immense it demands big furniture, which they haven't supplied, so there's an empty feel to some of the common areas. The guest rooms, however, are cozy and comfortable, three with kiva fireplaces, all with furniture hand-built by local craftspeople, and Mexican tile in the bathrooms. The full breakfast is tasty (though a little skimpy for my appetite), as are the snacks served in the afternoons. There's an outdoor swimming pool and Jacuzzi, as well as rooms for people with disabilities.

Willows Inn

412 Kit Carson Rd. (at Dolan St.; P.O. Box 6560 NDCBU), Taos, NM 87571. ☎ **800/525-8267** or 505/758-2558. Fax 505/758-5445. E-mail: willows@taos.newmex.com. 5 units. $95–$130 double. Rates include full breakfast and hors d'oeuvres. AE, MC, V.

What sets this inn apart from the rest is that it sits on the estate of E. Marin Hennings (one of the Taos Society artists). Built in the 1920s, the inn has thick adobe walls and kiva fireplaces in each guest room. It lies just a half mile from the Plaza, but within a tall adobe wall so it's very secluded. The grassy yard is decorated with fountains, and, most impressively, shaded by gargantuan weeping-willow trees that may be over 300 years old.

The common area is cozy and comes equipped with a TV, VCR, and CD player with access to innkeepers Janet and Doug Camp's extensive music collection—over 450 classical and jazz CDs. The guest rooms are also cozy and have rich personality. Built around a courtyard, they have old latch doors, oak floors, tin light fixtures, and kiva fireplaces. I recommend the Santa Fe Room, which has a nice sitting area in front of the fireplace and looks out toward the garden. Hennings's spacious studio still has paint splattered on the floor. It has a Jacuzzi tub in the bathroom. Breakfast specialties include apricot-stuffed French toast served with bacon, and chile-cheese egg soufflé served with applesauce muffins and sausage. The inn offers guided fly-fishing trips for novices to experts. Smoking is permitted outdoors only.

INEXPENSIVE

Abominable Snowmansion Skiers' Hostel

Taos Ski Valley Rd., Arroyo Seco (P.O. Box 3271), Taos, NM 87571. ☎ **505/776-8298.** Fax 505/776-2107. http://taoswebb.com/hotel/snowmansion. E-mail: snowman@new mex.com. 60 beds. $13–$22 for bed; $38–$60 private double, depending on size of accommodation and season; $12 cabins and tepees, $10 camping. Rates include full breakfast in winter. DISC, MC, V.

Since I was a kid, I've travleled past this hostel; it was a treat for me to finally experience the inside. Set in the quaint village of Arroyo Seco, about 8 miles north of Taos and 10 miles from the Taos Ski Valley, it offers clean beds for reasonable prices, and a nice community experience. The common room has a pool table, piano, and circular fireplace. The dorm rooms (2 men's and 2 women's) have 8 to

10 beds, and sheets, towels and blankets are provided free in winter or for a small fee in summer. Each dorm room has its own shower and bathroom. The private rooms are spacious, though the decor is only passable. Best of all are the tepees which sit out around a grassy yard. They sleep 2 to 4 people and have an outdoor kitchen, showers, and toilets nearby.

El Pueblo Lodge

412 Paseo del Pueblo Norte, Taos, NM 87571. ☎ **800/433-9612** or 505/758-8700. Fax 505/758-7321. http://taoswebb.com/hotel/el pueblo/. E-mail: elpueblo@newmex.com. 65 units. TV TEL. $68–$82 double; $105–$215 suite. Call for Christmas rates. Extra person $7–$10. Rates include continental breakfast. AE, DISC, MC, V. Pets are permitted for an extra $10.

Considering its location and setting, this hotel is a bargain, especially for families, although you'll want to reserve carefully. It's set on 3½ grassy, cottonwood-shaded acres, on the north end of town, a reasonable walk from the Plaza. Three buildings form a U-shape, each with its own high and low points. The oldest part to the south was once a 1950s court motel, and it maintains that cozy charm, with heavy vigas and tiny kitchenettes. This section could use some updating, but it's worth the price. To the north is a 2-story building, constructed in 1972, that seems frail and lacks charm, but provides lots of space. The newest section (to the west) is one of Taos's best bargains, with nicely constructed suites and double rooms decorated in blonde pine with kiva fireplaces and doors that open onto the center yard or, if you're on the second floor, onto a balcony. There are also fully equipped condominium units (with 1970s construction) that are good for large families. An outdoor swimming pool and hot tub are on the premises, and there's free use of laundry facilities.

La Fonda de Taos

South Plaza (P.O. Box 1447), Taos, NM 87571. ☎ **800/833-2211** or 505/758-2211. Fax 505/758-8508. 27 units. TEL. $65 double; $110 suite. AE, MC, V.

If this hotel can make it through a difficult transition time, it could be worth the stay. Recently, its flamboyant owner Saki Karavas died, and the hotel came under new ownership; the owners had big plans to remodel, but are being held up in litigation with Karavas' estate. Though the lobby is charming, with antique hand-carved pine furniture and bright Mexican-painted trim, all under a high ceiling with skylights, the hotel needs work. The only lodging on the Plaza, La Fonda once hosted many of Taos's most glamorous guests in the 1940s, 1950s, and 1960s. Through the years it has been known for its art collection, much of which remained with the previous owner's family. However, the strange, erotic oil paintings by D. H. Lawrence are still on view—pictures he brought to Taos in 1929 when they, along with his novel *Lady Chatterley's Lover*, were banned in England. Currently, the rooms have rather downtrodden furniture and decor.

Indian Hills Inn

233 Paseo del Pueblo Sur (P.O. Box 1229), Taos, NM 87571. ☎ **800/444-2346** or 505/758-4293. www.taosnet.com/indianhillsinn. E-mail: indianhills@taosnet.com. 55 units. A/C TV TEL. $49–$99 double; group and package rates available. Rates include continental breakfast. AE, DC, DISC, MC, V.

With its close location to the Plaza (3 blocks), this is a good choice if you're looking for a decent, functional night's stay. There are two sections to the hotel: one built in the 1950s, the other completed in 1996. The older section has just received a major face-lift: new carpet, new doors, artwork, drapes, bedspreads, sinks, and vanities. However, for a few more dollars you can stay in the newer section, where the rooms are larger, the bathrooms fresher. The buildings are set around a broad lawn studded with big blue spruce trees. There are picnic tables, barbecue grills, and a pool. The hotel offers golf, ski, and rafting packages at reduced rates.

Laughing Horse Inn

729 Paseo del Pueblo Norte (P.O. Box 4889), Taos, NM 87571. ☎ **800/776-0161** or 505/758-8350. Fax 505/751-1123. 13 units (3 with bathroom). TV. $49–$105 double; $105–$120 suite. AE, DISC, MC, V. Pets are welcome. Children are too.

In 1924, a man named Spud Johnson bought the building now occupied by the Laughing Horse Inn (an unmistakable stucco structure with lilac-purple trim located just a mile north of the Plaza) and established a print shop known as "The Laughing Horse Press." Johnson was a central figure in the cultural development of Taos, and he often provided rooms to writers (for example, D. H. Lawrence) who needed a place to hang their hats.

Today, guests who don't mind hippie charm can choose between sunny dorm rooms, cozy private rooms, a solar-heated penthouse, or guest houses. The private rooms feature sleeping lofts, cassette decks, TVs, VCRs, and some have fireplaces. Bathrooms are shared, and they are rustic, with lots of rough-sawed wood. The penthouse has a private solar bedroom and enclosed sleeping loft, a private bathroom, a woodstove, a big-screen TV, and video and audio decks (my guess is this would be very hot in the summer). The guest houses include living rooms, fireplaces, private bathrooms, and queen lofts; one has a full kitchen. These guest houses adjoin for large parties. The inn offers a common room around a big fireplace, a games room, a kitchen area where continental breakfasts (not included in the rates) are served, and a refrigerator (which is stocked for use on the honor system). There's an outdoor hot tub, a masseuse (by appointment), and mountain bikes for guests' free use. Frankly, for what you get here, the prices seem high to me.

Quality Inn

1043 Camino del Pueblo Sur, Taos, NM 87571. ☎ **800/845-0648** or 505/758-2200. Fax 505/758-9009. 101 units. A/C TV TEL. $59–$99 single or double; $150 suite. Extra person $7. Children under 18 stay free in parents' room. Rates include full breakfast. AE, CB, DC, DISC, EU, JCB, MC, V.

Another south-of-town budget hotel, this place will meet your needs while providing a relaxing stay. It's an L-shaped building built in 1974 about 2 miles from the Plaza. Remodeled in 1989, with more remodeling ongoing, it has a courtyard area with lots of grass surrounding a nice-sized pool, open year-round. The rooms are large and have decorative touches such as handmade Mexican furniture, mirrors framed with copperwork, and R. C. Gorman prints. All rooms are set off interior corridors and recently received comfortable new mattresses. There are 11 units with king-size beds; two suites offer kitchenettes, and half the rooms have microwaves and minirefrigerators. Request a north-facing room for a view of grass, swimming pool, and mountains, rather than the parking lot. There's a restaurant, lounge, and hot tub. The breakfast includes your choice of eggs, pancakes, French toast, or cereal, accompanied by bacon.

✪ Sun God Lodge

919 Paseo del Pueblo Sur (5513 NDCBU), Taos, NM 87571. ☎ **800/821-2437** or 505/ 758-3162. Fax 505/758-1716. 55 units. TV TEL. $45–$99 double; $100–$150 casita. AE, MC, DISC, V. Pets are allowed with $50 deposit.

For a comfortable, economical stay—with a Northern New Mexico ambience—this is my choice. This hotel, a 5-minute drive from the Plaza, has three distinct parts spread across 1½ acres of landscaped grounds. The oldest was solidly built in 1958 and has some court-motel charm with a low ceiling and large windows. To update the rooms, owners added Talavera tile sinks, Taos-style furniture, and new carpeting. To the south is a recently remodeled section, built in 1988. The rooms are small but have little touches that make them feel cozy, such as pink accent walls, little *nichos*, and hand-carved furnishings. In back to the east are the newest buildings built in 1994. These are 2-story with portal-style porches and balconies. Some rooms have kitchenettes, which include microwaves, refrigerators, and stoves (all rooms have coffeemakers), while others have kiva fireplaces. The two rooms on the northeast corner of the property are the quietest and have the best views. There is a Jacuzzi.

3 Taos Ski Valley

For information on the skiing and the facilities offered at Taos Ski Valley, see "Skiing," in chapter 14.

EXPENSIVE
HOTELS
Alpine Village Suites

P.O. Box 98, Taos Ski Valley, NM 87525. ☎ **800/576-2666** or 505/776-8540. Fax 505/ 776-8542. 24 units. TV TEL. Summer $60–$85 suite for 2 (includes continental breakfast); ski season $140–$200 suite for 2, $240–$260 suite that sleeps up to 6. AE, DISC, MC, V. Covered valet parking $10 per night.

Alpine Village is a small village within the Ski Valley a few steps from the lift. Owned by John and Barbara Cottam, the complex also houses a ski shop and bar/restaurant. The Cottams began with 7 rooms, still nice rentals, above their ski shop. Each has a sleeping loft for the agile who care to climb a ladder, as well as sunny windows. The newer section has nicely decorated rooms, with attractive touches such as Mexican furniture and inventive tile work done by locals. As with most accommodations at Taos Ski Valley, the rooms are not especially soundproof. Fortunately, most skiers go to bed early. All rooms have VCRs and small kitchenettes equipped with stoves, microwaves, and minirefrigerators. In the newer building, rooms have fireplaces and private balconies. Request a south-facing room for a view of the slopes. The Jacuzzi has a fireplace and a view of the slopes. There's a sauna on premises as well as massage facilities with a massage therapist.

Chalet Montesano

P.O. Box 77, Taos Ski Valley, NM 87525. ☎ **800/723-9104** or 505/776-8226. Fax 505/ 776-8760. http://taoswebb.com/chaletmontesano. E-mail: chalet@taosnm.com. 7 units. TV TEL. Ski season $118–$188 double; $163–$276 suite; Summer $85–$90 double; $110–$165 suite. Weekly rates range from $750–$2,307, depending on type of room and number of people. AE, DISC, MC, V. Children 14 and older are welcome.

This chalet constructed from a turn-of-the-century miner's cabin, is a nice romantic ski vacation retreat. A 5-minute walk from restaurants and the lift, you wouldn't expect to find such a woodsy, secluded place, but that's what innkeepers Victor and Karin Frohlich, who have been in Taos Ski Valley since the 1960s, have successfully created. All rooms have a Bavarian feel, with nice touches such as CD players, VCRs, coffeemakers, and minirefrigerators, and all but the standard rooms have fireplaces. In the studios, you'll find Murphy beds that fold into handcrafted chests to leave plenty of room for daytime living. These and the 1-bedroom apartment have full kitchens, with stove, oven, microwave, and dishwasher. On the west side of the building is a picturesque lap pool, health club, and Jacuzzi banked by windows with views of the runs and forest. No smoking here.

Hotel Edelweiss

P.O. Box 83, Taos Ski Valley, NM 87525. ☎ **800/I-LUV-SKI** or 505/776-2301. Fax 505/776-2533. www.taosnet.com/edelweiss. E-mail: edelweiss@taos.newmex.com. 10 units. TEL. May–Oct $65 double; ski season $170 double; summer "Gourmet" B&B package $49 per person. Ski season packages also available. Rates include full breakfast. AE, MC, V.

The big drawing card for this A-frame hotel built in 1973 and remodeled in 1996 is its location. Set between the beginner's hill and the main lift, it's a good place for families. You can look forward to a full breakfast (included in room packages) as well as Asian noodle lunches served in the sunny cafe. For dinner, guests get to dine at the famed and exclusive St. Bernard, well worth a visit. Families are very welcome here, and the most desirable rooms can accommodate them well. Baby-sitting can be arranged. I recommend rooms on the second and third floors, because the ground floor tends to be noisy. The upper rooms are separated from each other by stairs, so they're more quiet. All rooms have full-length robes, minirefrigerators, humidifiers, and hair dryers. There's a Jacuzzi with a view of the beginner's hill.

There is also a ski locker room with boot dryers and a full-service ski shop on the premises. Most important, with its proximity to the lifts, you can ski to and from your room. The owners, as well as others in the area, are promoting summer visits to Taos.

✪ Inn at Snakedance

110 Sutton Place (P.O. Box 89), Taos Ski Valley, NM 87525. ☎ **800/322-9815** or 505/776-2277. Fax 505/776-1410. 60 units. TV TEL. Early and late season $125 double; Christmas holiday and spring break $195–$270 double; rest of ski season $175–$195 double; summer $75 double. Closed April 11–May 20 and Oct 4–Nov 24. AE, MC, V. Free parking at Taos Ski Valley parking lot. Children over 6 are welcome.

This is my choice for on-slope accommodations. With all the luxuries of a full-service hotel, the Snakedance can please most family members, and it's just steps from the lift. The original structure that stood on this site (part of which has been restored for use today) was known as the Hondo Lodge. Before there was a Taos Ski Valley, Hondo Lodge served as a refuge for fishermen, hunters, and artists. Constructed from enormous pine timbers that had been cut for a copper mining operation in the 1890s, it was literally nothing more than a place for the men to bed down for the night. The Inn at Snakedance today offers comfortable guest rooms—the quietest in the valley—many of which feature wood-burning fireplaces. All of the furnishings are modern, the decor stylish, and the windows (many of which offer views) open to let in the mountain air. All rooms provide coffeemakers, hair dryers, minirefrigerators, wet bars (not stocked), humidifiers, and Spectravision movie channels. Some rooms adjoin, connecting a standard hotel room with a fireplace room—perfect for families. Smoking is prohibited in the guest rooms and most public areas.

Dining/Diversions: The **Hondo Restaurant and Bar** offers dining and entertainment daily during the ski season (schedules vary off-season) and also sponsors wine tastings and wine dinners. Grilled items, salads, and snacks are available on an outdoor deck. The slopeside bar provides great views.

Amenities: Shuttle service to nearby hotels, shops, and restaurants, video rentals, small health club (with Jacuzzi, sauna, exercise equipment, and massage facilities), massage therapist on site, conference rooms, sundeck, in-house ski storage and boot dryers, convenience store (with food, sundries, video rental, and alcoholic beverages).

Powderhorn Suites and Condominiums

P.O. Box 69, Taos Ski Valley, NM 87525. ☎ **800/776-2346** or 505/776-2341. Fax 505/776-2341 ext. 103. http://taoswebb.com/hotel/powderhorn/. E-mail: powder@newmex.

com. 17 units. TV TEL. Ski season $99–$150 double; $125–$190 suite; $190–$375 condo. Summer $59–$129 from 2–6 person occupancy. MC, V. Free parking near the inn.

For some time, the Ski Valley has needed this newer, moderately priced lodging just a 2-minute walk from the lift. Completely remodeled from a gutted structure in 1989, 2 years ago it came under new and very enthusiastic ownership. You'll find consistency here, not quite the quality of the Snakedance, nor the rustic nature of the Thunderbird and Edelweiss. There are a variety of types of units, all fairly roomy with spotless bathrooms and comfortable beds. Each also has a microwave, coffeemaker, and minirefrigerator. The larger suites have stoves, balconies, and fireplaces. Decorated in pastels that don't especially appeal to me, the rooms do have a sunny feel. All have views. There's a Jacuzzi on the 4th floor. If you're elderly or out of shape, request a room on the lower floors, as the only conveyance is stairs. Smoking is not allowed.

CONDOMINIUMS
Kandahar Condominiums
P.O. Box 72, Taos Ski Valley, NM 87525. ☎ **800/756-2226** or 505/776-2226. Fax 505/776-2481. E-mail: kandahar@laplaza.org. 27 units. A/C TV TEL. Ski season $250–$375; May–Oct $100–$125. Rates are based on 4 to 6 people per unit. AE, MC, V.

These condos have almost the highest location on the slopes—and with it, ski-in/ski-out access; you actually ski down to the lift from here. Built in the 1960s, the condos have been maintained well and are sturdy and functional. Two stories and private bedrooms allow for more privacy than most condos offer. Each unit is privately owned, so decor varies, although a committee makes suggestions to owners for upgrading. Facilities include a very small health club, a Jacuzzi, Laundromat, steam room, professional massage therapist, and small conference/party facility. Situated just above the children's center, it offers good access for families with young children.

Sierra del Sol Condominiums
P.O. Box 84, Taos Ski Valley, NM 87525. ☎ **800/523-3954** or 505/776-2981. Fax 505/776-2347. http://taoswebb.com/hotel/sierradelsol. E-mail: sol@newmex.com. 32 units. TV TEL. Prices range from $65 for a studio in summer to $370 for a 2-bedroom condo in high season. AE, DISC, MC, V. Free parking.

I have wonderful memories of these condominiums, which are just a 2-minute walk from the lift; family friends used to invite me to stay with them when I was about 10. I was happy to see that the units, built in the 1960s with additions through the years, have been well maintained. Though they're privately owned, and therefore decorated at the whim of the owners, management does inspect them every year and make suggestions. They're smartly built and come in a few sizes, which they term studio, one-bedroom, and two-bedroom. The one- and two-bedroom units have big living rooms with fireplaces and porches that look out on the ski runs. The bedrooms are spacious and some come with sleeping lofts. There's a full kitchen with a dishwasher, stove, oven, and refrigerator. Most rooms also have microwaves and humidifiers, and all have VCRs. There are indoor Jacuzzis and saunas. Two-bedroom units sleep up to six. There's also a business center, conference rooms, and a Laundromat. It's open in summer.

MODERATE
LODGES & CONDOMINIUMS
Austing Haus Hotel
Taos Ski Valley Rd. (P.O. Box 8), Taos Ski Valley, NM 87525. ☎ **800/748-2932** or 505/776-2649. Fax 505/776-8751. 45 units. TV TEL. $49–$170 double. Rates include continental breakfast. AE, DISC, MC, V.

About 1½ miles from the ski resort, the Austing Haus is a beautiful example of a timber-frame building. It was hand-built by owner Paul Austing, who will gladly give you details of the process. Though an interesting structure, at times it feels a bit fragile. The guest rooms have a Victorian feel; they're comfortable if a little cutesy. Each room has its own ski locker, and there's a nice hot tub. Tasty continental cuisine is served in a sunny dining room. *Beware:* Water runs very hot from the taps—don't burn yourself.

Taos Mountain Lodge

Taos Ski Valley Rd. (P.O. Box 698), Taos Ski Valley, NM 87525. ☎ **800/530-8098** or 505/776-2229. Fax 505/776-8791. 10 units. A/C TV TEL. Ski season $168–$275 suite; May–Oct $79.50–$122 suite. AE, MC, V.

About 1 mile west of the Ski Valley on the road from Taos, these loft suites (which can accommodate up to six) provide airy, comfortable lodging for a good price. Under new ownership, this lodge, built in 1990, is undergoing some renovation. I wouldn't expect a lot of privacy in these condominiums, but they're good for a romping ski vacation. Each unit has a small bedroom downstairs and a loft-bedroom upstairs, as well as a fold-out or futon couch in the living room. All rooms have microwaves and coffeemakers. Regular rooms have kitchenettes, with minirefrigerators and stoves, and deluxe rooms have more full kitchens, with full refrigerators, stoves, and ovens. There's daily maid service.

Thunderbird Lodge

P.O. Box 87, Taos Ski Valley, NM 87525. ☎ **800/776-2279** or 505/776-2280. Fax 505/776-2238. 32 units. $99–$142 per person, which includes 3 full meals. 7-day Ski Week Package $1,080–$1,350 per adult, double occupancy (7 days room, 21 meals, 6 lift tickets), depending on season and type of accommodation (if lift rates go up, these rates may change a little). AE, MC, V. Free valet parking.

Owners Elisabeth and Tom Brownell's goal at this Bavarian-style lodge is to bring people together, and they accomplish it, sometimes a little too well. The lodge sits on the sunny side of the ski area. The lobby has a stone fireplace, raw pine pillars, and tables accented with copper lamps. There's a sunny room ideal for breakfast and lunch, with a bank of windows looking out toward the notorious Al's Run and the rest of the ski village. Adjoining is a large bar/lounge with booths, a grand piano, and fireplace, where live entertainment plays during the evenings through the winter. The rooms are small, some tiny, and noise travels up and down the halls, giving these 3 stories a dormitory atmosphere. I suggest when making reservations that you request their widest room; otherwise, you may feel as though you're stuck in a train car.

Across the road, the lodge also has a chalet with larger rooms and a brilliant sunporch. Food is the big draw here. Included in your stay, you get three gourmet meals—some of the best food available in the region. For breakfast, we had blueberry pancakes and bacon, with our choice from a table of continental breakfast accompaniments, and for dinner, we had four courses highlighted by rack of lamb Provençale. You can eat at your own table or join the larger communal one and get to know the guests, some of whom have been returning for as many as 28 years. You'll find saunas, Jacuzzi, and a small conference/living area on the ground floor.

4 RV Parks & Campgrounds

Carson National Forest

208 Cruz Alta Rd., Taos, NM 87571. ☎ **505/758-6200.**

There are nine national-forest campsites within 20 miles of Taos, all open from April or May until September or October, depending on snow conditions. For information on other public sites, contact the **Bureau of Land Management,** 226 Cruz Alta Rd., Taos, NM 87571 (☎ **505/758-8851**).

Enchanted Moon Campground

7 Valle Escondido Rd. (on US 64 E.), Valle Escondido, NM 87571. ☎ **505/758-3338.** 69 sites. Full RV hookup, $17 per day. Closed Nov–Apr.

At an elevation of 8,400 feet, this campground is surrounded by pine-covered mountains and sits up against Carson National Forest. There's a reasonably priced restaurant on-site.

Questa Lodge

Junction of NM 522 and 38 (P.O. Box 155), Questa, NM 87556. ☎ **505/586-0300.** 24 sites. Full RV hookup, $15 per day, $175 per month. Four cabins for rent in summer. AE, DISC, MC, V. Closed Nov–Apr.

On the banks of the Red River, this RV camp is just outside the small village of Questa. It's a nice pastoral setting. The cabins aren't in the best condition, but the RV and camping accommodations are pleasant—all with amazing mountain views.

Taos RV Park

Paseo del Pueblo Sur (P.O. Box 729), Ranchos de Taos, NM 87557. ☎ **800/323-6009** or 505/758-1667. Fax 505/758-1989. 33 spaces. $12 without RV hookup, $19.50 with RV hookup. DISC, MC, V.

This RV park, located on the edge of town, offers a convenient location, but a city atmosphere. It has very clean and nice bathrooms and showers. Two tepees rent for $25 each, but beware, they're right on the main drag and may be noisy. Located on a local bus line. Senior discounts are available.

✪ Taos Valley RV Park and Campground

120 Estes Rd., off NM 68 (7204 NDCBU), Taos, NM 87571. ☎ **800/999-7571** or 505/758-4469. Fax 505/758-4469. www.camptaos.com/rv/. 92 spaces. $15–$17 without RV hookup, $21–$26 with RV hookup. MC, V. Limited services Nov 1–Mar 1.

Just 1½ miles south of the Plaza, this campground is surrounded by sage, with views of the surrounding mountains. Each site has a picnic table and grill. There's a small store, laundry room, playground, and tent shelters, as well as a dump station and very clean rest rooms.

13 Where to Dine in Taos

Taos is one of my favorite places to eat. Informality reigns; at a number of restaurants you can dine on world-class food while wearing jeans or even ski pants. Nowhere is a jacket and tie mandatory. This informality doesn't extend to reservations, however; especially during the peak season, it is important to make reservations well in advance and keep them or else cancel.

In the listings below, **Expensive** refers to restaurants where most main courses are $15 or higher; **Moderate** includes those where main courses generally range from $10 to $15; and **Inexpensive** indicates that most main courses are $10 or less.

1 Expensive

Doc Martin's

In the Historic Taos Inn, 125 Paseo del Pueblo Norte. ☎ **505/758-1977.** Reservations recommended. Breakfast $3.95–$6.50; lunch $5.50–$10.50; dinner $13.50–$28; fixed-price menu $14.95–$16.95 Sun–Thurs AE, DC, MC, V. Daily 7:30am–11am, 11:30am–2:30pm, and 5:30–9pm. NEW AMERICAN.

Doc Martin's restaurant (not to be confused with those urban-warrior boots, *Doc Martens*) comprises Dr. Thomas Paul Martin's former home, office, and delivery room. In 1912, painters Bert Philips (Doc's brother-in-law) and Ernest Blumenschein hatched the concept of the Taos Society of Artists in the Martin dining room. Art still predominates here, in both the paintings that adorn the walls and the cuisine offered. The food is widely acclaimed, and the wine list has received numerous "Awards of Excellence" from *Wine Spectator* magazine.

The atmosphere is rich, with bins of yellow squash, eggplants, and red peppers set near the kiva fireplace. Recently redecorated, it follows a Southwestern decor. Breakfast might include local favorites: huevos rancheros (fried eggs on a blue-corn tortilla smothered with chile and Jack cheese) or "The Kit Carson" (eggs Benedict with a Southwestern flair). Lunch might include a porta-bello mushroom salad with bacon vinaigrette, or a shrimp burrito. For a dinner appetizer, I recommend one of the specials, such as black-bean cakes (on red chile sauce, with guacamole and goat-cheese cream) or chile rellenos. This might be followed by seared salmon with brioche-lime dressing or the Southwest lacquered duck (poached, roasted, and grilled duck breast served over julienne

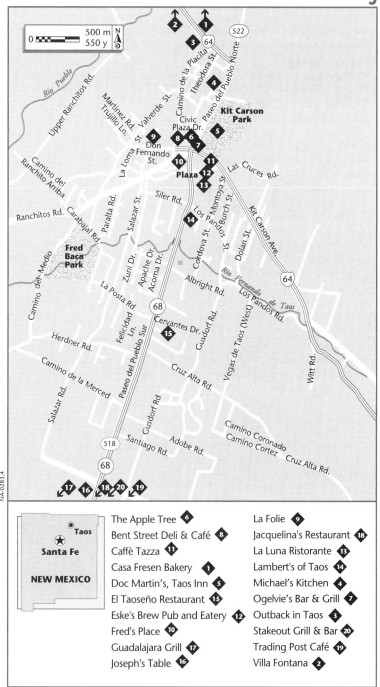

The Apple Tree **6**	La Folie **9**
Bent Street Deli & Café **8**	Jacquelina's Restaurant **18**
Caffè Tazza **11**	La Luna Ristorante **13**
Casa Fresen Bakery **1**	Lambert's of Taos **14**
Doc Martin's, Taos Inn **5**	Michael's Kitchen **4**
El Taoseño Restaurant **15**	Ogelvie's Bar & Grill **7**
Eske's Brew Pub and Eatery **12**	Outback in Taos **3**
Fred's Place **10**	Stakeout Grill & Bar **20**
Guadalajara Grill **17**	Trading Post Café **19**
Joseph's Table **16**	Villa Fontana **2**

duck-leg meat and red chile broth with posole and mango relish). If you still have room, there's always a nice selection of desserts—try the citrus cheesecake, a lemon-, lime-, and orange-flavored cheesecake served with an orange-tarragon sauce.

✪ Joseph's Table

4167 Highway 68, Ranchos de Taos. ☎ **505/751-4512.** Reservations recommended. Main courses $14–$20. AE, DC, DISC, MC, V. Tues–Thurs and Sun 5–10pm, Fri–Sat 5–11pm. NEW AMERICAN/MEDITERRANEAN.

Taos funk meets European flair at this intimate restaurant in Ranchos de Taos, about a 10-minute drive from the Plaza. In the original dining room, bird cages hang from the ceiling and medieval candles adorn the walls, while in a new room, opera plays while diners are surrounded by a whimsical El Greco motif. Between faux-painted walls, chef/owners Joseph and Gina Wrede serve up such dishes as steak au poivre and grilled Chilean sea bass. What's interesting is the way these dishes are served. The steak sits atop a layer of smooth mashed potatoes and is crowned with an exotic mushroom salad, while the sea bass rests on potatoes, as well as a layer of mashed squash, and is surrounded by a tomato puree. For dessert try such delicacies as bread pudding or the dark- and white-chocolate marquis, which Joseph describes as "creamy like the inside of a truffle." An eclectic selection of beers and wines by the bottle and glass is available.

Lambert's of Taos

309 Paseo del Pueblo Sur. ☎ **505/758-1009.** Reservations recommended. Main courses $8–$18.50. AE, DC, MC, V. Daily 5:50pm–closing, usually 9pm or so. CONTEMPORARY AMERICAN.

Zeke Lambert, a former San Francisco restaurateur who was head chef at Doc Martin's for 4 years, opened this fine dining establishment in late 1989 in the historic Randall Home near Los Pandos Road. It's a sparsely decorated place with contemporary art on the walls—a nice spot for a romantic evening. Though I've heard wonderful comments about the food here, I was not overly impressed. The service was friendly and efficient, and the meal always begins with a complimentary aperitif. I found the house salad nicely prepared with butter lettuce and raddicchio. Appetizers include a Mediterranean olive plate and chile-dusted rock shrimp. I ordered the restaurant's signature dish, the pepper-crusted lamb. If you like strong flavors, this is your dish—very peppery, served with a red wine demi-glace and linguine. I also tasted the shepherd's pie, lamb stew served with mashed potatoes, and wasn't overly impressed with the sauce. Others I've spoken to have enjoyed the grilled salmon with a tomato-sage sauce (at $16.50, a fair bargain). For dessert, the white-chocolate ice cream and Zeke's chocolate mousse with raspberry sauce are quite delicious. Espresso coffees, beers, and wines are served.

Stakeout Grill & Bar

101 Stakeout Dr. (just off NM 68). ☎ **505/758-2042.** www.stakeoutrestaurant.com. Reservations recommended. Main courses $11.95–$25.95. AE, CB, DC, DISC, MC, V. Daily 5–9:30pm. CONTINENTAL.

Drive about a mile up a dirt road toward the base of the Sangre de Cristo Mountains, and dine looking down upon the Taos gorge while the sun sets over the Jemez Range. That's the experience at the Stakeout, south of Taos. You're enveloped in the warmth of rustic decor (which is a great contrast to the almost-white exterior). There are paneled walls, creaking hardwood floors, and a crackling fireplace in the winter. The fare, which focuses on steak and seafood, is fresh, thoughtfully prepared, and conscientiously served. You can start with baked Brie served with sliced almonds and apples or escargots baked with walnuts, herbs, white wine, and garlic.

Move on to a filet mignon, served with béarnaise sauce and cooked to your liking. Or for something more exotic, try the duck Cumberland (half a duck roasted with apples and prunes and served with an orange-currant sauce). Among the seafood offerings are salmon, Alaskan king crab legs (steamed and served with drawn butter), scallops, and shrimp. Finish your meal with a fresh pastry and a cappuccino. Try to time your reservation so you can see the sunset. A full bar, extensive wine list, and cigars are available.

Villa Fontana

NM 522, 5 miles north of Taos. ☎ **505/758-5800.** www.silverhawk./com/villafontana/taos/. E-mail: villafon@aol.com. Reservations recommended. Main courses $19–$25. AE, CB, DC, DISC, MC, V. Mon–Sat 5:30–9pm. ITALIAN.

Carlo and Siobhan Gislimberti have received wide acclaim for their restaurant on the north end of town. They like to talk about *"peccato di gola"* (lust of the palate), which they brought with them to Taos when they left their home in the Italian Dolomites, near the Austrian border. They have their own herb garden, and Carlo, a master chef, is a member of the New Mexico Mycological Society—wild mushrooms play an important role in many of his kitchen preparations. The decor is country European, salmon-colored walls accented with kelly green and bright, cheerful (though amateurish) paintings (some of the chef's works).

Romantic opera plays, while tuxedoed waiters carefully serve each course. Meals are truly gourmet, but the word around town is that the food is not always consistent, and I have to agree. A must for a starter is the cream of wild mushroom soup, light and buttery. You also may want to try the shrimp marinara served with bruschetta. For a main course, the duck with green peppercorn sauce was very flavorful, except that the duck, which must have been cooked earlier and been refrigerated, wasn't warmed through. Considering the prices here, this counted heavily. The osso buco is a house specialty as well. Dinners are served with fresh vegetables and potatoes, rice, or polenta. For dessert, the profiterole is excellent. Outdoor dining in the summer offers pleasant mountain and valley views.

2 Moderate

Apple Tree

123 Bent St. ☎ **505/758-1900.** http://taoswebb.com/menu/appletree/.html. E-mail: appletree@newmex.com. Reservations recommended. Lunch $5.25–$9.95; dinner $10.95–$18.95. AE, CB, DC, DISC, MC, V. Mon–Sat 11:30am–3pm; light meals and snacks daily 3–5:30pm; daily 5:30–9pm; brunch Sun 10am–3pm. INTERNATIONAL.

Eclectic music pervades the four adobe rooms of this restaurant, a block north of the Plaza. Original paintings by Taos masters watch over the candlelit service indoors. Outside, diners sit at wooden tables on a graveled courtyard beneath a spreading apple tree.

This restaurant is popular among locals and travelers, but it doesn't appeal much to me. The recipes try too hard. I suggest ordering what looks simplest, either from the menu or from the daily specials. The Apple Tree salad (greens sprinkled with dried cranberries, walnuts, and blue cheese served with a vinaigrette) is very good, as is the posole (hominy with chile). A very popular dish, though too sweet for me, is mango chicken enchiladas (chicken simmered with onions and spices, layered between blue corn tortillas with mango chutney, sour cream, and salsa fresca and smothered with green chile). I prefer the Thai red curry (either vegetarian or with shrimp). The best thing here is the chile-jalapeño bread, served with the meal. The Apple Tree has an award-winning wine list, and the desserts are prepared fresh daily.

Bent Street Deli & Cafe

120 Bent St. ☎ **505/758-5787.** Reservations accepted. Breakfast $1.25–$6; lunch $2.50–$8; dinner $10–$16. MC, V. Mon–Sat 8am–9pm. DELI/INTERNATIONAL.

This popular cafe a short block north of the Plaza has inventive, reliable food in a country-home atmosphere. Outside, a flower box surrounds sidewalk cafe–style seating that is heated in winter. Inside, baskets and bottles of homemade jam accent wooden tables. The menu features breakfast burritos and homemade granola in the morning; for lunch, you can choose from 18 deli sandwiches, plus a "create-your-own" column. At dinner, the menu becomes a bit more sophisticated, with dishes such as beef tenderloin médaillons served over fettuccine with a chipotle-Fontina cream sauce, or roja shrimp (black tiger shrimp, red chile, and jicama, cilantro, and corn relish). All dinner entrees are served with a salad and freshly baked bread. If you'd like to grab a picnic to go, the deli offers carry-out service.

Jacquelina's Restaurant

1541 Paseo del Pueblo Sur. ☎ **505/751-0399.** Reservations recommended. Main courses $7.75–$14.95. AE, DISC, MC, V. Tues–Fri and Sun 11am–2pm; Tues–Sun 5–9pm. CREATIVE SOUTHWESTERN.

In a kiva-style, round dining room full of loud Mexican curios, this restaurant serves traditional and innovative Southwestern cuisine. Service is fast and efficient, and the clientele here are locals, often with kids who can color at a little play table near the entrance. You'll find the usual enchiladas and burritos, and many more elegant dishes such as fillet of salmon Southwest-style with black beans and pico de gallo. The price for two large pieces of salmon is quite good. The flavor, though tasty, is a little bland. Jacquelina's signature dish—chipotle chile and honey-marinated pork tenderloin, served with hush puppies—is spicy and tender.

La Luna Ristorante

223 Paseo del Pueblo Sur. ☎ **505/751-0023.** Reservations recommended. Main courses $7.95–$19.95. AE, DISC, MC, V. Daily 5pm–closing (approximately 10pm). ITALIAN.

This bright, airy restaurant is reminiscent of a cafe in Italy. Persimmon walls accent one area with tables nicely placed, some on a raised level. Another area has yellow walls and more intimate booths. In the warmer months there are tables outside, though, since it's a refurbished shopping center, the setting is a bit on the tarmac side. The restaurant surrounds a ceramic pizza/bread oven which lends warmth throughout. Service is friendly and efficient. The restaurant came under new ownership as of August 1997, and locals are waiting to see if its good, though not stellar, reputation holds. Appetizers are pretty basic, with various salads, including a Caesar. For an entree, I like the salmon, which is seared and served with rice and a honey-roasted shallot cream sauce. My friend's vegetarian pizza was crispy-crusted, with eggplant, mushrooms, artichoke hearts and bell peppers—very tasty. I won't, however, recommend the pollo alla parmesan, which was dry. There are also meat dishes and a variety of pastas. My favorite: *orechiette con salsiccia,* ear-shaped pasta with spicy Italian sausage and tomato sauce. You may want to try one of the daily specials. Beer and wine are available by the glass or bottle.

Ogelvie's Bar & Grill

1031 East Plaza. ☎ **505/758-8866.** No reservations. Lunch $5.95–$9.50; dinner $8.50–$18.50. AE, MC, V. Daily 11am–closing. INTERNATIONAL.

The only real reason to go to this restaurant is to have a cocktail right on the Plaza. In the warm months, there's a nice balcony where diners can sit and drink a margarita and indulge in chips or other appetizers, such as potato skins, or even a burger. Otherwise, the food here is not flavorful, and the atmosphere inside is dated.

⊕ Family-Friendly Restaurants

El Taoseño Restaurant *(see page 198)*   The jukebox and games room will keep the kids happy while you chow down on a breakfast burrito, tacos, or enchiladas.

Jacquelina's Restaurant *(see page 196)*   With all its brightly colored Mexican curios and a little play table, kids will be entertained while parents dine on fairly inexpensive, well-prepared food.

Michael's Kitchen *(see page 200)*   With a broad menu, comfy booths, and a very casual, diner-type atmosphere, both kids and their parents will feel at home here.

Outback in Taos *(see below)*   The pizza will please both parents and kids, and so will all the odd decorations, such as the chain with foot-long links hanging over the front counter.

✪ Outback in Taos

712 Paseo del Pueblo Norte (just north of Allsup's). ☎ **505/758-3112.** Reservations recommended on holidays. Pizzas $11.25–$23.95; pastas and calzones $6.50–$9.25. MC, V. Summer, daily 11am–10pm; winter, Sun–Thurs 11am–9pm, Fri–Sat 11am–10pm. PASTA AND GOURMET PIZZA.

My kayaking buddies always go here after a day on the river. That will give you an idea of the level of informality (very), as well as the quality of the food and beer (great), and the size of the portions (large). It's a raucous old hippie-decorated adobe restaurant, with a friendly and eager wait staff. There are three rooms: an enclosed porch, the main room (my favorite), decorated with such works as an old gas pump topped by a lampshade, and the back (through the kitchen) where most of the tables are booths. What to order? I have one big word here. Pizza. Sure the spicy Greek pasta is good, as is the Veggie Zone (a calzone filled with stir-fried veggies and two cheeses)—but, why? The pizzas are incredible. All come with a delicious thin crust (no sogginess here) that's folded over on the edges and sprinkled with sesame seeds. The sauce is unthinkably tasty, and the variations are broad. There's Thai chicken pizza (pineapple, peanuts, and a spicy sauce); The Killer, with sun-dried tomatoes, gorgonzola, green chile, and black olives; and my favorite, pizza Florentine, (spinach, basil, sun-dried tomatoes, chicken breast, mushrooms, capers, and garlic, sautéed in white wine). Of course, you can get the Carnivore Special if you like pepperoni and sausage. Don't leave without a Dalai Lama bar in hand (coconut, chocolate, and caramel) or without sharing the Devil Down Under (a "mongo" chocolate-chip cookie with ice cream, whipped cream, and chocolate sauce). Check out the small selection of wines and large selection of microbrews.

✪ Trading Post Café

4179 Paseo del Pueblo Sur. Ranchos de Taos. ☎ **505/758-5089.** No reservations except for parties of 5 or more. Menu items $6–$25. CB, DC, DISC, MC, V. Mon–Sat 11:30am–9:30pm. NORTHERN ITALIAN/INTERNATIONAL.

One of my tastiest writing assignments was when I did a profile of this restaurant for the *New York Times*. Chef/owner René Mettler spent 3 hours serving us course after course of dishes prepared especially for us. If you think this gastronomical orgy might color my opinion, just ask anyone in town where they most like to eat. Even notables such as R.C. Gorman, Dennis Hopper, and Gene Hackman will likely name the Trading Post. What draws them is a gallery atmosphere, where rough plastered walls washed with an orange hue are set off by sculptures, paintings, and photographs from the Lumina Gallery. The meals are also artistically served. "You eat with your eyes," says Mettler. When you go, be prepared to wait for a table, and don't expect quiet romance here, unless you come on an off hour. The place bustles. A bar encloses an open-exhibition kitchen. If you're dining alone or just don't feel like waiting for a table, the bar is a fun place to sit. The menu lists a nice variety of items without distinguishing between appetizers and main courses. This small detail speaks volumes about the restaurant. Although the focus is on the fine food, diners can feel comfortable here, even if trying three appetizers and skipping the main course. The Caesar salad is traditional with an interesting twist—garlic chips. You've probably never had a Caesar salad this good. If you like pasta, you'll find a nice variety on the menu. The angel-hair pasta with chicken, wild mushrooms, and Gorgonzola cream is surprisingly light and flavorful. There's also a fresh fish of the day and usually nice stews and soups at very reasonable prices. A new addition is the creole pepper shrimp, with saffron rice and fried leeks. For dessert try the tarts.

3 Inexpensive

Caffè Tazza
122 Kit Carson Rd. ☎ **505/758-8706.** Reservations not accepted. All menu items under $10. No credit cards. Daily 8am–6pm (to 10pm on performance nights). CAFE.

This cozy three-room cafe, with a summer patio, is a gathering spot for local community groups, artists, performers, and poets. Plays, films, comedy, and musical performances are given here on weekends (and some weeknights in summer), including appearances by such notable authors as John Nichols (*Milagro Beanfield War*) and Natalie Goldberg (*Writing Down the Bones).* The walls are always hung with the works of local emerging artists who have not yet made it to the Taos gallery scene. Locals and travelers alike enjoy sitting in the cafe, taking in the scene or reading one of the assorted periodicals (including the *New York Times*) available while sipping a cappuccino or cafe Mexicano (espresso with steamed milk and Mexican chocolate). The food is also quite good. Usually, there are two homemade soups from which to choose. I recommend the veggie red chile with tofu. Breakfast burritos are also tasty, as are the pastries, which are imported from the Plaza Bakery in Santa Fe.

Casa Fresen Bakery
482 Hwy 150 (Ski Valley Rd.), Arroyo Seco. ☎ **505/776-2969.** All menu items under $10. Wed–Mon 7:30am–5pm. AE, DISC, MC, V. EUROPEAN CAFE.

Hardly a person passes through the quaint village of Arroyo Seco without stopping here for gourmet coffee and killer brownies or the indomitable *schneken* (pecan rolls). Many now also make it a destination in order to sit out under an apricot tree, or inside at oddly matched tables and eat delicacies ordered at the counter: a smoked turkey sandwich with brie and honey-cup mustard, applewood-smoked trout sandwich with basil pesto, or soups such as carrot-cilantro. If you're heading into the outdoors they'll pack you an unforgettable lunch.

El Taoseño Restaurant
819 S. Santa Fe Rd. ☎ **505/758-4142.** Main courses $3.10–$11.95. AE, MC, V. Mon–Fri 6am–9pm, Sat 6:30am–10pm, Sun 6:30am–2pm. NEW MEXICAN/AMERICAN.

For years I'd driven by this unimpressive brown adobe-style building, not caring to enter. But once I did, I was glad I had. Nothing fancy here. It's a New Mexico–style diner, with red print carpet that clashes with the blue-checkered tablecloths and a counter for loners. But the food, well, it's some of the best traditional New

Mexican food around. Best of all, you can get a breakfast burrito any time of day, and this is probably what you'll want to order: plenty of hash browns, scrambled eggs, and bacon wrapped in a flour tortilla smothered in chile and cheese, served with pinto beans and a sopaipilla. Red or green? Both are good, but the green is award-winning (though hotter). Since this diner is open all day and evening, it's a great place to go between meals. A low-fat menu is also available.

Eske's Brew Pub and Eatery

106 Des Georges Lane. ☎ **505/758-1517.** All menu items under $9. MC, V. Mar–Sept and during peak times such as winter and spring break daily 11:30am–10pm; rest of winter only open Sat and Sun 11:30am–1pm. SOUTHWESTERN PUB FARE.

I have a fondness for this place that one might have for an oasis in the desert. The first time I ate here, I'd been on assignment ice climbing and spent 8 hours out in the shadow of a canyon hacking my way up an 80-foot frozen waterfall. I sat down at one of the high tables in the main room, dipped into a big bowl of Wanda's green chile turkey stew, and felt the blood return to my extremities. My climbing buddies ordered The Fatty (a whole-wheat tortilla filled with beans, mashed potatoes, onions, feta and cheddar cheese, smothered in green chile turkey stew). But we all considered bangers and mash (bratwurst cooked in beer with homemade mashed potatoes and warm apple sauce). We also enjoyed some tasty brew—a black and tan, a mixture of barley wine and stout, the heavier beer sinking to the bottom, and a Mesa pale ale. When I asked the owner, Steve "Eske" Eskeback, which was his favorite beer, he replied "the one in my hand," meaning he recommends all the beers, which are his own recipes. The service is friendly and informal. The crowd is local, a few people sitting at the bar where they can visit and watch the beer-pouring and food preparation. At times it can be a rowdy place, but mostly it's just fun, lots of ski patrollers and mountain guides showing up to swap stories. In summer, you can eat on picnic tables outside.

✪ Fred's Place

332 Paseo del Pueblo Sur. ☎ **505/758-0514.** Main courses $5–$12. MC, V. Mon–Sat 5–9:30pm. NEW MEXICAN.

I was warned by a number of locals not to put Fred's Place in this guide. This is *our* place, they pleaded. But alas, the guide wouldn't be complete without mention of Fred's. God and the devil are at odds at this New Mexican food restaurant, and judging by the food, God has won out. The atmosphere is rich, though for some it may be a bit unnerving. Walls are hung with crucifixes and a vivid ceiling mural depicts a very hungry devil that appears to swoop down toward the dining tables.

Fred's offers New Mexican food, but it's not of the greasy-spoon variety. It's very refined, the flavors carefully calculated. You have to try Dee Dee's squash stew (squash, corn, beans, and vegetarian green chile, topped with cheese and fresh oregano). For me, Fred's chicken enchilada is heaven; however, you can't go wrong with a burrito either. Daily specials include grilled trout and carne asada served with a watercress salad. For dessert, try the warm apple crisp with ice cream.

Guadalajara Grill

1384 Paseo del Pueblo Sur. ☎ **505/751-0063.** All items under $10. MC, V. Mon–Sat 10:30am–9pm, Sun 11am–9pm. MEXICAN.

My organic lettuce farmer friend Joe introduced me to this authentic Mexican restaurant; then he disappeared into Mexico, only communicating occasionally by e-mail. Did the incredible food drive him south? I wonder. The restaurant is in an odd location. On the south end of town, it shares a building with a car wash. Don't be deceived, however; the food here is excellent (and very clean!). It's Mexican rather than New Mexican, a refreshing treat. I recommend the tacos, particularly pork or chicken, served in soft homemade corn tortillas, the meat artfully seasoned and grilled. The burritos are large and smothered in chile. Platos are served with rice and beans and half orders are available for smaller appetites. Recently, the chef added seafood to the menu. Try the *mojo de ajo* (shrimp cooked with garlic), served with rice, beans, and guacamole. Beer and wine are now available.

La Folie

122 Dona Luz. ☎ **505/758-8800.** www.silverhawk.com/taos/lafolie.html. Main courses $6.95–$12.75. AE, DC, DISC, MC, V. Tues–Sat 11am–2:30pm and 5:30–9:30pm; Sun 9am–3pm. ECLECTIC FRENCH/ASIAN.

This new restaurant opened by Mark and Lisa Felix promises delicate and rich flavors in a festive environment. Inside, you're surrounded by walls faux-painted with images of pillars and birds, and outside, tables are set around a charming courtyard with a fountain. For lunch, try the Thai peanut chicken salad, with julienned vegetables. For dinner, the mussels mariniere (with a sauce of parsley and garlic sautéed with cream and white wine, served over fettuccini) has a fresh taste. The beef bourguignon is also nice. For dessert, the piña colada mousse is surprisingly light. Due to the restaurant's proximity to a church, no alcoholic beverages are served.

Michael's Kitchen

304 C Paseo del Pueblo Norte. ☎ **505/758-4178.** No reservations. Breakfast $1.55–$7.95; lunch $3.25–$9.50; dinner $5–$13.95. AE, DISC, MC, V. Daily 7am–8:30pm (except major holidays). NEW MEXICAN/AMERICAN.

A couple of blocks north of the Plaza, this eatery is a throwback to earlier days, when big plates full of hearty food was the norm. Between its hardwood floor and viga ceiling are various knickknacks on posts, walls, and windows: a deer head here, a Tiffany lamp there, and several scattered antique woodstoves. Seating is at booths and tables. Breakfast dishes, including a large selection of pancakes and egg preparations (with names like the "Moofy," "Omelette Extra-ordinaire," and "Pancake Sandwich"), are served all day (because they're so good), as are lunch sandwiches (including Philly cheesesteak, tuna melt, chile burger, and a veggie sandwich). One of my favorite lunch dishes is generically (and facetiously) called "Health Food," a double order of fries with red or green chile and cheese. Dinners range from veal Cordon Bleu to plantation-fried chicken to enchiladas rancheros. Now, on Saturday evening you can get prime rib. Michael's has its own excellent full-service bakery.

What to See & Do in Taos

With a history shaped by pre-Colombian civilization, Spanish colonialism, and the Wild West; outdoor activities that range from ballooning to world-class skiing; and a clustering of artists, writers, and musicians, Taos has something to offer almost everybody. Its pueblo is the most accessible in New Mexico, and its museums, including the new Van Vechten Lineberry Taos Art Museum, represent a world-class display of regional history and culture.

SUGGESTED ITINERARIES

If You Have Only 1 Day

Spend at least 2 hours at the Taos Pueblo. You'll also have time to see the Millicent Rogers Museum and to browse in some of the town's fine art galleries. Try to make it to Ranchos de Taos to see the San Francisco de Asis Church and to shop on the Plaza there.

If You Have 2 Days

On the second day, explore the Kit Carson Historic Museums—the Martinez Hacienda, the Kit Carson Home, and the Ernest L. Blumenschein Home. Then. head out of town to enjoy the view from the Rio Grande Gorge Bridge.

If You Have 3 Days or More

On your third day, drive the "Enchanted Circle" through Red River, Eagle Nest, and Angel Fire or head to the Van Vechten Lineberry Taos Art Museum. You may want to allow a full day for shopping or perhaps drive up to the Taos Ski Valley for a chairlift ride or a short hike. Of course, if you're here in the winter with skis, the mountain is your first priority.

If You're an Outdoorsperson

Start with the first day recommendation, just to get a feel for the culture of Taos. Then, if it's spring or early summer, plan a raft trip down the Taos Box Canyon (a full day event). It it's spring, summer, or fall, contact one of the bicycle rental or touring companies and have them show you the way or take you to some of the mountain rides in the area or the West Rim of the Taos Box Canyon.

The next day, head up to Wheeler Peak (13,161 feet), the highest point in New Mexico (a good full-day hike up and back), where you'll have a 360° view of Northern New Mexico. Or, you may want to spend the day hiking and visiting ruins around Bandelier National Monument near Los Alamos. If it's winter, plan at least a day of skiing at the world-acclaimed Taos Ski Valley; however, you also might want to take skinny (cross-country) skis up into the mountains. You can also snowshoe or backcountry ski in the area. For rock climbing, there's a great site just to the west of Taos.

A Note on Taos Museums: If you would like to visit all seven museums that comprise the Museum Association of Taos—Blumenschein Home, Fechin Institute, Hacienda Martinez, Harwood Museum, Kit Carson Home and Museum, Millicent Rogers Museum, and Van Vechten Lineberry Taos Art Museum—it might be worthwhile to purchase a combination ticket for $20.

1 The Top Attractions

Taos Pueblo

P.O. Box 1846, Taos Pueblo, NM 87571. ☎ **505/758-1028.** Cost is $6 for parking and $4 per person for admission; $1 for children. If you would like to use a still camera, the charge is $10; for a video camera $20; if you would like to sketch or paint, written permission is required. Other charges apply for commercial use of imagery. Photography is not permitted on feast days. Winter daily 8:30am–4:30pm; summer daily 8am–5pm, with a few exceptions. Closed for 1 month every year in late winter or early spring (call to find out if it will be open at the time you expect to be in Taos). Also, since this is a living community, you can expect periodic closures.

It's amazing that in our frenetic world, 200 Taos Pueblo residents still live much as their ancestors did a thousand years ago. When you enter the pueblo you'll see where they dwell in two large buildings, each with rooms piled on top of each other, forming structures that echo the shape of Taos Mountain (which sits to the northeast). Here, a portion of Taos residents live without electricity and running water. The remaining 2,000 residents of Taos Pueblo live in conventional homes on the Pueblo's 95,000 acres.

The main buildings' distinctive flowing lines of shaped mud, with a straw-and-mud exterior plaster, are typical of Pueblo architecture throughout the Southwest. It's architecture that blends in with the surrounding land—which makes sense, given that it is itself made of earth. Bright blue doors are the same shade as the sky that frames the brown buildings.

The northernmost of New Mexico's 19 pueblos, Taos has been home to the Tiwa tribes for more than 900 years. Many residents here still practice ancestral rituals. The center of their world is still nature, many still bake bread in hornos, and most still drink water that flows down from the sacred Blue Lake. Meanwhile, arts and crafts and other tourism-related businesses support the economy, along with government services, ranching, and farming.

The village looks much the same today as it did when a regiment from Coronado's expedition first came upon it in 1540. Though the Tiwa were essentially a peaceful agrarian people, they are perhaps best remembered for spearheading the only successful revolt by Native Americans in history. Launched by Pope ("Pó pay") in 1680, the uprising drove the Spanish from Santa Fe until 1692 and from Taos until 1698.

As you explore the pueblo, you can visit the residents' studios, munch on homemade bread, look into the new **San Geronimo Chapel,** and wander past the fascinating ruins of the old church and cemetery. You're expected to ask permission from individuals before taking their photos; some will ask for a small payment, but that's for you to negotiate. Kivas and other ceremonial underground areas are restricted.

Taos Attractions

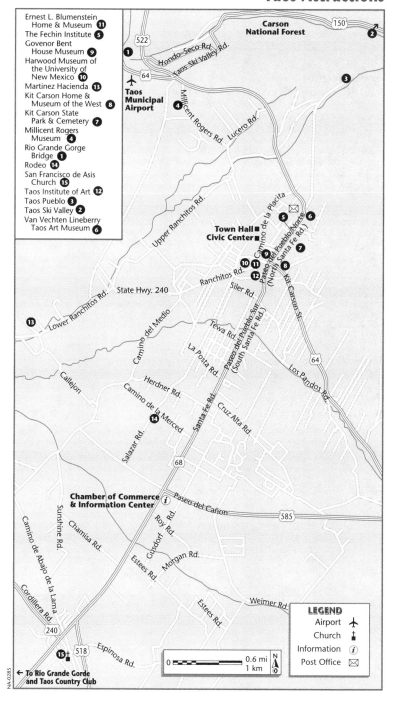

Ernest L. Blumenstein
Home & Museum ⑪

The Fechin Institute ⑤

Govenor Bent
House Museum ⑨

Harwood Museum of
the University of
New Mexico ⑩

Martinez Hacienda ⑬

Kit Carson Home &
Museum of the West ⑧

Kit Carson State
Park & Cemetery ⑦

Millicent Rogers
Museum ④

Rio Grande Gorge
Bridge ①

Rodeo ⑭

San Francisco de Asis
Church ⑮

Taos Institute of Art ⑫

Taos Pueblo ③

Taos Ski Valley ②

Van Vechten Lineberry
Taos Art Museum ⑥

Carson
National Forest

Taos
Municipal
Airport

Town Hall ■
Civic Center ■

Chamber of Commerce
& Information Center

To Rio Grande Gorde
and Taos Country Club

Upper Ranchitos Rd.

Lower Ranchitos Rd.

State Hwy. 240

Ranchitos Rd.

Siler Rd.

Camino del Medio

Tewa Rd.

La Posta Rd.

Camino de la Placita

Paseo del Pueblo Norte
(North Santa Fe Rd.)

Kit Carson St.

Los Pandos Rd.

Paseo del Pueblo Sur
(South Santa Fe Rd.)

Santa Fe Rd.

Cruz Alta Rd.

Herdner Rd.

Camino de la Merced

Salazar Rd.

Callejon

Paseo del Cañon

Roy Rd.

Gusdorf Rd.

Estees Rd.

Morgan Rd.

Chamisa Rd.

Sunshine Rd.

Camino de Abajo de la Lama

Cordillera Rd.

Espinosa Rd.

Estees Rd.

Weimer Rd.

Hondo - Seco Rd.

Taos Ski Valley Rd.

Millicent Rogers Rd.

Lucero Rd.

LEGEND

Airport ✈

Church ✝

Information ⓘ

Post Office ✉

0   0.6 mi
1 km

N

203

San Geronimo is the patron saint of the Taos Pueblo, and his feast day (September 30) combines Catholic and pre-Hispanic traditions. The **Old Taos Trade Fair** on that day is a joyous occasion, with foot races, pole climbs, and crafts booths. Dances are performed the evening of September 29. Other annual events include a **turtle dance** on New Year's Day, **deer or buffalo dances** on Three Kings Day (January 6), and **corn dances** on Santa Cruz Day (May 3), San Antonio Day (June 13), San Juan Day (June 24), Santiago Day (July 23), and Santa Ana Day (July 24). The **Taos Pueblo Powwow,** a dance competition and parade that brings together tribes from throughout North America, is held the weekend after July 4 on reservation land off NM 522. **Christmas Eve bonfires** mark the start of the children's corn dance, the **Christmas Day deer dance,** and the 3-day-long **Matachines dance.**

During your visit to the pueblo you will have the opportunity to purchase traditional fried and oven-baked bread as well as a variety of arts and crafts. If you would like to try traditional feast-day meals, **Tiwa Kitchen,** near the entrance to the pueblo, is a good place to stop. Close to Tiwa Kitchen is the **Oo-oonah Children's Art Center,** where you can see the creative works of pueblo children.

As with many of the other pueblos in New Mexico, Taos Pueblo has opened a **casino,** featuring slot machines, blackjack, and poker. Free local transportation is available. Call ☎ **505/758-4460** for details.

✪ Millicent Rogers Museum of Northern New Mexico

Off NM 522, 4 miles north of Taos. ☎ **505/758-2462.** Admission $6 adults, $5 students, $1 children 6–16. Daily 10am–5pm. Closed Mon in Nov–Mar, Easter, San Geronimo Day (Sept 30), Thanksgiving, Dec 25, and Jan 1.

This museum is small enough to give a glimpse of some of the finest Southwestern arts and crafts you'll see without being overwhelmed. It was founded in 1953 by family members after the death of Millicent Rogers. Rogers was a wealthy Taos émigré who in 1947 began acquiring a magnificent collection of beautiful Native American arts and crafts. Included are Navajo and Pueblo jewelry, Navajo textiles, pueblo pottery, Hopi and Zuni kachina dolls, paintings from the Rio Grande Pueblo people, and basketry from a wide variety of Southwestern tribes. The collection continues to grow through gifts and museum acquisitions. The museum also presents changing exhibitions of Southwestern art, crafts, and design.

Since the 1970s, the scope of the museum's permanent collection has been expanded to include Anglo arts and crafts and Hispanic religious and secular arts and crafts, from Spanish and Mexican colonial to contemporary times. Included are *santos* (religious images), furniture, weavings, colcha embroideries, and decorative tin work. Agricultural implements, domestic utensils, and craftspeople's tools dating from the 17th and 18th centuries are also displayed.

The museum gift shop has a fine collection of superior regional art. Classes and workshops, lectures, and field trips are held throughout the year.

✪ Kit Carson Historic Museums

P.O. Drawer CCC, Taos, NM 87571. ☎ **505/758-0505.** Three museums $10 adults (ages 16 and over), $5 children 6–15; family rate, $20. Two museums $7.50 adults, $4 children; family rate, $15. One museum $5 adults, $2.50 children; family rate, $10. All museums free for children under 6. Summer, Kit Carson Home daily 8am–6pm; Martinez Hacienda daily 9am–5pm; Blumenschein Home daily 9am–5pm. Winter, Kit Carson Home daily 9am–5pm; Martinez Hacienda daily 10am–4pm; Blumenschein Home daily 11am–4pm.

Three historical homes are operated as museums, affording visitors a glimpse of early Taos lifestyles. The Martinez Hacienda, Kit Carson Home, and Ernest Blumenschein home each has unique appeal.

The **Martinez Hacienda,** Lower Ranchitos Road, Hwy. 240 (☎ **505/ 758-1000**), is the only Spanish colonial hacienda in the United States that's open to the public year-round. This was the home of the merchant and trader Don Antonio Severino Martinez, who bought it in 1804 and lived here until his death in 1827. Located on the west bank of the Rio Pueblo de Taos about 2 miles southwest of the Plaza, the museum is remarkably beautiful, with thick, raw adobe walls and no exterior windows, to protect against raids by Plains tribes.

Twenty-one rooms were built around two *placitas,* or interior courtyards. They give you a glimpse of the austerity of frontier lives, with only a few pieces of modest period furniture in each. You'll see bedrooms, servants' quarters, stables, a kitchen, and even a large fiesta room. Exhibits in one newly renovated room tell the story of the Martinez family and life in Spanish Taos between 1598 and 1821, when Mexico gained control.

Don Antonio Martinez, who for a time was *alcalde* (mayor) of Taos, owned several caravans that he used in trade on the Chihuahua Trail to Mexico. This business was carried on by his youngest son, Don Juan Pascual, who later owned the hacienda. His eldest son was Padre Antonio José Martinez, Northern New Mexico's controversial spiritual leader from 1826 to 1867.

Kit Carson Historic Museums has developed the hacienda into a living museum with weavers, blacksmiths, and wood carvers. Demonstrations are scheduled daily, and even more often during the **Taos Trade Fair** (the last weekend in September) when they run virtually nonstop. The Trade Fair commemorates the era when Native Americans, Spanish settlers, and mountain men met here to trade with each other. The Martinez Hacienda is currently home to a new santos exhibit.

The **Kit Carson Home and Museum of the West,** East Kit Carson Road (☎ **505/758-4741**), located a short block east of the Plaza intersection, is the town's only general museum of Taos history. The 12-room adobe home, with walls 2½-feet thick, was built in 1825 and purchased in 1843 by Carson, the famous mountain man, Indian agent, and scout, as a wedding gift for his young bride, Josefa Jaramillo. It remained their home for 25 years, until both died (exactly a month apart) in 1868.

A living room, bedroom, and kitchen are furnished as they might have been when occupied by the Carsons. The Indian Room contains artifacts crafted and utilized by the original inhabitants of Taos Valley; the Early American Room has a variety of pioneer items, including many antique firearms and trappers' implements; and the Carson Interpretive Room presents memorabilia from Carson's unusual life. In the kitchen is a Spanish plaque that reads: *Nadie sabe lo que tiene la olla mas que la cuchara que la menea* (Nobody better knows what the pot holds than the spoon that stirs it). New permanent exhibits in the Carson home include Native American prehistory and history as well as "Kit Carson: Life and Times."

The museum bookshop, with perhaps the town's most comprehensive inventory of New Mexico historical books, is adjacent to the entry.

The **Ernest L. Blumenschein Home & Museum,** 222 Ledoux St. (☎ **505/ 758-0505**), 1½ blocks southwest of the Plaza, re-creates the lifestyle of one of the founders of the Taos Society of Artists (founded 1915). An adobe home with garden walls and a courtyard, parts of which date from the 1790s, it became the home and studio of Blumenschein (1874–1960) and his family in 1919. Period furnishings include European antiques and handmade Taos furniture in Spanish colonial style.

Blumenschein was born and raised in Pittsburgh. In 1898, he arrived in Taos somewhat by accident. After training in New York and Paris, he and fellow painter Bert Phillips were on assignment for *Harper's* and *McClure's* magazines of New York when a wheel of their wagon broke while they were traversing a mountain 30 miles north of Taos. Blumenschein drew the short straw and thus was obliged to bring the wheel by horseback to Taos for repair. He later recounted his initial reaction to the valley he entered: "No artist had ever recorded the New Mexico I was now seeing. No writer had ever written down the smell of this air or the feel of that morning sky. I was receiving . . . the first great unforgettable inspiration of my life. My destiny was being decided."

That spark later led to the foundation of Taos as an art colony. An extensive collection of works by early-20th-century Taos artists is on display in several rooms of the home, including some by Blumenschein's daughter, Helen.

2 More Attractions

Kit Carson Park and Cemetery
Paseo del Pueblo Norte.

Major community events are held in the park in summer. The cemetery, established in 1847, contains the graves of Carson and his wife, Governor Charles Bent, the Don Antonio Martinez family, Mabel Dodge Luhan, and many other noted historical figures and artists. Their lives are described briefly on plaques.

✪ Fechin Institute
227 Paseo del Pueblo Norte (P.O. Box 832), Taos, NM 87571. ☎ **505/758-1710.** Admission $4. Oct–May Wed–Sun 10am–2pm; May–Oct Wed–Sun 10am–5pm.

The home of Russian artist Nicolai Fechin (Feh-shin) from 1927 until 1933, this historic building commemorates the career of a 20th-century Renaissance man. Born in Russia in 1881, Fechin came to the United States in 1923, already acclaimed as a master of painting, drawing, sculpture, architecture, and woodwork. In Taos, he renovated a large adobe home and embellished it with hand-carved doors, windows, gates, posts, fireplaces, and other features of a Russian country home. The house and adjacent studio are now used for Fechin Institute educational activities, as well as concerts, lectures, and other programs. Fechin died in 1955.

Governor Bent House Museum
117 Bent St. ☎ **505/758-2376.** Admission $1 adults, 50¢ children. Summer daily 9am–5pm; winter daily 10am–4pm.

Located a short block north of the Plaza, this was the residence of Charles Bent, New Mexico Territory's first American governor. Bent, a former trader who established Fort Bent, Colorado, was murdered during the 1847 Native American and Hispanic rebellion, while his wife and children escaped by digging through an adobe wall into the house next door. The hole is still visible. Period art and artifacts are on display.

Harwood Museum of the University of New Mexico
238 Ledoux St. ☎ **505/758-9826.** Admission $4. Tues–Sat 10am–5pm, Sun noon–5pm.

With its high ceilings and broad wood floors, this recently restored museum has become a lovely place to wander among New Mexico–inspired images, old and new. A cultural and community center since 1923, the museum displays paintings, drawings, prints, sculpture, and photographs by Taos-area artists from 1800 to the present. Featured are paintings from the early days of the art colony by members of the Taos Society of Artists, including Oscar Berninghaus, Ernest Blumenschein, Herbert Dunton, Victor Higgins, Bert Phillips, and Walter Ufer. Also included are works by Emil Bisttram, Andrew Dasburg, Leon Gaspard, Louis Ribak, Bea Mandelman, Agnes Martin (seven new paintings in 1997), Larry Bell, and Thomas Benrimo.

Upstairs are 19th-century pounded-tin pieces and *retablos,* religious paintings of saints that have traditionally been used for decoration and inspiration in the homes and churches of New Mexico. The permanent collection includes sculptures by Patrociño Barela, one of the leading Hispanic artists of 20th-century New Mexico—well worth seeing, especially his 3-foot-tall "Death Cart" a rendition of Doña Sebastiána, the bringer of death.

The museum also schedules five or six changing exhibitions a year, many of which feature works by celebrated artists currently living in Taos.

D. H. Lawrence Ranch
San Cristobal. ☎ **505/776-2245.**

The shrine dedicated to this controversial early-20th-century author is a pilgrimage site for literary devotees. A short uphill walk from the ranch home, it's a bit of a forgotten place, with a broken gate, peeling paint, and an eagle on an altar, where people have left a few mementos such as juniper berries and sticks of gum. Most interesting is the guest book. Reading it you really get a sense that this *is* a pilgrimage spot. One couple had tried for 24 years to get here from England.

Lawrence lived in Taos on and off between 1922 and 1925. The ranch was a gift to his wife, Frieda, from the art patron Mabel Dodge Luhan. Lawrence repaid Luhan the favor by giving her the manuscript of *Sons and Lovers.* When Lawrence died in southern France in 1930 of tuberculosis, his ashes were returned here for burial. The grave of Frieda, who died in 1956, is outside the shrine.

The shrine is the only public building at the ranch, which is operated today by the University of New Mexico as an educational and recreational retreat. To reach the site, head north from Taos about 15 miles on NM 522, then another 6 miles east into the forested Sangre de Cristo Range via a well-marked dirt road. The views getting there and upon arrival are spectacular.

✪ Rio Grande Gorge Bridge
US 64, 10 miles west of Taos.

This impressive bridge, west of the Taos airport, spans the Southwest's greatest river. At 650 feet above the canyon floor, it's one of America's highest bridges. If you can withstand the vertigo, it's interesting to come more than once, at different times of day, to observe how the changing light plays tricks with the colors of the cliff walls. A curious aside is that the wedding scene in the controversial movie, *Natural Born Killers,* was filmed here.

✪ San Francisco de Asis Church
P.O. Box 72, Ranchos de Taos ☎ **505/758-2754.** Donations appreciated, $2 minimum. Mon–Sat 9am–noon and 1–4pm. Visitors may attend mass Sat at 6pm (mass rotates from this church to the 3 mission chapels) and Sun at 7 (Spanish), 9, and 11:30am. Closed to the public the first 2 weeks in June, when repairs are done; however, services still take place.

From NM 68, about 4 miles south of Taos, this famous church appears as a modern adobe sculpture with no doors or windows. This is the image that has often been photographed (by Ansel Adams, among others) and painted (for example, by Georgia O'Keeffe). Visitors must walk through the garden on the east side of this remarkable 2-story church to enter and get a full perspective of its massive walls, authentic adobe plaster, and beauty.

The church office and gift shop are just across the driveway north of the church. A video presentation is given here every hour on the half hour. Also, displayed on the wall is an unusual painting, *The Shadow of the Cross,* by Henri Ault (1896). Under ordinary light it portrays a barefoot Christ at the Sea of Galilee; in darkness, however, the portrait becomes luminescent, and the perfect shadow of a cross forms over the left shoulder of Jesus' silhouette. The artist reportedly was as shocked as everyone else to see this. The reason for the illusion remains a mystery. Several nice galleries and crafts shops surround the square.

Van Vechten Lineberry Taos Art Museum

501 Paseo del Pueblo Norte. ☎ **505/758-2690.** Admission $5 adults, $3 students. Tues–Fri 11am–4pm, Sat–Sun 1:30–4pm.

Taos's newest museum, the Van Vechten Lineberry Taos Art Museum, offers visitors works of the Taos Society of Artists, which give a sense of what Taos was like in the late 19th and early 20th centuries. The museum was the brainchild of Ed Lineberry, who lives in the spectacular home adjacent to the museum; he conceived of it as a memorial to his late wife, Duane Van Vechten. An artist herself, Duane spent much time working in her studio, which now serves as the entryway to the 20,000-square-foot main gallery of the museum. The works of the Taos Society of Artists are rich and varied, capturing panoramas as well as the personalities of the Native American and Hispanic villagers.

Among other things, the entryway features John Dunn's roulette wheel. Lineberry traveled throughout Europe studying techniques for preservation and storage, as well as the display space, climate control, and lighting of fine museums. As a result, the museum is state-of-the-art. There are works by Van Vechten, as well as some less accomplished local work. The museum is also actively acquiring new works. Besides the main gallery space, there are smaller areas available for traveling exhibitions and a wonderful library that will be open by appointment to researchers.

ART CLASSES

Perhaps you're visiting Taos because of its renown as an arts community, but galleries and studio visits may not satisfy your own urge to create. If you'd like to pursue an artistic adventure of your own here, check out the weeklong classes in such media as writing, sculpture, painting, jewelry making, photography, clay working, and textiles that are available at the **Taos Institute of Arts,** 108-B Civic Plaza Dr., Taos, NM 87571 (☎ **800/822-7183** or 505/758-2793; www.taosnet. com/tia/; e-mail: tia@taosnet.com). Class sizes are limited, so if you're thinking about giving these workshops a try, call for information well in advance. The fees vary from class to class but are generally quite reasonable; however, they usually don't include the cost of materials.

3 Organized Tours

Damaso Martinez's **Pride of Taos Tours,** P.O. Box 5271, Taos, NM 87571 (☎ **800/273-8340** or 505/758-8340), offers two tours a day, April through October, of the historical streets in Taos, Taos Pueblo, and Ranchos de Taos Church ($25 adults, $5 children 12 and under). The tour takes about 3 hours, and the cost includes admission to the sites.

An excellent opportunity to explore the historic downtown area is offered by **Taos Historic Walking Tours** (☎ **505/758-4020**). Tours cost $10 and take 1½ to 2 hours. Call for schedule.

If you'd really like a taste of Taos history and drama call **Enchantment Dreams Walking Tours** (☎ **505/776-2562**). Roberta Courtney Meyers, a theater artist, dramatist, and composer will tour you through Taos' history while performing a number of characters such as Georgia O'Keeffe and Kit Carson. I've seen her do a spicy performance piece of D. H. Lawrence's three women companions in life: Frieda Lawrence, Lady Dorothy Brett, and Mabel Dodge Luhan.

4 Skiing

DOWNHILL

Five alpine resorts are within an hour's drive of Taos; all offer complete facilities, including equipment rentals. Although exact opening and closing dates vary according to snow conditions, the season usually begins around Thanksgiving and continues into early April.

Ski clothing can be purchased, and ski equipment rented or bought, from several Taos outlets. Among them are **Cottam's Ski & Outdoor Shops,** with four locations (call ☎ **800/322-8267** or 505/758-2822 for the one nearest you); **Taos Ski Valley Sportswear, Ski & Boot Co.,** in Taos Ski Valley (☎ **505/776-2291**); and **Stay Tuned,** also in the Ski Valley (☎ **505/776-8839**).

✪ **Taos Ski Valley** (P.O. Box 90), Taos Ski Valley, NM 87525 (☎ **505/776-2291**) http://taoswebb.com/nmusa/), is the preeminent ski resort in the southern Rocky Mountains. It was founded in 1955 by a Swiss-German immigrant, Ernie Blake. According to local legend, Blake searched for 2 years in a small plane for the perfect location for a ski resort comparable to what he was accustomed to in the Alps. He found it at the abandoned mining site of Twining, high above Taos. Today, under the management of two younger generations of Blakes, the resort has become internationally renowned for its light, dry powder (320 inches annually), its superb ski school, and its personal, friendly service.

Taos Ski Valley, however, can best be appreciated by the more experienced skier. It offers steep, high-alpine, high-adventure skiing. The mountain is more intricate than it might seem at first glance, and it holds many surprises and challenges—even for the expert. The *London Times* called the valley "without any argument the best ski resort in the world. Small, intimate, and endlessly challenging, Taos simply has no equal." And, if you're sick of dealing with yahoos on snowboards, you will be pleased to know that they're not permitted on the slopes of Taos Ski Valley (the only ski area in New Mexico that forbids them). The quality of the snow here (light and dry) is believed to be due to the dry Southwestern air and abundant sunshine.

Between the 11,819-foot summit and the 9,207-foot base, there are 72 trails and bowls, more than half of them designated for expert and advanced skiers. Most of the remaining trails are suitable for advanced intermediates; there is little flat terrain for novices to gain experience and mileage. However, many beginning skiers find that after spending time in lessons they can enjoy the **Kachina Bowl,** which offers spectacular views as well as wide-open slopes.

The area has an uphill capacity of 15,000 skiers per hour on its five double chairs, one triple, four quads, and one surface tow. Tickets for all lifts, depending on the season, cost $29 to $42 for adults for a full day, $26 half-day; $18 to $26 for children 12 or younger for a full day, $16 half-day; teen ticket (13- to 17-year-olds) $24 to $34 for a full day, $21 half-day; $27 seniors ages 65 to 69 for a full day, $22 half-day; free for seniors over 70. Novice lift tickets cost $20 for all ages. Full rental packages are $12 for adults and $6 for children. Taos Ski Valley is open daily from 9am to 4pm from Thanksgiving to the second week of April. It should be noted that Taos Ski Valley has one of the best ski schools in the country. This school specializes in teaching people how to negotiate steep and challenging runs.

With its children's ski school, Taos Ski Valley has always been an excellent location for skiing families, but with the 1994 addition of an 18,000-square-foot children's center (Kinderkäfig Center), skiing with your children in Taos is even better. Kinderkäfig offers every service imaginable, from equipment rental for children to baby-sitting services. Call ahead for more information.

Taos Ski Valley has many lodges and condominiums with nearly 1,500 beds. (See "Taos Ski Valley," in chapter 12, for details on accommodations.) All offer ski-week packages; four of them have restaurants. There are two more restaurants on the mountain in addition to the many facilities of Village Center at the base. For reservations, call the **Taos Valley Resort Association** (☎ **800/776-1111** or 505/776-2233).

Not far from Taos Ski Valley is **Red River Ski Area,** (P.O. Box 900), Red River, NM 87558 (☎ **505/754-2223** for information, 800/331-7669 for reservations). One of the bonuses of this ski area is the fact that lodgers at Red River can walk out their doors and be on the slopes. Two other factors make this 37-year-old, family-oriented area special: First, most of its 57 trails are geared toward the intermediate skier, though beginners and experts also have some trails; and second, good snow is guaranteed early and late in the year by snowmaking equipment that can work on 75% of the runs, more than any other in New Mexico. However, be aware that this human-made snow tends to be icy, and the mountain is full of inexperienced skiers, so you really have to watch your back. Locals in the area refer to this as "Little Texas" because it's so popular with Texans and other Southerners. A very friendly atmosphere, with a touch of red-neck attitude, prevails.

There's a 1,600-foot vertical drop here to a base elevation of 8,750 feet. Lifts include four double chairs, two triple chairs, and a surface tow, with a skier capacity of 7,920 skiers per hour. The cost of a lift ticket for all lifts is $39 for adults for a full day, $29 half-day; $34 for teens 13 to 19 for a full day, $24 half-day; $25 for children 12 and under and seniors (60 and over) for a full day, $18 half-day. Full rental packages start at $14 for adults, $9 for children. Lifts run daily from 9am to 4pm from Thanksgiving to about March 28.

Also quite close to Taos is **Angel Fire Resort** (P.O. Drawer B), Angel Fire, NM 87710 (☎ **800/633-7463** or 505/377-6401). If you don't feel up to skiing steeper Taos Mountain (or your kids don't), Angel Fire is a good choice. The 62 trails are heavily oriented to beginner and intermediate skiers and snowboarders, with a few runs for more advanced skiers and snowboarders. I hadn't skied in Angel Fire since college until recently and was pleasantly surprised. Under new ownership, the mountain has received over $7 million in improvements in the past 2 years. This is not an old village like you'll find at Taos and Red River. Instead, it's a Vail-style resort, built in 1960, with a variety of activities other than skiing (see "A Driving Tour of the Enchanted Circle," below). The snowmaking capabilities here are excellent, and the ski school is good, though I hear so crowded it's difficult to get in during spring break. With its new high-speed quad lift (the only one in New Mexico) you can get to the top fast and have a long ski to the bottom. There are also four double lifts and one surface lift. There's a large snowboard park as well as some new hike-access advanced runs; however, the hike is substantial. All-day lift tickets cost $39 for adults, $31 for teens (13 to 17 years old) and $23 for children (7 to 12 years old). Kids 6 and under and seniors 65 and over ski free. Open from

---

Shredders (Snowboarders) Unite!

As you drive around the area you may see graffiti proclaiming "Free Taos" on the sides of buildings or roadside signs. With recent developments in Montana and Texas, you might think that these are the marks of a local separatist militia. On the contrary, they are part of a campaign by mostly young people (with many of the area's lodgers behind it as well) to open the ski area up to snowboarders. Traditional downhill skiers don't look kindly on sharing the mountain with the shredders, who they claim make the sport more dangerous. Currently, Taos is one of only a handful of ski resorts in the West that bans boarders completely from its slopes. However, many of the area's lodgers feel they are losing out on significant business from families and young adults who are into snowboarding. In the spring of 1997, the "Free Taos" message appeared in 100-foot-high letters emblazoned in the snow across an open slope above the ski area.

---

approximately Thanksgiving to March 29 (depending on the weather) daily from 9am to 4:30pm.

The oldest ski area in the Taos region, founded in 1952, **Sipapu Ski Area** (P.O. Box 29), Vadito, NM 87579 (☎ 505/587-2240), is 25 miles southeast, on NM 518 in Tres Ritos Canyon. It prides itself on being a small local area, especially popular with schoolchildren. It has just one triple chair and two surface lifts, with a vertical drop of 865 feet to the 8,200-foot base elevation. There are 18 trails, half classified as intermediate. Unfortunately, beginners are limited to only a few runs here, as are advanced skiers. Still, it's a nice little area, tucked way back in the mountains, with excellent lodging rates. Be aware that since the elevation is fairly low, runs get very icy. Lift tickets are $29 for adults for a full day, $21 half-day; $22 for children under 12 for a full day, $17 half-day; $20 for seniors (65 and 69) for a half or full day; and free for seniors age 70 and over, as well as children 5 and under. A package including lift tickets, equipment rental, and a lesson costs $45 for adults and $38 for children. Sipapu is open from about December 18 to the end of March, and lifts run daily from 9am to 4pm.

Just south of the Colorado border is **Ski Rio** (P.O. Box 159), Costilla, NM 87524 (☎ **800/2-ASK-RIO** or 505/758-7707), a broad (and often cold and windy) ski area that can't quite get over its financial problems. In fact, you'll want to call before driving up there, as the resort may not make it into the next season. It's a pity because there's a lot on this mountain. Half of its 83 named trails are for the intermediate skier, 30% for beginners, and 20% for advanced skiers. There are also snowboard and snow-skate parks, as well as 13 miles of cross-country trails. Annual snowfall here is about 260 inches, and there are three chairlifts (two triple, one double) and three tows. At the ski base you can rent skis, snowboards, snowshoes, and snow skates, as well as find lodgings, restaurants, and a sports shop. Sleigh rides, dogsled tours, and snowmobile tours are also available. The ski school offers private and group clinics (for adults and children) in cross-country and downhill skiing, snow skating, and snowboarding. Lift tickets are in the mid-$30 range for adults and mid-$20 range for juniors. Ski Rio is open on a limited basis, generally weekends and only a few weekdays, from 9am to 4pm from November through April. Call to be sure it's open at all and for details. For information via the World Wide Web, try: **http://laplaza.com/tp/skirio/.**

CROSS COUNTRY

Numerous popular Nordic trails exist in Carson National Forest. If you call or write ahead, they'll send you a booklet titled "Where to Go in the Snow," which gives cross-country skiers details about the maintained trails. One of the more popular trails is **Amole Canyon,** off NM 518 near the Sipapu Ski Area, where the Taos Nordic Ski Club maintains set tracks and signs along a 3-mile loop. It's closed to snowmobiles, a comfort to lovers of serenity. Several trails are open only to cross-country skiers.

Just east of Red River, with 22 miles of groomed trails in 600 acres of forest lands atop Bobcat Pass, is the **Enchanted Forest Cross Country Ski Area** (☎ 505/ 754-2374). Full-day trail passes, good from 9am to 4:30pm, are $10 for adults, $7 for children, and free for seniors age 70 and over. Equipment rentals and lessons can be arranged at **Miller's Crossing** ski shop on Main Street in Red River (☎ 505/ 754-2374). Nordic skiers can get instruction in skating, mountaineering, and telemarking.

Taos Mountain Outfitters, 114 South Plaza (☎ **505/758-9292**), offers telemark and cross-country sales, rentals, and guide service, as does **Los Rios Whitewater Ski Shop** (☎ **505/776-8854**).

Southwest Nordic Center (☎ **505/758-4761**) offers rental of four *yurts* (Mongolian-style huts) in the Rio Grande National Forest near Chama. These are insulated and fully equipped accommodations, each with a stove, pots, pans, dishes, silverware, mattresses, pillows, a table and benches, and wood-stove heating. Skiers trek into the huts, carrying their clothing and food in backpacks. Guide service is provided, or people can go in on their own, following directions on a map. The yurts are rented by the night and range from $65 to $90 per group. Call for reservations as much in advance as possible as they do book up. The season is mid-November through April, depending on snow conditions.

5 More Outdoor Activities

Taos County's 2,200 square miles embrace a great diversity of scenic beauty, from New Mexico's highest mountain, 13,161-foot Wheeler Peak, to the 650-foot-deep chasm of the Rio Grande Gorge. Carson National Forest, which extends to the eastern city limits of Taos and cloaks a large part of the county, contains several major ski facilities as well as hundreds of miles of hiking trails through the Sangre de Cristo Range.

Recreation areas are mainly in the national forest, where pine and aspen provide refuge for abundant wildlife. Forty-eight areas are accessible by road, including 38 with campsites. There are also areas on the high desert mesa, carpeted by sagebrush, cactus, and frequently wildflowers. Two beautiful areas within a short drive of Taos are the Valle Vidal Recreation Area, north of Red River, and the Wild Rivers Recreation Area, near Questa. For complete information, contact **Carson National Forest,** 208 Cruz Alta Rd., Taos, NM 87571 (☎ **505/758-6200**), or the **Bureau of Land Management,** 226 Cruz Alta Rd., Taos, NM 87571 (☎ **505/758-8851**).

BALLOONING   As in many other towns throughout New Mexico, hot-air ballooning is a top attraction. Recreational trips over the Taos Valley and Rio Grande Gorge are offered by **Paradise Hot Air Balloon Adventure** (☎ **505/751-6098**).

The **Taos Mountain Balloon Rally,** P.O. Box 3096, Taos, NM 87571 (☎ **800/ 732-8267**), is held each year the last full weekend of October. (See "Northern New Mexico Calendar of Events," in chapter 2, for details.)

BIKING   Even if you're not an avid cyclist, it won't take long for you to realize that getting around Taos by bike is preferable to driving. You won't have the usual parking problems, and you won't have to sit in the line of traffic as it snakes through the center of town. If you feel like exploring the surrounding area, Carson National Forest rangers recommend several biking trails in the greater Taos area, including those in Garcia Park and Rio Chiquito for beginner to intermediate mountain bikers, and Gallegos and Picuris peaks for experts. Inquire at the U.S. Forest Service office, 208 Cruz Alta Rd. (☎ **505/758-6200**) for excellent materials that map out trails; tell you how to get to the trailhead; specify length, difficulty, and elevation; and inform you about safety tips. You can also purchase the Taos Trails map (created jointly by the Carson National Forest, Native Sons Adventures, and Trail Illustrated). It's readily available at area bookstores and is designed to withstand water damage. Once you're out riding in Carson National Forest, you'll find trails marked in green (easy), blue (moderate), or gray (expert).

Bicycle rentals are available from the **Gearing Up Bicycle Shop,** 129 Paseo del Pueblo Sur (☎ **505/751-0365**); daily rentals run $20 for a mountain bike with front suspension, $40 for one with full suspension. **Hot Tracks Cyclery,** 214 Paseo del Pueblo Sur (☎ **505/751-0949**), rents front-suspension mountain bikes and full-suspension bikes for $18/half-day and $25/full day. The knowledgeable staff will supply you with a map and directions to bike trails; and **Native Sons Adventures,** 1033-A Paseo del Pueblo Sur (☎ **800/753-7559** or 505/758-9342), rents regular (unsuspended) bikes for $15/half-day and $20/full day, front-suspension bikes for $20 half-day and $35/full day, and full-suspension bikes for $30/half-day and $45/full day; they also rent car racks for $5. All of these prices include use of helmets and water bottles.

Annual touring events include Red River's **Enchanted Circle Century Bike Tour** (☎ **505/754-2366**) on the weekend following Labor Day.

FISHING   The fishing season in the high lakes and streams opens April 1 and continues through December, though spring and fall tend to be the best times. Naturally, the Rio Grande is a favorite fishing spot, but there is also excellent fishing in the streams around Taos. Taoseños favor the Rio Hondo, Rio Pueblo (near Tres Ritos), Rio Fernando (in Taos Canyon), Pot Creek, and Rio Chiquito. Rainbow, cutthroat, German brown trout, and kokanee (a freshwater salmon) are commonly stocked and caught. Pike and catfish have been caught in the Rio Grande as well. Jiggs, spinners, or woolly worms are recommended as lure, or worms, corn, or salmon eggs as bait; many experienced anglers prefer fly-fishing.

Licenses are required, of course and are sold, along with tackle, at several Taos sporting-goods shops. For backcountry guides, try **Deep Creek Wilderness Outfitters and Guides,** P.O. Box 721, El Prado, NM 87529 (☎ **505/776-8423**), or **Taylor Streit Flyfishing Service,** 405 Camino de la Placita (P.O. Box 2759), Taos, NM 87571 (☎ **505/751-1312**).

FITNESS FACILITIES   The **Taos Spa and Court Club,** 111 Dona Ana Dr. (☎ **505/758-1980**), is a fully equipped fitness center that rivals any you'd find in a big city. There are treadmills, step machines, climbing machines, rowing machines, exercise bikes, NordicTrack, weight-training machines, saunas, indoor and outdoor Jacuzzis, a steam room, and indoor and outdoor pools. Thirty-five aerobic step classes a week, as well as stretch aerobics, aqua aerobics, and classes specifically designed for senior citizens are also offered. In addition, there are five tennis and two racquetball courts. Therapeutic massage is available daily by appointment. Children's programs include tennis and swimming camp, and baby-sitting programs are available in the morning and evening. The spa is open Monday through Friday from 5:30am to 9pm; Saturday and Sunday from 7am to 8pm. Monthly, weekly, and daily memberships are available for individuals and families. For visitors, there's a daily rate of $10.

The **Northside Health and Fitness Center,** at 1307 Paseo del Pueblo Norte, in Taos (☎ **505/751-1242**), is also a full-service facility, featuring top-of-the-line Cybex equipment, free weights, and cardiovascular equipment. Aerobics and Jazzercise classes are scheduled daily, and there are indoor/outdoor pools and four tennis courts, as well as children's and senior citizens' programs.

GOLF Since the summer of 1993 the 18-hole golf course at the **Taos Country Club,** Ranchos de Taos (☎ **800/758-7375** or 505/758-7300), has been open to the public. Located on NM 570 west, just 4 miles south of the Plaza, it's a first-rate championship golf course designed for all levels of play—in fact, it is ranked as the third-best course in New Mexico. It has open fairways and no hidden greens. The club also features a driving range, practice putting and chipping green, and instruction by PGA professionals. Greens fees in 1998 were $32 during the week, $40 weekends (includes Friday) and holidays for 18 holes. Twilight fee is $23. Cart and club rentals are also available. It's always advisable to call ahead for tee times one week in advance, but it's not unusual for people to show up unannounced and still manage to find a time to tee off.

The par-72, 18-hole course at the **Angel Fire Resort Golf Course** (☎ **800/633-7463** or 505/377-3055) is PGA-endorsed. Surrounded by stands of ponderosa pine, spruce, and aspen, at 8,500 feet, it's one of the highest regulation golf courses in the world. It also has a driving range and putting green. Carts and clubs can be rented at the course, and the club pro provides instruction.

For 9-hole play, stop at the golf course at **Valle Escondido** residential village (☎ **505/758-3475**) just off US 64. It's a par-36 course with mountain and valley views. Clubs and pull-carts are available for rental, and the clubhouse serves refreshments.

Another golf course is under construction in Red River. At press time 9 holes were open. Call **Red Eagle Golf Course** (☎ **505/754-6569**).

HIKING There are hundreds of miles of hiking trails in Taos County's mountain and high-mesa country. They're especially well traveled in the summer and fall, although nights turn chilly and mountain weather may be fickle by September.

Maps (for a nominal fee) and free materials and advice on all **Carson National Forest** trails and recreation areas can be obtained from the **Forest Service Building,** 208 Cruz Alta Rd. (☎ **505/758-6200**), and from the office adjacent to the Chamber of Commerce on Paseo del Pueblo Sur. Both are open Monday through Friday from 8am to 4:30pm. Detailed USGS topographical maps of backcountry areas can be purchased from **Taos Mountain Outfitters** on the Plaza (☎ **505/758-9292**). This is also the place to rent camping gear, if you came without your own. Tent rentals are $15 and sleeping bags are $10 each per day. Backpacks can be rented for $15 a day. Ask about special deals on weekend packages. They also have a weekly rock-climbing class.

Two wilderness areas close to Taos offer outstanding hiking possibilities. The 19,663-acre **Wheeler Peak Wilderness** is a wonderland of Alpine tundra encompassing New Mexico's highest peak (13,161 feet). The 20,000-acre **Latir Peak Wilderness,** north of Red River, is noted for its high lake country. Both are under the jurisdiction of the **Questa Ranger District,** P.O. Box 110, Questa, NM 87556 (☎ **505/586-0520**).

HORSEBACK RIDING The **Taos Indian Horse Ranch,** on Pueblo land off Ski Valley Road, just before Arroyo Seco (☎ **505/758-3212**), offers a variety of guided rides. Open by appointment, the ranch provides horses for all types of riders (English, Western, Australian, and bareback) and ability levels. Call ahead to reserve. Rates start at $32 and go up to $65 to $95 for a 2-hour trail ride. Horse-drawn hay wagon rides are also offered in summer. From late November to March, the ranch provides afternoon and evening sleigh rides to a bonfire and marshmallow roast at $25 to $37.50 per person; ask for prices for a steak cookout. Also ask about the Paddle and Saddle Club "designed for the adrenaline junky," 8-hour or overnight programs, which include riding, a raft trip, and pack trip for $185 to $495.

Horseback riding is also offered by the **Shadow Mountain Guest Ranch,** 6 miles east of Taos on US 64 (☎ **800/405-7732** or 505/758-7732); **Rio Grande Stables** (P.O. Box 2122), El Prado (☎ **505/776-5913**); and **Llano Bonito Ranch** (P.O. Box 99), Peñasco, about 40 minutes from Taos (☎ **505/587-2636;** fax 505/587-2636). Rates at Llano Bonito Ranch are $22.50 for a 1-hour trail ride, $70 per person for a half-day ride ($95 for breakfast ride), and $125 per person for a full-day ride. In addition to trail rides, Llano Bonito Ranch offers 3-day pack trips for $595 per person. On the 3-day trip you'll spend 2 nights in the high-country wilderness, and during the day you'll ride to an altitude of 12,500 feet. Meals are included on the pack trip. Minimum of four people. They also have wagon rides for $25 per person.

Most riding outfitters offer lunch trips and overnight trips. Call for further details.

HUNTING Hunters in Carson National Forest bag deer, turkey, grouse, band-tailed pigeons, and elk by special permit. On private land, where hunters must be accompanied by qualified guides, there are also black bear and mountain lions. Hunting seasons vary year to year, so it's important to inquire ahead with the **New Mexico Game and Fish Department in Santa Fe** (☎ 505/827-7882).

Several Taos sporting-goods shops sell hunting licenses, including **Cottam's Ski and Outdoor Shop,** 207-A Paseo del Pueblo Norte and in Taos Ski Valley (☎ 505/758-2822); and **Wal-Mart,** 925 Paseo del Pueblo Sur (☎ 505/758-3116). Backcountry guides include **Moreno Valley Outfitters** (☎ 505/377-3512) in Angel Fire, and **Rio Costilla Park** (☎ 505/586-0542) in Costilla.

ICE-SKATING For ice-skating, **Kit Carson Park Ice Rink** (☎ 505/758-8234), located in Kit Carson Park, is open from Thanksgiving through February. Skate rentals are available for adults and children.

JOGGING You can jog anywhere (except on private property) in and around Taos. I would especially recommend stopping by the Carson National Forest office in the Chamber of Commerce building to find out what trails they might recommend.

LLAMA TREKKING For a taste of the unusual, **El Paseo Llama Expeditions** (☎ 800/455-2627 or 505/758-3111; www.elpaseollama.com) utilizes U.S. Forest Service–maintained trails that wind through canyons and over mountain ridges. The llamas will carry your gear and food, allowing you to walk and explore, free of any heavy burdens. They're friendly, gentle animals that have a keen sense of sight and smell. Often, other animals, such as elk, deer, and mountain sheep, are attracted to the scent of the llamas and will venture closer to hikers if the llamas are present. Llama expeditions are scheduled from May to mid-October; and day hikes are scheduled year-round. Gourmet meals are provided. Half-day hikes cost $49, day hikes $70, and 2- to 8-day hikes run up to $850.

Wild Earth Adventures (☎ **800/758-LAMA** or 505/586-0174; http://members.aol.com/llamatrek. E-mail: llamatrek@aol.com.) offers a "Take a llama to llunch hike"—a day-hike into the Sangre de Cristo Mountains, and a gourmet lunch for $75, with discounts for children under 12. Wild Earth owner Stuart Rosenberg also offers a variety of custom multi-day guided pack trips tailored to travelers needs and fitness levels. A 2-day overnight is $210; 3-day and longer, $120 per day per person. Camping gear and food are provided. On the trips, Rosenberg provides information on edible and medicinal plants, animal tracking, history, and geology.

RIVER RAFTING   Half- or full-day white-water rafting trips down the Rio Grande and Rio Chama originate in Taos and can be booked through a variety of outfitters in the area. The wild **Taos Box,** a steep-sided canyon south of the Wild Rivers Recreation Area, offers a series of class IV rapids that rarely lets up for some 17 miles. The water drops up to 90 feet per mile, providing one of the most exciting 1-day white-water tours in the West. May and June, when the water is rising, is a good time to go. Experience is not required, but you will be required to wear a life jacket (provided), and you should be willing to get wet.

One convenient rafting service is **Rio Grande Rapid Transit,** Box A, Pilar, NM 87531 (☎ **800/222-RAFT** or 505/758-9700). In addition to Taos Box ($69 to $89 per person), Rapid Transit also runs the **Pilar Racecourse** ($30 to $35 per person) on a daily basis. A full-day Pilar trip takes a more leisurely route before getting to the Racecourse and includes lunch ($69). The new evening dinner floats—great for older people, little kids, or people with disabilities—have no white water, but plenty of scenery ($30). They let out at Embudo Station, where rafters can dine and drink microbrewed beer. Rapid Transit's headquarters is at the entrance to the BLM-administered **Orilla Verde Recreation Area,** 16 miles south of Taos, where most excursions through the Taos Box end. Several other serene but thrilling floats through the Pilar Racecourse start at this point.

Other rafting outfitters in the Taos area include **Los Rios River Runners,** P.O. Box 2734, ☎ **800/544-1181** or 505/776-8854); **Native Sons Adventures,** 1033-A Paseo del Pueblo Sur (☎ **800/753-7559** or 505/758-9342); and **Far Flung Adventures** (☎ **800/359-2627** or 505/758-2628).

Safety Warning: Taos is not the place to experiment if you are not an experienced rafter. Do yourself a favor and check with the **Bureau of Land Management** (☎ **505/758-8851**) to make sure that you're fully equipped to go white-water rafting without a guide. Have them check your gear to make sure that it's sturdy enough—this is serious rafting!

ROCK CLIMBING   Mountain Skills (☎ **800/584-6863** or 505/758-9589) offers rock-climbing instruction for all skill levels, from basic beginners to more advanced climbers who would like to fine-tune their skills or just find out the best area climbs.

SPAS   Mountain Massage & Spa Treatments (at Casa de las Chimeneas B&B), 405 Cordoba Rd., (☎ **505/758-9156**), though a small place, has large treatments. I tried the herbal steam tent, aromatherapy facial, and salt glow body scrub and felt like I'd found heaven. Massages are also excellent, and there is a sauna and Jacuzzi.

SWIMMING   The **Don Fernando Pool** (☎ **505/737-2622**), on Civic Plaza Drive at Camino de la Placita, opposite the new Convention Center, admits swimmers over age 8 without adult supervision.

SNOWMOBILING   **Native Sons Adventures,** 1033-A Paseo del Pueblo Sur (☎ **800/753-7559** or 505/758-9342), runs fully guided tours in the Sangre de Cristo Mountains. Rates run $60 to $135. Advanced reservation required.

TENNIS   **Quail Ridge Inn** (see chapter 12) has six outdoor and two indoor tennis courts. **Taos Spa and Tennis Club** (see "Fitness Facilities" above) has five courts, and the **Northside Health and Fitness Center** (see above) in El Prado has three tennis courts. In addition, there are four free public courts in Taos, two at **Kit Carson Park,** on Paseo del Pueblo Norte, and two at **Fred Baca Memorial Park,** on Camino del Medio south of Ranchitos Road.

6 Shopping

Given the town's historical associations with the arts, it isn't surprising that many visitors come to Taos to buy fine art. Some 50-odd galleries are located within easy walking distance of the Plaza, and a couple dozen more are just a short drive from downtown. Galleries are generally open 7 days a week, especially in high season. Some artists show their work by appointment only.

The best-known artist in modern Taos is R. C. Gorman, a Navajo from Arizona who has made his home in Taos for more than 2 decades. Now in his 50s, Gorman is internationally acclaimed for his bright, somewhat surrealistic depictions of Navajo women. His **Navajo Gallery,** at 210 Ledoux St. (☎ **505/758-3250**), is a showcase for his widely varied work: acrylics, lithographs, silk screens, bronzes, tapestries, hand-cast ceramic vases, etched glass, and more.

A good place to begin exploring galleries is the **Stables Fine Art Gallery,** operated by the Taos Art Association at 133 Paseo del Pueblo Norte (☎ **505/ 758-2036**). A rotating group of fine arts exhibits features many of Taos's emerging and established artists. All types of work are exhibited, including painting, sculpture, printmaking, photography, and ceramics. Admission is free; it's open year-round daily from 10am to 5pm.

My favorite place to shop in Taos is in the **St. Francis Plaza** in Rancho de Taos, just a few miles south of the Plaza. This is what shopping in Northern New Mexico once was. Forget T-shirt shops and fast food. Here, you'll find small shops, where the owner often presides. There's even a little cafe where you can stop to eat, and of course, you'll want to visit the San Francisco de Asis Church (discussed earlier in this chapter).

Here are a few shopping recommendations, listed according to their specialties:

ART

Act I Gallery
226D Paseo del Pueblo Norte. ☎ **800/666-2933** or 505/758-7831.

This gallery has a broad range of works in a variety of media; you'll find watercolors, retablos, furniture, paintings, Hispanic folk art, pottery, jewelry, and sculpture.

✪ Philip Bareiss Contemporary Exhibitions
15 Ski Valley Rd. ☎ **505/776-2284.**

The works of some 30 leading Taos artists, including sculptor Gray Mercer and watercolorist Patricia Sanford, are exhibited here. In 1995, Philip Bareiss opened "Circles and Passageways," a sculptural installation by Gray Mercer, on the 2,500-acre Romero Range located just west of Taos. This is true land art; a four-wheel-drive vehicle is recommended in order to get there.

Desurmont Art Gallery

118 Camino de la Placita. ☎ **505/758-3299.**

Here, you'll find abstract and impressionist oils and watercolors, sculpture, ceramics, and jewelry.

Fenix Gallery

228B N. Pueblo Rd. ☎ **505/758-9120.**

The Fenix Gallery focuses on Taos artists with national and/or international collections and reputations who live and work in Taos. The work is primarily nonobjective and very contemporary. Some "historic" artists are represented as well. Recent expansion has doubled the gallery space.

Franzetti Metalworks

120-G Bent St. ☎ **505/758-7872.**

This work appeals to some more than others. The designs are surprisingly whimsical for metalwork. Much of the work is functional; you'll find laughing-horse switch plates and "froggie" earthquake detectors.

Gallery A

105–107 Kit Carson Rd. ☎ **505/758-2343.**

The oldest gallery in town, Gallery A has contemporary and traditional paintings, sculpture, and graphics, including Gene Kloss oils, watercolors, and etchings.

Hirsch Fine Art

146 Kit Carson Rd. ☎ **505/758-2478.**

If you can find this gallery open, it's well worth the visit. Unfortunately, the hours posted are not always maintained. Spread through a beautiful old home are watercolors, etchings and lithographs, and drawings by early Southwestern artists, including the original Taos founders.

✪ Lumina of New Mexico

239 Morada Rd. ☎ **505/758-7282.**

Located in the historic Victor Higgins home, next to the Mabel Dodge Luhan estate, Lumina is one of the loveliest galleries in New Mexico. You'll find a large variety of fine art, including paintings, sculpture, and photography. This place is as much a tourist attraction as any of the museums and historic homes in town.

Look for wonderful Picasso-esque paintings of New Mexico village life by Andrés Martinez, and take a stroll through the new 3-acre outdoor sculpture garden with a pond and waterfall—where you'll find large outdoor pieces from all over the United States.

✪ New Directions Gallery

107B North Plaza. ☎ **800/658-6903** or 505/758-2771.

Here, you'll find a variety of contemporary abstract works such as Larry Bell's unique mixed-media "Mirage paintings." My favorites, though, are the impressionistic works depicting Northern New Mexico villages by Tom Noble.

Quast Galleries—Taos

229 and 133 E. Kit Carson Rd. ☎ **505/758-7160** or 505/758-7779.

You won't want to miss this gallery, where you'll find representational landscapes and figurative paintings and distinguished sculpture. Rotating national and international exhibits are shown here.

R. B. Ravens
70 St. Francis Church Plaza, Ranchos de Taos. ☎ **505/758-7322.**

A trader for many years, including 15 on the Ranchos Plaza, R. B. Ravens is skilled at finding incredible period artwork. Here, you'll see (and have the chance to buy) a late 19th-century Plains elk-tooth woman's dress, as well as moccasins, Navajo rugs, and pottery, all in the setting of an old home, with raw pine floors and hand-sculpted adobe walls.

Shriver Gallery
401 Paseo del Pueblo Norte. ☎ **505/758-4994.**

Traditional paintings, drawings, etchings, and bronze sculpture.

Taos Gallery
403 Paseo del Pueblo Norte. ☎ **505/758-2475.**

Here, you'll find Southwestern impressionism, traditional Western art, contemporary fine art, and bronze sculpture.

BOOKS

Brodsky Bookshop
218 Paseo del Pueblo Norte. ☎ **505/758-9468.**

Exceptional inventory of fiction, nonfiction, Southwestern and Native American studies, children's books, topographical and travel maps, cards, tapes, and CDs.

Kit Carson Home
E. Kit Carson Rd. ☎ **505/758-4741.**

Fine collection of books about regional history.

✪ Moby Dickens Bookshop
124A Bent St. ☎ **888/442-9980** or 505/758-3050.

This is one of Taos's best bookstores. You'll find children's and adults' collections of Southwest, Native American, and out-of-print books. A renovation has added 600 square feet, much of it upstairs, where there's a comfortable place to sit and read.

Taos Book Shop
122D Kit Carson Rd. ☎ **505/758-3733.**

Founded in 1947, this is the oldest general bookstore in New Mexico. Taos Book Shop specializes in out-of-print and Southwestern titles.

CRAFTS

Clay & Fiber Gallery
126 W. Plaza Dr. ☎ **505/758-8093.**

Clay & Fiber represents over 150 artists from around the country; merchandise changes frequently, but you should expect to see a variety of ceramics, fiber arts, jewelry, and wearables.

Southwest Moccasin & Drum
803 Paseo del Pueblo Norte. ☎ **800/447-3630** or 505/758-9332.

Home of the All One Tribe Drum, this favorite local shop carries a large variety of drums in all sizes and styles, handmade by master Native American drum makers from Taos Pueblo. Southwest Moccasin & Drum also has the country's second-largest selection of moccasins, as well as an incredible inventory of indigenous world instruments and tapes, sculpture, weavings, rattles, fans, fetishes, bags, decor, and many handmade one-of-a-kind items. A percentage of the store's profits goes to support Native American causes.

✪ Taos Artisans Cooperative Gallery
109 Bent St. ☎ **505/758-1558.**

This eight-member cooperative gallery, owned and operated by local artists, sells local handmade jewelry, wearables, clay work, glass, drums, baskets, leather work, garden sculpture, and woven Spirit Women. You'll always find an artist in the shop.

Taos Blue
101A Bent St. ☎ **505/758-3561.**

This gallery has fine Native American and contemporary handcrafts; it specializes in clay and fiber work.

Twining Weavers and Contemporary Crafts
135 Paseo del Pueblo Norte. ☎ **505/758-9000.**

Here, you'll find an interesting mix of handwoven wool rugs and pillows by owner Sally Bachman, as well as creations by other gallery artists in fiber, basketry, and clay.

Weaving Southwest
216 Paseo del Pueblo Norte. ☎ **505/758-0433.**

Contemporary tapestries by New Mexico artists, as well as one-of-a-kind rugs, blankets, and pillows, are the woven specialties found here.

FASHIONS

Mariposa Boutique
120-F Bent St. ☎ **505/758-9028.**

What first caught my eye in this little shop were bright chile-pepper-print overalls for kids. Closer scrutiny brought me to plenty of finds for myself such as suede and rayon broomstick skirts and Mexican-style dresses, perfect for showing off turquoise jewelry.

Overland Sheepskin Company
NM 522 (a few miles north of town). ☎ **505/758-8822.**

You can't miss the romantically weathered barn sitting on a meadow north of town. Inside, you'll find anything you can imagine in leather: gloves, hats, slippers, coats. The coats here are exquisite, from oversized ranch styles to tailored blazers in a variety of leathers from sheepskin to buffalo hide.

FOOD

Amigos Co-op Natural Grocery
136 Paseo del Pueblo Sur. ☎ **505/758-8493.**

If you've had your fill of rich food, this is the place to find healthy treats. In the front of the store are organic fruits and vegetables. And in the back, there's a small cafe, where you can eat or take out sandwiches, healthy green chile stew, or my favorite, a huge plate of stir-fried veggies over brown rice. You'll also find baked goods such as muffins and brownies.

The Cookie Gallery
127 Bent St. ☎ **505/758-5867.**

Ready for a mid-morning or mid-afternoon snack? Here, you'll find Chinese sesame cookies, pumpkin cookies that must be kin to cupcakes, and melt-in-your-mouth

Mexican wedding cookies. For a more substantial snack try the veggie empañadas. During warm months you can sit outside at tree-shaded tables.

FURNITURE

Country Furnishings of Taos
534 Paseo del Pueblo Norte. ☎ **505/758-4633.**

Here, you'll find unique hand-painted folk-art furniture that has become popular all over the country. The pieces are as individual as the styles of the local folk artists who make them. There are also home accessories, unusual gifts, clothing, and jewelry.

Greg Flores Furniture of Taos
120 Bent St. ☎ **800/880-1090** or 505/758-8010.

This is a great little find. Greg Flores, native of Taos, fashions Southwestern furniture out of native ponderosa pine; he uses wood joinery and hand rubs each piece with an oil finish. You'll also find charming paintings by his wife Johanna Flores.

Lo Fino
201 Paseo del Pueblo Sur. ☎ **505/758-0298.**

With a name meaning "the refined," you know that this expansive showroom is worth taking time to wander through. You'll find a variety of home furnishings, from driftwood lamps and exotic masks made of dried flowers, to wagon-wheel furniture and finely painted *trasteros* (armoires), as well as handcrafted traditional and contemporary Southwestern furniture. Lo Fino specializes in custom building furniture.

The Taos Company
124K John Dunn Plaza, Bent St. ☎ **800/548-1141** or 505/758-1141.

This interior design showroom specializes in unique Southwestern antique furniture and decorative accessories. Especially look for wrought-iron lamps and iron-and-wood furniture.

GIFTS & SOUVENIRS

Big Sun
2 St. Francis Church Plaza, Ranchos de Taos. ☎ **505/758-3100.**

This folk-art gallery and curio emporium is packed with beautiful objects, from rugs made by the Tarahumara Indians in Mexico to local tinwork made in Dixon and authentic Navajo throw rugs, made by beginning weavers, that cost around $70.

El Rincón
114 Kit Carson Rd. ☎ **505/758-9188.**

This shop has a real trading-post feel. It's a wonderful place to find turquoise jewelry, whether you're looking for contemporary or antique. In the back of the store is a museum full of Native American and Western artifacts.

JEWELRY

Artwares Contemporary Jewelry
Taos Plaza. ☎ **800/527-8850** or 505/758-8850.

The gallery owners here call their contemporary jewelry "a departure from the traditional." Indeed, each piece here offers a new twist on traditional Southwestern and Native American design.

Leo Weaver Gallery
62 St. Francis Plaza (P.O. Box 1596), Ranchos de Taos. ☎ **505/751-1003.**

This shop carries the work of more than 50 local silversmiths. There's an expansive collection of concho belts and some very fresh work, using a variety of stones from turquoise to charolite to lapis.

Taos Gems & Minerals
637 Paseo del Pueblo Sur. ☎ **888/510-1664** or 505/758-3910.

This is a great place to explore; you can buy items like fetishes at prices much more reasonable than most galleries. Now in its 30th year of business, Taos Gems & Minerals is a fine lapidary showroom. You can also buy jewelry, carvings, and antique pieces at reasonable prices.

MUSICAL INSTRUMENTS

Taos Drum Company
5 miles south of Taos Plaza (off NM 68). ☎ **505/758-3796.**

Drum making is an age-old tradition that local artisans give continued life to in Taos. The drums are made of hollowed-out logs stretched with rawhide, and they come in all different shapes, sizes, and styles. Taos Drums has the largest selection of Native American log and hand drums in the world. In addition to drums, the showroom displays Southwestern and wrought-iron furniture, cowboy art, and over 60 styles of rawhide lampshades, as well as a constantly changing selection of primitive folk art, ethnic crafts, Native American music tapes, books, and other information on drumming. To find Taos Drum Company, look for the tepees and drums off NM 68. Ask about the tour that demonstrates the drum-making process.

POTTERY & TILES

Stephen Kilborn Pottery
136D Paseo del Pueblo Norte. ☎ **800/758-0136,** 505/758-5760, or 505/758-0135 (studio).

Visiting this shop in town is a treat, but for a real adventure go 17 miles south of Taos toward Santa Fe to Stephen Kilborn's studio in Pilar, open Monday through Saturday from 10am to 5pm, and noon to 5pm on Sunday. There, you'll see him throw, decorate, and fire pottery that's fun, fantastical, and functional.

Vargas Tile Co.
South end of town on NM 68. ☎ **505/758-5986.**

Vargas Tile has a great little collection of hand-painted Mexican tiles at good prices. You'll find beautiful pots with sunflowers on them and colorful cabinet doorknobs, as well as inventive sinks.

7 Taos After Dark

For a small town, Taos has its share of top entertainment. Performers are attracted to Taos because of the resort atmosphere and the arts community, and the city enjoys annual programs in music and literary arts. State troupes, such as the New Mexico Repertory Theater and New Mexico Symphony Orchestra, make regular visits.

Many events are scheduled by the **Taos Art Association,** 133 Paseo del Pueblo Norte, Taos, NM 87571 (☎ **505/758-2052**), at the **Taos Community Auditorium** (☎ **505/758-4677**). The TAA imports local, regional, and national performers in theater, dance, and concerts (Roy Hargrove, the Lula Washington Dance

The Major Concert & Performance Halls

Taos Civic Plaza and Convention Center, 121 Civic Plaza Dr. (☎ 505/758-4160).

Taos Community Auditorium, Kit Carson Memorial State Park (☎ 505/758-4677).

Theater, and Theater Grottesco have performed here, and the American String Quartet still performs each year). Also, look for a weekly film series offered year-round.

You can obtain information on current events in the *Taos News,* published every Thursday. The **Taos County Chamber of Commerce** (☎ **800/732-TAOS** or 505/758-3873) publishes semiannual listings of "Taos County Events," as well as an annual *Taos Country Vacation Guide* that also lists events and happenings around town.

THE PERFORMING ARTS
MAJOR ANNUAL PROGRAMS

Fort Burgwin Research Center
6580 NM 518, Ranchos de Taos, NM 87557. ☎ **505/758-8322.**

This historic site (of the 1,000-year-old Pot Creek Pueblo), located about 10 miles south of Taos, is a summer campus of Dallas's Southern Methodist University. From mid-May through mid-August, the SMU-In-Taos curriculum (such as studio arts, humanities, and sciences) includes courses in music and theater. There are regularly scheduled orchestral concerts, guitar, and harpsichord recitals, and theater performances available to the community, without charge, throughout the summer.

Music from Angel Fire
P.O. Box 502, Angel Fire, NM 87710. ☎ **505/377-3233** or 505/989-4772.

This acclaimed program of chamber music begins in mid-August with weekend concerts and continues up to Labor Day. Based in the small resort community of Angel Fire (located about 21 miles east of US 64), it also presents numerous concerts in Taos, Las Vegas, and Raton.

Taos Poetry Circus
Office mailing address: 5275 NDCBU, Taos, NM 87571. ☎ **505/758-1800.** Events take place at various venues around town.

Aficionados of the literary arts appreciate this annual event, held during 8 days in mid-June. Billed as "a literary gathering and poetry showdown among nationally known writers," it includes readings, seminars, performances, public workshops, and a poetry video festival. The main event is the **World Heavyweight Championship Poetry Bout,** 10 rounds of hard-hitting readings—with the last round extemporaneous.

Taos School of Music
P.O. Box 1879, Taos, NM 87571. ☎ **505/776-2388.** Tickets for chamber-music concerts $15 adult, $12 for children under 16.

Sponsored by the Taos Art Association, the Taos School of Music was founded in 1963. It is located at the Hotel St. Bernard in Taos Ski Valley. From mid-June to mid-August there is an intensive 8-week study and performance program for advanced students of violin, viola, cello, and piano. Students receive daily coaching by the American String Quartet and pianist Robert McDonald.

The 8-week **Chamber Music Festival,** an important adjunct of the school, offers 16 concerts and seminars for the public; performances are given by pianist Robert McDonald, guest musicians, and the international young student artists. In 1998, guests included the American String Quartet, and violist Michael Tree (1998) of the Guarneri Quartet. Performances are held at the Taos Community Auditorium and the Hotel St. Bernard.

✪ Taos Talking Picture Festival

1337 Gusdorf Rd., Suite. F. (7217 NDCBU), Taos, NM 87571. ☎ **505/751-0637.** Fax 505/751-7385. www.taosnet.com/ttpix/. E-mail: ttpix@taosnet.com.Individual screenings $7. Fast pass $300–$350. For 1999, the festival is scheduled April 15–18; screenings run 9am–11pm.

Filmmakers and film enthusiasts from the Southwest and as far away as Finland gather—8,000 strong in 1998—to view a variety of films, from serious documentaries to lighthearted comedies. The festival also offers lectures about the culture of films and filmmaking, a media conference, workshops, pre-showing discussions, and parties. You'll see locally made films as well as films involving Hollywood big-hitters. Each year, 5 acres of land is given as a prize to encourage filmmakers to take a fresh approach to storytelling. In 1998, the festival's Land Grant Award went to Native American filmmaker Chris Eyre. His film, *Smoke Signals,* shown opening night, is the first Native-written and -directed film to be introduced into national distribution. The festival's 1998 Cineaste Award went to Latino filmmaker Moctesuma Esparza, whose work includes *Selena, The Disappearance of Garcia Lorca,* and *The Milagro Beanfield War.*

THE CLUB & MUSIC SCENE

Adobe Bar

In the Historic Taos Inn, 125 Paseo del Pueblo Norte. ☎ **505/758-2233.** No cover. Noon–10:30pm.

A favorite gathering place for locals and visitors, the Adobe Bar is known for its live music series (nights vary) devoted to the eclectic talents of Taos musicians. The schedule offers a little of everything—classical, jazz, folk, Hispanic, and acoustic. The Adobe Bar features a wide selection of international beers, wines by the glass, light New Mexican dining, desserts, and an espresso menu.

Alley Cantina

121 Teresina Lane. ☎ **505/758-2121.** Cover for live music only.

This new bar has become the hot late-night spot in Taos. The focus is on interaction—so there's no TV. Instead, patrons play shuffleboard and pool, as well as chess and backgammon, in this building, which is said to be the oldest house in Taos. Pastas, sandwiches, and other dishes are served until past midnight.

Hideaway Lounge

At the Holiday Inn, 1005 Paseo del Pueblo Sur. ☎ **505/758-4444.** No cover.

This hotel lounge, built around a large adobe fireplace, offers live entertainment and an extensive hors d'oeuvre buffet. Call for schedule.

Sagebrush Inn

Paseo del Pueblo Sur (P.O. Box 557), Taos, NM 87571. ☎ **505/758-2254.** No cover.

This is a real hot spot for locals. The atmosphere is Old West, with a rustic wooden dance floor and plenty of smoke. Dancers generally two-step to country performers nightly, year-round, from 9pm.

Thunderbird Lodge
Taos Ski Valley. ☎ **505/776-2280.** No cover, except occasionally on holidays; then, the cost varies widely.

Throughout the winter, the Thunderbird offers a variety of nightly entertainment at the foot of the ski slopes. You'll also find wine tastings and two-step dance lessons here.

8 Exploring Beyond Taos: A Driving Tour of the Enchanted Circle

If you're in the mood to explore, take this 90-mile loop north of Taos through the old Hispanic villages of Arroyo Hondo and Questa, into a pass the Apaches, Kiowas, and Comanches once used to cross through the mountains to trade with the Taos Indians. You'll come to the Wild-West mining town of Red River, pass through the expansive Moreno Valley, and along the base of some of New Mexico's tallest peaks. Then, you'll skim the shores of a high mountain lake at Eagle Nest, pass through the resort village of Angel Fire, and head back to Taos along the meandering Rio Fernando de Taos. Although one can drive the entire loop in 2 hours from Taos, most folks prefer to take a full day, and many take several days.

ARROYO HONDO   Traveling north from Taos via NM 522, it's a 9-mile drive to this village, the remains of an 1815 land grant along the Rio Hondo. Along the dirt roads that lead off NM 522, you may find a windowless Morada or two, marked by plain crosses in front, places of worship for the still-active Penitentes, a religious order known for self flagellation. This is also the turn-off point for trips to the Rio Grande Box, an awesome 1-day, 17-mile white-water run for which you can book trips in Santa Fe, Taos, Red River, and Angel Fire. Arroyo Hondo was also the site of the New Buffalo commune in the 1960s. Hippies flocked here looking to escape the mores of modern society. Over the years, the commune members have dispersed throughout Northern New Mexico, bringing an interesting creative element to the food, architecture, and philosophy of the state. En route north, the highway passes near **San Cristobal,** where a side road turns off to the D. H. Lawrence Ranch (see "More Attractions," above) and **Lama,** site of an isolated spiritual retreat.

QUESTA   Next, Highway 522 passes through Questa, most of whose residents are employed at a molybdenum mine about 5 miles east of town. Mining molybdenum (an ingredient in lightbulbs, television tubes, and missile systems) in the area has not been without controversy. The process has raked across hillsides along the Red River, and though Molycorp, the mine's owner, treats the water they use before returning it to the river, studies show it has adversely affected the fishlife. Still, the mine is a major employer in the area, and locals are grateful for the income it generates.

If you turn west off NM 522 onto NM 378 about 3 miles north of Questa, you'll descend 11 miles on a gravel road into the gorge of the Rio Grande at the Bureau of Land Management–administered **Wild Rivers Recreation Area** (☎ **505/ 770-1600**). Here, where the Red River enters the gorge, is the most accessible starting point for river-rafting trips through the infamous Taos Box. Some 48 miles of the Rio Grande, south from the Colorado border, are protected under the national Wild and Scenic River Act of 1968. Information on geology and wildlife, as well as hikers' trail maps, can be obtained at the visitor center here. Ask for directions to the impressive petroglyphs in the gorge. River-rafting trips can be booked in Taos, Santa Fe, Red River, and other communities. (See the "Outdoor Activities" sections in chapter 7 and above for booking agents in Santa Fe and Taos, respectively.)

The village of **Costilla,** near the Colorado border, is 20 miles north of Questa. This is the turnoff point for four-wheel-drive jaunts and hiking trips into **Valle Vidal,** a huge U.S. Forest Service–administered reserve with 42 miles of roads and many hiking trails. A day hike in this area can bring you sightings of hundreds of elk.

RED RIVER   However, to continue on the Enchanted Circle loop, turn east at Questa onto NM 38 for a 12-mile climb to Red River, a rough-and-ready 1890s gold-mining town that has parlayed its Wild West ambience into a pleasant resort village that's especially popular with families from Texas and Oklahoma.

This community, at 8,750 feet, is a center for skiing and snowmobiling, fishing and hiking, off-road driving and horseback riding, mountain biking, river rafting, and other outdoor pursuits. Frontier-style celebrations, honky-tonk entertainment, and even staged shootouts on Main Street are held throughout the year.

Though it can be a charming and fun town, Questa's food and accommodations are mediocre at best. Its patrons are down-home folks, happy with a bed and a diner-style meal. If you decide to stay, try **The Lodge at Red River,** P.O. Box 189, Red River, NM 87558 (☎ **800/91-LODGE** or 505/754-6280); www.redrivernm. com/lodgeatrr/, in the center of town. It offers hotel rooms beginning at $42, though I'd spend a bit more, $68 to $78, for a room with a window opening to the outside. Knotty pine throughout, the accommodations are clean and comfortable. Downstairs, the restaurant serves standard breakfasts and family-style dinners: fried chicken, steaks, trout, and pork chops.

If you're passing through and want a quick meal, the **Past Times Deli,** 316 E. Main St. (☎ **505/754-3400**), has brought some excellent flavors to the little village. You'll find tasty home-baked muffins and stuffed baked potatoes, soups, and sub sandwiches under $8. Don't leave without trying a macadamia-nut white-chocolate chip cookie.

The **Red River Chamber of Commerce,** P.O. Box 870, Red River, NM 87558 (☎ **800/348-6444** or 505/754-2366), lists more than 40 accommodations, including lodges and condominiums. Some are open winters or summers only.

EAGLE NEST   About 16 miles east of Red River, on the other side of 9,850-foot Bobcat Pass, is the village of Eagle Nest, resting on the shore of Eagle Nest Lake in the Moreno Valley. Gold was mined in this area as early as 1866, starting in what is now the ghost town of **Elizabethtown** about 5 miles north; Eagle Nest itself (population 200) wasn't incorporated until 1976. The 4-square-mile lake is considered one of the top trout producers in the United States and attracts ice fishermen in winter as well as summer anglers. Sailboats and windsurfers also use the lake, although swimming, waterskiing, and camping are not permitted.

If you're heading to Cimarron or Denver, proceed east on US 64 from Eagle Nest. But if you're circling back to Taos, continue southwest on US 38 and US 64 to Agua Fría and Angel Fire.

Shortly before the Agua Fría junction, you'll see the **DAV Vietnam Veterans Memorial.** It's a stunning structure with curved white walls soaring high against the backdrop of the Sangre de Cristo Range. Consisting of a chapel and underground visitor center, it was built by Dr. Victor Westphall in memory of his son, David, a marine lieutenant killed in Vietnam in 1968. The chapel has a changing gallery of

Taos Area (Including Enchanted Circle)

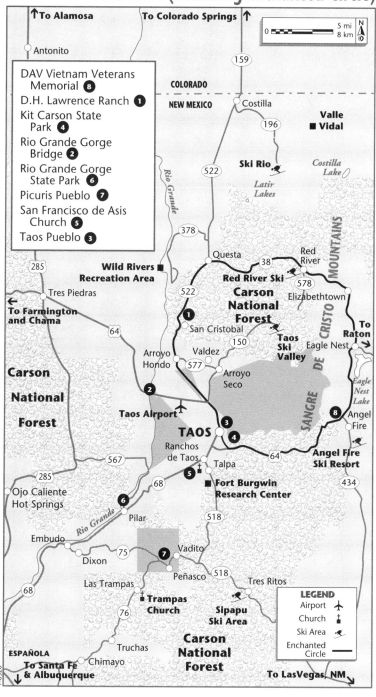

To Alamosa

To Colorado Springs

5 mi
8 km

0

N

Antonito

DAV Vietnam Veterans Memorial 8
D.H. Lawrence Ranch 1
Kit Carson State Park 4
Rio Grande Gorge Bridge 2
Rio Grande Gorge State Park 6
Picuris Pueblo 7
San Francisco de Asis Church 5
Taos Pueblo 3

159

COLORADO

NEW MEXICO

Costilla

196

Valle
■ **Vidal**

522

Rio Grande

Ski Rio

Costilla Lake

Latir Lakes

378

Questa

38

Red River

285

Wild Rivers Recreation Area

522

Red River Ski

578

Carson National Forest

Elizabethtown

Tres Piedras

To Farmington and Chama

64

1

San Cristobal

150

To Raton

Eagle Nest

Taos Ski Valley

Arroyo Hondo

Valdez

577

Arroyo Seco

SANGRE DE CRISTO MOUNTAINS

Eagle Nest Lake

Carson National Forest

2

Taos Airport

3

TAOS

Ranchos de Taos

4

567

Talpa

5

8 Angel Fire

Angel Fire Ski Resort

285

Ojo Caliente Hot Springs

68

■ **Fort Burgwin Research Center**

64

434

6

Pilar

Rio Grande

518

Embudo

75

7 Vadito

Dixon

Peñasco

518

Tres Ritos

68

Las Trampas

✝ **Trampas Church**

Sipapu Ski Area

LEGEND
Airport ✈
Church ✝
Ski Area ⚤
Enchanted Circle ──

76

Carson National Forest

ESPAÑOLA

Truchas

Chimayo

To Santa Fe & Albuquerque

To LasVegas, NM

1-0326

227

photographs of Vietnam veterans who lost their lives in the Southeast Asian war, but no photo is as poignant as this inscription written by young David Westphall, a promising poet:

> *Greed plowed cities desolate.*
> *Lusts ran snorting through the streets.*
> *Pride reared up to desecrate*
> *Shrines, and there were no retreats.*
> *So man learned to shed the tears*
> *With which he measures out his years.*

ANGEL FIRE   If you like the clean efficiency of a resort complex, you may want to plan a night or two here—any time of year. Angel Fire is approximately 150 miles north of Albuquerque, 21 miles east of Taos. Opened in the late 1960s, this resort offers a hotel with spacious, comfortable rooms, as well as condominiums and cabins. Winter is the biggest season. This medium-sized beginner and intermediate mountain is an excellent place for families to roam about (see "Skiing," above). A new high-speed quad lift zips skiers to the top quickly while allowing them a long ski down. The views of the Moreno Valley are awe-inspiring. Recently, a Nordic trail has been added, running around the snow-covered golf course, and visitors can also snowmobile and take sleigh rides, including one out to a sheepherder's tent with a plank floor and a wood stove where you can eat dinner cooked over an open fire. Contact **Roadrunner Tours** (☎ **800/377-6416,** 505/377-6416, or 505/377-2811).

During spring, summer, and fall the resort offers golf, tennis, hiking, mountain biking (you can take your bike up on the quad lift), fly-fishing, river rafting, and horseback riding.

There are other fun family activities such as the Human Maze, 5,200 square feet of wooden passageway within which to get lost and find your way (basically seek your lower rat-like self). There's an indoor climbing wall, video arcade, miniature golf course, theater performances, and, throughout the year, a variety of festivals including a hot-air balloon festival, Winterfest, and concerts of both classical and popular music.

The unofficial community center is the **Angel Fire Resort,** North Angel Fire Road (P.O. Drawer B), Angel Fire, NM 87710 (☎ **800/633-7463** or 505/377-6401) www.angelfireresort.com, a 150-unit hotel with spacious, comfortable rooms. Rates start at $70 in the summer, $145 during holidays.

For more information on the Moreno Valley, including full accommodations listings, contact the **Angel Fire Chamber of Commerce,** P.O. Box 547, Angel Fire, NM 87710 (☎ **800/446-8117** or 505/377-6353; fax 505/377-3034).

A fascinating adventure you may want to try here is a 1-hour, 1-day, or overnight horseback trip with **Roadrunner Tours and Elkhorn Lodge Ltd.,** P.O. Box 274, Angel Fire, NM 87710 (☎ **800/377-6416,** 505/377-6416, or 505/377-2811). From Angel Fire, Nancy and Bill Burch guide adventurers on horseback trips through private ranchland to taste the life of the lonesome cowboy. The cattle-drive trip is no bland trail ride. The first day, you'll travel 15 miles through ponderosa forests, across meadows of asters and sunflowers, with bald peaks in the distance. Once at camp, riders bed down in an authentic mountain cowboy cabin. The second day, you'll move as many as 300 cows through the Moreno Valley. One-hour rides are $20; day rides $95; cattle drives $184 (includes overnight stay in a cow camp). Cattle drives take place in July and August; book early, because space is limited.

WHERE TO DINE

Aldo's Cantina

Angel Fire Resort ☎ **505-377-6401.** Lunch $5.95–$11.95; dinner $12.95–$21.95. Daily 11am–2pm; après ski (during winter) 2–5pm; dinner 5–9pm. During summer the restaurant may close on Mon; call first. HAUTE MEXICAN.

Even if you're just driving through, plan to dine at Aldo's Cantina. Located at the base of the ski mountain and owned by the Angel Fire Resort, this little nouveau Mexican restaurant is a grateful respite from the mediocre food you'll find around the rest of the Enchanted Circle. In the warm months, diners can enjoy tables on a wooden deck. Inside, amidst persimmon walls, diners often begin with a strawberry margarita. This is *not* New Mexican food, nor is it typical Mexican. It is elegant fare that people all over Northern New Mexico are raving about. Lunches include *Ensalada del Parque de Chapultepec* (jicama, cucumber, mango, and orange over greens). Try the *Truchas del Lago Parangaricutirimicuaro* (I did check the spelling), (trout marinated with tamarind, chipotle, and lime served with green rice and vegetables). The dinner entrees include *Tampiquena* (grilled T-bone steak marinated in Tecate, lime, and salt), served with an enchilada, beans, guacamole, and green rice. There are also fish dishes, but what you MUST order here is the vegetarian surprise (have the chef throw in some shrimp, meat, or chicken if you'd like). This three-course meal is different every time. Mine began with a black-bean tostada seasoned with cilantro, moved onto a portabello-mushroom enchilada with an amazing green chile sauce, and ended with a chimichanga (fried burrito), all artfully presented. For dessert, try the fried plantain with ice cream.

15 | Albuquerque

Albuquerque is the gateway to Northern New Mexico, the portal through which most domestic and international visitors pass before traveling on to Santa Fe and Taos. While Albuquerque is now a big city, it's worth stopping in for a day or two in order to get a feel of the whole history of this area.

From the rocky crest of Sandia Peak at sunset, one can see the lights of this city of almost half a million people spread out across 16 miles of high desert grassland. As the sun drops beyond the western horizon, it reflects off the Rio Grande, flowing through Albuquerque more than a mile below.

This waterway is the bloodline for the area, what allowed a city in this vast desert to spring up, and it continues to be at the center of the area's growth. Farming villages that line its banks are being stampeded by expansion. As the west side of the city sprawls, more means for transporting traffic across the river have had to be built, breaking up the pastoral valley area.

The railroad, which set up a major stop here in 1880, prompted much of Albuquerque's initial growth, but that economic explosion was nothing compared with what has happened since World War II. Designated a major national center for military research and production, Albuquerque became a trading center for this state, whose populace is spread widely across the land. That's why the city may strike visitors as nothing more than one big strip mall. Look closely and you'll see ranchers, Native Americans, and Hispanic villagers stocking up on goods to take back to the New Mexico boot heel or the Texas panhandle.

Climbing out of the valley is Route 66, well worth a drive, if only to see the rust that time has left. Old court hotels still line the street, many with their funky '50s signage. One enclave on this route is the University of New Mexico district, with a number of hippie-ish cafes and shops.

Farther downhill, you'll come to downtown Albuquerque. During the day, this area is all suits and heels, but at night it becomes a hip nightlife scene. People from all over the state come to Albuquerque to check out the live music and dancing clubs, most within walking distance from each other.

The section called Old Town is worth a visit. Though it's the most touristy part of town, it's also a unique Southwestern village with a beautiful and intact plaza. Also in this area are Albuquerque's new aquarium and botanical gardens, as well as its continually upgrading zoo.

Greater Albuquerque

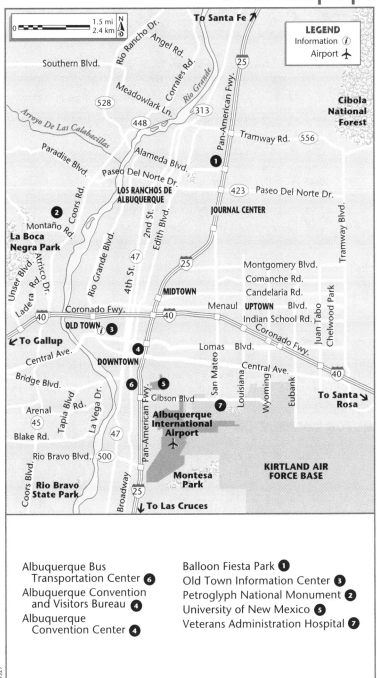

To Santa Fe ↗

LEGEND
Information ⓘ
Airport ✈

1.5 mi
2.4 km
N

Rio Rancho Dr.
Angel Rd.
Southern Blvd.
Corrales Rd.
Meadowlark Ln.
Rio Grande
528
313
448
Arroyo De Las Calabacillas
Paradise Blvd.
Alameda Blvd.
Paseo Del Norte Dr.
LOS RANCHOS DE
ALBUQUERQUE
Coors Rd.
Montaño Rd.
La Boca
Negra Park
Unser Blvd.
Atrisco Rd. Dr.
Ladera
40
To Gallup
OLD TOWN ⓘ ❸
Central Ave.
Bridge Blvd.
DOWNTOWN
Arenal
45
Blake Rd.
Rio Grande Blvd.
2nd St.
Edith Blvd.
47
4th St.
MIDTOWN
Coronado Fwy.
40
Tapia Blvd.
La Vega Dr.
47
Rio Bravo Blvd.
500
Coors Blvd.
Rio Bravo
State Park
Broadway
25
To Las Cruces ↓

Pan-American Fwy.
25

Tramway Rd.
556
Cibola
National
Forest
❶
423
Paseo Del Norte Dr.
JOURNAL CENTER
❷
25
Montgomery Blvd.
Comanche Rd.
Candelaria Rd.
Menaul UPTOWN Blvd.
Indian School Rd.
Coronado Fwy.
40
Lomas Blvd.
Central Ave.
To Santa ↘
Rosa
San Mateo
Louisiana
Wyoming
Eubank
Juan Tabo
Chelwood Park
Tramway Blvd.
❹
❻ ❺
Gibson Blvd
Albuquerque
International
Airport ✈
❼
Montesa
Park
KIRTLAND AIR
FORCE BASE

Albuquerque Bus
  Transportation Center ❻
Albuquerque Convention
  and Visitors Bureau ❹
Albuquerque
  Convention Center ❹

Balloon Fiesta Park ❶
Old Town Information Center ❸
Petroglyph National Monument ❷
University of New Mexico ❺
Veterans Administration Hospital ❼

1-0327

1 Orientation

ARRIVING

Since Albuquerque is the transportation hub for New Mexico, getting in and out of town is easy. For more detailed information, see "Getting There," in chapter 2.

BY PLANE The **Albuquerque International Airport** is in the south-central part of the city, between I-25 on the west and Kirtland Air Force Base on the east, just south of Gibson Boulevard. Sleek and efficient, the airport is served by nine national airlines and two local ones.

Most hotels have courtesy vans to meet their guests and take them to their respective destinations. In addition, **Shuttlejack** (☎ **505/243-3244**) and **Checker Airport Express** (☎ **505/765-1234**) run services to and from city hotels. **Sun Tran** (☎ **505/843-9200**), Albuquerque's public bus system, also makes airport stops. There is efficient taxi service to and from the airport, plus numerous car-rental agencies.

BY TRAIN **Amtrak's** "Southwest Chief" arrives and departs daily to and from Los Angeles and Chicago. The station is at 214 First St. SW, 2 blocks south of Central Avenue (☎ **800/USA-RAIL** or 505/842-9650). *Note:* A new train station is currently in the planning stage, so call ahead to make sure the address listed here is still current.

BY BUS **Greyhound/Trailways** (☎ **800/231-2222** for schedules, fares, and information) and **TNM&O Coaches** (☎ **505/243-4435**) arrive and depart from the Albuquerque Bus Transportation Center, 300 Second St. SW (at the corner of Lead and Second, near the train station).

BY CAR If you're driving, you'll probably arrive via either the east–west I-40 or the north–south I-25. Exits are well marked. For information and advice on driving in New Mexico, see "Getting There," in chapter 2.

VISITOR INFORMATION

The main office of the **Albuquerque Convention and Visitors Bureau** is at 20 First Plaza NW (☎ **800/284-2282** or 505/842-9918). It's open Monday through Friday from 8am to 5pm. There are information centers at the airport, on the lower level at the bottom of the escalator, open daily from 9:30am to 8pm; and in Old Town at 303 Romero St. NW (Suite 107), open daily from 9am to 5pm. Tape-recorded information about current local events is available from the bureau after 5pm weekdays and all day Saturday and Sunday. Call ☎ **800/284-2282.** If you have access to the World Wide Web, the address for the Albuquerque Convention and Visitors Bureau is **www.abqcvb.org.**

CITY LAYOUT

The city's sprawl takes a while to get used to. A visitor's first impression is of a grid of arteries lined with shopping malls and fast-food eateries, with residences tucked behind on side streets.

If you look at a map of Albuquerque, the first thing you'll notice is that it lies at the crossroads of I-25 north–south and I-40 east–west. Refocus your attention on the southwest quadrant: Here, you'll find both downtown Albuquerque and Old Town, site of many tourist attractions. Lomas Boulevard and Central Avenue, the old Route 66 (US 66), flank downtown on the north and south. They come together 2 miles west of downtown near the Old Town Plaza, the historical and spiritual heart of the city. Lomas and Central continue east across I-25, staying about half a mile apart as they pass by the University of New Mexico and the New Mexico State Fairgrounds. The airport is directly south of the UNM campus, about 3 miles via Yale Boulevard. Kirtland Air Force Base—site of Sandia National Laboratories and the National Atomic Museum—is an equal distance south of the fairgrounds on Louisiana Boulevard.

Roughly paralleling I-40 to the north is Menaul Boulevard, the focus of mid-town and uptown shopping as well as the hotel districts. As Albuquerque expands northward, the Journal Center business park area, about 4½ miles north of the freeway interchange, is getting more attention. East of Eubank Boulevard are the Sandia Foothills, where the alluvial plain slants a bit more steeply toward the mountains.

When looking for an address, it is helpful to know that Central Avenue divides the city into north and south, and the railroad tracks—which run just east of First Street downtown—comprise the dividing line between east and west. Street names are followed by a directional: NE, NW, SE, or SW.

MAPS   The most comprehensive Albuquerque street map is distributed by the Convention and Visitors Bureau.

2 Getting Around

Albuquerque is easy to get around, thanks to its wide thoroughfares and grid layout, combined with its efficient transportation systems.

BY PUBLIC TRANSPORTATION   Sun Tran of Albuquerque (☎ **505/ 843-9200**) cloaks the arterials with its city bus network. Call for information on routes and fares.

BY TAXI   Yellow-Checker Cab (☎ **505/765-1234**) serves the city and surrounding area 24 hours a day.

BY CAR   The Yellow Pages list more than 30 car-rental agencies in Albuquerque. Among them are the following well-known national firms: **Alamo,** 2601 Yale Blvd. SE (☎ 505/842-4057); **Avis,** at the airport (☎ 505/842-4080); **Budget,** at the airport (☎ 505/768-5900); **Dollar,** at the airport (☎ 505/842-4304); **Hertz,** at the airport (☎ 505/842-4235); **Rent-A-Wreck,** 500 Yale Blvd. SE (☎ 505/ 232-7552); and **Thrifty,** 2039 Yale Blvd. SE (☎ 505/842-8733). Those not located at the airport itself are close by and can provide rapid airport pickup and delivery service.

Parking is generally not difficult in Albuquerque. Meters operate weekdays from 8am to 6pm and are not monitored at other times. Only the large downtown hotels charge for parking. Traffic is a problem only at certain hours. Avoid I-25 and I-40 at the center of town around 5pm.

FAST FACTS: Albuquerque

Airport   See "Orientation," above.

American Express   The American Express office is at 5031 Indian School Rd. NE, Building C, Suite. 200 (☎ **800/219-1023**; fax 505/332-5911). To report lost credit cards, call ☎ 800/528-2122.

Area Code   The telephone area code for all of New Mexico is 505.

Car Rentals   See "Getting There," in chapter 2, or "Getting Around," above.

Climate   See "When to Go," in chapter 2.

Currency Exchange   Foreign currency can be exchanged between 9am and 2pm at NationsBank, 303 Roma St. NW, ☎ **505/765-2211**); or at any of the branches of First Security Bank (its main office is at Forty-First Plaza NW, ☎ **505/765-4000**).

Dentists   Call the Albuquerque District Dental Society at ☎ **505/260-7333** for emergency service.

Doctors   Call the University of New Mexico Medical Center Physician Referral Service at ☎ **505/843-0124** for a recommendation.

Embassies/Consulates   See "Fast Facts: For the Foreign Traveler," in chapter 3.

Emergencies   For police, fire, or ambulance, dial ☎ **911.**

Hospitals   The major facilities are Presbyterian Hospital, 1100 Central Ave. SE (☎ **505/841-1234,** 505/841-1111 for emergency services); and University of New Mexico Hospital, 2211 Lomas Blvd. NE (☎ **505/272-2111,** 505/843-2411 for emergency services).

Liquor Laws   The legal drinking age is 21 throughout New Mexico. Bars may remain open until 2am Monday through Saturday and until midnight on Sunday. Wine, beer, and spirits are sold at licensed supermarkets and liquor stores, but there are no package sales on election days until after 7pm. It is illegal to transport liquor through most Native American reservations.

Newspapers & Magazines   The two daily newspapers are the *Albuquerque Tribune,* published mornings, and the *Albuquerque Journal,* published evenings.

Police   For emergencies, call ☎ **911.** For other business, contact the Albuquerque City Police (☎ **505/768-1986**) or the New Mexico State Police (☎ **505/841-9256**).

Post Offices   The Main Post Office, 1135 Broadway NE (☎ **505/245-9561**), is open daily from 7:30am to 6pm. There are 25 branch offices, with about another dozen in surrounding communities.

Radio/TV   Albuquerque has some 30 local radio stations catering to all musical tastes. Albuquerque television stations include KOB, Channel 4 (NBC affiliate); KOAT, Channel 7 (ABC affiliate); KGGM, Channel 13 (CBS affiliate); KNME, Channel 5 (PBS affiliate); and KGSW, Channel 14 (Fox and independent). There are, of course, numerous local cable channels as well.

Taxes   In Albuquerque, the hotel tax is 10.5625%; it will be added to your bill.

Taxis   See "Getting Around," above.

Time Zone   Albuquerque is on Mountain Time, 1 hour ahead of the West Coast and 2 hours behind the East Coast.

Transit Information   Sun Tran of Albuquerque is the public bus system. Call ☎ **505/843-9200** for schedules and information.

Useful Telephone Numbers   For time and temperature, call ☎ **505/247-1611;** for road information, call ☎ **800/432-4269;** and for emergency road service (AAA), call ☎ **505/291-6600.**

3 Where to Stay

Albuquerque's hotel glut is good news to travelers looking for quality rooms at a reasonable cost. Except during peak periods—specifically, the New Mexico Arts and Crafts Fair (late June), the New Mexico State Fair (September), and the Kodak

Central Albuquerque Accommodations

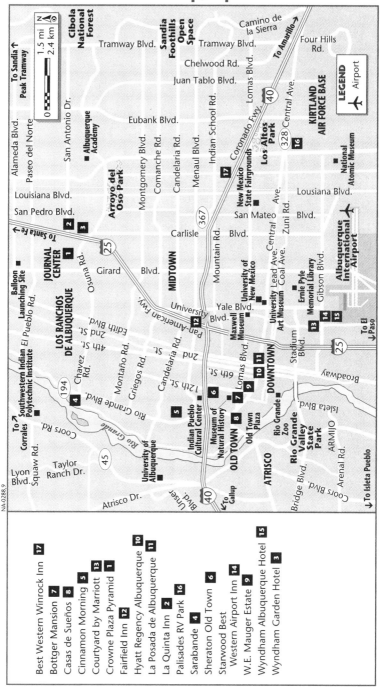

Best Western Winrock Inn **17**
Bottger Mansion **7**
Casas de Sueños **8**
Cinnamon Morning **5**
Courtyard by Marriott **13**
Crowne Plaza Pyramid **1**
Fairfield Inn **12**
Hyatt Regency Albuquerque **10**
La Posada de Albuquerque **11**
La Quinta Inn **2**
Palisades RV Park **16**
Sarabande **4**
Sheraton Old Town **6**
Starwood Best
  Western Airport Inn **14**
W.E. Mauger Estate **9**
Wyndham Albuquerque Hotel **15**
Wyndham Garden Hotel **3**

Albuquerque International Balloon Fiesta (early October)—most of the city's hotels have vacant rooms, so guests can frequently request and get a lower room rate than the one posted.

In the following listing, hotels are categorized by price range: **Expensive** means that a double room costs $110 or more per night; **Moderate** includes doubles for $75 to $110; and **Inexpensive** refers to doubles for $75 and under.

A tax of 10.5625% is added to every hotel bill. All hotels listed offer rooms for nonsmokers and travelers with disabilities; all the bed-and-breakfasts do as well.

EXPENSIVE

Crowne Plaza Pyramid
5151 San Francisco Rd. NE, Albuquerque, NM 87109. ☎ **800/544-0623** or 505/821-3333. Fax 505/822-8115. 365 units. A/C TV TEL. $139–$184 double; $140–$275 suite. Ask about special weekend and package rates. AE, CB, DC, MC, V. Free parking.

About a 15-minute drive from Old Town and downtown is this Aztec pyramid-shaped structure reached via the Paseo del Norte exit (exit 232) from I-25. Previously the Holiday Inn Pyramid, this structure, built in 1986, has recently come under the Crowne Plaza name and with it received a $4.5-million renovation. The 10 guest floors are grouped around a hollow skylit atrium. Vines drape from planter boxes on the balconies, and water falls five stories to a pool between the two glass elevators.

The rooms are spacious, though not extraordinary, all with picture windows and ample views. The renovation has added Spectravision movie channels, coffee-makers, hair dryers, makeup mirrors, irons, and ironing boards. The morning newspaper is delivered to your door. Rooms on the 10th-floor executive level offer more space and a few more amenities.

With lots of convention space at the hotel, you're likely to encounter name-tagged conventioneers here, though the service seems to be good enough to handle the crowds without inconvenience to you. However, the two elevators can't quite accommodate the crowds and the stairs are locked on the ground floor, so guests often must wait.

Dining/Diversions: The Terrace Restaurant offers American cuisine with a Southwestern flair. There are also two lounges on the premises.

Amenities: Concierge, room service, valet laundry, newspaper delivery, express check-out, indoor/outdoor pool, medium-sized health club, Jacuzzi, sauna, jogging track, business center, conference rooms, sundeck.

✪ Hyatt Regency Albuquerque
330 Tijeras Ave. NW, Albuquerque, NM 87102. ☎ **800/233-1234** or 505/842-1234. Fax 505/766-6710. 409 units. A/C TV TEL. Weekdays $150–$175 double; weekends $89 double; $310–$725 suite. AE, CB, DC, DISC, MC, V. Self-parking $8, valet $11.

If you like luxury and want to be right downtown, this is the place to stay. This $60-million hotel, which opened in 1990, is pure shiny gloss and art deco. The lobby features a palm-shaded fountain beneath a pyramidal skylight, and throughout the hotel's public areas is an extensive art collection, including original Frederic Remington sculptures. The spacious guest rooms enhance the feeling of richness with mahogany furnishings, full-length mirrors, and big views of the mountains. Each room has Spectravision movie channels, a coffeemaker, and hair dryer. This is a nice location if you want to sample Albuquerque's nightlife as well as seasonal events on the recently renovated Civic Plaza. The hotel has a number of shops and is located right next door to the Galeria, a shopping area.

Dining/Diversions: McGrath's serves three meals daily in a setting of forest-green upholstery and black-cherry furniture. Bolo Saloon is noted for its whimsical oils of "where the deer and the antelope play" (at the bar).

Amenities: Concierge, room service, dry cleaning, laundry service, newspaper delivery, baby-sitting, secretarial services, express check-out, valet parking. You'll also find an outdoor swimming pool, small health club, sauna, business center, conference rooms, car-rental desk, beauty salon, boutiques.

Sheraton Old Town

800 Rio Grande Blvd. NW, Albuquerque, NM 87104. ☎ **800/325-3535** or 505/843-6300. Fax 505/842-9863. 208 units. A/C TV TEL. $120–$130 double; $150 suite. Children stay free in parents' room. AE, CB, DC, DISC, MC, V. Free parking.

No Albuquerque hotel is closer to top tourist attractions than the Sheraton. It's only a 5-minute walk from the Old Town Plaza and two important museums. Constructed in 1975 and remodeled in 1993, with more updating in 1998, the building has mezzanine-level windows lighting the adobe-toned lobby, an airiness that carries into the rooms. They have unique handmade furniture such as *trasteros* (free-standing closets, like armoires) accented with willow shoots. Request a south-side room and you'll get a balcony overlooking Old Town and the pool, which is heated year-round. All rooms now offer coffeemakers, hair dryers, and irons and ironing boards.

Dining: The Customs House Restaurant, specializing in seafood and regional cuisine, serves weekday lunches and nightly dinners. The Café del Sol is the Sheraton's coffee shop.

Amenities: Concierge, room service, valet laundry, secretarial and baby-sitting services. There's also the Old Town Place, an attached shopping center, which has arts-and-crafts dealers, a bookstore, beauty salon, and Explora Science Center for children.

MODERATE

✪ Courtyard by Marriott

1920 Yale Blvd. SE, Albuquerque, NM 87106. ☎ **800/321-2211** or 505/843-6600. Fax 505/843-8740. 164 units. A/C TV TEL. $104 double; $99–$130 suite. Weekend rates available. AE, DC, DISC, MC, V.

If you don't like high-rises such as the Wyndham Albuquerque Hotel, this is the best selection for airport area hotels. Opened in 1990, this four-story member of the Marriott family is built around an attractively landscaped courtyard reminiscent of a village green. Families appreciate the security system—access is only by key card between 11pm and 6am—though most of the hotel's clients are business travelers. The units are roomy and comfortable, with walnut furniture and firm beds. Ask for a balcony room on the courtyard. Among the nicer touches are coffee and tea service from a 190° faucet, on-command movie channel, full-size writing desks, irons and ironing boards, hair dryers, voice mail, clock radios, and massage showerheads.

The coffee shop is open daily for breakfast and dinner. There is an adjacent lounge. The hotel provides valet laundry and a courtesy van. Don't miss a trip to the lovely indoor pool and spacious whirlpool. There's also a Laundromat and a small exercise room.

✪ La Posada de Albuquerque

125 Second St. NW (at Copper Ave.), Albuquerque, NM 87102. ☎ **800/777-5732** or 505/242-9090. Fax 505/242-8664. 114 units. AC TV TEL. $89–$115 double; $195–$275 suite. AE, DISC, MC, V. Valet parking $5.

Built in 1939 by Conrad Hilton as the famed hotelier's first inn in his home state of New Mexico, this hostelry on the National Register of Historic Places feels like old Spain. Though remodeled in 1996, the owners have kept the finer qualities. An elaborate Moorish brass-and-mosaic fountain stands in the center of the tiled lobby floor while new carpet, drapes, and furniture in 1997 set off touches such as old-fashioned tin chandeliers hanging from the 2-story ceiling. The lobby is surrounded on all sides by high archways, creating the feel of a 19th-century hacienda courtyard.

As in the lobby, all guest room furniture is handcrafted, but here it's covered with cushions of Southwestern design. There are spacious rooms with big windows looking out across the city and toward the mountains. If you want a feel for downtown Albuquerque as well as easy access to the Civic Plaza, nightclubs, and Old Town, this hotel will suit you well.

Conrad's Downtown, La Posada's elegantly redesigned restaurant, features Southwestern cuisine from Jane Butel who has a cooking school on the premises. The Lobby Bar is a favorite gathering place and has entertainment Thursday through Saturday evenings.

The hotel offers room service, dry cleaning, laundry service, express check-out, valet parking, and access to a nearby health club.

Wyndham Albuquerque Hotel

2910 Yale Blvd. SE, Albuquerque, NM 87106. ☎ **800/227-1117** or 505/843-7000. Fax 505/843-6307. 276 units. A/C TV TEL. $69–$149 double. AE, CB, DC, DISC, EURO, JCB, MC, V. Free parking. Small pets welcome with prior approval.

This recently remodeled hotel right at the airport now has an elegant feel. The lobby, grill, and lounge areas employ a lot of sandstone, wood, copper, and tile to lend an Anasazi feel. The hotel caters to air travelers with a 24-hour desk, shuttle service, and same-day valet laundry. But it could also be a wise choice for a few days of browsing around Albuquerque, as it has good access to freeways and excellent views. Of course, you will hear some jet noise. The hotel recently came under the Wyndham name and with it came a multimillion-dollar remodel.

The Anasazi feel carries into the rooms of the 15-story hotel. Each room has a balcony, data ports, Nintendo on the TV, a hair dryer, coffeemaker, iron, ironing board, and *USA Today*. Deluxe club rooms on the 15th floor offer oversized towels and bottled water, as well as a concierge lounge with complimentary hors d'oveures. Room service is also available. Facilities include an outdoor swimming pool, self-service Laundromat, two all-weather tennis courts, business center, and gift shop. The Rojo Grill serves a variety of American and Southwestern dishes, from tostadas to Ostrich medaillons.

INEXPENSIVE

Best Western Winrock Inn

18 Winrock Center NE, Albuquerque, NM 87110. ☎ **800/866-5252** or 505/883-5252. Fax 505/889-3206. 175 units. A/C TV TEL. $55–$125 single or double; $73–$145 suite. Rates include full breakfast buffet. AE, CB, DC, DISC, MC, V.

Located just off I-40 at the Louisiana Boulevard interchange, the Winrock is attached to one of Albuquerque's largest shopping centers: Winrock Center. This is a mall-like area featuring movies and discount-store shopping—and lots of traffic. Built in 1962 and remodeled in 1995, the hotel's two separate buildings are wrapped around a garden and private lagoon with Mandarin ducks, giant koi (carp), and an impressive waterfall. The comfortable rooms, many of which have private patios overlooking the lagoon (request a ground-floor room, poolside; this will help minimize traffic noise from the freeway), feature a pastel Southwestern-motif decor. A full, hot breakfast is served in the Club Room every morning. Valet laundry service is available. On the premises you will find a heated outdoor pool and guest laundry.

Fairfield Inn

1760 Menaul Rd. NE, Albuquerque, NM 87102. ☎ **800/228-2800** or 505/889-4000. Fax 505/872-3094. 188 units. A/C TV TEL. $62.95 double. Extra person $6. Children 18 and under stay free in parents' room. Continental breakfast included in the price of the room. AE, CB, DC, DISC, MC, V.

Owned by Marriott, this hotel has exceptionally clean rooms and a location with easy access to freeways that can quickly get you to Old Town, downtown, or the heights. Ask for an east-facing room to avoid the noise and a view of the highway. Rooms are medium-sized and have new bedspreads, lamp shades, carpet, and bathroom tile. Each has a balcony or terrace. Local phone calls are free and valet laundry service is available. There's an indoor/outdoor swimming pool with saunas and a Jacuzzi as well as a medium-sized health club. You probably couldn't get more for your money (in a chain hotel) anywhere else.

La Quinta Inn

5241 San Antonio Dr. NE, Albuquerque, NM 87109. ☎ **800/531-5900** or 505/821-9000. Fax 505/821-2399. 130 units. A/C TV TEL. $70–$75 double (higher during Balloon Fiesta). Children 18 and under stay free in parents' room. AE, CB, DC, DISC, MC, V. Pets welcome.

With its "new rooms" campaign, La Quinta is charging ahead in the inexpensive room category, and after my visit to this hotel I can see why. Though the bed was a little hard, the rest of the accommodation was ergonomically right; these fairly spacious rooms have a table and chairs where you need them, and a bathroom you can move around in. They are decorated tastefully in greens with art deco tile in the bathroom. If you're headed to the Balloon Fiesta, this is a good choice, since it's not far from the launch site, though you'll have to reserve as much as a year in advance. The lobby breakfast room is comfortable, with pillars that lend a dignified air. A bean-shaped heated pool, open May through October, offers respite from Albuquerque's hot summers. King rooms have a recliner, and 2-room suites are available.

If you like these inns, and want to stay at one near the airport, you can make reservations at the above 800 number for **La Quinta Airport Inn** #816 at 2116 Yale Blvd. SE.

Starwood Best Western Airport Inn

2400 Yale Blvd. SE, Albuquerque, NM 87106. ☎ **800/528-1234** or 505/242-7022. Fax 505/243-0620. 122 units. A/C TV TEL. $63–$69 double. Rates include continental breakfast. AE, CB, DC, DISC, MC, V.

Struggling to keep pace with the newer Comfort Inns and La Quintas springing up in the area, this hotel is receiving a remodel from the lobby to the rooms. At press time the lobby was getting a new balcony area where breakfast was to be served. The rooms have new dark wood furniture, bedspreads, carpet, and TVs. Units are still average sized, except for the newer east wing where they are a little larger. Each is equipped with a hairdryer, iron, and ironing board; some have balconies and patios. All offer free local phone calls. Deluxe units are equipped with refrigerators. A courtesy van is available from 5am to midnight (hotel will pay for a taxi during odd hours), and the hotel also offers valet laundry service. Guests can enjoy an outdoor swimming pool and Jacuzzi, surrounded by grass.

Wyndham Garden Hotel

6000 Pan American Fwy. NE (I-25 at San Mateo Blvd.), Albuquerque, NM 87109. ☎ **800/ 996-3426** or 505/821-9451. Fax 505/858-0239. 151 units. A/C TV TEL. $59–$99 single or double. AE, CB, DC, DISC, MC, V.

From the outside, this 5-story stucco structure doesn't look like much, but a recent remodeling has done wonders with the inside. Located off I-25, it's about 15 minutes from Old Town and downtown, but has good access to many restaurants on San Mateo, just minutes away. The hotel does a lot of corporate and some group business, but is still a good spot for travelers. It features a lobby atrium decorated in a Southwest fishing-lodge decor that carries into the rooms, which are richly decorated in warm tones. Some rooms are quite large and they cost the same as the others, so request one of them. All rooms have private balconies (patios on the ground floor), city or mountain views, On Command movies, coffeemakers, safes, irons and ironing boards, and data ports. *USA Today* is delivered to guest rooms weekdays. The Garden Cafe is open daily for a full breakfast buffet (included with room rate weekdays), lunch, and dinner. The Atrium Lounge is a quiet, comfortable place to enjoy cocktails or after-dinner drinks. Room service is available from 5am to 10pm. There's a guest laundry, fax, and copy service, as well as a small health club, Jacuzzi, sauna, and indoor/outdoor heated swimming pool.

BED & BREAKFASTS

EXPENSIVE

Casas de Sueños

310 Rio Grande Blvd. SW, Albuquerque, NM 87104. ☎ **800/CHAT-W/US** or 505/ 247-4560. 21 units. TV TEL. $95–$250 single or double. Rates include full breakfast and afternoon snacks. AE, CB, DC, DISC, MC, V. Children 12 and older are welcome, but pets are not accepted.

The principal attraction of this B&B is its location. It's within walking distance from the Plaza, the aquarium, and botanical garden—even the zoo, though it's farther. You'll recognize Casas de Sueños by the bright sign and the snail-shaped front of the main building, which was designed by famed renegade architect Bart Prince. The buildings that comprise the Casas were once private homes—a compound that was part of a gathering place for artists and their admirers. Most of them face a garden courtyard filled with roses and exotic sculptures.

Each of the rooms has an individual theme; one room is designed to follow the color schemes of Monet's paintings, while another has an Asian motif, with a shadow puppet from Bali and a two-person Jacuzzi. The rooms are interesting though not pristine, better described as artsy in their design and upkeep. Some are equipped with kitchens, a few have their own Jacuzzis (some indoor, some out), and a number have fireplaces. Outside the garden area are two newer rooms that I found spacious and efficient, though lacking in charm. Every accommodation has its own entrance.

A delicious full breakfast buffet is served in the main building every morning. You'll find specialties such as asparagus soufflé and apple or pear cobbler. Massage therapy is available. No smoking is permitted indoors.

MODERATE

Bottger Mansion

110 San Felipe NW, Albuquerque, NM 87104. ☎ **800/758-3639** or 505/243-3639. 7 rooms. $79–$139 double. Rates include full breakfast. AE, DC, MC, V. Children are welcome, pets are not.

This fun B&B has the corner on the market of Spanish/Victorian style in Albuquerque. Clearly, proprietor Patsy Garcia grew up around the Spanish New Mexico tradition and has awakened the Victorian in this historic 1912 mansion right in Old Town. There's lots of white lace about, and enough floral prints on synthetic fabrics so that some might find the place gaudy; I found it refreshing. My favorite room is Mercedes, with a pink tile floor, a queen bed, and Jacuzzi tub. Julia has a King and is, as are all the rooms except Marcelina, spacious. All rooms have nice-sized bathrooms with ceramic tile, and the larger rooms have TV and VCR. Those facing south are sunnier but pick up a bit of street noise from nearby Central Avenue. Breakfast is another reason to come here. Patsy goes all out. In one sitting, I was served, and ate, French toast, bacon, eggs with a tasty salsa, yogurt, juice and fruit, all deliciously prepared. It's served in a sunny indoor patio.

Casa del Granjero

414C de Baca Lane NW, Albuquerque, NM 87114. ☎ **800/701-4144** or 505/897-4144. Fax 505/897-4144. 7 units. $89–$159 double. Extra person $20. Rates include full breakfast. DISC, MC, V.

From the pygmy goats to the old restored wagon out front, Casa del Granjero ("The Farmer's House") is true to its name. Located north of town—about a 15-minute drive from Old Town—it is quiet and has a rich, homey feeling. Butch and Victoria Farmer have transformed this residence—the original part of which is 120 years old—into a fine bed-and-breakfast. The great room has an enormous sculptured adobe fireplace, comfortable bancos for lounging, a library, and is almost cluttered with Southwestern artifacts. There's a 52-inch TV in the den.

The guest rooms, with Spanish nicknames, are beautifully furnished and decorated. Most have fireplaces. Cuarto del Rey features Mexican furnishings and handmade quilts and comforters. Cuarto de Flores has French doors that open onto a portal, and Cuarto Alegre has a king-size canopy bed done up in lace and satin. The newer Guest House has comfortable rooms and access to a kitchen, but a less luxurious and Southwestern feel. In the morning, a full breakfast is served at long tables decorated with colorful Mexican cloths or on the portal. Specialties include *chiliquilles* (an enchilada-like recipe from Yucatán), served with Cuban rice custard, coffee cake, and fruit. Catered lunches and dinners are also available by arrangement. There's an organic garden and raspberry patch, as well as a new Jacuzzi and sauna, conference room, and office center equipped with fax and computer. Smoking is permitted outdoors only, and no pets except horses are permitted. There are accommodations for travelers with disabilities. *A warning to women:* These are country folk, and the men will tend to call you "hon" and "darlin'."

Cinnamon Morning

2700 Rio Grande Blvd. NW, Albuquerque, NM 87104. ☎ **800/214-9481** or 505/345-3541. 4 units, 1 suite. $65–$150 double (more for 1-night stay). Rates include full breakfast. AE, DISC, MC, V.

This is a good place to stay if you want a room near Old Town but don't want to pay a lot. Sue and Dick Percilick have turned a contemporary home in the north valley just 2 miles from Old Town into a comfortable, informal inn. Decorated in a down-home style, Sue has used touches such as art deco tile and Mexican tin mirrors to bring flair to the rooms, and each has robes and a hair dryer. Request the room with the gas fireplace and you'll sleep in a four-poster king bed. The suite has two bedrooms and a turquoise painted kitchen, a good buy for a family. Breakfasts are complete and delicious, with such specialties as eggs béarnaise and, of course, cinnamon buns. The inn does pick up noise from Rio Grande Boulevard, so if you're a light sleeper go somewhere else.

✪ Hacienda Antigua

6708 Tierra Dr. NW, Albuquerque, NM 87107. ☎ **800/201-2986** or 505/345-5399. Fax 505/345-3855. www.haciendaantigua.com/bnb/. E-mail: antigua@swcp.com. 5 units. A/C TEL. $85–$159 double. Extra person $25. Rates include breakfast. AE, DISC, MC, V.

Located on the north side of Albuquerque, just off Osuna Road, is Hacienda Antigua, a 200-year-old adobe home that was once the first stagecoach stop out of Old Town in Albuquerque. When Ann Dunlap and Melinda Moffit bought it, they were careful to preserve the building's historic charm while transforming it into an elegant bed-and-breakfast. The artistically landscaped courtyard, with its large cottonwood tree and abundance of greenery (including a large raspberry patch), offers a welcome respite for today's tired travelers.

The rooms are gracefully and comfortably furnished with antiques. There's the Don Pablo Suite with a king-size bed (covered with a stunning blue quilt), a sitting room with a kiva fireplace, and a bathroom with a wonderful old pedestal bathtub/shower; and La Capilla, the home's former chapel, which is furnished with a queen-size bed, a fireplace, and a beautiful carving of San Ysidro (the patron saint of farmers). All the rooms have such regional touches. They are also equipped with fireplaces, Caswell Massey soaps, hair dryers, coffeemakers, and unstocked minirefrigerators. A gourmet breakfast is served in the garden during warm weather and by the fire in winter. Guests also have use of the pool and Jacuzzi. Just a 20-minute drive from the airport, Hacienda Antigua is a welcome change from the anonymity of the downtown Albuquerque high-rise hotels, and Ann and Melinda are terrific hosts.

Sarabande

5637 Rio Grande Blvd. NW, Albuquerque, NM 87107. ☎ **888/506-4923** or 505/345-4923. Fax 505/345-9130. www.sarabandebb.com. E-mail: Janie@sarabandebb.com. 3 units. A/C TV TEL. $85–$125 double. Rates include breakfast. AE, DISC, MC, V. Free parking.

A bit of grandmotherly comfort describes this place situated in the North Valley, a lovely 10-minute drive from Old Town. Once you pass through the front gate and into the well-tended courtyard gardens with fountains, you'll forget that you're staying on the fringes of a big city. With cut-glass windows, lots of pastels, traditional antiques, and thick carpet (in all but the poolside room), you'll be well pampered here. Innkeepers Betty Vickers and Margaret Magnussen have filled the home with fine art as well as comfortable modern furniture. The Rose Room has a Japanese soaking tub and kiva fireplace. The Iris Room, with its stained-glass window depicting irises, has a king-size bed. Both rooms open onto a wisteria-shaded patio where breakfast can be taken in the morning. Out back are a 50-foot heated lap pool and a Jacuzzi (which can be used through the winter). There is a library stocked with magazines, books by local authors, and books about New Mexico (including local sports and recreation). Betty and Margaret are avid hikers and will be happy to recommend hiking options for you. All-terrain bikes are available for guest use free of charge. Breakfast (fresh fruit, fresh squeezed juice, coffee, and homemade breads) may be served in the courtyard or the dining room. Don't miss the chocolate-chip cookies offered in the afternoon.

The W. E. Mauger Estate

701 Roma Ave. NW, Albuquerque, NM 87102. ☎ **800/719-9189** or 505/242-8755. Fax 505/842-8835. www.thuntek.net/tc_arts/mauger 8 units, 1 suite. A/C TV TEL. $89–$179 double. Rates include full breakfast. AE, DC, DISC, MC, V. Children welcome ($15), as are small pets by prior arrangement ($30).

A restored Queen Anne–style home constructed in 1897, this former residence of wool baron William Mauger is listed on the National Register of Historic Places. Today, it is a wonderfully atmospheric Old West/Victorian–style bed-and-breakfast, with high ceilings and rich brass appointments. It's located close to downtown and Old Town, just 5 blocks from the convention center and only 5 miles from the airport. All rooms feature period furnishings, private bathrooms with showers, and one has a balcony. Each also has a coffeemaker, unstocked refrigerator, and hair dryer. A full breakfast is served each morning, in indoor and outdoor dining rooms.

NEAR ALBUQUERQUE

Hacienda Vargas

El Camino Real (P.O. Box 307), Algodones/Santa Fe, NM 87001. ☎ **800/261-0006** or 505/867-9115. Fax 505/867-1902, www.swcp.com.hacvar//. E-mail: hacvar@swcp.com. 7 units. $79–$149 double. Extra person $15. MC, V.

Unassuming in its elegance, Hacienda Vargas is located right on old Route 66. Owned and operated by the DeVargas family, the inn is situated in the small town of Algodones (about 20 miles from Albuquerque) and is a good place to stay if you're planning to visit both Santa Fe and Albuquerque but don't want to stay in one of the downtown hotels in either city. There's a real Mexican feel to the decor, with brightly woven place mats in the breakfast room and Spanish suits of armor hanging in the common area. Each guest room has a private entrance, many opening onto a courtyard. All rooms are furnished with New Mexico antiques, are individually decorated, and have handmade kiva fireplaces. Many have Jacuzzi tubs. Each of the four suites has a Jacuzzi tub, fireplace, and private patio. Hosts Jule and Paul DeVargas are extremely gracious and helpful—they'll make you feel right at home. A full breakfast is served every morning in the dining room. The only drawback here is the train tracks near the back of the house, and during my stay the last train went by around midnight. At all other times the inn is quiet and restful.

La Hacienda Grande

21 Baros Lane, Bernalillo, NM 87004. ☎ **505/867-1887.** Fax 505/867-4621. 6 units (all with bathroom). A/C. $99–$129 double. Extra person $15. Rates include breakfast. AE, DISC, MC, V. Free parking.

Twenty minutes from Albuquerque, this is the place to stay if you want to experience the feel of historic adobe architecture at its finest. The 250-year-old structure built around a courtyard was once a stagecoach stop on El Camino Real, the route north from Mexico. Three years ago it was purchased by Shoshana Zimmerman, who did a complete interior renovation, adding bathrooms to each unit, yet preserving the spirit of the old place. Two-foot-thick walls and brick or flagstone floors, as well as elegant vigas, distinguish the architecture. A real attention to soul comfort distinguishes the decorating. Shoshana has implemented some feng shui principles in her choice of music in the main room (often Native American flute), scents, and textures. All the rooms offer views out toward country meadows. My favorite room is the San Felipe, with a queen bed, Jacuzzi tub, and a freestanding ceramic fireplace (five of the rooms have wood-burning kiva fireplaces). If you love morning sun, request the Santa Clara. Most of the bathrooms are small and have showers rather than bathtubs. Early each morning, coffee and tea are left in thermoses outside your door. Breakfast is served in a sunny room that was once a chapel. My favorite is the huevos motuleños, a mixture of tortillas, eggs, green chile, and goat cheese. Other favorites are Amaretto French toast and pumpkin pancakes. There are phone jacks in each room, and phones are available at the front desk. In addition, TVs and VCRs are available upon request. Smoking is prohibited except on the patio.

The Sandhill Crane Bed-and-Breakfast

389 Camino Hermosa, Corrales, NM 87048. ☎ **800/375-2445** or 505/898-2445. Fax 505/792-8515. www.sandhillbb.com/thorpe. 5 units. A/C TV TEL. $75–$145 double. Rates include continental breakfast on weekdays, full breakfast on weekends. AE, MC, V. Free parking.

This lovely bed-and-breakfast, run by Carol Hogan and Phil Thorpe, is about 20 minutes from Albuquerque in the sleepy little town of Corrales. It's a great place to stay if you want to explore the city but don't want to be right downtown. Wisteria-draped walls surround the renovated adobe hacienda, and each room is uniquely decorated in an elegant, traditional Southwestern style. For families or friends traveling together, the ominously named Outlaw Wing (two rooms with connecting bathroom, small kitchen, and private entrance) is a great choice. All rooms have cable TV and phone jacks for those who want a telephone. Be aware that this is a home, and with it comes close-quarters coziness, not necessarily the choice for those who like their own outdoor entrance. Carol has decorated the guest rooms with her charming collection of bird decoys and birdhouses, while Phil is responsible for breakfasts that include fruit drinks, bagels, muffins, or homemade bread, as well as, on weekends, a special hot entree such as his frittata (an Italian omelet) served with focaccia. In warmer weather, breakfast is served on the patio, where you're likely to see a roadrunner pass by. Currently, plans are in the works to add three new rooms. Rooms for nonsmokers and travelers with disabilities are available.

RV PARKS

Albuquerque Central KOA

12400 Skyline Rd. NE, Albuquerque, NM 87123. ☎ **800/562-7781** or 505/296-2729. $22 tent site; $30–$32 RV site, depending on the hook-up; $38 1-room cabin; $48 2-room cabin. All prices are valid for up to 2 people; additional adult $5. AE, DISC, MC, V.

This RV park sits in the foothills east of Albuquerque. It features a bathhouse, Laundromat, Jacuzzi, outdoor swimming pool (open summers only), miniature golf course and playground, a convenience store, and bicycles to rent during summer. Cabins are available.

Albuquerque North KOA

555 Hill Rd., Bernalillo, NM 87004. ☎ **505/867-5227.** $20 tent site; $25–$30 RV site, depending on the hook-up; $32 1-bedroom cabin; and $40.95 2-bedroom cabin. All prices include a pancake breakfast and are valid for up to 2 people; additional adult $3. DISC, MC, V.

Over 1,000 cottonwood and pine trees shade this park, and in the warm months there are many flowers. Located at the foot of the mountains 14 miles from Albuquerque, this campground has a Laundromat, outdoor swimming pool (open May to October), playground, convenience store, cafe, and free outdoor movies. There's a free pancake breakfast daily. Reservations are recommended. There are also 6 camping cabins available.

Palisades RV Park

9201 Central Ave. NW, Albuquerque, NM 87121. ☎ **505/831-5000.** Fax 505/352-2983. 110 sites. $20 per day; $100 per week; $220 plus electricity per month. MC, V.

Sitting out on the barren west mesa, this RV park does have nice views of the Sandia Mountains and is the closest RV park to Old Town and the new Biopark (10-minute drive); however, it is also in a fairly desolate setting, with only a few trees about. In mid-summer it will be hot. The owner is on site and there's a bathhouse, Laundromat, reception room, small convenience store, and propane is available.

4 Where to Dine

In these listings, the following categories define price ranges: **Expensive,** most dinner main courses are priced over $15; **Moderate,** most dinner main courses $10 to $15; **Inexpensive,** $10 and under.

IN OR NEAR OLD TOWN
EXPENSIVE

Antiquity
112 Romero NW (in Old Town). ☎ **505/247-3545.** Reservations recommended. Main courses $15.65–$24.95. AE, DC, DISC, MC, V. Daily 5–9pm. FRENCH/CONTINENTAL.

I'd heard people rave about this small restaurant in a 200-year-old building in Old Town, but I wasn't overly impressed. The atmosphere is cozy with Southwestern touches and the food is well-prepared, but the place seems a little behind the times. In some respects it's a positive thing. Rather than succumbing to the à la carte plague that's run through restaurants these days, most entrees come with salad, bread, a vegetable, and rice or baked potato. On the other hand, my salmon, which was cooked perfectly in parchment paper with a champagne sauce, was topped with *dried* dill—with fresh dill it really would have sung. If you don't mind a quite rich dinner, order the Henry IV (filet mignon, on artichoke leaves, topped with the artichoke heart smothered with béarnaise). There's also a chicken cashew with red chile in it that's quite tasty. Service here is conscientious, if a little slow. Beer and wine are available.

✪ Maria Teresa
618 Rio Grande Blvd. NW. ☎ **505/242-3900.** Reservations recommended. Lunch $7–$10.95; dinner $12.95–$23. AE, DC, MC, V. Daily 11am–2:30pm and 5–9pm. NEW MEXICAN/CONTINENTAL.

If you're looking for excellent food in a Victorian Old West atmosphere, walk a block north of the Plaza and eat here. In summer, there's a small enclosed patio that's enchanting. This 1840s Salvador Armijo House, a National Historic property, has 32-inch-thick adobe walls and is furnished with Victorian antiques and paintings. Tables are well spaced through 7 rooms, a great place for an intimate meal. Service is formal and professional, though, on a busy day, it may be slow. Lunches include a variety of pasta and salad dishes. I enjoyed the crispy crab cake served with thick asparagus spears, though you may prefer it with Southwestern pasta salad. Or try the Old Town tortilla roll filled with cheese, veggies, and your choice of meat or fish, served with guacamole. Dinner entrees include soup or salad, and range from fish to meats. My favorite is the sautéed jumbo prawns, but others prefer the seared filet of beef tenderloin, topped with béarnaise sauce. For dessert, you may want to choose from a variety of specialty drinks such as a Chocolate Cream Fizz (Godiva chocolate liqueur topped with cream and spritzed with club soda). There's a full bar.

MODERATE

High Noon Restaurant and Saloon
425 San Felipe St. NW. ☎ **505/765-1455.** Reservations recommended. Main courses lunch $4.75–$8.50; dinner $9.50–$21.50. AE, CB, DC, DISC, MC, V. Mon–Sat 11am–3pm and 5–10pm, Sun noon–9pm. STEAKS/SEAFOOD/NEW MEXICAN.

Located in one of Albuquerque's oldest buildings, this 25-year-old restaurant has three rooms, each with its own theme. My favorite is the Hispanic Room, near the bar, where carved santos sit within lighted nichos. There's also the Anglo Room, with historical photos on the walls. One photo depicts the original 1785 structure, which now comprises the building's foyer and Santo Room. The Native American Room has weavings on the walls and a skylight. All have stuccoed walls and thick ceiling beams. Though the food here isn't outstanding, the restaurant is a good choice for parties with a variety of desires. There are fish, meat, and chicken dishes—my Spanish chicken was tasty, spiced with peppers and garlic. There are burgers—even a tasty buffalo burger—and there's good New Mexican fare such as enchiladas and burritos. There's a full bar and free parking, a definite plus in this part of town.

✪ La Crêpe Michel

400 San Felipe C2. ☎ **505/242-1251.** Reservations accepted. Main courses $3.50–$17.50. MC, V. Tues–Sun 11:30am–2pm; Thurs–Sat 6–9pm. FRENCH.

This small find is tucked away in a secluded walkway not far from the Plaza. Run by chef Claudie Zamet-Wilcox from France, it has a cozy, informal European feel, with checked table coverings and simple furnishings. Service is friendly and calm, which makes this a good place for a romantic meal. You can't miss with any of the crêpes. I found the crêpe aux fruits de mer (blend of sea scallops, bay scallops, and shrimp in a velouté sauce with mushrooms) especially nice, as is the crêpe à la volaille (chunks of chicken in a cream sauce with mushrooms and Madeira wine). For a heartier meal, try one of the specials listed on the board on the wall. My mahi Basquaise came in a light vegetable sauce, and my companion's fillet de boeuf had a delicious béarnaise. Both were served with vegetables cooked just enough to leave them crisp and tasty. For dessert, don't leave without having a crêpe aux fraises (strawberry crêpe). Because of its proximity to a church, no alcoholic beverages are served.

La Hacienda Restaurant

302 San Felipe St. NW (at North Plaza). ☎ **505/243-3131.** Reservations recommended for large parties. Lunch $4.95–$9.95; dinner $8.50–$14.95. AE, CB, DC, MC, V. Daily 11am–9:30pm. NEW MEXICAN/AMERICAN.

This restaurant, like its neighbor La Placita, offers more atmosphere than flavor. Appealing mostly to tourist traffic, the food is a muted version of real Northern New Mexican cuisine. If you want the real thing, I suggest Duran Central Pharmacy, a few blocks from the Plaza.

Still, this place is full of history. It's set in a 100-year-old adobe structure and has been in business for 65 years. A mural girding La Hacienda's outer wall depicts the construction of this Villa de Albuquerque at the turn of the 18th century, and President Clinton ate here during a 1998 visit. Diners enter through a large gift shop. The interior, with an intimate, laid-back atmosphere, has brightly painted tables and chairs set very close together. In summer, choose the sidewalk dining with a view of the Plaza. Most like to start with one of the big margaritas in a variety of flavors from strawberry to pineapple. The specialty here is the chimichanga, a fried burrito stuffed with carne adovada and topped with guacamole and sour cream, tasty but *muy rico* (very rich). The chicken enchilada is also a nice choice. Meals come with chips and salsa and good sopaipillas. The servers are friendly but elusive.

INEXPENSIVE

Chef du Jour

119 San Pasquale SW. ☎ **505/247-8998.** Menu items lunch $2.50–$7.50; dinner $4–$14. MC, V. Mon–Fri 11am–2pm; Fri–Sat 5:30–8:30pm. ECLECTIC.

This small, quiet, and informal one-room cafe serves elegantly prepared food at very reasonable prices. When I was here recently, I ran into an old friend, who said that when the place first opened, she ate lunch here every day and took home dinner

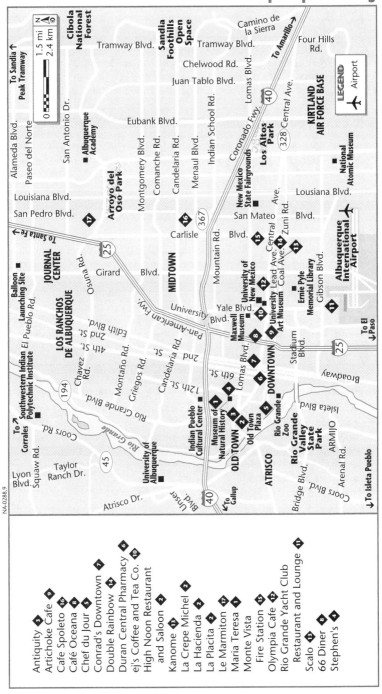

from here at night. She claims that, thus, she didn't cook for a year. The chef confirmed that she was barely exaggerating. The restaurant is a little difficult to find; travel south from the Plaza, cross Lomas and find San Pasquale. Inside, there's an open kitchen along one side and oddly matched tables. Original floral paintings and a red floor make it very bright. Once you get a taste of what's on the menu (which changes every week), you'll be coming back for more. Take special note of the condiments, all of which—from the ketchup to the salsa—are homemade. Recent menu offerings included spicy garlic soup, a great garden burger, green-corn tamales (served with Southwest mango salsa), and marinated fish on a French roll. There is also a salad du jour. Chef du Jour has some outdoor tables. If you call in advance, the restaurant will fax you a copy of their current menu. They're now serving microbrew beers and hard ciders.

Duran Central Pharmacy

1815 Central Ave. NW. ☎ **505-247-4141.** Menu items $4.20–$7.50. No credit cards. Mon–Fri 9am–6:30pm, Sat 9am–2pm. NEW MEXICAN.

Sounds like an odd place to eat, I know. Although you could go to one of the touristy New Mexican restaurants in the middle of Old Town and have lots of atmosphere and mediocre food, you can also come here, where locals eat, and feast. It's a few blocks up Central, east of Old Town. On your way through the pharmacy, you may want to stock up on specialty soaps; there's a pretty good variety here.

The restaurant itself is plain, with a red tile floor and small tables, as well as a counter. For years, I used to come here for a bowl of green chili and a homemade tortilla, which is still an excellent choice. Now I go for the full meals, such as the blue-corn enchilada plate or the huevos rancheros (eggs over corn tortillas, smothered with chili). The menu is short, but you can count on authentic Northern New Mexican food. No smoking is permitted.

La Placita

208 San Felipe St. NW (Old Town Plaza). ☎ **505/247-2204.** Reservations recommended for large parties. Lunch $4.25–$7.25; dinner $6.25–$14.50. AE, DC, DISC, MC, V. Daily 11am–9pm. NEW MEXICAN/AMERICAN.

You won't find many locals frequenting this restaurant; it's a tourist spot, and though the atmosphere is lively, the food is mediocre. It has a nice ambience, though, right on the Plaza. Native American artisans spread their wares on the sidewalk outside the building, which is called the old Casa de Armijo. It was built by a wealthy Hispanic family in the early 18th century. The 283-year-old adobe hacienda, which faces the Old Town Plaza, features hand-carved wooden doorways, deep-sunken windows, and an ancient patio. Fine regional art and furnishings decorate the five dining rooms and an upstairs gallery. You might want to try the Old Town Special (two sopaipillas, one stuffed with chicken, the other with beef, topped with cheese and chili), or the chicken burrito, served with beans and rice. All dishes come with sopaipillas. There is also a variety of beef, chicken, and fish selections.

DOWNTOWN
EXPENSIVE

Stephens

1311 Tijeras Ave. NW (at 14th St. and Central Ave.). ☎ **505/842-1773.** Reservations recommended. Main courses $18.95–$24.95. AE, CB, DISC, MC, V. Mon–Sun 5:30–9:30pm. CONTEMPORARY AMERICAN.

This is the place many Albuquerqueans go to celebrate. My father usually takes me here on my birthday. The decor by noted designer Richard Worthen is very traditional, with lots of fine wood and brass, yet the atmosphere is comfortable, not stuffy. French windows provide a view of lush gardens surrounding a fountain. For an appetizer, I've enjoyed the baked brie with almonds, apples, and honey in a puff pastry as well as the smoked salmon. Entrees include a number of meat dishes as well as some chicken, polenta, and pasta. I'm partial to the steak Diane tenderloin. There's a spa menu, with entrees lower in fat and calories, which is also nice. I enjoy the ruby red trout, grilled, with piñones and julienne vegetables. The award-winning wine list features more than 300 choices. There are daily dessert specials.

MODERATE

✪ Artichoke Café

424 Central Ave. SE. ☎ **505/243-0200.** Reservations recommended. Main courses $9.95–$19.95. AE, DISC, MC, V. Mon–Fri 11am–2:30pm; Mon–Sat 5:30–10pm. CONTINENTAL.

An art gallery as well as a restaurant, this popular near-downtown spot has startling paintings and sculptures set against azure walls, a hint at the innovative dining experience offered here. Set in three rooms, with dim lighting, this is a nice romantic place. The waitstaff is friendly and efficient, though a little slow on a busy night. I was impressed by the list of special drinks available, a variety of interesting waters that included my favorite Ame, as well as ginger beer, Jamaican ice coffee, microbrews, and an excellent list of California and French wines. Of course, you'll want to start with an artichoke; you can have one steamed with three dipping sauces or roasted and stuffed with forest mushrooms and rock shrimp. For lunch, there are a number of salads and gourmet sandwiches, as well as entrees such as flash-fried sea scallops with ginger and lime sauce. Check out the dinner specials. My favorite was a wahoo on glass noodles with a miso broth. From the menu, try the pumpkin ravioli with butternut squash, spinach and ricotta filling with a hazelnut–sage butter sauce with Madeira wine.

THE NORTHEAST HEIGHTS
EXPENSIVE

High Finance Restaurant and Tavern

40 Tramway Rd., NE (atop Sandia Peak). ☎ **505/243-9742.** Reservations requested. Main courses $13.95–$35. Tramway $10 with dinner reservations ($13 without). AE, DC, DISC, MC, V. Summer, daily 4:30–10pm; winter, daily 4:30–8pm. CONTINENTAL.

People don't rave about the food at this restaurant, but they do rave about the experience of eating here. Set high above Albuquerque, at the top of the Sandia Peak Tramway, it offers a fun and romantic adventure. The decor follows the name's theme, with lots of shiny brass and comfortable furniture, and the service is decent. You might start with the sesame fried calamari, served with greens and a Thai dipping sauce. There are a number of pasta dishes, which are nice, or you can try skillet-roasted ahi tuna served with a curry glaze, udon noodles, and stir-fried vegetables. For the meat lovers, there's prime rib or a nice filet. Drinks from a full bar, as well as from a nice wine and beer list, are available.

MODERATE

✪ Cafe Spoleto

2813 San Mateo NE. ☎ **505/880-0897.** Reservations recommended. Main courses $12–$18. Tues–Sat 5:30–9:30pm. AE, DISC, MC, V. MEDITERRANEAN.

Bathed in candlelight, this quiet contemporary restaurant offers one of the best dining experiences in Albuquerque. It's set with simple pine tables accented by subdued modern art, a nice place for a romantic dinner or a night out before theater. Service is friendly and efficient. The menu changes every 2 weeks, so be prepared for some innovation. You might start with bruschetta with grilled pears, caramelized onions, and Gorgonzola or wild mushroom and leek soup. My favorite entree here is the unconventional paella, made with risotto, chicken, Italian sausage, mussels, cranberry beans, and red and gold peppers. The grilled mahimahi is also nice, served with baby beets, rosti potatoes, and green beans.

The County Line

9600 Tramway Blvd. NE. ☎ **505/856-7477.** Reservations not accepted. Main courses $8.95–$14.95. AE, CB, DC, DISC, MC, V. Mon–Thurs 5–9pm, Fri–Sat 5–10pm, Sun 4–9pm. BARBECUE AND STEAKS.

My brother and his wife like to take their kids to this restaurant after visiting the nearby ice-skating rink. The place is popular and doesn't take reservations, but if you call before you leave your hotel, they'll put your name on the waiting list; by the time you get there you'll probably be next in line. If not, you can always wait at the ever-crowded bar. The restaurant is loud and always busy, but it has a spectacular view of the city lights. It's decor is Old Route 66, with wagon-wheel furniture, aged license plates, and cowboy-boot lamps.

When you finally get a table, you'll be given a Big Chief Writing Tablet menu offering great Southwestern barbecue at very reasonable prices. The service is so good it borders on pushy, but it's friendly too. We all like the garlic mashed potatoes, and most of us order the baby back ribs, but there's also a mixed platter that has a spicy sausage. They've also added grilled fish to the menu. A kid's menu, paper and markers, and take-home cups make it a treat for the little ones. If you're not very hungry you should probably consider going somewhere else.

UNIVERSITY & NOB HILL
MODERATE

Kanome: An Asian Diner

3128 Central Ave. SE. ☎ **505/265-7773.** Main courses $4.50–$12.50. AE, MC, V. Mon–Thurs 11am–10pm, Fri 11am–11pm, Sat 4–11pm, Sun 4–10pm. PACIFIC RIM.

I heard friends talk of this new restaurant long before I tried it. The comments on the food were all good, though some joked about the restaurant's theme: "inspired by Asian communal meals" and the way the waiter comes and explains the concept of sharing dishes, as though this were new to an Asian dining experience. But this place is *not* typical. It has a contemporary airy atmosphere with burnished orange walls and wonderful collaged tables: pumpkin seeds, chinese noodles, and vintage post cards embedded in clear plastic. It's not a cozy place, but the service is very friendly and efficient. The food is served with a flair and you eat with fine wooden chopsticks. My favorite is the Balinese skewered pork and cashews. The Chinese duck with Tsing Tao peanut sauce is also tasty. The chef uses free range chicken and organic vegetables. Save room for the homemade ice cream. I tried three flavors and my favorite was the java, but each was excellent.

Monte Vista Fire Station

3201 Central Ave. NE, Nob Hill. ☎ **505/255-2424.** Reservations recommended. Main courses $12.95–$17.95. AE, CB, DC, DISC, MC, V. Mon–Fri 11am–2:30pm; Sun–Thurs 5–10:30pm, Fri–Sat 5–11pm. Bar open to 2am Mon–Sat, to midnight Sun. CONTEMPORARY AMERICAN.

This restaurant is on to a very novel idea. Each month it brings in a chef from a different city. You may savor New Orleans–style Cajun food in April and New

American food with a dash of San Francisco–Asian flavor in July. The setting is unique too. It actually was a fire station, built in Pueblo Revival style in 1936. Now the decor is art deco, a little cold feeling, perhaps, but fun. There are menu standards such as the cornmeal-dusted calamari on wild baby greens with chipotle chile aïoli, a starter. From visiting chef Barbara Miachika from San Francisco, I tried a risotto of sun-dried tomatoes, porcini, and fresh mushrooms, but I've also enjoyed a number of good pastas and chicken or meat dishes. There's fish as well. If you want something simpler, there are sandwiches, including the fire burger, served with caramelized red onions, green chili, and mozzarella cheese on home-baked bread. For dessert, you have to try the Monte Vista chocolate "bombe" with gold leaf and crème Anglaise. There's a popular singles bar on the second-floor landing.

✪ Scalo

3500 Central Ave. SE, Nob Hill. ☎ **505/255-8782.** Reservations recommended. Main courses $7.95–$16.95; lunch $5.75–$9. AE, CB, DC, DISC, MC, V. Mon–Sat 11:30am–2:30pm and 5:30–11:30pm, Sun 5–9pm. Bar Mon–Sat 11am–1am. NORTHERN ITALIAN.

Ask anyone in "Burque" where they go to eat Italian, and they will most likely say Scalo. And with a new chef, in the past year the food has become even better. The place has a simple bistro-style elegance, with white linen-clothed tables indoors, plus outdoor tables in a covered, temperature-controlled patio. The kitchen, which makes its own pasta and breads, specializes in contemporary adaptations of classical Northern Italian cuisine.

Seasonal menus focus on New Mexico–grown produce. Featured appetizers include *calamaretti fritti* (fried baby squid served with a spicy marinara and lemon aïoli) and *caprini con pumante* (local goat cheese with fresh focaccia, capers, tapenade, and a roasted garlic spread). There's a selection of pastas (excellent ravioli) for lunch and dinner, as well as meat, chicken, and fish dishes. The *filetto con salsa balsamica* (grilled filet of beef with rosemary, green peppercorns, garlic, and a balsamic demi glace sauce) is one of my favorites, and the fish specials are worth trying. Dessert selections change daily.

INEXPENSIVE

Double Rainbow

3416 Central Ave. SE. ☎ **505/255-6633.** Reservations not accepted. All menu items under $9. AE, DISC, MC, V. Daily 6:30am–midnight. CAFE/BAKERY.

Albuquerque's literati hang out at this cafe, as do university professors and hippies. They come for the many coffee drinks such as chocolate cappuccino or iced java (made with cream and chocolate), as well as for salads and sandwiches, and to read from a decent selection of magazines and newspapers. In the warm months, people eat on small tables on the sidewalk. Any time of year, the three rooms inside set around a mural of cirrus clouds are often bustling. You'll find soups such as New Mexico chicken and rice or broccoli cheddar, various kinds of quiche, and an incredible huevos rancheros (flour tortilla, black beans, cheese, and home fries). There's a pot roast for the hungry and a schezwan chicken salad for the lighter appetite. For dessert, try one of the elaborate baked goods such as a tricolor mousse with white, milk, and dark chocolate, or sample from a variety of ice-cream flavors. Double Rainbow has another branch at 4501 Juan Tabo NE (☎ **505/275-8311**), which features a large outdoor patio and a slightly more extensive menu.

Olympia Cafe

2210 Central Ave. SE. ☎ **505/266-5222.** Menu items $1.50–$10.25. AE, DC, DISC, MC, V. Mon–Fri 11am–10pm, Sat noon–10pm. GREEK.

Ask any Northern New Mexico resident where they go for Greek food and the hands-down favorite is Olympia. It's very informal (you order at a counter and wait for your number to pick up food), right across from the university, and diners eat there at all times of day. It has a lively atmosphere, with the sound bursts of enthusiastic Greek emanating from the kitchen. With a full carry-out menu, it's also a great place to grab a meal on the run. In the summer months, I like to get the Greek salad, served with fresh pita bread, and white bean soup. A standard is the falafel sandwich with tahini. The restaurant is well known for its gyros (slices of beef and lamb broiled on a vertical spit wrapped in pita), and I hear the moussaka is excellent. For dessert try the baklava.

66 Diner

1405 Central Ave. NE. ☎ **505/247-1421.** www.66diner.com. Menu items $3–$6.99. AE, DISC, MC, V. Mon–Thurs 11am–11pm, Fri 11am–midnight, Sat 8am–midnight, Sun 8am–10pm. AMERICAN.

Like a trip back in time to the days when Martin Milner and George Maharis got "their kicks on Route 66," this thoroughly 1950s-style diner comes complete with Seeburg jukebox and full-service soda fountain. The white caps make great green-chile cheeseburgers, along with meatloaf sandwiches, grilled liver and onions, and chicken-fried steaks. Ham-and-egg and pancake breakfasts are served on weekends. Beer and wine are available.

SOUTHEAST NEAR THE AIRPORT

Rio Grande Yacht Club Restaurant & Lounge

2500 Yale Blvd. SE. ☎ **505/243-6111.** Reservations recommended at dinner. Main courses lunch $5.25–$9.95; dinner $9.95–$32.95. AE, CB, DC, DISC, MC, V. Mon–Fri 11am–2pm; daily 5:30–10:30pm. SEAFOOD.

This is a festive restaurant with decent seafood and steaks. Red, white, and blue sails are draped beneath the skylight of a large room dominated by a tropical garden. The walls, hung with yachting prints and photos, are made of wood strips, like those of a ship's deck. The lunch menu features burgers, sandwiches, salads, and a few New Mexican specialties. At dinner, however, fresh fish is the main attraction. Swordfish, sea scallops, ahi tuna, fresh oysters, and other denizens of the deep are prepared broiled, poached, blackened, teriyaki, Vera Cruz, au gratin, mornay, stuffed, and more. If you'd rather have something else, the chef also prepares certified Angus beef, shrimp, Alaskan king crab, several chicken dishes, and even barbecued baby-back pork ribs. If you find it difficult to choose one of these, you might want to try a steak and seafood combination. The bar here is a good place for evening drinks. You'll hob-nob with flight crews and sample such delicacies as smoked trout and lahvosh (Armenian cracker bread covered with havarti and parmesan, baked until bubbly.) Don't leave without sharing an Aspen snowball (vanilla ice cream rolled in walnuts and covered in hot fudge).

OUT OF TOWN

Prairie Star

1000 Jemez Canyon Dam Rd., Bernalillo. ☎ **505/867-3327.** Reservations recommended. Main courses $14–$26. AE, CB, DC, DISC, MC, V. Sun–Thurs 5–9pm, Fri–Sat 5–10pm (lounge opens at 4pm). CONTEMPORARY REGIONAL.

A new chef has gotten people talking about the food at this elegant restaurant by adding a Native American touch to the cuisine. Located on the Santa Ana Pueblo about 30 minutes north of Albuquerque, the restaurant is set in a 6,000-square-foot sprawling adobe home, with a marvelous view across the high plains and a golf course.

It was built in the 1940s in Mission architectural style. Exposed vigas and full latilla ceilings, as well as hand-carved fireplaces and bancos, complement the thick adobe walls in the dining room. There is a lounge at the top of the circular stairway.

Diners can start with blue-corn crab cakes, with a chile tartar or a variety of salads. For an entree try the salmon paillard, topped with prickly-pear sauce and served with new potatoes. There is a variety of grilled items such as a filet mignon and even a grilled ostrich filet, as well as some New Mexican dishes. Desserts vary nightly.

✪ Range Cafe

925 Camino del Pueblo, Bernalillo. ☎ **505/867-1700.** www.rangecafe.com. No reservations. Breakfast/lunch $2.95–$8.95; dinner $6.50–$19.95. AE, DISC, MC, V. Daily 7:30am until closing (at least 9pm). NEW MEXICAN/AMERICAN.

This cafe on the main drag of Bernalillo, about 15 minutes north of Albuquerque, is a perfect place to stop on your way out of town. However, the food's so good you may just want to make a special trip here. Housed in what was once an old drugstore, the restaurant has tin molding on the ceiling and is decorated with Western touches, such as cowboy boots and period photos. There's a soda fountain in the center of the large space, and all the tables and chairs are hand-painted with whimsical stars and clouds.

The food ranges from New Mexican enchiladas and burritos to chicken-fried steak to sandwiches and elegantly prepared meals. The proprietors here have come from such notable restaurants as Scalo in Albuquerque and Prairie Star on Santa Ana Pueblo, and the chef was quickly nabbed from the Double A in Santa Fe after it closed, so you can count on exquisite food. For breakfast, try the pancakes or the breakfast burrito. For lunch or dinner, I recommend Tom's meatloaf, served with roasted-garlic mashed potatoes, mushroom gravy, and sautéed vegetables. For dinner, you might try Range scallops, with a grilled tomato and cilantro cream sauce with pine nuts over red chile linguine. Taos Cow ice cream is the order for dessert, served in cones or malts, shakes, or sundaes, or try the baked goods and specialty coffees. No smoking is permitted. Next door, the Range has opened a retail space selling local arts and crafts.

5 What to See & Do

Albuquerque's original town site, known today as Old Town, is the central point of interest for visitors. Here, grouped around the Plaza, are the venerable Church of San Felipe de Neri and numerous restaurants, art galleries, and crafts shops. Several important museums are situated close by. Within a few blocks are the recently completed Albuquerque Aquarium and the Rio Grande Botanic Garden (near Central Avenue and Tingley Drive NW). The project includes a 25,000-square-foot aquarium and a 50-acre botanical garden, both well worth the visit.

But don't get stuck in Old Town. Elsewhere you will find the Sandia Peak Tramway, Kirtland Air Force Base and the National Atomic Museum, the University of New Mexico with its museums, and a number of natural attractions. Within day-trip range are several pueblos and a trio of significant monuments (see "Exploring Nearby Pueblos & Monuments," below).

THE TOP ATTRACTIONS

Old Town

Northeast of Central Ave. and Rio Grande Blvd. NW.

A maze of cobbled courtyard walkways leads to hidden patios and gardens, where many of Old Town's 150 galleries and shops are located. Adobe buildings, many refurbished in the Pueblo Revival style of the 1950s, are grouped around the tree-shaded **Plaza,** created in 1780. Pueblo and Navajo artisans often display their pottery, blankets, and silver jewelry on the sidewalks lining the Plaza.

The buildings of Old Town once served as mercantile shops, grocery stores, and government offices, but the importance of Old Town as Albuquerque's commercial center declined after 1880, when the railroad came through 1¼ miles east of the Plaza and businesses relocated to be closer to the trains. Old Town clung to its historical and sentimental roots, but the quarter fell into disrepair until the 1930s and 1940s, when it was rediscovered by artisans and other shop owners, and the tourism industry burgeoned.

When Albuquerque was established in 1706, the first building erected by the settlers was the **Church of San Felipe de Neri,** which faces the Plaza on its north side. It's a cozy church with wonderful stained-glass windows and vivid retablos. This house of worship has been in almost continuous use for about 290 years.

It's sad to see the changes the past 10 years or so have wrought on Old Town shopping. When I was growing up in the area, this was the place to go to buy gifts. Now, many of the interesting shops (such as the basket shop right on the Plaza, which used to be packed with thousands of dusty baskets) have become trinket stores. However, you can still find good buys from the Native Americans selling jewelry on the Plaza. Look especially for silver bracelets and strung turquoise. If you want to take something fun home and spend very little, buy a dyed corn necklace. Your best bet when wandering around Old Town is to just peek into shops, but there are a few places you'll definitely want to spend time in. See the shopping section for a list of recommendations. An excellent Old Town historic walking tour originates at the Albuquerque Museum (see below) at 11am Tuesday through Sunday during spring, summer, and fall.

✪ Indian Pueblo Cultural Center

2401 12th St. NW. ☎ **800/766-4405** or 505/843-7270. Admission $4 adults, $3 seniors, $1 students; free for children 4 and under. Daily 9am–5:30pm; restaurant 7:30am–4pm. Closed Jan 1, Thanksgiving Day, and Dec 25.

Owned and operated as a nonprofit organization by the 19 pueblos of New Mexico, this is a fine place to begin an exploration of Native American culture. Located about a mile northeast of Old Town, this museum—modeled after Pueblo Bonito, a spectacular 9th-century ruin in Chaco Culture National Historic Park—consists of several parts.

Begin your exploration in the basement, where a permanent exhibit depicts the evolution from prehistory to present of the various pueblos, including displays of the distinctive handcrafts of each community. Note especially how pottery differs in concept and design from pueblo to pueblo. You'll also find a small screening room where you can see films of some of New Mexico's most noted Native American artists making their wares, including San Ildefonso potter María Martinez firing her pottery with open flames.

The Pueblo House Children's Museum, located in a separate building, is a hands-on experience that gives children the opportunity to learn about and understand the evolution of Pueblo culture. There they can touch pot sherds, play with heishi (shell) drills, even don fox tails and dance.

Upstairs is an enormous (10,000-square-foot) gift shop featuring fine pottery, rugs, sandpaintings, kachinas, drums, and jewelry, among other things. Southwestern clothing and souvenirs are also available. Prices here are quite reasonable.

Every weekend throughout the year, Native American dancers perform at 11am and 2pm in an outdoor arena surrounded by original murals. Often, artisans

Central Albuquerque Attractions

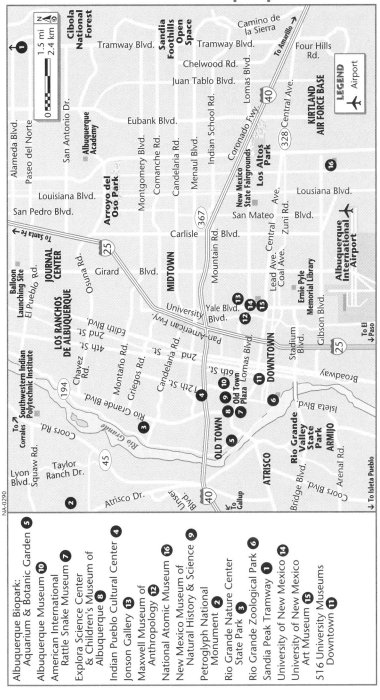

Albuquerque Biopark:
Aquarium & Botanic Garden ⑤
Albuquerque Museum ⑩
American International
Rattle Snake Museum ⑦
Explora Science Center
& Children's Museum of
Albuquerque ⑧
Indian Pueblo Cultural Center ④
Jonson Gallery ⑬
Maxwell Museum of
Anthropology ⑫
National Atomic Museum ⑯
New Mexico Museum of
Natural History & Science ⑨
Petroglyph National
Monument ②
Rio Grande Nature Center
State Park ③
Rio Grande Zoological Park ⑥
Sandia Peak Tramway ①
University of New Mexico ⑭
University of New Mexico
Art Museum ⑮
516 University Museums
Downtown ⑪

demonstrate their crafts expertise there as well. During certain weeks of the year, such as the Balloon Fiesta, dances are performed daily.

A restaurant serves traditional Native American foods. I wouldn't eat a full meal here, but you might want to stop in for some Indian fry bread and a bowl of *posole*.

Albuquerque Museum

2000 Mountain Rd. NW. ☎ **505/243-7255.** Free admission, but donations are appreciated. Tues–Sun 9am–5pm. Closed major holidays.

Take an interesting journey down into the caverns of New Mexico's past in this museum on the outskirts of Old Town. Drawing on the largest U.S. collection of Spanish colonial artifacts, displays here include Don Quixote–style helmets, swords, and even horse armor. You can wander through an 18th-century house compound with adobe floor and walls, and see gear used by *vaqueros*, the original cowboys who came to the area in the 16th century. A weaving exhibition allows kids to try spinning wool, and a trapping section provides them with pelts to touch. In an old-style theater, two films on Albuquerque history are shown. In the History Hopscotch area, kids can explore an old trunk or play with antique blocks and other toys. An Old Town walking tour originates here at 11am Tuesday through Sunday during spring, summer, and fall. In the upper floors there are permanent art collections, and best of all, a huge exhibit space where you'll find some extraordinary shows. The 1999 schedule includes *Imagenes de Oro: Colonial & Modern Images from Guatemala and New Mexico; WPA Photographs; Intermountain Weavers;* and *Impressionism.* A gift shop sells books, jewelry, and has a nice selection of Navajo dolls.

Rio Grande Nature Center State Park

2901 Candelaria Rd. NW. ☎ **505/344-7240.** www.unm.edu/natrcent. E-mail: natrcent@ unm.edu. Admission $1 adults, 50¢ children 6 and older, free for children under 6. Daily 10am–5pm. Closed Jan 1, Thanksgiving, and Dec 25.

Whenever I'm in Albuquerque and want to get away from it all, I come here. The Center, located just a few miles north of Old Town, spans 270 acres of riverside forest and meadows which include stands of 100-year-old cottonwoods and a 3-acre pond. Located on the Rio Grande Flyway, an important migratory route for many birds, it's an excellent place to see sandhill cranes, Canada geese, quail—over 260 species have made this their temporary or permanent home. In a protected area where dogs aren't allowed (you can bring dogs on most of the 2 miles of trails) you'll find exhibits of native grasses, wildflowers, and herbs. Inside a building built half above and half below ground, you can sit next to the pond in a glassed-in viewing area and comfortably watch ducks and other birds in their avian antics. There are 21 self-guided interpretive exhibits as well as photo exhibits, a library, a small nature store, and children's resource room. On Saturday mornings you can join in a guided nature walk. Other weekend programs are available for adults and children including nature photography and bird and wildflower identification classes. Call for a schedule.

See the "Especially for Kids" section for more museums and attractions in the Old Town area.

✪ Sandia Peak Tramway

10 Tramway Loop NE. ☎ **505/856-7325.** www.sandiapeak.com. Admission $14 adults, $10 seniors and children 5–12, free for children under 5. AE, DISC, MC, V. Memorial Day–Labor Day daily 9am–10pm; spring and fall Thurs–Tues 9am–8pm, Wed 5–8pm; ski season Mon–Tues and Thurs–Fri 9am–8pm, Wed noon–8pm, Sat–Sun 8:30am–8pm. To reach the base of the tram, take I-25 north to Tramway Rd. (exit 234), then proceed east about 5 miles on Tramway Rd. (NM 556); or take Tramway Blvd., exit 167 (NM 556), north of I-40 approximately 8½ miles. Turn east the last half mile on Tramway Rd.

This is a fun and exciting half-day or evening outing, allowing incredible views of the Albuquerque landscape and wildlife. The Sandia Peak Tram is a "jigback"; in other words, as one car approaches the top, the other nears the bottom. The two pass halfway through the trip, in the midst of a 1½-mile "clear span" of unsupported cable between the second tower and the upper terminal.

Several hiking trails are available on Sandia Peak and one of them—La Luz Trail—is partly flat and quite easy. The views in all directions are extraordinary. *Note:* The trails on Sandia may not be suitable for children.

There is a popular and expensive restaurant, High Finance Restaurant & Tavern, at Sandia's summit, (see "Where to Dine," earlier in this chapter). Special tram rates apply with dinner reservations.

OTHER ATTRACTIONS

✪ National Atomic Museum

Wyoming Blvd. and K St. (P.O. Box 5800), Kirtland Air Force Base. ☎ **505/284-3243.** www.sandia.gov/AtomMus/AtomMus.htm. Admission $2 adults, $1 children 7–18 and seniors, free for children 6 and under. Visitors must obtain passes (and a map) at the Wyoming or Gibson Gate of the base. Children under 12 not admitted without parent or adult guardian. Daily 9am–5pm. Closed Jan 1, Easter, Thanksgiving, Dec 25.

"I am become death, the shatterer of worlds." Shortly after the successful detonation of the first atomic bomb, Robert Oppenheimer, who headed the Manhattan Project, said this, quoting from ancient Hindu texts. This and other valuable information highlight the 51-minute film *Ten Seconds That Shook the World,* which is shown daily at 10:30 and 11:30am, and 2 and 3pm at this museum, an experience worth fitting into a busy schedule. The museum itself offers the next-best introduction to the nuclear age after the Bradbury Science Museum in Los Alamos. The film has lots of actual footage from the days of the race to build the first nuclear weapon, and though it does present a quite positive view of the bombing of Japan, viewers really get a sense of the historical context within which the decision was made.

The museum itself makes for an interesting hour to 2 hour perusal. It traces the history of nuclear weapons development beginning with the top-secret Manhattan Project of the 1940s, including a copy of the letter Albert Einstein wrote to President Franklin D. Roosevelt suggesting the possible need to beat the Germans at creating an atomic bomb—a letter which surprisingly went ignored for nearly 2 years.

You'll find a permanent Marie Curie exhibit in the lobby and full-scale models of the "Fat Man" and "Little Boy" bombs, as well as displays and films on the peaceful application of nuclear technology and other alternative energy sources. Fusion is explained in a manner that laypeople can understand; other exhibits deal with the use and development of robotics, with plenty of strange R-2, D-2 types moving around for kids to enjoy. Outdoor exhibits include a B-52 "Stratofortress," an F-105D "Thunderchief," and a 280mm atomic cannon. The museum is directly across the street from the Interservice Nuclear Weapons School—do you think they offer summer courses?—adjacent to Sandia National Laboratory.

Petroglyph National Monument

6001 Unser Blvd. NW (west of Coors Rd.). ☎ **505/899-0205.** Admission $1 per vehicle weekdays, $2 weekends. MC, V. Summer, daily 9am–6pm; winter, daily 8am–5pm. Visitor center daily 8am–5pm. Closed Jan 1 and Dec 25.

In the past few years this monument has made national news, and for good reason; a struggle has raged in Congress over whether or not to allow a road through these lava flows that were once a hunting and gathering area for prehistoric Native Americans, who left a chronicle of their beliefs etched on the dark basalt boulders. The issue is heated not only because such a road would disturb the 15,000 petroglyphs, but also because it would set a precedent that might allow roads through other national monuments around the country. One ranger said he sees Albuquerque expanding so fast that the monument is "like a speed bump in the development of the West Mesa." It's a sad, but true analogy. History-in-progress aside, this place is worth visiting, a nice outdoor adventure after a morning in a museum. You'll want to stop at the visitor center to get a map, check out the new interactive computer, and, in summer, hook up with a ranger-led tour. From there, drive north to the Boca Negra area where you'll have a choice of three trails. Take the Mesa Point Trail (30 minutes) that climbs quickly up the side of a hill offering many petroglyph sightings as well as an outstanding view of the Sandia Mountains. If you're traveling with your dog, you can bring her along on the Rinconada Trail. It's fun because hikers have to search the rocks more for the petroglyphs, and there are many to be found. This trail (located a few miles south of the visitor center) runs for miles around a huge *rincon* (corner) at the base of the lava flow. Camping is not permitted in the park; it's strictly for day use, with picnic areas, drinking water, and rest rooms provided.

University of New Mexico

Yale Blvd. NE (north of Central Ave.). ☎ **505/277-0111.**

The state's largest institution of higher learning stretches across an attractive 70-acre campus about 2 miles east of downtown Albuquerque, north of Central Avenue and east of University Boulevard. The five campus museums, none of which charges admission, are constructed (like other UNM buildings) in a modified Pueblo style. Popejoy Hall, in the south-central part of the campus, hosts many performing-arts presentations, including those of the New Mexico Symphony Orchestra; other public events are held in nearby Keller Hall and Woodward Hall.

I've found the best way to see the museums and parts of the campus is on a walking tour which can make for a nice 2- to 3-hour morning or afternoon outing. Begin on the west side of campus at the Maxwell. You'll find parking meters there, as well as Maxwell Museum parking for which you can get a permit inside.

The **Maxwell Museum of Anthropology,** situated on the west side of the campus on Redondo Drive at Ash Street NE (☎ 505/277-4404), is an internationally acclaimed repository of Southwestern anthropological finds. What's really intriguing here is not just the ancient pottery, tools, and yucca weavings, but the anthropological context within which these items are set. You'll see a reconstruction of an archaeological site complete with string markers, brushes, and field notes, as well as microscope lenses you can examine to see how archaeologists perform temper analysis to find out where pots were made, and pollen analysis to help reconstruct past environments. It's open Tuesday to Friday from 9am to 4pm, Saturday from 10am to 4pm, and Sunday from noon to 4pm; closed holidays. From the Maxwell, walk east into the campus until you come to the Duck Pond and pass Mitchell Hall; then, turn south (right) and walk down a lane until you reach Northrup Hall.

In Northrup Hall (☎ 505/277-4204), about halfway between the Maxwell Museum and Popejoy Hall in the southern part of the campus, the adjacent **Geology Museum** (☎ 505/277-4204) and **Meteorite Museum** (☎ 505/277-1644) cover the gamut of recorded time from dinosaur bones to moon rocks. Within the Geology Museum, you'll see stones that create spectacular works of art, from little black-on-white orbs of orbicular granite to the brilliant blue of dioptase. In the Meteorite Museum, 550 meteorite specimens comprise the sixth-largest collection in the United States. You'll see and touch a sink-sized piece of a meteorite that weighs as much as a car, as well as samples of the many variations of stones that fall from the sky. The Geology Museum is open Monday to Friday from 7:30am to noon and 1 to 4:30pm; the Meteorite Museum, Monday to Friday from 9am to noon and 1 to 4pm.

Right next door and to the south, in the basement of the Biology Department at Castetter Hall, the **Museum of Southwestern Biology,** (☎ 505/277-4392), is a working research museum. In order to see it you need a reservation. It has extensive research holdings of global flora and fauna, especially representative of Southwestern North America, Central America, South America, and parts of Asia.

From here, you walk east straight through a mall that will take you by the art building to the Fine Arts Center.

The **University of New Mexico Art Museum** (☎ **505/277-4001**) is located here, just north of Central Avenue and Cornell Street. The museum features changing exhibitions of 19th- and 20th-century art. Its permanent collection includes Old Masters paintings and sculpture, significant New Mexico artists, Spanish colonial artwork, the Tamarind Lithography Archives, and one of the largest university-owned photography collections in the country. This is my favorite part. You'll see modern and contemporary works, images that will remain in your psyche for years. It's open Tuesday to Friday from 9am to 4pm; Tuesday evening from 5 to 8pm; and Sunday from 1 to 4pm; closed holidays. A gift shop offers a variety of gifts and posters. Admission is free.

By now you'll probably want a break. Across the mall to the north is the Student Union Building, where you can get anything from muffins to pizza. Campus maps can be obtained here, along with directions. Once you're refreshed, head out the north door of the SUB and walk west through Smith Plaza, then turn north by the bus stop to Las Lomas Road, where you'll turn right and walk a half block to the intimate **Jonson Gallery,** at 1909 Las Lomas Blvd. NE (☎ **505/277-4967**), on the north side of the central campus. This museum displays more than 2,000 works by the late Raymond Jonson, a leading modernist painter in early 20th-century New Mexico, as well as works by contemporary artists. This is my least favorite of the campus museums, so if you're going to miss one, make it this one. The gallery is open Tuesday to Friday from 9am to 4pm and Tuesday evening from 5 to 8pm.

From the Jonson you can walk west on Las Lomas to Redondo Road, where you'll turn south and arrive back at the Maxwell where your car is parked. If you have the time, drive straight down Central to a branch of the University of New Mexico's Art Museum, **516 University Museums Downtown** (☎ **505/ 242-8244**), at 516 Central Ave. SW. Its two floors of exhibition space feature changing exhibitions drawn from art and anthropological collections of the University Art Museum and Maxwell Museum of Anthropology, as well as works by significant New Mexico and regional artists. Gallery talks, lectures, and demonstrations are featured regularly. It's open Tuesday to Saturday from 11am to 4pm (closed holidays). There is a gift shop offering cards, posters, jewelry, and art gift items. Admission is free.

Once you leave there, step next door to **Skip Maisel's,** (see "Shopping," below) where, adorning the outside of the store, there are murals painted in 1933 by notable Navajo painter Harrison Begay and Pueblo painter Pablita Velarde.

COOKING SCHOOLS

If you've fallen in love with New Mexican and Southwestern cooking during your stay (or even before you arrived), you might like to sign up for cooking classes with Jane Butel, a leading Southwest cooking authority and author of 14 cookbooks. At **Jane Butel's Cooking School,** 125 Second St. NW (La Posada de Albuquerque), (☎ **800/472-8229** or 505/243-2622; fax 505/243-8297), you'll learn the history and techniques of Southwestern cuisine and have ample opportunity for hands-on preparation. If you choose the weeklong session, you'll start by learning about chiles. The second and third days you'll try your hand at native breads and dishes, the fourth focuses on more innovative dishes, and the fifth and last day covers appetizers, beverages, and desserts. Weekend sessions are also available. Call or fax for current schedules and fees.

6 Especially for Kids

✪ Albuquerque Bio Park: Aquarium and Botanic Garden

2601 Central Ave. NW. ☎ **505/764-6200.** Admission $2.50 for ages 3–5 and over 65; $4.50 for ages 16–64. Daily 9am–4:30pm; Sat–Sun during June, July, and August 9am–6pm. Ticket sales stop at 4:30pm to allow time to view the facilities. Closed Jan 1, Thanksgiving, and Dec 25.

For those of us born and raised in the desert, this attraction quenches years of soul thirst. The self-guided aquarium tour begins with a beautifully produced 9-minute film that describes the course of the Rio Grande River from its origin to the Gulf Coast. Then, you'll move on to the touch pool, where at certain times of day children can gently touch hermit crabs and starfish. You'll pass by a replica of a salt marsh, where a gentle tidal wave moves in and out, and you'll explore the eel tank, through which you get to walk since it's an arched aquarium over your path. There's a colorful coral-reef exhibit, as well as the culminating show, in a 285,000-gallon shark tank, where many species of fish and 15 to 20 sand tiger, brown, and nurse sharks swim around looking ominous.

Within a state-of-the-art 10,000-square-foot conservatory, you'll find the botanical garden split into two sections. The smaller one houses the desert collection and features plants from the lower Chihuahuan and Sonoran deserts, including unique species from Baja California. The larger pavilion exhibits the Mediterranean collection and includes many exotic species native to the Mediterranean climates of southern California, South Africa, Australia, and the Mediterranean Basin. Allow at least 2 hours to see both parks. There is a restaurant on the premises.

American International Rattlesnake Museum

202 San Felipe St. NW. ☎ **505/242-6569.** Admission $2 adults, $1 children. AE, DISC, MC, V. Daily 10am–6:30pm.

This unique museum, located just off Old Town Plaza, has living specimens of common, uncommon, and very rare rattlesnakes of North, Central, and South America in naturally landscaped habitats. Oddities such as albino and patternless rattlesnakes are included, as is a display popular with youngsters—baby rattlesnakes. More than 30 species can be seen, followed by a 7-minute film on this contributor to the ecological balance of our hemisphere. Throughout the museum are rattlesnake artifacts from early American history, Native American culture, medicine, the arts, and advertising.

You'll also find a gift shop that specializes in Native American jewelry, T-shirts, and other memorabilia related to the natural world and the Southwest, all with an emphasis on rattlesnakes.

Explora Science Center and Children's Museum of Albuquerque

800 Rio Grande Blvd. NW, Suite 10. ☎ **505/842-1537.** Admission $4 ages 13–64, $2 ages 3–12 and 65 or over, and free for children 2 and under. Tues–Sat 9am–4pm, Sun noon–5pm.

At this exploration center there's something for everyone: bubbles, whisper disks, a puppet theater, a giant loom, a dress-up area, zoetropes, a capture-your-shadow wall, art activities, science demonstrations, and a giant pin-hole camera. The museum also sponsors wonderful educational workshops. "The Me I Don't Always See" was a health exhibit designed to teach children about the mysteries of the human body, and a Great Artists Series featured live performances about artists' lives and work followed by a related art activity. You'll also find hands-on science and technology exhibits. Kids will learn about air pressure by flying a model plane and floating a ball on a stream of air. A new facility is planned to open in 2000 at 18th Street and Mountain.

✪ New Mexico Museum of Natural History and Science

1801 Mountain Rd. NW. ☎ **505/841-2800.** Admission $5.25 adults, $4.20 seniors, $2.10 children 3–11. Museum and Dynamax, $8.40 adults, $6.30 seniors, $3.15 children 3–11. Children under 12 must be accompanied by an adult. MC, V. Daily 9am–5pm. Closed non-holiday Mon in Jan and Sept, and Dec 25.

A trip through this museum will take you through 12 billion years of natural history, from the formation of the universe to the present day. Begin looking at a display of stones and gems, then stroll through the "Age of Giants" display, where you'll find dinosaur skeletons cast from the real bones. As you walk beneath an allosaurus, stegosaurus, and others, you can examine real teeth and even feel the weight and texture of a real bone. Moving along, you come into the Cretaceous Period and learn of the progression of flooding in the Southwestern United States beginning 100 million years ago and continuing until 66 million years ago, when New Mexico became dry. This exhibit takes you through a tropical oasis, with aquariums of alligator gars, fish that were here 100 million years ago and still exist today. Next, step into the Evolator (kids love this!), a simulated time-travel ride that moves and rumbles taking you 2,000 meters up (or down) and through 38 million years of history. Then, you'll feel the air grow hot as you walk into a cave and see the inner workings of a volcano including simulated magma flow. Soon, you'll find yourself in the age of the mammoths, and moving through the ice age. Other stops along the way include a Naturalist Center, where kids can peek through microscopes and make their own bear or raccoon footprints in sand, and Fossilworks, where real archaeologists work behind glass excavating bones of a seismosaurus. Don't miss the computer-generated sound of a parasaurolophus nearby. For an additional charge, the Dynamax theater surrounds you with images and sound. And look for the large new space accommodating traveling exhibitions. A gift shop on the ground floor sells imaginative nature games and other curios. This museum has good access for people with disabilities, including scripts for people who have hearing impairment, and exhibit text written in braille.

Rio Grande Zoological Park

903 10th St. SW. ☎ **505/764-6200.** Admission $4.25 adults, $2.25 children and seniors, free for children 2 and under. Children under 12 must be accompanied by an adult. Daily 9am–4:30pm, and on summer weekends until 6pm. Closed Jan 1, Thanksgiving, Dec. 25.

More than 1,200 animals from 300 species live on 60 acres of riverside bosque among ancient cottonwoods. Open-moat exhibits with animals in naturalized habitats are a treat for zoo-goers. Major exhibits include the polar bears, giraffes, sea lions (with underwater viewing), the cat walk, the bird show, and ape country with its gorilla and orangutans. The zoo has an especially fine collection of elephants, mountain lions, koalas, reptiles, and native Southwestern species. A children's petting zoo is open during the summer. There are numerous snack bars on the zoo grounds, and La Ventana Gift Shop carries film and souvenirs.

7 Outdoor Activities

BALLOONING Visitors not content to just watch the colorful craft rise into the clear-blue skies have a choice of several hot-air balloon operators; rates start at about $130 per person per hour: **Braden's Balloons Aloft,** 3900 Second St. NW (☎ 505/345-6199); **Rainbow Ryders,** 10305 Nita Place NE (☎ 505/293-0000); and **World Balloon Corporation,** 4800 Eubank Blvd. NE (☎ 505/293-6800).

The annual **Kodak Albuquerque International Balloon Fiesta** is held the first through second weekends of October (see "Frommer's Favorite Northern New Mexico Experiences," in chapter 1, and "Northern New Mexico Calendar of Events," in chapter 2, for details).

BIKING Albuquerque is a major bicycling hub in the summer, both for road racers and mountain bikers. Bikes can be rented from **Rio Mountain Sport,** 1210 Rio Grande NW (☎ 505/766-9970), and they come with helmets, maps, and locks. A great place to bike is Sandia Peak in Cíbola National Forest. You can't take your bike on the tram, but chairlift no. 1 is available for up- or downhill transportation with a bike. If you'd rather not rent a bike from the above-mentioned sports store, bike rentals are available at the top and bottom of the chairlift. The lift ride one-way with a bike is $7; all day with a bike will cost you $12. Helmets are mandatory. Bike maps are available; the clearly marked trails range from easy to very difficult. Mountain Bike Challenge Events are held on Sandia Peak in May, July, August, and September.

Down in the valley, there's a bosque trail that runs along the Rio Grande and is easily accessible to Old Town and the Biopark. To the east, the Foothills Trail runs along the base of the mountains. Across the Rio Grande, on the west mesa, Petroglyph National Park is a nice place to ride. If you're looking for more technical mountain biking, head up through Tijeras Canyon to Cedro Peak. For information about other mountain-bike areas, contact the Albuquerque Convention and Visitors Bureau. See "Orientation," above.

BIRD WATCHING **Bosque del Apache National Wildlife Refuge** (☎ 505/835-1828) is a haven for migratory waterfowl such as snow geese and cranes. It's located 90 miles south of Albuquerque on I-25, and is well worth the drive. You'll find 7,000 acres of carefully managed riparian habitat, which include marshlands, meadows, agricultural fields, and old-growth cottonwood forests lining the Rio Grande River. Particularly if you're here from November through March, the experience is thrilling, not only for the variety of birds—over 300 species—but for the sheer numbers of them. Huge clouds of snow geese and sandhill cranes take flight at dawn and dusk, the air filling with the sounds of their calls and wing flaps. In early December, the refuge may harbor as many as 45,000 snow geese, 57,000 ducks of many different species, and 18,000 sandhill cranes. You may even be fortunate enough—as I was on my last visit—to see a whooping crane or two. There are also plenty of raptors about including numerous red-tailed hawks and northern harriers (sometimes called marsh hawks), Cooper's hawks and kestrels, and even bald and golden eagles. The refuge has a 15-mile auto-tour loop, which you should drive very slowly. The southern half of the loop travels past numerous water impoundments, where the majority of the ducks and geese are, and the northern half has the meadows and farmland, where you'll see roadrunners and other landbirds, and where the cranes and geese feed from mid-morning through the afternoon.

FISHING   There are no real fishing opportunities in Albuquerque as such, but there is a nearby fishing area known as **Shady Lakes.** Nestled among cottonwood trees, it's located near I-25 on Albuquerque's north side. The most common catches are rainbow trout, black bass, bluegill, and channel catfish. To reach Shady Lakes, take I-25 north to the Tramway exit. Follow Tramway Road west for a mile and then go right on NM 313 for a half mile. Call ☎ **505/898-2568** for information. **Sandia Lakes Recreational Area** (☎ **505/897-3971**), also located on NM 313, is another popular fishing spot. There is a bait and tackle shop there.

GOLF   There are quite a few public courses in the Albuquerque area. The **Championship Golf Course at the University of New Mexico,** 3601 University Blvd. SE (☎ **505/277-4546**), is one of the best in the Southwest and was rated one of the country's top-25 public links by *Golf Digest.* **Paradise Hills Golf Course,** 10035 Country Club Lane NW (☎ **505/898-7001**), is a popular 18-hole golf course that has recently been completely renovated.

Other Albuquerque courses to check with for tee times are **Ladera,** 3401 Ladera Dr. NW (☎ **505/836-4449**); **Los Altos,** 9717 Copper Ave. NE (☎ **505/298-1897**); **Puerto del Sol,** 1800 Girard Blvd. SE (☎ **505/265-5636**); and **Arroyo del Oso,** 6401 Osuna Rd. NE (☎ **505/888-8115**).

If you're willing to drive a short distance just outside Albuquerque, you can play at the **Santa Ana Golf Club at Santa Ana Pueblo,** 288 Prairie Star Rd. (P.O. Box 1736), Bernalillo, NM 87004 (☎ **505/867-9464**), which was rated by the *New York Times* as one of the best public golf courses in the country. Rentals are available (call for information), and greens fees range from $29 to $35.

In addition, **Isleta Pueblo,** 4001 Hwy. 47, has recently completed building an 18-hole golf course (☎ **505/869-0950**).

HIKING   The 1.6-million-acre **Cíbola National Forest** offers ample hiking opportunities. In the Sandia Ranger District alone there are 16 recreation sites, including Sandia Crest, though only Cedro Peak allows overnight camping. For details, contact **Sandia Ranger Station,** NM 337 south toward Tijeras (☎ **505/281-3304**).

Elena Gallegos/Albert G. Simms Park, near the base of the Sandia Peak Tramway at 1700 Tramway Blvd. NE (☎ **505/768-5300**), is a 640-acre mountain picnic area with hiking-trail access to the Sandia Mountain Wilderness.

HORSEBACK RIDING   There are a couple of places in Albuquerque that offer guided or unguided horseback rides. At **Sandia Trails Horse Rentals,** 10601 N. 4th St. (☎ **505/898-6970**), you'll have the opportunity to ride on Sandia Indian Reservation land along the Rio Grande. The horses are friendly and are accustomed to children. In addition, **Turkey Track Stables, Inc.,** 1306 US 66 E. Tijeras (☎ **505/281-1772**), located about 15 miles east of Albuquerque, offers rides on trails in the Manzano foothills.

RIVER RAFTING   This sport is generally practiced farther north, in the area surrounding Santa Fe and Taos.

In mid-May each year, the **Great Race** takes place on a 7.5-mile stretch of the Rio Grande through Albuquerque. Many categories of craft, including rafts, kayaks, canoes, and homemade craft, race down the river. Call ☎ **505/768-3483** for details.

SKIING   The **Sandia Peak Ski Area** is a good place for family skiing. There are plenty of beginner and intermediate runs. However, if you're looking for more challenge or more variety, you'd better head north to Santa Fe or Taos. The ski area has twin base-to-summit chairlifts to its upper slopes at 10,360 feet and a 1,700-foot vertical drop. There are 30 runs (35% beginner, 55% intermediate, 10% advanced) above the day lodge and ski-rental shop. Four chairs and two pomas accommodate 3,400 skiers an hour. All-day lift tickets are $34 for adults, $25 for children and seniors (age 62 and over), and free for those age 72 and over; rental packages are $15 for adults, $12 for kids. The season runs from mid-December to mid-March. Contact **10 Tramway Loop NE** (☎ **505/242-9133**) for more information, or call the hotline for ski conditions (☎ **505/857-8977**).

Cross-country skiers can enjoy the trails of the Sandia Wilderness from the ski area, or they can go an hour north to the remote Jemez Wilderness and its hot springs.

TENNIS   There are 29 public parks in Albuquerque with tennis courts. Because of the city's size, your best bet is to call the Albuquerque Convention and Visitors Bureau to find out which park is closest to your hotel. See "Orientation," in this chapter.

8 Spectator Sports

BASEBALL   The Albuquerque Dukes, 1994 champions of the Class AAA Pacific Coast League, are a farm team of the Los Angeles Dodgers. They play 72 home games from mid-April to early September in the city-owned 10,500-seat Albuquerque Sports Stadium, 1601 Stadium Blvd. SE (at University Boulevard; ☎ **505/243-1791**).

BASKETBALL   The University of New Mexico team, nicknamed "The Lobos," plays an average of 16 home games from late November to early March. Capacity crowds cheer the team at the 17,121-seat University Arena (fondly called "The Pit") at University and Stadium boulevards. The arena was the site of the National Collegiate Athletic Association championship tournament in 1983.

FOOTBALL   The UNM Lobos football team plays a September-to-November season, usually with five home games, at the 30,000-seat University of New Mexico Stadium, opposite both Albuquerque Sports Stadium and University Arena at University and Stadium boulevards.

HORSE RACING   The **Downs at Albuquerque,** New Mexico State Fairgrounds (☎ **505/266-5555** for post times), is near Lomas and Louisiana boulevards NE. Racing and betting—on thoroughbreds and quarter horses—take place on weekends from October to December and during the state fair in September. The Downs has a glass-enclosed grandstand, exclusive club seating, valet parking, and complimentary racing programs and tip sheets. General admission is free; reserved second-floor seating is $2.

9 Shopping

Visitors seeking regional specialties will find many local artists and galleries of interest, although neither group is as concentrated as in Santa Fe and Taos. The galleries and regional fashion designers around the Plaza in Old Town comprise a kind of a shopping center for tourists, with more than 40 merchants represented. The Sandia Pueblo runs its own crafts market at the reservation off I-25 at Tramway Road, just beyond Albuquerque's northern city limits.

Albuquerque has three of the largest shopping malls in New Mexico, two within 2 blocks of each other on Louisiana Boulevard just north of I-40—Coronado Center and Winrock Center. The other is on the west mesa at 10,000 Coors Blvd. NW (☎ **505/899-SHOP**).

Business hours vary, but shops are generally open Monday to Saturday from 10am to 6pm; many have extended hours; some have reduced hours; and a few, especially in shopping malls or during the high tourist season, are open on Sunday.

The Albuquerque sales tax is 5.5625%.

BEST BUYS

The best buys in Albuquerque are Southwestern regional items, including **arts and crafts** of all kinds—traditional Native American and Hispanic as well as contemporary works. In local Native American art, look for silver and turquoise jewelry, pottery, weavings, baskets, sand paintings, and Hopi kachina dolls. Hispanic folk art—handcrafted furniture, tinwork and retablos, and religious paintings—is worth seeking out. The best contemporary art is in paintings, sculpture, jewelry, ceramics, and fiber art, including weaving.

Other items of potential interest are fashions in Southwestern print designs; gourmet foods/ingredients, including blue-corn flour and chile ristras; and unique regional souvenirs, especially local Native American and Hispanic creations.

By far the greatest concentration of **galleries** is in Old Town; others are spread around the city, with smaller groupings in the university district and the northeast heights. Consult the brochure published by the Albuquerque Gallery Association, "A Select Guide to Albuquerque Galleries," or Wingspread Communications' annual *The Collector's Guide to Albuquerque,* widely distributed at shops. Once a month, usually from 5 to 9pm on the third Friday, the Albuquerque Art Business Association (☎ 505/842-9918 for information) sponsors an **ArtsCrawl** to dozens of galleries and studios. If you're in town, it's a great way to meet the artists.

You'll find some interesting shops in the Nob Hill area, which is just west of the University of New Mexico. This whole area has an art deco feel.

ARTS & CRAFTS

Amapola Gallery
2045 S. Plaza St. NW (Old Town). ☎ 505-/242-4311.

Fifty artists and craftspeople show their talents at this lovely cooperative gallery off a cobbled courtyard. You'll find pottery, paintings, textiles, carvings, baskets, jewelry, and other items.

La Piñata
No. 2 Patio Market (Old Town). ☎ 505/242-2400.

This shop features what else?—piñatas, in shapes from dinosaurs to parrots to pigs, as well as paper flowers, puppets, toys, and crushable bolero hats decorated with ribbons.

Mariposa Gallery
113 Romero St. NW (Old Town). ☎ 505/842-9097.

Fine contemporary crafts, including fiber arts, jewelry, clay works, sculptural glass, and other media, are sold here.

Mineral and Fossil Gallery
2011 Mountain Rd. NW, Suite E-1 (San Felipe Plaza, Old Town). ☎ 800/354-6213 or 505/843-8297.

A great place to find natural art, from fossils to geodes to cave-bear skeletons.

✪ Skip Maisel's
510 Central Ave. SW. ☎ 505/242-6526.

If you want a real bargain in Native American arts and crafts this is the place to shop. You'll find a broad range of quality and price here in goods such as pottery, weavings, and kachinas. Take note! Adorning the outside of the store are murals painted in 1933 by notable Navajo painter Harrison Begay and Pueblo painter Pablita Velarde.

Tanner Chaney Galleries
410 Romero NW (Old Town). ☎ **800/444-2242** or 505/247-2242.

In business since 1875, this gallery has fine jewelry, pottery, and rugs.

BOOKS

Borders Books and Music
Winrock Center, 2100 Louisiana Blvd. NE. ☎ **505/884-7711.**

With close to 200 stores nationwide, this chain provides a broad range of books, music, and videos, and hosts in-store appearances by authors, musicians, and artists.

Bookstar
2201 Louisiana Blvd. NE. ☎ **505/883-2644.**

Pick a title, any title, and this 18,000-square-foot store, owned by Barnes and Noble, is likely to have it—probably at a discounted price.

Barnes & Noble
3701 Ellison Dr. NW #A. ☎ **505/792-4234.**

On the west side, just north of Cottonwood Mall, this huge bookstore offers plenty of browsing room and a Starbucks Cafe for lounging. The store is known for its large children's section and weekly story-time readings.

FOOD

The Candy Lady
524 Romero NW (Old Town). ☎ **800/214-7731** or 505/243-6239. www.thecandylady.com.

Making chocolate for over 18 years, The Candy Lady is especially known for 21 varieties of fudge, including jalapeño flavor.

SOUTHWESTERN APPAREL

Albuquerque Pendleton
1100 San Mateo NE, Suite 4. ☎ **505/255-6444.**

Cuddle up within a large selection of blankets and shawls, and haul them away in a handbag.

Jeanette's Originals
205-B San Felipe NW (Old Town). ☎ **505/842-1093.**

Stop by here for those all-important, matching mother-daughter fashions, as well as men's Navajo and ribbon shirts. You'll also find velvet broomstick skirts and denim skirts and tops.

10   Albuquerque After Dark

Albuquerque has an active performing-arts and nightlife scene, as befits a city of half a million people. As also befits this area, the performing arts are multicultural, with Hispanic and (to a lesser extent) Native American productions sharing stage space with Anglo works, including theater, opera, symphony, and dance. Albuquerque also attracts many national touring companies. Country music predominates in nightclubs, though aficionados of rock, jazz, and other forms of music can find them here as well.

Complete information on all major cultural events can be obtained from the **Albuquerque Convention and Visitors Bureau** (☎ 800/284-2282 for recorded information after 5pm). Current listings appear in the two daily newspapers; detailed weekend arts calendars can be found in the Thursday evening *Tribune* and the Friday morning *Journal*. The monthly *On the Scene* also carries entertainment listings.

Tickets for nearly all major entertainment and sporting events can be obtained from TicketMaster, 4004 Carlisle Blvd. NE (☎ 505/884-0999). Discount tickets are often available for midweek and matinee performances. Check with specific theaters or concert halls.

THE PERFORMING ARTS
CLASSICAL MUSIC

Chamber Orchestra of Albuquerque
2730 San Pedro Dr. NE, Suite H-23. ☎ **505/881-0844.** www.aosys.com/coa. Tickets $14–$25, depending on seating and performance.

This 32-member professional orchestra performs from September to June, primarily at St. John's United Methodist Church, 2626 Arizona St. NE. There is a subscription series of seven classical concerts. The orchestra regularly features guest artists of national and international renown.

New Mexico Ballet Company
4200 Wyoming Blvd. NE, Suite B (P.O. Box 21518). ☎ **505/292-4245.** www.mandala.net/nmballet. Tickets $15`–$25 adults, half-price for children under 12 and students.

Founded in 1972, the state's oldest ballet company performs two or three times a year at Popejoy Hall. Typically there is a fall production such as *The Legend of Sleepy Hollow*, a December performance of *The Nutcracker* or *A Christmas Carol*, and a contemporary spring production.

New Mexico Symphony Orchestra
3301 Menaul Blvd. NE, Suite 4. ☎ **800/251-6676** for tickets and information, or 505/881-9590. Ticket prices vary with concert; call for details.

My first introduction to symphony was with the NMSO. Though I didn't quite understand the novelty of hearing live symphony, I loved picking out the distinct sounds and following as they melded together. The NMSO first played in 1932 (long before I attended, thank you), and has continued as a strong cultural force throughout the state. The symphony performs classics and pops, family and neighborhood concerts. It plays for more than 20,000 grade school students and visits communities throughout the state in its annual tour program. Concert venues are generally Popejoy Hall on the University of New Mexico campus, the Albuquerque productions are staged for three consecutive weekends, including some Sunday matinees.

Albuquerque Little Theatre

224 San Pasquale Ave. SW. ☎ **505/242-4750.** Tickets $9–$13. Box office Mon–Fri 12–6pm.

The Albuquerque Little Theatre has been offering a variety of productions ranging from comedies to dramas to musicals since 1930. Six plays are presented here annually during a September-to-May season. Located across from Old Town, Albuquerque Little Theatre offers plenty of free parking.

La Compañía de Teatro de Albuquerque

P.O. Box 884, Albuquerque, NM 87103-0884. ☎ **505/242-7929.** Tickets $9 adults, $7 students ages 18 and above and seniors, $6 children under 18.

Productions given by the company can provide a focused view into New Mexico culture. One of the few major professional Hispanic companies in the United States and Puerto Rico, La Compañía stages a series of bilingual productions (most original New Mexican works) every year from late September through May. Comedies, dramas, and musicals are offered, along with an occasional Spanish-language play. Performances take place in the KiMo Theater (see above), South Broadway Cultural Center (1025 Broadway SE), and in other venues regionally. A recent production titled *The Merchant of Santa Fe,* was a spin off of *The Merchant of Venice,* and involved the crypto-Jews of Northern New Mexico.

Vortex Theatre

Buena Vista (just south of Central Ave.). ☎ **505/247-8600.** Tickets $8 adults, $7 students and seniors; $6 for everyone on Sun.

A 20-year-old community theater known for its innovative productions, the Vortex is Albuquerque's "Off-Broadway" theater, presenting a range of plays from classic to original. An original short play festival is scheduled for 4 weeks every year. *Antony and Cleopatra* played in 1988. Performances take place on Friday and Saturday at 8pm and on Sunday at 6pm. The black-box theater seats 90.

THE CLUB & MUSIC SCENE
COMEDY CLUBS/DINNER THEATER

Laffs Comedy Caffé

3100-D Juan Tabo Blvd. (at Candelaria Rd. NE). ☎ **505/296-5653.**

Top acts from each coast, including comedians who have appeared on *The Late Show with David Letterman* and HBO, are booked at Albuquerque's top comedy club. Shows Wednesday, Thursday, and Sunday begin at 8:30pm ($5 per person with a two-item minimum purchase); on Friday and Saturday, shows start at 8:30 and 10:30pm ($7 per person with a two-item minimum purchase). Wednesday is nonsmoking night. The club serves a full dinner menu with all items under $10. You must be 21 or older to attend.

Mystery Cafe

2601 Wyoming Blvd. NE, Suite 115-E, Albuquerque, NM 87112. Performances held at Sheraton Uptown (at Menaul and Louisana). Performances Friday and Saturday evenings at 7pm. Approximately $33.☎ **505/237-1385.**

If you're in the mood for a little interactive dinner theater, the Mystery Cafe might be just the ticket. You'll help the characters in this ever-popular, delightfully funny show solve the mystery as they serve you a four-course meal. Reservations are a must.

COUNTRY MUSIC

Midnight Rodeo

4901 McLeod Rd. NE (near San Mateo Blvd.). ☎ **505/888-0100.** No cover Sun–Thurs, $3 Fri–Sat.

The Southwest's largest nightclub of any kind, this place has bars in all corners; it even has its own shopping arcade, including a boutique and gift shop. A DJ spins records nightly until closing; the hardwood dance floor is so big (5,500 square feet) that it resembles an indoor horse track. Free dance lessons are offered on Sunday from 5:30 to 7pm and Thursday from 7 to 8pm. A busy kitchen serves simple but hearty meals to dancers who work up appetites. Now, there's even a rock-and-roll dance bar within Midnight Rodeo.

ROCK/JAZZ

In recent years an interesting club scene has opened up downtown. Almost any night of the week, but particularly Thursday through Saturday nights, the place is hopping, as people wander from one club to another. The 20-something crowd should try **The Zone and The Z-Pub** (that's one joint) at 120 Central SW (☎ **505/343-7933**).

Brewsters Pub

312 Central Ave. SW (Downtown). ☎ **505/247-2533.**

Tuesday through Sunday, Brewsters Pub offers live blues or light rock entertainment in a sports bar–type setting. There are 29 beers on tap, as well as a wide variety of bottled beer. Sports fans can enjoy the game on a big-screen TV. Barbecue is served at lunch and dinner.

The Cooperage

7220 Lomas Blvd. NE. ☎ **505/255-1657.** Cover $3–$5.

Salsa on Thursday and Saturday nights and rhythm and blues on Friday nights keep dancers hopping inside this gigantic wooden barrel.

Dingo Bar

313 Gold Ave. SW (Downtown). ☎ **505/243-0663.** Cover charge varies with performance, but can run up to $20 per person.

The Dingo Bar is one of Albuquerque's premier rock clubs. Nightly live entertainment runs from punk rock to classic rock 'n' roll to blues and jazz. The atmosphere is earthy, with patrons ranging from hippies to suits.

MORE ENTERTAINMENT

Albuquerque's best nighttime attraction is the **Sandia Peak Tramway** (see "What to See & Do," above) and the restaurant High Finance at the summit (see "Where to Dine," above). Here, you can enjoy a view nonpareil of the Rio Grande Valley and the city lights.

The best place to catch foreign films, art films, and limited-release productions is the **Guild Cinema,** 3405 Central Ave. NE (☎ **505/255-1848**). For film classics, check out the **Southwest Film Center,** on the UNM campus (☎ **505/277-5608**), with double features Wednesday through Sunday, changing nightly (when classes are in session).

There are a number of first-run movie theaters whose numbers you can find in the local telephone directory.

The **Isleta Gaming Palace,** 11,000 Broadway SE (☎ **800/460-5686** or 505/869-2614), is a luxurious, air-conditioned casino (blackjack, poker, slots, bingo, and keno) with a full-service restaurant, no-smoking section, and free bus transportation on request. Open Monday through Thursday from 9am to 5am; Friday through Sunday 24 hours a day.

11 Exploring Nearby Pueblos & Monuments

Ten Native American pueblos are located within an hour's drive from central Albuquerque. One national and two state monuments preserve another five ancient pueblo ruins.

The active pueblos nearby include Acoma, Cochiti, Isleta, Jemez, Laguna, Sandia, San Felipe, Santa Ana, Santo Domingo, and Zia. Of these, Acoma is the most prominent.

When you visit pueblos, it is important to observe certain **rules of etiquette:** Remember to respect the pueblos as people's homes; don't peek into doors and windows or climb on top of the buildings. Stay out of cemeteries and ceremonial rooms (such as kivas), since these are sacred grounds. Don't speak during dances or ceremonies or applaud after their conclusion; silence is mandatory. Most pueblos require a permit to carry a camera or to sketch or paint on location. Several pueblos prohibit picture taking at any time.

Acoma Pueblo

To reach Acoma from Albuquerque, drive west on I-40 approximately 52 miles to the Acoma–Sky City exit (exit 108), then about 12 miles southwest.

This spectacular "Sky City," a walled adobe village perched high atop a sheer rock mesa 365 feet above the 6,600-foot valley floor, is believed to have been inhabited at least since the 11th century—the longest continuously occupied community in the United States. Native legend claims that it has been inhabited since before the time of Christ. Both the pueblo and **San Estevan del Rey Mission** are National Historic Landmarks.

The Keresan-speaking Acoma (Ack-oo-mah) Pueblo boasts 6,005 inhabitants, but only about 50 people reside year-round on the 70-acre mesa top. They make their living from tourists who come to see the large church containing examples of Spanish colonial art and to purchase the pueblo's thin-walled white pottery with polychrome designs.

The pueblo's address is P.O. Box 309, Acoma, NM 87034 (☎ **800/747-0181** or 505/470-4966). The admission charge is $8 for adults, $7 for seniors (60 and over), $6 for children 6 through 17, and free for children under 6. Group discounts apply to parties of 15 or more, and there's also a discount for Native American visitors. The charge to take still photographs is $10; *no video cameras are allowed.* The pueblo is open daily in the summer from 8am to 7pm; daily in the spring, fall, and winter from 8am to 4:30pm. One-hour tours begin every 30 minutes, depending on the demand; the last tour is scheduled 1 hour before closing. The pueblo is closed the first or second weekend in October and also July 10 to 13.

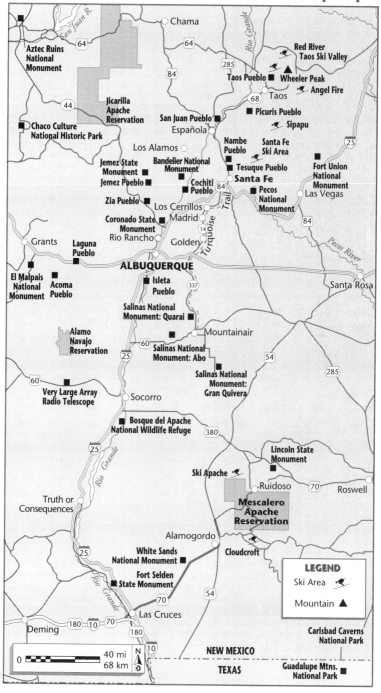

Chama

Aztec Ruins
National
Monument

64

64

285

Red River
Taos Ski Valley

Taos Pueblo   Wheeler Peak

44

Jicarilla
Apache
Reservation

84

68   Taos   Angel Fire

Chaco Culture
National Historic Park

San Juan Pueblo   Picuris Pueblo

Española   Sipapu

Los Alamos

Nambe
Pueblo

Santa Fe
Ski Area

25

Jemez State
Monument

Bandelier National
Monument

Tesuque Pueblo

Fort Union
National
Monument

Jemez Pueblo

Cochiti
Pueblo

84

Santa Fe

Las Vegas

Zia Pueblo

Los Cerrillos

Pecos
National
Monument

Coronado State
Monument

Madrid

14

84

Grants

Rio Rancho

Golden

Pecos River

Laguna
Pueblo

ALBUQUERQUE

Santa Rosa

El Malpais
National
Monument

Acoma
Pueblo

Isleta
Pueblo

337

Salinas National
Monument: Quarai

Alamo
Navajo
Reservation

Mountainair

60

25

Salinas National
Monument: Abo

54

60

Very Large Array
Radio Telescope

Socorro

285

Salinas National
Monument:
Gran Quivera

Bosque del Apache
National Wildlife Refuge

380

Lincoln State
Monument

25

Ski Apache

Ruidoso

70   Roswell

Truth or
Consequences

Mescalero
Apache
Reservation

Alamogordo

Lincoln State Monument

White Sands
National Monument

Cloudcroft

Fort Selden
State Monument

70

LEGEND

Ski Area

Mountain ▲

Deming

180   10   70

Las Cruces

54

180

0   40 mi
68 km   N

Carlsbad Caverns
National Park

NEW MEXICO

TEXAS

Guadalupe Mtns.
National Park

Start your tour at the **visitor center** at the base of the mesa. There's a **museum, cafe,** and **gift shop** here. A 16-seat **tour bus** climbs through a rock garden of 50-foot sandstone monoliths and past precipitously dangling outhouses to the mesa's summit. There's no running water or electricity in this medieval-looking village; a small reservoir collects rainwater for most purposes, but drinking water is transported up from below. Wood-hole ladders and mica windows are prevalent among the 300-odd adobe structures.

Salinas Pueblo Missions National Monument

P.O. Box 517, Mountainair, NM 87036. ☎ **505/847-2585.** Free admission. Sites daily 9am–6pm in summer, 9am–5pm the rest of the year. Visitor center in Mountainair, daily 8am–5pm. Closed Jan 1 and Dec 25. Abo is 9 miles west of Mountainair on US 60. Quarai is 8 miles north of Mountainair on NM 55. Gran Quivira is 25 miles south of Mountainair on NM 55. All roads are paved.

The Spanish conquistadors' Salinas Jurisdiction, on the east side of the Manzano Mountains (southeast of Albuquerque), was an important 17th-century trade center because of the salt extracted by the Native Americans from the salt lakes. Franciscan priests, utilizing native labor, constructed missions of Abo red sandstone and blue-gray limestone for the native converts. The ruins of some of the most durable missions—along with evidence of preexisting Anasazi and Mogollon cultures—are the highlights of a visit to Salinas Pueblo Missions National Monument. The monument consists of three separate units: the ruins of Abo, Quarai, and Gran Quivira. They are situated around the quiet town of **Mountainair,** 75 miles southeast of Albuquerque at the junction of US 60 and NM 55.

Abo (☎ **505/847-2400**) boasts the 40-foot-high ruins of the **Mission of San Gregorio de Abo,** a rare example of medieval architecture in the United States. Quarai (☎ **505/847-2290**) preserves the largely intact remains of the **Mission of La Purísima Concepción de Cuarac** (1630). Its vast size, 100 feet long and 40 feet high, contrasts with the modest size of the pueblo mounds. A small museum in the visitor center has a scale model of the original church, along with a selection of artifacts found at the site. **Gran Quivira (☎ 505/847-2770**) once had a population of 1,500. Las Humanes has 300 rooms and seven kivas. Rooms dating back to 1300 can be seen. There are indications that an older village, dating back to 800, may have previously stood here. Ruins of two churches (one almost 140 feet long) and a Convento have been preserved. A museum with many artifacts from the site, a 40-minute movie showing the excavation of some 200 rooms, plus a short history video of Las Humanes can be seen at the visitor center.

All three pueblos and the churches that were constructed above them are believed to have been abandoned in the 1670s. Self-guided tour pamphlets can be obtained at the units' respective visitor centers and at the **Salinas Pueblo Missions National Monument Visitor Center** in Mountainair, on US 60 1 block west of the intersection of US 60 and NM 55. The visitor center offers an audiovisual presentation on the region's history, a bookstore, and an art exhibit.

Coronado State Monument

NM 44 (P.O. Box 95), Bernalillo, NM 87004. ☎ **505/867-5351.** Admission $3 adults, free for children 16 and under. Daily 8am–5pm. Closed major holidays. To get to the site (20 miles north of Albuquerque), take I-25 to Bernalillo and NM 44 west for 1 mile.

When the Spanish explorer Coronado traveled through this region in 1540–41 while searching for the Seven Cities of Cíbola, he wintered at a village on the west bank of the Rio Grande—probably one located on the ruins of the ancient Anasazi Pueblo known as Kuaua. Those excavated ruins have been preserved in this state monument.

Traditional Native American Bread Baking

While visiting the pueblos in New Mexico, you'll probably notice outdoor ovens (they look a bit like giant ant hills), known as hornos, which Native Americans have used to bake bread for hundreds of years. For Native Americans, making bread is more than simply preparing a staple of daily life; it is a tradition that links them directly to their ancestors. The long process of mixing and baking also brings mothers and daughters together for what today we might call quality time.

Usually, in the evening the bread dough (ingredients: white flour, lard, salt, yeast, and water) is made and kneaded, and the loaves are shaped. They are then allowed to rise overnight. In the morning, the oven is stocked with wood and a fire lighted. After the fire burns down to ashes and embers, the oven is cleared, and the ashes are shoveled away. Unlike modern ovens, hornos don't come equipped with thermometers, so the baker must rely on her senses to determine when the oven is the proper temperature. At that point, the loaves are placed into the oven with a long-handled wooden paddle. They bake for about an hour.

If you would like to try a traditional loaf, you can buy one at the Indian Pueblo Cultural Center in Albuquerque (and elsewhere throughout the state).

Hundreds of rooms can be seen, and a kiva has been restored so that visitors can descend a ladder into the enclosed space, once the site of sacred rites. Unique multicolored murals, depicting human and animal forms, were found on successive layers of wall plaster in this and other kivas here; some examples are displayed in the monument's small archaeological museum.

Jemez State Monument

NM 4 (P.O. Box 143), Jemez Springs, NM 87025. ☎ **505/829-3530.** Admission $3 adults, free for children 16 and under. Daily 8:30am–5pm. Closed Jan 1, Easter Sunday, Thanksgiving, Dec 25. From Albuquerque, take NM 44 to NM 4, and then continue on NM 4 for about 18 miles.

All that's left of the Mission of San José de los Jemez, founded by Franciscan missionaries in 1621, is preserved at this site. Visitors will find massive walls standing alone; sparse small door and window openings underscore the need for security and permanence in those times. The mission was excavated between 1921 and 1937, along with portions of a prehistoric Jemez Pueblo. The pueblo, near the Jemez Hot Springs, was called Giusewa—"place of the boiling waters."

A small **museum** at the site displays artifacts found during the excavation, describes traditional crafts and foods, and weaves the thread of history of the Jemez peoples to the 21st century in a series of exhibits. An instructional trail winds through the ruins.

THE TURQUOISE TRAIL

Known as "The Turquoise Trail," NM 14 begins about 16 miles east of downtown Albuquerque, at I-40's Cedar Crest exit, and winds some 46 miles to Santa Fe along the east side of the Sandia Mountains. This state-designated scenic and historic route traverses the revived ghost towns of Golden, Madrid, and Cerrillos, where gold, silver, coal, and turquoise were once mined in great quantities. Modern-day settlers, mostly artists and craftspeople, have brought a renewed frontier spirit to the old mining towns.

GOLDEN   Golden is approximately 10 miles north of the Sandia Park junction on NM 14. Its sagging houses, with their missing boards and the wind whistling through the broken eaves, make it a purist's ghost town. There's a general store widely known for its large selection of well-priced jewelry, as well as a bottle seller's "glass garden." Nearby are the ruins of a pueblo called **Paako,** abandoned around 1670. Such communities of mud huts were all that the Spaniards ever found during their avid quest for the gold of Cíbola.

MADRID   Madrid (pronounced with the accent on the first syllable) is about 12 miles north of Golden. Madrid and neighboring Cerrillos were in a fabled turquoise-mining area dating back to prehistory. Gold and silver mines followed, and when they faltered, there was coal. The Turquoise Trail towns supplied fuel for the locomotives of the Santa Fe Railroad until the 1950s, when the railroad converted to diesel fuel. Madrid used to produce 100,000 tons of coal a year, but the mine closed in 1956. Today, this is a village of artists and craftspeople seemingly stuck in the 1960s: Its funky, ramshackle houses have many counterculture residents who operate several crafts stores and import shops.

The **Old Coal Mine Museum** (☎ **505/473-0743**) invites visitors to go down into a real mine that was saved when the town was abandoned. You can see the old mine's offices, steam engines, machines, and tools. It's called a living museum because blacksmiths, metalworkers, and leatherworkers ply their trades here in restoring parts and tools found in the mine. It's open daily; admission is $3 for adults and seniors, and $1 for children 6 to 12; children under 6 are free.

Next door, the **Mine Shaft Tavern** continues its colorful career by offering a variety of burgers on the menu and presenting live music Saturday and Sunday afternoons and some Friday and Saturday nights; it's open for dinner Wednesday and Friday through Sunday, and attracts folks from Santa Fe and Albuquerque. Next door is the **Madrid Opera House,** possibly the only such establishment on earth with a built-in steam locomotive on its stage. (The structure had been an engine repair shed; the balcony is made of railroad track.)

CERRILLOS   Cerrillos, about 3 miles north of Madrid, is a village of dirt roads that sprawls along Galisteo Creek. It appears to have changed very little since it was founded during a lead strike in 1879; the old hotel, the saloon, and even the sheriff's office look very much like an Old West movie set. It's another 15 miles to Santa Fe and I-25.

Appendix: Useful Toll-Free Numbers & Web Sites

LODGINGS

Best Western International
☎ 800/528-1234 in North America
☎ 800/528-2222 TDD
www.bestwestern.com/best.html

Clarion Hotels
☎ 800/CLARION in the continental U.S. and Canada
☎ 800/228-3323 TDD
www.clarioninn.com

Comfort Inns
☎ 800/228-5150 in the continental U.S. and Canada
☎ 800/228-3323 TDD
www.comfortinn.com

Courtyard by Marriott
☎ 800/321-2211 in the continental U.S. and Canada
☎ 800/228-7014 TDD
www.marriott.com

Days Inn
☎ 800/329-7466 in the continental U.S. and Canada
☎ 800/329-7155 TDD
www.daysinn.com

Econo Lodges
☎ 800/553-2666 in the continental U.S. and Canada
☎ 800/228-3323 TDD
www.hotelchoice.com

Embassy Suites
☎ 800/362-2779 in the continental U.S. and Canada
☎ 800/458-4708 TDD
www.embassy-suites.com

Hampton Inn
☎ 800/HAMPTON in the continental U.S. and Canada
☎ 800/451-HTDD TDD
www.hampton-inn.com

Hilton Hotels Corporation
☎ 800/HILTONS in the continental U.S. and Canada
☎ 800/368-1133 TDD
www.hilton.com

Holiday Inn
☎ 800/HOLIDAY in the continental U.S. and Canada
☎ 800/238-5544 TDD
www.holiday-inn.com

Howard Johnson
☎ 800/654-2000 in the continental U.S. and Canada
☎ 800/654-8442 TDD
www.hojo.com

ITT Sheraton
☎ 800/325-3535 in the continental U.S. and Canada
☎ 800/325-1717 TDD

La Quinta Motor Inns
☎ 800/531-5900 in the continental U.S. and Canada
☎ 800/426-3101 TDD

Marriott Hotels
☎ 800/228-9290 in the continental U.S. and Canada
☎ 800/228-7014 TDD
www.marriott.com

Motel 6
☎ 800/466-8356 in the continental U.S. and Canada

Quality Inns
☎ 800/228-5151 in the continental U.S. and Canada
☎ 800/228-3323 TDD
www.qualityinn.com

Radisson Hotels International
☎ 800/333-3333 in the continental U.S. and Canada

Ramada
☎ 800/272-6232 in the continental U.S. and Canada
☎ 800/228-3232 TDD
www.ramada.com/ramada.html

Residence Inn by Marriott
☎ 800/331-3131 in the continental U.S. and Canada
☎ 800/228-7014 TDD
www.marriott.com

Rodeway Inns
☎ 800/228-2000 in the continental U.S. and Canada
☎ 800/228-3323 TDD
www.hotelchoice.com

Super 8 Motels
☎ 800/800-8000 in the continental U.S. and Canada
☎ 800/533-6634 TDD
www.super8motels.com

Travelodge
☎ 800/578-7878 in the continental U.S. and Canada
☎ 800/578-7878 TDD
www.travelodge.com

CAR-RENTAL AGENCIES

Advantage Rent-A-Car
☎ 800/777-5500 in the continental U.S. and Canada

Alamo Rent A Car
☎ 800/327-9633 in the continental U.S. and Canada
www.goalamo.com

Avis
☎ 800/331-1212 in the continental U.S.
☎ 800/TRY-AVIS Canada
☎ 800/331-2323 TDD
www.avis/com

Budget Rent A Car
☎ 800/527-0700 in the continental U.S. and Canada
☎ 800/826-5510 TDD
www.budgetrentacar.com

Dollar Rent A Car
☎ 800/800-4000 in the continental U.S. and Canada
☎ 800/232-3301 TDD
www.dollarcar.com

Enterprise Rent-A-Car
☎ 800/325-8007 in the continental U.S. and Canada
www.pickenterprise.com

Hertz
☎ 800/654-3131 in the continental U.S. and Canada
☎ 800/654-2280 TDD
www.hertz.com

National Car Rental
☎ 800/CAR-RENT in the continental U.S. and Canada
☎ 800/328-6323 TDD
www.nationalcar.com

Thrifty Rent-A-Car
☎ 800/367-2277 in the continental U.S. and Canada
☎ 800/358-5856 TDD
www.thrifty.com

AIRLINES

Alaska Airlines
☎ 800/426-0333 in the U.S. and Canada
☎ 800/682-2221 TDD
www.alaskaair.com

America West
☎ 800/235-9292 in the continental U.S. and Canada
☎ 800/682-2221 TDD
www.americawest.com

American Airlines
☎ 800/433-7300 in the continental U.S. and western Canada
☎ 800/543-1586 TDD
www.americanair.com

Continental Airlines
☎ 800/525-0280 in the continental U.S.
☎ 800/343-9195 TDD
www.flycontinental.com

Delta Air Lines
☎ 800/221-1212 in the continental U.S.
☎ 800/831-4488 TDD
www.delta-air.com

Horizon Airlines
☎ 800/547-9308 in the continental U.S. and Canada
☎ 800/843-1338 TDD
www.horizon.com

Northwest Airlines
☎ 800/225-2525 in the continental U.S. and Canada
☎ 800/328-2298
www.nwa.com

Reno Air
☎ 800/736-6247
www.renoair.com

Southwest Airlines
☎ 800/435-9792 in the continental U.S. and Canada
☎ 800/533-1305 TDD
www.iflyswa.com

Trans World Airlines
☎ 800/221-2000 in the continental U.S.
☎ 800/421-8480 TDD
www.twa.com

United Airlines
☎ 800/241-6522 in the continental U.S. and Canada
☎ 800/323-0170 TDD
www.ual.com

Index

ACCOMMODATIONS

Santa Fe

Taos

Frommer's® Complete Travel Guides

Alaska
Amsterdam
Arizona
Atlanta
Australia
Austria
Bahamas
Barcelona, Madrid & Seville
Belgium, Holland & Luxembourg
Bermuda
Boston
Budapest & the Best of Hungary
California
Canada
Cancún, Cozumel & the Yucatán
Cape Cod, Nantucket & Martha's Vineyard
Caribbean
Caribbean Cruises & Ports of Call
Caribbean Ports of Call
Carolinas & Georgia
Chicago
China
Colorado
Costa Rica
Denver, Boulder & Colorado Springs
England
Europe
Florida
France

Germany
Greece
Greek Islands
Hawaii
Hong Kong
Honolulu, Waikiki & Oahu
Ireland
Israel
Italy
Jamaica & Barbados
Japan
Las Vegas
London
Los Angeles
Maryland & Delaware
Maui
Mexico
Miami & the Keys
Montana & Wyoming
Montréal & Québec City
Munich & the Bavarian Alps
Nashville & Memphis
Nepal
New England
New Mexico
New Orleans
New York City
New Zealand
Nova Scotia, New Brunswick & Prince Edward Island
Oregon
Paris
Philadelphia & the Amish Country
Portugal

Prague & the Best of the Czech Republic
Provence & the Riviera
Puerto Rico
Rome
San Antonio & Austin
San Diego
San Francisco
Santa Fe, Taos & Albuquerque
Scandinavia
Scotland
Seattle & Portland
Singapore & Malaysia
South Pacific
Spain
Switzerland
Thailand
Tokyo
Toronto
Tuscany & Umbria
USA
Utah
Vancouver & Victoria
Vermont, New Hampshire & Maine
Vienna & the Danube Valley
Virgin Islands
Virginia
Walt Disney World & Orlando
Washington, D.C.
Washington State

Frommer's® Dollar-a-Day Guides

Australia from $50 a Day
California from $60 a Day
Caribbean from $60 a Day
England from $60 a Day
Europe from $50 a Day
Florida from $60 a Day

Greece from $50 a Day
Hawaii from $60 a Day
Ireland from $50 a Day
Israel from $45 a Day
Italy from $50 a Day
London from $75 a Day

New York from $75 a Day
New Zealand from $50 a Day
Paris from $70 a Day
San Francisco from $60 a Day
Washington, D.C., from $60 a Day

Frommer's® Portable Guides

Acapulco, Ixtapa & Zihuatanejo
Alaska Cruises & Ports of Call
Bahamas
California Wine Country
Charleston & Savannah
Chicago

Dublin
Las Vegas
London
Maine Coast
New Orleans
New York City
Paris

Puerto Vallarta, Manzanillo & Guadalajara
San Francisco
Sydney
Tampa & St. Petersburg
Venice
Washington, D.C.

FROMMER'S® NATIONAL PARK GUIDES

Family Vacations in the
National Parks
Grand Canyon

National Parks of the
American West
Yellowstone & Grand Teton

Yosemite & Sequoia/
Kings Canyon
Zion & Bryce Canyon

FROMMER'S® MEMORABLE WALKS

Chicago
London

New York
Paris

San Francisco
Washington D.C.

FROMMER'S® IRREVERENT GUIDES

Amsterdam
Boston
Chicago

London
Manhattan

New Orleans
Paris

San Francisco
Walt Disney World
Washington, D.C.

FROMMER'S® DRIVING TOURS

America
Britain
California

Florida
France
Germany

Ireland
Italy
New England

Scotland
Spain
Western Europe

THE COMPLETE IDIOT'S TRAVEL GUIDES

Boston
Cruise Vacations
Planning Your Trip to Europe
Hawaii

Las Vegas
London
Mexico's Beach Resorts
New Orleans

New York City
San Francisco
Walt Disney World
Washington D.C.

THE UNOFFICIAL GUIDES®

Branson, Missouri
California with Kids
Chicago
Cruises
Disney Companion

Florida with Kids
The Great Smoky &
Blue Ridge
Mountains

Las Vegas
Miami & the Keys
Mini-Mickey
New Orleans

New York City
San Francisco
Skiing in the West
Walt Disney World
Washington, D.C.

SPECIAL-INTEREST TITLES

Frommer's Britain's Best Bike Rides
The Civil War Trust's Official Guide
   to the Civil War Discovery Trail
Frommer's Caribbean Hideaways
Frommer's Gay & Lesbian Europe
Israel Past & Present
Monks' Guide to California
Monks' Guide to New York City
New York City with Kids
New York Times Weekends
Outside Magazine's Adventure Guide
   to New England
Outside Magazine's Adventure Guide
   to Northern California

Outside Magazine's Adventure Guide
   to Southern California & Baja
Outside Magazine's Adventure Guide
   to the Pacific Northwest
Outside Magazine's Guide
   to Family Vacations
Places Rated Almanac
Retirement Places Rated
Washington, D.C., with Kids
Wonderful Weekends from Boston
Wonderful Weekends from New York City
Wonderful Weekends from San Francisco
Wonderful Weekends from Los Angeles

www.frommers.com

WHEREVER YOU TRAVEL, *H*ELP IS NEVER FAR AWAY.

From planning your trip to

providing travel assistance along

the way, American Express®

Travel Service Offices

are always there to help

you do more.

American Express Travel Service
Offices are found in central locations
throughout Santa Fe, Taos and Albuquerque.

do more **AMERICAN EXPRESS**
®
Travel

http://www.americanexpress.com/travel